FROM DIXIE TO ROCKY TOP

From Dixie to Rocky Top

Music and Meaning in
Southeastern Conference Football

CARRIE TIPTON

Vanderbilt University Press

NASHVILLE, TENNESSEE

Library of Congress Cataloging-in-Publication Data

Names: Tipton, Carrie, 1978– author.
Title: From Dixie to Rocky Top : music and meaning in Southeastern
    Conference football / Carrie Tipton.
Description: Nashville : Vanderbilt University Press, 2023. | Includes
    bibliographical references.
Identifiers: LCCN 2023030345 (print) | LCCN 2023030346 (ebook) | ISBN
    9780826506399 (paperback) | ISBN 9780826506405 (hardcover) | ISBN
    9780826506412 (epub) | ISBN 9780826506429 (pdf)
Subjects: LCSH: Fight songs—Southern States—History and criticism. |
    Music and sports—Southern States. | Popular music—Southern
    States—20th century—History and criticism. | Racism in higher
    education—Southern States. | Allen, Thornton W. (Thornton Whitney),
    1890–1944. | Southeastern Conference.
Classification: LCC ML3477 .T57 2023 (print) | LCC ML3477 (ebook) | DDC
    782.421/5940976—dc23/eng/20230705
LC record available at https://lccn.loc.gov/2023030345
LC ebook record available at https://lccn.loc.gov/2023030346

Contents

Introduction

When I was thirteen, we moved within earshot of Davis Wade Stadium, football field of the Mississippi State University Bulldogs. Quite suddenly, fall afternoons were punctuated with roaring crowds, blaring brass, and stentorian announcers. From our yard, individual words and notes issuing from the stadium dissolved into an undifferentiated sonic mass, yet together they constituted the unmistakable sounds of war. Urging the troops forward was "Hail State," written in the mid-1930s by Joseph Burleson Peavey, whose son went on to invent the guitar amps that bear the family name. Peavey's tune leapfrogs up through an octave in four quick opening notes, a distinctive melodic contour still indelible in my mind. After graduation, I found myself in Athens, Georgia, trying with noble and naïve optimism to use the university library during the season's first University of Georgia home football game. Mired in traffic that inched tortuously through a sea of red tents, I smelled smoke from the grills, saw Sanford Stadium rear its leonine head, heard the band bleat "Glory to Old Georgia," and knew that although I might not make it to the library, I was already home.[1]

My experience is one of many similar ones across the US South, where big-time college football—with a soundscape that forms first impressions and enduring memories—has forged a powerful sense of meaning and identity. Unlike other parts of the United States, the South had no professional football teams to rally around until the middle of the twentieth century, almost fifty years later than midwestern and northern states. Instead, since the early 1890s, college football united southern students, alumni, and locals as they cheered for the closest university team. The annual recurrence of the sport—blazing and brief, like autumn leaves—provided sorely-needed rhythm to a region increasingly unmoored from the agrarian calendar that once ordered its collective life. And from the beginning, this short, colorful, pageantry-filled season had a memorable soundtrack: fight songs. First borrowed from northern schools, minstrel songs, and Civil War tunes, later Southeastern Conference fight songs were composed by students, alumni, and professional songwriters, sometimes lifted outright from popular music. Although the musical profiles of these songs get flattened out in a marching band context, they span the stylistic spectrum of US popular music, including ragtime, jazz, bluegrass, and Broadway. In our own time, they sound stylistically frozen as the wider musical world moves on around them, these short, spunky pieces that derive power from stasis, simplicity, and a sense of "always-been-there-ness."

Football has historically linked campus to material and imagined community, nationally and in the US South, through

> shared emblems and experiences. . . For the majority of Americans living in the age of mass media, the defining characteristics of a particular college or university have not resided in the curriculum or [academic laurels]. Rather, the measure of a school in popular consciousness often rests on its athletic record . . . and the host of signs and symbols that emphasize the distinctiveness of an institution also advertise its involvement in a national pastime.[2]

Fight songs are the most potent and portable of these "shared emblems and experiences," audible "signs and symbols" of college football culture. Historically disseminated through the dominant channels of the music industry in any given era—sheet music, live performances, recordings, radio, television—fight songs have long moved beyond the boundaries of campus life. In the football-haunted South, these songs have become the hymns of a regional college football culture that scholar Eric Bain-Selbo describes as a religion, the soundtrack of a region that regards sports as "central" to its "modern . . . identity."[3]

Despite the significance of college fight songs in southern culture, and US culture more broadly, they figure minimally in academic research. Mentions of fight songs in college football scholarship tend toward the anecdotal and brief: quoting lyrics; stating bare facts of a song's composition; describing a song's affective power.[4] Simon J. Bronner's *Campus Traditions: Folklore from the Old-Time College to the Modern Mega-University* devotes merely eight pages to fight songs and alma maters.[5] In *Football: The Ivy League Origins of an American Obsession*, Mark Bernstein even writes that

> the great age of fight songs [the 1920s] was drawing to a close . . . [unable to] survive changing tastes or the disruption of World War I, which brought back to campus mature veterans less interested in musical trifles. By the late 1920s, new songs had all but ceased to appear—a loss to future generations of fans.[6]

If Bernstein's statement applies not only to Ivy League schools but to universities across the United States—an interpretation suggested by its context—it is wrong. As the book shows, the bulk of Southeastern Conference fight songs were written in the 1930s, with some written or adopted as late as the early 1970s. Even in books on football at predominantly white southern universities, neither scholars nor journalists have documented and analyzed sources for, historical contexts of, and complex meanings generated by southern fight songs as a body of music.[7] (The exception is "Dixie," which I will discuss shortly.) The only books devoted to college fight songs, southern or otherwise, are a few dictionaries and encyclopedias containing brief, sometimes erroneous entries about tune sources, composers, lyricists, and dates of introduction, with no historical, musical, or social analyses or arguments.[8] They cover schools across the United States and do not engage the notion of a regionally distinctive history, development, or reception of fight songs.

In contrast, this book treats SEC fight songs as a cohesive repertory, geographically and historically contingent, bound not by common musical style but by the political, social, and cultural investments of the white South from the late nineteenth to the late twentieth centuries and situated within broader US commercial music history. In documenting and analyzing this understudied category of vernacular music-making, the book responds to Elijah Wald's rebuke of popular music scholarship that neglects music significant to wide swaths of people in the past simply because it strikes contemporary listeners as unoriginal or pedestrian.[9] Yet as this book shows, for long stretches of time, especially from the 1910s through the 1940s, college songs (including what we now call fight songs) formed a vibrant sector of the US commercial music industry. They were written, arranged, published, advertised, sold, recorded, danced to, and performed on and off campus, in football contexts and otherwise, by a broad range of US consumers and producers.

Treating SEC fight songs as a regional repertory embedded within US commercial music history documents a new dimension of southern investment in the consumption and production of mainstream popular music and culture. Here the book builds on Karl Hagstrom Miller's *Segregating Sound*, which argues that from 1890 to 1920, southerners consumed and performed far more mainstream commercial music than the historiography of southern music often suggests.[10] Treating SEC fight songs as a regionally cohesive repertory also means considering how such simple songs have generated complex individual and collective meanings that coalesce polyphonically around several main themes. As Ken McLeod notes, "music and sports intersect on many levels . . . almost invariably, this nexus serve[s] to construct, contest, and/or promote one identity or another."[11] The book shows how the nexus of SEC football and fight songs is animated by musical constructions and expressions of race, gender, and regional identity, spinning out in fixed and fluid ways across more than a century, which publishers and composers have used to commodify the nebulous concept of "school spirit."

Before providing chapter summaries, I'll preview how these broad categories of thematic analysis work themselves out across the book. Regarding race and regional identity as constructed and expressed by southern college fight songs, this book makes new and significant contributions. First, it documents and explores the use of minstrel songs in SEC football to shape and reflect white fantasies about antebellum plantation life, arguing that southern universities' later post-integration reliance on unpaid Black athletic labor echoed and paralleled the earlier musical phenomenon. Here my book extends the work of scholars who have documented the use of "Dixie"—initially a minstrel song—in white southern college football to perpetuate "Lost Cause" mythology, an issue that has made headlines in recent years via the University of Texas's "Eyes of Texas" song controversy.[12] The book draws on Matthew Morrison's "Blacksound" concept to explore the cultural politics of SEC schools' use of minstrel songs, based on white imaginings of Black expressive culture, to build their football pageantry while excluding Black citizens from institutional life.[13] Related to this, the book explores how SEC football music has "embraced black musical styles without addressing the cultural implications of that embrace," using Black styles such as jazz or ragtime in fight songs and halftime shows, especially in eras when the SEC barred Black Americans from admission—part of a larger cultural and historic trend of predominantly white institutions (PWIs) reaping financial and cultural profits from Black musical innovation.[14] The interconnected themes of race and regional identity are centered in Chapter 2, Chapter 11, and the Epilogue and are interwoven in many other chapters. At the same time, the book documents how SEC fight song history also evinces white southern college students' participation in and contribution to national collegiate culture—a subject foregrounded in Chapters 6 and 7 and which threads its way through most other chapters.

Regarding gender, the book is the first to explore the musical participation of women in southern college football as fight song composers, arrangers, performers, and consumers. The scant research on women's engagement with college football often reduces their agency to the roles of cheerleaders, sponsors, or passive spectators. Gerald Gems's chapter on "Feminism and Football" describes 1880 to 1920 as a period of US masculine retrenchment against feminism, with college football a bulwark against "encroaching females."[15] According to Gems, women's participation in football culture was limited to the "traditional Victorian functions for female spectators" re-inscribed by "the male-dominated media."[16] Aside from a few examples of women who engaged with college football culture, such as coaches' wives or writers who covered the sport, Gems concludes that "women served as recipients or the audience for male sports."[17] As this book demonstrates, Gems and other scholars of sport have missed how women have shaped college football pageantry through musical activities.[18] This is true even in SEC football, situated within larger traditional regional gender hierarchies: we just have to look hard to find evidence of it.

To flesh out this line of inquiry, the book discusses women well-known in contemporary music circles whose contributions to the southern college football soundscape have gone unnoticed by scholars. These include May Singhi Breen, who popularized college songs in the 1920s with her ukulele and banjo arrangements; Emma Ashford, Nashville composer who wrote Vanderbilt songs in the early twentieth century; and Felice Boudreaux, country music songwriter and co-author of "Rocky Top," the unofficial fight song and cult hit of the University of Tennessee. The book also documents examples of women students, alumni, and fans who wrote, arranged, and performed college fight songs before World War II, when women's agency in campus life at coeducational southern universities was circumscribed. By foregrounding women's voices in a soundscape that often codes hypermasculine, I respond to Hazel V. Carby's formulation of Michel-Rolph Trouillot's call for scholars to counter "inequalities of power in knowledge of the past [with] scanty evidence . . . repositioned to generate new narratives."[19] While some of this material is distributed throughout the book, Chapter 5 centers the subject by documenting women's pre–World War II musical engagement with the militaristic football pageantry of Texas A&M University. A related thread of gendered inquiry is how SEC fight song history illustrates the durability of southern orthodoxies around white masculinity across the long period encompassed in the book, a subject taken up in Chapter 1 and Chapter 11.

Finally, *From Dixie to Rocky Top* uses SEC fight song history as a novel way to engage college football's longtime tension between tradition and commercialism by treating these songs as what they are: commodities, shaped by market forces, that exist as copyrighted entities within the US music industry. When prominent southern sportswriter Grantland Rice co-wrote a Texas Christian University fight song in 1938, he noted primly that the song was prepared "without compensation" in a "signal recognition of clean sportsmanship."[20] Rice's comments index a common belief among fans, students, and alumni—southern and otherwise—that college football's symbols and songs are non-commercial traditions springing from the hazy mists of collective sentiment. In contrast to and sometimes in tension with this belief, this book "follows the money" by documenting the once-strong college song market in the US music industry, nationally and in the South, and situating SEC fight songs within that market. A category that emerged from mid-nineteenth-century US college songbooks, the college song flourished in the sheet music market and recording industry of the 1910s through 1940s.[21] The book provides a rich trove of sources and analysis on this once-vibrant yet understudied sector of US popular music, starting with the history of the hit 1910 southern fight song "Washington and Lee Swing," and its publisher,

Thornton Wilder Allen (1890–1944), who built a college song publishing empire on the strength of the "Swing," documented in Chapter 4.[22] Until his death in 1944, Allen acquired, wrote, copyrighted, published, and marketed dozens of college songs for schools across the US, including key SEC fight songs, in piano, ukulele, dance band, and glee club arrangements. Sources from the 1920s through 1940s show that Allen vigorously defended his college song copyrights, thereby shaping the southern college fight song repertory. Chapter 5 draws on these sources to show that Allen's threatened litigation around unauthorized use of the "Washington and Lee Swing" spurred the composition of new fight songs at the University of Alabama and Tulane University in 1925 and 1926. Despite Allen's significance as a shaper of regional and national collegiate musical taste and his commodification of school spirit for the popular song market, no research exists on him. His national and southern work in college song publishing is also centered in Chapters 4 and 6 and figures prominently in many other chapters.

Along related economic lines, the book contains the first deep exploration of Louisiana Governor Huey P. Long's musical activities at Louisiana State University (LSU) from 1930 to 1935, in Chapter 9. The chapter is the first scholarship to document and analyze Long's roles as a fight song composer, substitute band director, consumer of college songs, and collaborator with Castro Carazo, the composer and bandleader Long hired in late 1934 to direct the LSU band. It highlights the nebulous, unquantifiable ways that football music and pageantry can generate public relations value for a university. John Sayle Watterson writes that "like other college sports, football [always] posed as an amateur sport"—a historically accurate statement that may surprise and distress fans who cling to enduring myths about amateurism in their beloved game.[23] By illuminating the unfolding of the college song genre as an *industry*, and the fight song as a commodity in that industry, through the activities of Allen, Long, and others, *From Dixie to Rocky Top* connects longstanding concerns over amateurism and "purity" in college football discourse with the belief of football fans and university communities that fight songs arose organically from the hazy mists of tradition, insulated from capitalistic forces.[24]

These themes—the US music industry's commodification of school spirit and the construction and expression of race, regional identity, and gender in SEC football pageantry—link and overlap within and across chapters. Chapter 1 begins with a brief overview of college football's spread in the 1890s from New England to the South, including white southern universities' adaption or emulation of Ivy League pageantry. The chapter then documents the chants, yells, and cheers that largely made up the early white southern college football soundscape and locates the roots of that oral expression in the pre-football campus culture of social, fraternal, rhetorical, and literary clubs. The chapter also reconstructs how this soundscape unfolded in public southern urban spaces in the late nineteenth and early twentieth centuries, with Nashville and Atlanta as case studies, and explores the gendered and racialized significance of this use of public space. Chapter 2 documents the use of minstrel and Civil War songs in white southern football culture of the same era, highlighting football music as a malleable cultural text which has allowed southern students to participate in national collegiate culture and to project regional or sectional identity. By embedding minstrel and Civil War songs in early football culture, southern universities planted seeds that blossomed in the regional fight song repertory for decades to come: an obsession with "Lost Cause" mythology and an unyielding celebration of sectional identity.

Chapter 3, the first to cover individual SEC football songs, documents the emergence of Georgia Tech's "Ramblin' Wreck" (ca. 1890s) and the University of Florida's "We Are the Boys of Old Florida (ca. 1919). With their scarce printed sources, conflicting origin stories, and decades-long authorship debates, these songs highlight the challenge of assigning copyright and ownership to early fight songs that used pre-existing tunes, circulated orally in student culture, and employed texts that likely developed collectively and spontaneously. The chapter frames these case studies as early examples of recurring conflicts in SEC fight song history over tensions between commercialism and tradition, which often refracted competing notions of musical authorship operative in early twentieth-century US commercial music. Chapter 4 continues to situate southern fight songs within the commercial music industry by documenting the early history of the 1910 "Washington and Lee Swing" and its publisher; the song and the man profoundly shaped the broader college song genre and the SEC fight song repertory. Chapter 5 documents how women musically engaged with the hypermasculine football culture of pre–World War II white southern college football pageantry. After a primary case study of women and football music at the militaristic Texas A&M

University, which also provides the history of its "Aggie War Hymn" (ca. 1919), the chapter briefly explores women's pre–World War II musical involvement in football culture at several other proto-SEC schools.

Chapter 6 moves into the 1920s, when white southern college football teams entered the national sports arena, showing how southern football culture retained some songs rooted in antebellum sectional identity while also generating unique fight songs with no ties to the Old South, such as the University of Kentucky's "On, On, U of K." The chapter documents how commercial and legal pressure generated two proto-SEC fight songs: the University of Alabama's ragtime-inflected "Yea Alabama" and Tulane University's "Roll On, Tulane." Chapter 7 lays conceptual and historical groundwork for understanding the 1930s profusion of SEC fight songs by documenting the flourishing 1930s college song industry, created and sustained by a vibrant network of regional and national "collegiate" performers and music publishers. Chapter 8 documents how the writing and adoption of SEC fight songs reached its zenith in the 1930s after the Southeastern Conference was formed in 1932. Throughout the Depression, SEC football prospered, with music a key part of its spectacle and spirit. In this decade, SEC schools turned toward promotion and marketing to define institutional identities, solidify ties with alumni and donors, and advertise themselves to potential students. Increased administrative and student urgency around these imperatives led to a flurry of new SEC fight songs in the 1930s: the University of Mississippi's "Forward Rebels (Rebels March)," Mississippi State University's "Hail State," the University of Arkansas's "Arkansas Fight" (written ca. 1913 but not used until ca. 1932), Vanderbilt's "Dynamite," the University of Tennessee's "Fight, Vols, Fight," and LSU's "Touchdown for LSU" and "Fight for LSU," among others.

Nowhere was the belief in college football's economic power stronger than in Louisiana, where populist governor Huey P. Long micromanaged LSU's football program and marching band to new heights of success—or, at least, new heights of publicity. Chapter 9 historicizes Long's musical relationship with LSU and with college songs as a hyperbolic confluence of two regional 1930s trends: SEC schools' crystallization of football pageantry in order to promote institutional identities and white southern investment in the "collegiate" trope ubiquitous in US popular culture of the time. The chapter frames Long's political use of the LSU marching band as a projection of the bellicose voice of the state—the voice of New-Deal-era white southern democracy.

Chapter 10 documents the emergence of three final SEC fight songs between 1955 and 1972, at Auburn University ("War Eagle"), the University of South Carolina ("Fighting Gamecocks Lead the Way"), and the University of Tennessee ("Rocky Top"). Developed and adopted much differently than earlier SEC fight songs, these songs appeared in the wake of postwar changes that swept the US South, including higher education, where the economic and cultural importance of SEC football mushroomed. Emerging in the context of increasingly sophisticated marching band pageantry, these final SEC fight songs demonstrate how marching bands, boosters, and band directors shaped postwar college football pageantry, in contrast to student-driven fight song creation of earlier eras, showing that southern powerbrokers were increasingly aware of music's role in building and sustaining football fandom and media attention.

The book concludes in Chapter 11, which evaluates thematic continuity and change in the SEC football soundscape across the century that the book spans. The chapter traces the decline of sectionally resonant fight songs in the context of the SEC's academic and athletic integration through documenting the "Dixie" debates that roiled the conference from the late 1960s to the mid-1970s. It also explores the reception history and complex meanings of Lynyrd Skynyrd's "Sweet Home Alabama," used as an unofficial University of Alabama fight song since the 1990s. Arguing that the song turns the stadium into a space that projects durable white southern orthodoxies around gender, race, and regional identity, the chapter creates symmetry with the analysis of southern students' late nineteenth-century use of public urban space in Chapter 1. Chapter 11 concludes by exploring how SEC fight song history can engage and test the limits of the historiographic concept of southern exceptionalism. A brief epilogue uses the fight song history of the University of Missouri, SEC latecomer, to explore another question that animates southern historiography, journalistic discourse, and everyday chatter: "where exactly is the South?"

These chapters coalesce to create a nested organizational scheme that discusses songs by school within a larger thematic and chronological framework, enabling readers to find information about a school's songs in one location, in most cases, while also showing how individual song histories and their potential for generating meaning unfolded within larger trajectories across broader cultural and social contexts. These trajectories, discernibly linear in shape by the end of the book, include SEC schools' longtime use of sectionally resonant songs, fading only in the 1960s under the duress of integration; the burst of SEC fight songs in the late 1920s and 1930s, stimulated by a conference-wide turn toward public relations; the post-1940s fading of college songs from the popular music industry as dance bands waned and marching bands became more important in football pageantry; and the internal institutional creation of fight songs through the early 1940s, followed from the 1950s through the early 1970s by a few final fight songs from external sources, reflective of college football's professionalization.

Since 1932, the Southeastern Conference has come to dominate the economic and, arguably, the cultural landscape of college football. As of Spring 2023, SEC schools have won thirteen out of the last seventeen national college football championships and regularly produce more NFL players and pay head football coaches more than other collegiate athletic conferences. By any metric, SEC television viewership and annual football revenues are superlative, supported by a massive and rabid fan base. In 2022, the conference consists of fourteen current members, primarily land-grant state schools:

Texas A&M University	the University of Kentucky
the University of Arkansas	the University of Alabama
Louisiana State University	Auburn University
Mississippi State University	the University of South Carolina
the University of Mississippi	the University of Georgia
Vanderbilt University	the University of Missouri
the University of Tennessee	University of Florida

There are three former members:

Sewanee (the University of the South)
the Georgia Institute of Technology (Georgia Tech)
Tulane University

Prior to the SEC's 1932 formation, most of these schools were in the Southern Conference. From the late nineteenth century, these universities have shaped the political and social trajectory of the South, working to fortify white democracy in the region well into the twentieth century.[25] The powerful cultural, historical, and social role that SEC schools have played in US and regional history merits a study of their musical contributions to the pageantry of US college football, and to the nation's popular music industry.

These are the schools whose fight songs are covered in this book, although the book does not give equal time to every official and unofficial fight song ever used on each campus. For example, Sewanee left the SEC and big-time college sports in 1940, at the close of the decade in which many SEC schools found their enduring fight songs, and therefore never acquired a notable and lasting fight song, although sources related to Sewanee's early football songs and cheers appear in this book's early pages. I also mostly do not discuss other elements that the current college football soundscape comprises, such as chants, song fragments, popular music, or sound effects. Instead, I focus on one or two songs per current and former SEC school, chosen for their endurance as official university songs or fan favorites; notable circumstances of composition, publication, and reception; and availability of relevant sources. Kolan Thomas Morelock writes that "campus cultures are complex, consisting of student, faculty, and administrative subcultures" that interact among themselves and against the larger "surrounding community," and the vast, rich array of sources this project uses reflect those vibrant interconnected relationships.[26] In addition to scholarship and interpretive frameworks from multiple disciplines, the book draws on manuscript collections, football programs, sheet music, photographs, student and alumni publications, and other sources found in the digital and physical archives of SEC schools and other repositories. The project also uses regional and national newspapers—a reflection of longtime press coverage of southern college football—music trade publications, recordings, legal records, and sheet music.[27]

The book necessarily omits non-SEC southern schools with vibrant football traditions and iconic, beloved fight songs: smaller schools; major universities in other athletic conferences (Florida State University, the University of North Carolina, and the University of Virginia, for example); and historically Black colleges and universities (HBCUs). The fight songs of predominantly white southern universities not covered in this book may fit into the historical narratives developed in the book, including the early use of minstrel and Civil War songs, although further research would be required to confirm this. Southern HBCUs, with their distinctive football rituals and music, deserve a breadth and depth of attention that would form the subject of many books.[28] For instance, Nashville's Tennessee State University uses the Black gospel song "I'm So Glad" as a fight song, with minimal lyrical tweaks, suggestive of rich differences in repertory roots and meanings compared to fight songs of predominantly white southern institutions. Rich research into HBCU fight songs would require situating their repertoire and performance practice within HBCU history, animated by an awareness of the role HBCU marching bands play as culture bearers of Black musical and expressive practices and histories. It is good to remember that despite the Southeastern Conference's economic and media hegemony and the bluster of its pageantry, it does not represent the entirety of southern college football.

As I researched this book, Confederate monuments came down at universities across the US South, accompanied by varying degrees of celebration and mourning, depending on whom you ask. The Southeastern Conference voted to admit two additional members, the Universities of Texas and Oklahoma, stimulating new rounds of the eternal debate around what, exactly, constitutes the geographical and cultural South. Since the 2016 and 2020 elections, topics of race, gender, regional identity, and their intersections—necessary starting points for understanding southern identity and history—have surged to the forefront of national discourse, with books, podcasts, and think pieces galore trying to parse a region that still baffles us all. In what Walker Percy calls "that perennial American avocation," everybody inside and outside the South keeps trying to explain it, and I'd like to think that this book provides one more piece of the puzzle.[29] As Carolin Dutlinger wrote of Walter Benjamin, "For Benjamin, historical inquiry is no conservationist project. His aim is not to reconstruct the past but to bring past events into a dialogue with the present, so that they take on a sudden relevance and become culturally and politically illuminating for the present-day observer."[30] I am no Walter Benjamin, but my book pursues his aims. I only hope that I have not, in the process, outkicked my coverage.

CHAPTER 1

"Hideous with Unearthly Noises"

Early Football Sounds and Spaces

In November 1909, when Clemson University came to Atlanta to play Georgia Tech, several thousand students "invaded" downtown, rending the city air asunder with their "leather lungs," cheers, yells, and a brass band.[1] After defeating Clemson, Georgia Tech students marched through Atlanta two abreast: "Carrying megaphones, tin horns, cow bells, and every other imaginable noise-making device, they came whooping, singing, yelling."[2] Accounts of these noisy bacchanals highlight two key aspects of the soundscape of early white southern college football, which this chapter explores: students' use of a broad sonic palette—cheers, yells, instruments and noisemakers—prior to the emergence of distinctive fight songs, and their privileged marshaling of public spaces in southern cities where football games were played before the advent of regional campus stadiums.[3]

White southern college students were shouting in the Atlanta streets about a new and rough game born in the Ivy League in 1869, two decades before it traveled south.[4] College football was first played by informal, student-led teams competing intramurally or with local athletic clubs, but New England and midwestern university administrators quickly formalized the sport into intercollegiate programs. By the 1890s, these universities ran their football programs like businesses, part of the valorization of modern, industrial, and corporate values that marked Gilded-Age higher education.[5] This historical reality challenges enduring fan beliefs about a spirit of "amateurism"—a nineteenth-century Oxbridge concept indexing elitist ideas about sport as upper-class leisure—that supposedly animates football in its "pure" collegiate form.[6] Tensions between commercialism and tradition, rooted in the amateurism myth, have marked the creation, consumption, reception, and dissemination of fight songs, as this book will show. In the 1890s, professional football also took shape in northern and midwestern states, a development delayed for decades in the South.

Football helped turn the US into a turn-of-the-century "sporting republic," where a popular craze for sport was buttressed by discourse linking athletic prowess with social progress, modernity, civic values, democracy, and military power.[7] In addition to this sophisticated ideological rationale, football spread through college culture because it fit neatly on campuses awash in social clubs and organizations. In its early intramural version, football was only one of many campus societies. Literary, rhetorical, oratorical, and fraternal clubs equipped students for a combative capitalist marketplace, using the martial language of "battles" and "opponents" to describe their competitions.[8] Early college football echoed these clubs' competitive ethos and pageantry, which included rowdy parades, "ever-present band music," "raucous college yells and cheers," and "flying banners."[9] Like these earlier clubs, college football used sonic "insider" symbols to demarcate collective identity: mottos, handshakes, chants, yells, cheers, and songs. These symbols allowed "rooters" to audibly participate in the football spectacle.

A separate but related campus phenomenon predating and informing early football culture was the college song, a loose category which in the nineteenth century referred to a nebulous repertory of songs that college students enjoyed singing.[10] College songbooks from the second half of the nineteenth century were largely compilations of parlor songs, light classical and operetta numbers, minstrel songs, marches, spirituals, drinking songs, and folk songs—styles and repertory that permeated a burgeoning US mass popular culture. The songbooks' few explicitly "collegiate" songs, such as "Fair Harvard," "Old Yale," "Old Nassau," and Cornell's alma mater, came from the Ivy League.[11] Ivy League students sang these stately, hymn-like school songs at early games and pep rallies and soon created peppier, football-specific songs, such as Yale's "Boolah Boolah," which emerged around 1900 from uncertain origins.

In the late nineteenth century, feeding the public's budding fascination with the allure of college life, Ivy League football songs and cheers circulated beyond campus culture and outside New England. A 1901 *Topeka Herald* article exemplified this rhetoric, framing Ivy League songs and cheers as "old" and established:

> Directly the leader starts them off, not on the new war-chant, but on the old one, the "always one." At Princeton it is of "Nassau," and "Tigers" and "Prince-t-o-n." At Yale it is of "Blue," of "Elis" [referring to founder Eli Yale] and "undying pluck." At Harvard, it is of "That's the way they do at Old Harvard." At Pennsylvania, it is of "Pennsyl, Pennsyl, we sing the chorus free," and so on down the list. All have their yells, all are peculiar to the school from whence they sprang. [Then] the singing commences. And it is strange to note, how fond college students are of the tune "Marching Through Georgia." At Princeton the following words are sung to it: "Nassau, Nassau, we sing the chorus free. Nassau, Nassau, we sing the chorus free." At Philadelphia the students have used the words "Pennsyl, Pennsyl, we sing the chorus free," and fastened them to the Georgia marching song. At Harvard one of the old battle songs carries this same air. Many of the smaller schools have also used the famous old song of the Civil War.[12]

Such fawning press coverage contextualized the Ivy League as the font of authentic college football pageantry, illustrating that "age, not modernity, bestowed prestige" in the public's conception of US higher education in this period.[13] Riding on the vector of Ivy League glamour, football came south in the 1890s, part of elite white southerners' longstanding engagement with New England higher education.[14] Since the eighteenth century, the white planter class sent its sons to the Ivies, with Princeton a favored destination due to its conservative faculty.[15] In the late nineteenth century, New South business and civic leaders touted New England universities as models for southern higher education, with football a high-profile way for southern schools to demonstrate modernizing progress.[16]

High-circulation southern newspapers midwifed football into the region through breathless coverage of Ivy League rituals, colors, mascots, and songs, stimulating local interest in the years before radio mediated the game soundscape to listeners. The *Atlanta Constitution* account of the 1905 Princeton-Yale match lionized the power of music:

The singing at the game was inspiring as it always is, but Princeton had more lung power and had the courage to hurl their catchy songs across the field, Yale's reply becoming enfeebled as interest in the game increased. . . . It required Princeton's hymn, "For Old Nassau," to bring about some of the stonewall defense for which old Nassau is noted.[17]

The article's subtitle foregrounded music's affective influence: "Not Daunted by the Certain Defeat Due Their Team, the Princeton Backers Outsung the Yale Contingent With 'Old Nassau.'"[18] The earliest major southern intercollegiate game, the 1892 Georgia-Auburn game in Atlanta, was hyped for weeks by the *Atlanta Constitution*, which laid down an earnest benchmark: "to have this game as 'swell' in every respect as the Yale and Princeton games."[19]

Unsurprisingly, the first southern universities to adopt football consciously tried "to associate their games with those of more established institutions in the northeast."[20] The University of Mississippi chose Yale blue and Harvard crimson as school colors and the University of Georgia used Yale's bulldog mascot.[21] Cross-regional borrowing extended to songs, too. An 1895 Sewanee football songbook paired the "Yale Drinking Song" with Sewanee lyrics, and as late as 1913, Sewanee still set football texts to the tunes of Ivy League fight songs.[22] Such homage "reflect[ed southern] students' ambivalence concerning regional loyalties and their quest to become a part of a more expansive college culture"—a tension that permeates the book.[23] Like students throughout the US, southern college students transferred the concept of yells and cheers from earlier campus societies to the new sport. They were ready to raise the roof.

Sounds: Oral Culture and Instruments

It is not always clear exactly *what* students yelled, chanted, sang, or played in early southern football contexts—only that they did so loudly and, quite often, in public urban spaces. The soundscape of southern PWI football in its first two decades was fluid, with most schools yet to solidify a distinctive sonic identity through lasting and unique fight songs, and encompassed a wide range of sonic phenomena: cheers, yells, chants, and a chaotic use of instruments and noisemakers.

A preview of the 1892 southern championship games in Atlanta stated that the city eagerly anticipated receiving "men from all the principal colleges of the southern states . . . with their 'hur-rah-rahs' and their respective college yells."[24] The University of Georgia already had its own yell in 1892: "Hoo – rah – rah! Hoo – rah – rah! Hoo – rah – rah! Georgia," which UGA students taught a train engineer to replicate on the train whistle. Brazenly and successfully, the students then petitioned Atlanta Mayor William A. Hemphill to override an ordinance forbidding train whistles within city limits so that the train could toot its UGA way through the city.[25] To generate excitement (and sales) before games, newspapers published college cheers, regardless of how inane they appeared on the page. Before the Vanderbilt-Sewanee match—already a major event in 1893— the *Nashville American* reproduced the rivals' cheers:

Vanderbilt! Hoorah! Hoorah!
Vanderbilt! Hoorah! Hoorah!
Hoorah! Hoorah! 'Varsity?
'Varsity! Rah! Rah! Rah!

Sewanee! Rah! Sewanee! Rah!
Sewanee! Tiger! Sis Boom, Ah![26]

Judging from such accounts, oral practice must have differentiated these banal collections of syllables from one another, although print sources flatten them to the point of absurdity.[27] More distinctive southern college yells used novelty syllables, such as Georgia Tech's "Techity-teck! Hoo-reck!" and two of Auburn's early yells:[28]

Prek-e-ge-gek, prek-e-ge-gek
Who-wa, Who-wa.
Siss-boom—hulla-baloo, Auburn.

Ghe-har! Ghe-har!
Ghe-har-har-har-har!
Auburn! Auburn!!
Rah-rah-rah!"[29]

Some early cheers centered on specific rivalries. The Sewanee-Vanderbilt axis stimulated targeted yells, such as one conveying the elite Episcopal university's perspective on their cross-state Methodist rival: "Vanderbilt,

Vanderbilt, leave 'em in the lurch! Down with the Methodists, up with the church!"[30]

In the era before marching bands and cheerleaders carried the sonic burden at football games, southern college students took cheering duty seriously. Cheers and yells were transmitted in print by broadsides, school newspapers, and football programs and orally at campus pep rallies.[31] In the early years of Sewanee football, cheer practices convened *nightly* in the Forensic Hall. Pep rallies or cheer practices typically occurred in chapels, gyms, and cafeterias with their capacious seating and prime acoustics. An October 1909 account of a Vanderbilt pep meeting describes a typical such event: three hundred students gathered in the dining hall to practice yells and songs, hear speeches, and elect a male student "cheer leader for the rest of the season" due to his "considerable experience in leading the yells and songs." The report emphasized students' belief in the affective power of cheering at football games and their moral obligation to display school spirit.[32] Early cheerleaders were important not for acrobatic tumbling and synchronized routines, which came later, but for their vocal pedagogy.

Southern city newspapers covered pep rallies as an important part of emerging football culture and a glimpse of the college mystique. Sportswriter Grantland Rice's report on a 1907 Vanderbilt cheer practice—one of a series of nightly rallies leading up to the Michigan game—exemplifies such coverage: "The mass meeting in chapel tonight gives promise of being a nectarine. There will be a long signal practice in songs as a starter, followed by a heavy scrimmage of the cheering squad. Every student in the university able to attend is expected."[33] Rice named individual yell leaders, and another Nashville newspaper reported that Vanderbilt students practiced Michigan songs and yells to welcome the visiting team, a common practice at the time.[34]

Although historians sometimes argue that college football fundamentally broke with earlier forms of campus culture, the examples in this chapter demonstrate continuity with pre-football rhetorical, oratorical, and literary activities.[35] Football channeled these impulses in a new direction, resulting in a flurry of songs, yells, cheers, and poems. A two-page section of cheers and songs in the 1897 University of Georgia yearbook, "The Weapons of Georgia's Lung Brigade," illustrates this flowering of football-related oral culture, which permeated turn-of-the-century southern yearbooks, student newspapers, and broadsides.[36] These publications also printed overwrought football poems, such as the University of Alabama's 1893 "Narratio Tristis Quaedam" which in neo-classical terms lamented a 32–22 loss to Auburn:

> We'd brought our trumpets to the field, which now in vain we sought
> to shield
> Since only fit to mock us; they soon beneath our coat were hid
> As quickly to the ground then slid; all hope was gone to use them.
> We had some songs we'd fixed to sing which sure had made the welkin
> [heavens] ring
> And touched off Auburn lightly . . . [37]

At southern PWIs, football became an earnest rhetorical object of turn-of-the-century student literary and oral culture, extending rather than supplanting it.

"Narratio Tristis Quaedam" is also notable for its references to early football music. Its mention of songs prepared for the Alabama-Auburn game aligns with contemporary descriptions of students rehearsing specific, ephemeral songs for certain games. The reference to trumpets, more ambiguous, might riff on martial tropes common in football culture, but it could refer to real brass instruments, which popped up early in southern college football pageantry. In the 1890s, civic and military brass bands performed at southern college football games and parades, although references to the songs they played are scarce.[38] Beginning around 1900, southern schools formed student bands for football games, sometimes borrowing personnel from civic and military groups. By 1901, Auburn University had a band that traveled to Atlanta for the Georgia-Auburn game, supplementing vigorous yelling.[39] The First Georgia Military Band, formed in 1906 by the University of Georgia Military Corps, became the foundation of the university's Redcoat band, numbering roughly thirty-four by 1910.[40] In 1906, Georgia Tech launched a fundraising campaign to "secure a band to work in opposition" to the UGA band by "playing martial and other airs" at football games and parades.[41] In 1907, Sewanee students subscribed to a brass band fund and the University of Kentucky launched a football band.[42] In November 1909, Vanderbilt's newly formed student band debuted at the Vanderbilt-Sewanee game.[43] The 1910

Georgia-Georgia Tech game in Atlanta featured a parade of five hundred Georgia students headed by the UGA band, while the Tech "band and rooters . . . march[ed] to town to lend their lusty throats to the bedlam."[44]

More chaotically, students also used random noisemakers at football events. In 1896, Georgia Tech students marching in downtown Atlanta employed "noise-making instruments of large proportions: tremendous horns, which they manufactured themselves, tested their lung capacity and made the air hideous with unearthly noises."[45] In November 1901, Auburn and Georgia fans in Atlanta "made their presence felt everywhere" with "horns and megaphones [making] the air hideous with discordant sound."[46] A 1909 postgame Georgia Tech parade featured students "carrying megaphones, tin horns, cow bells, and every other imaginable noise-making device."[47]

Early White Southern Football Events in Urban Public Spaces

As some of these sources show, football-crazed southern college students were making sonic mayhem in the public spaces of Birmingham, St. Louis, New Orleans, Montgomery, Atlanta, Nashville, and other southern cities in the late nineteenth and early twentieth centuries.[48] Before the post–World War I advent of southern campus stadiums, the region's pageantry unfolded in city streets with parades, carriages, and electric cars full of shouting fans; at municipal fairgrounds, fields, and parks during games; and in hotel lobbies and train depots where fans and teams amassed, cheered, and sang. Brian Ingrassia describes the college stadium as a "liminal" space, "a ritual zone where social and cultural meaning was malleable."[49] These urban southern public spaces were liminal, too, occupying a continuum of private-to-public zones, access to which was circumscribed by class, race, and gender.[50] Using Nashville and Atlanta as case studies, this section reconstructs those soundscapes. In this period, Nashville hosted Vanderbilt and Sewanee games and Atlanta hosted Georgia Tech and University of Georgia games.[51] Both cities, especially Atlanta, were centers of New South boosterism. Local newspapers therefore hyped the new sport that drew spectators and their dollars, yielding robust accounts of football pageantry which, in dialogue with other contemporary sources, create a rich interpretive window into the sonic pageantry of early southern college football.[52]

On fall Saturdays in the 1890s, trains conveyed football teams and large groups of southern students from college towns to cities.[53] Crowd size could swell impressively; five thousand people assembled at Atlanta's Piedmont Park for an 1893 game.[54] Boisterous students gave traveling fans and players rousing send-offs at train depots, as when five hundred fans "beating tin pins, singing songs and giving 'varsity yells'" dispatched the Vanderbilt team to its 1910 Yale game in New Haven.[55] After arriving at the destination depot, team members and student fans decamped to a hotel, on foot and loudly. Students commandeered hotel lobbies with cheers and songs, later parading to playing fields and, post-game, around central city districts. After a 1909 Vanderbilt-Sewanee game, Sewanee students wound their way through Nashville, bouncing back and forth between hotels:

> The city was Sewanee's last night. Yelling and singing and rah-rah-rah-ing, a line of the Purple marched from the Maxwell House to the Duncan [Hotel], badly scaring a horse en route, back to the Maxwell, over to the Tulane [Hotel] . . . back to the Maxwell and around the lobby several times, singing the song of the Tiger's [*sic*] victory. . . . At the Tulane Hotel, where the boys yelled for the benefit of golden colors floating from the mezzanine floor, they gave the Vanderbilt enemies fifteen cheers also.[56]

Roughly four blocks separated the Maxwell and Tulane hotels, with the Duncan Hotel another two blocks up North Cherry Avenue from the Maxwell. Traversing downtown streets between these points, raucous Sewanee men would have passed two churches, a fire engine house, and the Vanderbilt Law School, coming within shouting distance of the city jail four blocks away. That they avoided a stay there signified the legal immunity conferred upon them by social status, a subject to which we will return.[57]

For the inaugural Auburn-Georgia game in 1892, a noon train from Athens disgorged several hundred male students and their female dates at an Atlanta depot. Upon arriving at the Kimball House hotel, "they sounded the university college yell in thundering chorus, which at once brought every guest . . . to the corridors all the way up to the sixth floor." The Kimball House, partly financed in its second incarnation in the 1880s by New South booster extraordinaire Henry Grady, was preferred lodging for visiting students. Auburn students arriving from south Alabama by train also swarmed to the Kimball and "joined in mighty chorus to sound their college yell." A reporter wrote approvingly that "the big city of Atlanta belonged to the college boys yesterday. They gathered here from Georgia and Alabama in vast armies, and stormed Georgia's capital with their merry yells, songs, jokes and extravagant jollity."[58] When teams went home, fans loudly greeted them at the depot.[59] The 1909 report cited earlier suggests that the operatic scale of these football bacchanals could wildly disrupt urban life: four thousand fans marched in that year's Clemson-Georgia Tech pre-game parade.[60]

Andrew Doyle accurately and briefly notes that the "carnivalesque" and "outlandish misbehavior" on display in these spectacles indexed "assumptions of class privilege."[61] The most egregious of these customs, however, was one he didn't focus on: the nightshirt parade, a pajama-clad procession through city streets that baldly foregrounded the unassailable social position of its participants. In a 1907 post-game nightshirt parade, Vanderbilt students snaked through Nashville's business district, popping into theaters, hotels, and train stations to bellow college yells and songs. The late-night parade, headed by a drum corps, climaxed when students stormed the Bijou Theater stage to disrupt a play about college life with yells and songs![62] More than one thousand Vanderbilt students celebrated a 1910 tie with Yale "clad in nightshirts, pajamas and curtailed bonnets . . . march[ing] in undress parade through the streets of Nashville," stopping at hotels and ending up at Belmont, then a women's college. [63] Similar accounts exist of many college football nightshirt parades in southern cities of the time; at Vanderbilt, the custom continued well into the twentieth century.

Far from suffering legal or social repercussions for their public shenanigans, students garnered gleeful press coverage. A 1907 *Nashville American* article hailed one Vanderbilt nightshirt parade as "the greatest welcome given to [homecoming warriors] since the old First Tennessee [Confederate regiment] arrived." [64] An 1893 *Atlanta Constitution* report stated approvingly that "the great heart of Atlanta goes out to the happy-hearted gong-singers from college land this morning . . . let's all go and be young again, shouting ourselves hoarse and throwing our hats high up in the air.[65] Press coverage at times documented a lenient law enforcement response: "Police officers, realizing that they were up against it, smiled and said nothing."[66] For participants, such escapades were a boyish lark, an attitude preserved in a Sewanee song of the period:

> Hand in hand together, boys, we've wandered through the night,
> Steps and voice in unison and every heart was light,
> Always fit and ready, boys, for anything in sight,
> While we were boys at Sewanee.

> Yes; and there were maidens, boys, who heard our footsteps beat
> While the moonlight shone along the still-deserted street;
> We woke for them the echoes with our serenadin' sweet,
> While we were boys at Sewanee.[67]

It is doubtful, however, that city-dwellers of marginalized social status felt so indulgent toward masses of rampaging elite white men. As Marina Peterson writes, "urban public space is a key site for the expression and negotiation of citizenship in cities."[68] Her insight applies to these turn-of-the-century spectacles in which southern white males loudly expressed their privileged citizenship contemporary with the formation of Jim Crow. What would Black residents of Atlanta or Nashville have feared from such displays when at the time, spectacle in the form of public lynchings was a common tool for the maintenance of southern white political and social domination?[69] For them, hearing students' nocturnal "footsteps beat," as the Sewanee song put it, could sonically signify regionalized and terrifying power relations.[70]

When glowing press accounts of these boisterous events are read in tandem with other contemporary sources, the disconnect between laws governing public deportment and the illegal behavior of white male students highlights their social privilege. In the late nineteenth and early twentieth century, southern authorities worked to control the urban soundscape, part of a growing national effort to police urban noise in ways that refracted class conflict.[71] Atlanta's and Nashville's municipal codes of the time distinctly forbade the behaviors routinely displayed in college football revelry and lauded in city newspapers. The 1899 Atlanta City Code outlawed the following infractions on pain of a $100 fine or thirty days in jail: acting "in a disorderly manner," making "any noise at night calculated to disturb the public peace, or to annoy any of the citizens," "assembling and loitering on the streets in sufficient numbers . . . to be an obstruction" on streets or sidewalks, creating "unnecessary or unusual noise" such as "hooting" and "hallooing," and appearing in public "in an indecent" state of dress.[72] Nashville's turn-of-the-century city codes threatened "riotous and disorderly persons" guilty of "breaches of the peace, noise, disturbance, or disorderly assemblies" with arrest and imprisonment.[73] Its 1901 municipal codes directed people to avoid "wandering about the alleys or streets," congregating in front of public buildings, and obstructing sidewalks and streets. "Loud and unusual" or "tumultuous" noises were forbidden, along with appearing publicly in "indecent" dress.[74]

These codes read like a litany of the conduct exhibited with impunity by white male college students, reinforcing a longstanding regional notion that the white southern man is invested with "legitimate claims to power and control."[75] Here white male students enacted their social privilege, publicly using "insider" sonic symbols to "surround themselves with secrecy" and "stress their difference from the common world."[76] Their bombastic, mobile displays of conspicuous leisure declared to working-class observers, women, and people of color that participants had time, resources, and social capital with which to disport themselves—even in the face of codes that bound the rest of the citizenry.[77] Racialized and gendered southern custom, more powerful than law, legitimized the boisterous white masculinity on tap in these events. This kind of behavior remained visible in southern football culture over the next century, attesting to the durability of "broadly shared or at least broadly recognized notions of white southern manhood . . . central to southern culture."[78]

Additionally, these revelries and their press coverage likely drew "regular" citizens into the hubbub of southern college football, although a vocal contingent of southerners did lament unseemly student behavior around the sport.[79] Before the eras of radio, television, and professional football teams in the region, off-campus football events probably helped create non-student fandom in the South. Functioning as informal advertising, students' public revelry likely aroused curiosity about college life through sonic displays that hinted enticingly at their "membership in elite subculture."[80] Already in the late nineteenth century, college football was linked to increased enrollment.[81] Public urban football pageantry may have augmented that trend in the South. This pageantry unfolded during the "fulcrum of American urban history," when the nation "made the transition from a rural to a self-consciously urban society."[82] In this transitional time, football spectacles in Atlanta and Nashville helped shape gendered, racialized, and classed ideas about recreation and leisure in the new urban South.

Conclusion

Although the pageantry of southern college football in this period unfolded through public spectacles audible and visible to many off-campus observers, the sonic elements of the pageantry were focused on marking insider identity. Gendered, classed, and racialized privilege may have been on display in this pageantry in urban southern spaces, but the sounds involved—noisemakers, fragments of meaningless syllables—were likely incoherent to observers. Southern college students were not yet eager, as they would be in later years, to identify specific songs by which their schools' football programs would be rendered sonically legible to outsiders. Additionally, the nascent and rambunctious customs of southern PWI football emerged just as the South began "to feel the effects of an evolving national mass culture."[83] The sonic pageantry documented in this chapter reflected broader trends across the US, with few, if any, traces of sectional or regional identity, "mark[ing] the assimilation" of southern universities into "national intercollegiate culture."[84] Football was modern; it represented science and progress, ideologies with which southern flagship universities were eager to align themselves at the turn of the century. As tradition and custom surrounding southern football continued to develop in the early twentieth century, its music launched novel opportunities for southerners to consume and contribute to mass culture, sometimes in regionally distinctive ways and sometimes not, as the book will show. Old South myths and New South ideologies interfaced in dynamic ways in higher education at the time.[85] Football's customs and traditions served as a malleable cultural text that facilitated flexible expression, allowing southern students to not only participate in national culture, but also to project regional or sectional identity. Soon, southern students were using songs in their football pageantry that celebrated the honor-centric masculinity that animated Lost Cause mythology about the white South—the subject of the next chapter.

CHAPTER 2

Songs of the South

Football Music and the Lost Cause

If you flip through the 1910 University of Kentucky yearbook, you will run across a play titled "The Illinois Game," a thinly veiled fictional account of Kentucky's real-life victory over the University of Illinois in the 1909 football season.[1] In the play, Kentucky students sent off their northbound team at the Lexington depot to the sound of a band playing "Hail, Hail, the Gang's All Here," "Dixie," and "My Old Kentucky Home." Unsurprisingly, given the era and the intersectional nature of the match, the latter two songs were blackface minstrel numbers that articulated white plantation fantasies about the antebellum South.[2] From scattered sources such as this, a trend emerges: early white southern football used songs that projected Lost Cause fantasies and indexed sectional sentiment.[3] This chapter builds on Lost Cause scholarship to document how white southern football's early soundtrack foregrounded and contributed to white investment in regional symbolism that romanticized the antebellum South.[4]

White southerners forged the Lost Cause myth between 1890 and 1920 through educational materials, monuments, and public events such as Confederate Memorial Days, which peaked in intensity and frequency contemporary with college football's emergence in the South.[5] Both kinds of large-scale southern spectacles were created for and attended by white people, held outdoors in public spaces, and used ritualized pageantry, including the same constellation of minstrel and Civil War songs.[6] These commonalities are not hard to account for. Between 1890 and 1920, white southern youth grew up on a diet of core songs used in Lost Cause textbooks. Often published by the United Daughters of the Confederacy (UDC), these textbooks included "Dixie," "Bonnie Blue Flag," and "Maryland, My Maryland" and used "'My Old Kentucky Home' and other plantation melodies [sic] . . . as evidence of slave happiness."[7] "Dixie" and Stephen Foster songs appeared in the UDC's *Historical Catechism for Children of the Confederacy* and in the 1918 songbook *Echoes from Dixie*, compiled by J. Griff Edwards, director of UDC choirs.[8]

Wilmington, North Carolina, public schools celebrated Robert E. Lee's birthday in 1900 with "My Old Kentucky Home," "Dixie," and "Old Folks at Home."[9] That same year, a Confederate veterans' reunion in Kentucky featured the Confederate Glee Club's performance of "Dixie" and "My Old Kentucky Home."[10] An orchestra played "My Old Kentucky Home," "Maryland, My Maryland," "Way Down Upon the S'wanee [sic] River," "Dixie," and "The Bonnie Blue Flag" at a 1903 Confederate memorial banquet hosted by the New Orleans UDC.[11] At a 1901 Kentucky event sponsored by the Confederate Veterans Association and the UDC, "whooping and emotionalism found unanimous vent only when the band played 'Dixie' again and again and 'My Old Kentucky Home.'"[12] When early southern PWI football culture used this repertory, they were unambiguously expressing Lost Cause ideology and planting a musical seed that blossomed in the regional fight song repertory for decades to come.

Minstrel Songs in Southern Football

Blackface minstrelsy developed in the 1830s as a musical-theatrical entertainment in northern cities, first aimed at and consumed by the white working class. Its songs, dances, tropes, and stock characters were animated onstage by "mostly ethnic white men [who] performed imagined and witnessed aspects of black performativity."[13] This performativity encompassed music, choreography, archetypal gestures, slang, clothing, and dialects, yielding jumbled racialized caricatures. Dan Emmett and the Virginia Minstrels and Christy's Minstrels began touring the US in the mid-nineteenth century, reaching stardom and disseminating minstrelsy's theatrical conventions and repertory. Songs written for minstrel shows took on lives of their own through sheet music and performance in other contexts. Minstrel songs and performance styles reflected a cultural and aesthetic dynamic that Matthew Morrison theorizes as "Blacksound": a "dialectic construction" mingling "real and imagined black performance aesthetics," forming the "aesthetic basis" of minstrel songs by Stephen Foster and other composers.[14] The result was a genre that projected and constructed "whiteness . . . in relation not to 'being' but to performing the black 'other.'"[15] This sensibility threaded its way through the southern college football soundscape, a later extension of the nineteenth-century trend of white composers, actors, and impresarios primarily profiting from Blacksound in minstrelsy.[16] Minstrelsy so pervaded the founding of American mass popular culture in the nineteenth century that William Mahar argued that it did not merely "'touch' every form of popular *music*; it is linked to the very formation of antebellum popular *culture*."[17]

By the turn of the twentieth century, minstrelsy permeated US mass popular culture, where it endured well into the twentieth century.[18] In the South and elsewhere, the songs, dances, tropes, stock characters, and images of minstrelsy were ubiquitous in theater and concert culture, recordings, stories and poetry, and visual media such as advertising. Minstrelsy also saturated US college campuses, where turn-of-the-century glee clubs and quartets performed minstrel songs, printed them in songbooks, and staged minstrel shows as campus fundraisers and entertainments. By the time minstrel songs entered turn-of-the-century football culture at southern schools that educated mostly elite white men, the songs had attained middle-class respectability. Christy's Minstrels, for whom Stephen Foster composed, began performing "programs that emphasized 'respectability'" as early as the late 1840s.[19] Foster's Christy's Minstrels songs became middle-class parlor fare, sung by white and even Black entertainers at concerts outside minstrel show contexts.[20] Foster fitted the once-vulgar minstrel tradition to middle-class sensibilities through "heavy doses of nostalgia, sentiment . . . a gradual backgrounding of the rebellious free black, [and] an increasing turn to the character of the sentimental slave.[21] The narrative stance of the "sentimental slave" is articulated by the two Stephen Foster songs that entered southern football culture, "My Old Kentucky Home" and "Old Folks at Home."

"My Old Kentucky Home," chiefly used by the University of Kentucky among southern schools, appeared in school culture as early as 1907 when its chorus was first printed in the Kentucky yearbook.[22] (The 1903 yearbook printed a football contrafactum on the minstrel song "Hot Time in the Old Town Tonight," but it didn't "stick" in the school's football culture.[23]) By 1913, "My Old Kentucky Home" was ensconced in University of Kentucky football culture, often underscoring the team's entrance and exit from the field.[24] A 1915 alumni dinner featured "My Old Kentucky Home" alongside old and new college yells.[25] By the early 1920s, University of Kentucky fans and observers regarded it as the school's signature football song. An effusive 1923 student article praised the song's affective power and the university band for strategically playing this "battle hymn" at a Kentucky-Georgia Tech game—exploits noted by the *Atlanta American*, which stated that in an athletic context, the song "causes men to do things that they are not otherwise capable of doing."[26] An account of the 1924 Kentucky-Tennessee game mentioned "My Old Kentucky Home" four times, describing its "soul-stirring strains" and noting that the Tennessee band played it in deference to the victors.[27]

The text of "My Old Kentucky Home" brims with sentimentalized agrarian references. Its putative narrator romanticizes bright sunshine and "ripe corn tops" that in real life would have indexed backbreaking work in the heat by the enslaved people purportedly represented by the narrator. The chorus describes children rolling around cabin floors—contextually implying a reference to enslaved children—in a primitive, unbothered state, "merry, happy and bright." In 1914, University of Kentucky publication *The Idea* speculated about the song's composition in similar terms, stating that it was

> written as a sort of musical souvenir of . . . the prosperous days "before the war." One morning while the slaves were at work and the darkey children were romping in the quarters, the visitors [including Stephen Foster] were seated on a bench in front of the mansion . . . the trained ear of the composer caught the exquisite melody in the [mocking] bird's variations of the sweet music of the thrush and then and there . . . he jotted down the notes and scribbled several verses.[28]

The white student writer at *The Idea* used wildly euphemistic language ("the prosperous days 'before the war'"; "the slaves were at work") to "obscure and aestheticize" the reality of a southern economy built on the chattel labor.[29] The account also links race-based slavery to the natural world via birdsong, implying that this arrangement was a naturalized part of a bucolic social order—a pillar of Lost Cause mythology. Foster's text reframed grueling Black physical labor as recreational, rendering it a subject of light entertainment for white consumption.[30]

The University of Florida used "My Old Kentucky Home" too; it appeared in a short early twentieth century collection of football songs along with minstrel songs "Carry Me Back to Old Virginny," "Dixie," and "Massa's in de Cold, Cold Ground," which all looked back with undisguised longing at the antebellum South.[31] Stephen Foster's other plantation-centric minstrel song, "Old Folks at Home," also appeared in this University of Florida football songbook. Set on the Swanee (Suwannee) River, the song was written by Stephen Foster in 1851 for Christy's Minstrels. "Old Folks at Home" yearns for a sanitized antebellum plantation through the narrative perspective and dialect of an elderly Black person. Like "My Old Kentucky Home," the song's text obscures the historical reality of the plantation as a site of forced Black labor through nostalgic framing of the world outside the plantation as "sad and dreary." "Old Folks at Home" showed up in University of Florida football culture throughout the twentieth century in compilations of football songs.[32] An arrangement of the song used by the UF band late in the twentieth century confirmed its durability.[33]

Other minstrel songs popped up in early southern PWI football culture, including "Moonlight in Dixie," "Carry Me Back to Old Virginny," "Hot Time in the Old Town Tonight," "Levee Song" (the tune used for the University of Texas song "The Eyes of Texas"), and, of course, "Dixie."[34] Like Stephen Foster's songs, they obscured or minimized Black physical labor in the service of white plantation mythology. The well-worn words to "Dixie" speak flippantly of longing for a "land of cotton" where the past is remembered, handily concealing what "cotton" would have meant for enslaved African Americans. The common thread? Minstrel songs in early PWI football culture worked, like other elements of the plantation myth, to "veil" the realities of enslaved Black labor.[35]

There are other stakes to consider, economic though intangible, articulated in Matthew Morrison's "Blacksound" concept: PWIs used blackface minstrel songs—sonic fantasies about Black labor, imagined by many to represent Black musical culture—to build the pageantry of their million-dollar football enterprises while excluding Black citizens. Black men were physically excluded from faculties and student bodies of these schools at this time, despite their occasional use in football culture as a sort of human mascot.[36] But they were summoned spectrally in these songs, laboring ghosts that animated the soundscape of early southern college football. This musical stream was a grotesque antecedent or inverse of the labor structure of contemporary NCAA football, wherein young Black men animate PWI football with real—not imagined nor remembered—labor. SEC and other US schools' post-integration exploitative reliance on Black athletic labor has been documented and analyzed by William Rhoden and Billy Hawkins, who frame the economic dynamic in terms of the plantation, foregrounding the discomfiting ease with which the white South has historically consumed unpaid Black labor.[37]

Scholars have discussed "Dixie" in southern PWI football culture, although this literature tends to frame it as a Civil War song.[38] "Dixie" was first published in 1860 as a minstrel song, attributed to Daniel Emmett of the Virginia Minstrels.[39] After its entry into the nineteenth-century urban sheet music market as a minstrel song, this musical commodity was recycled as a symbol of authentic white southern identity, first as a Confederate marching song, then as a Lost Cause anthem and all-purpose signifier of white southern resistance on political, cultural, and social fronts. Despite the song's roots as a piece of notated music attributing the piece to a specific composer, it attained mythical folk-song status in the South, where "many southerners thought 'Dixie' appeared out of thin air."[40] Christian McWhirter documents white southerners' efforts to grapple with their anthem's northern authorship: from 1903 to 1905, the United Daughters of the Confederacy pushed to change the song's words, a move resisted by Confederate veterans. Some southerners dealt with Dan Emmett's geographic origins by recapitulating him as a regional hero; when he toured the South in 1895 with the A. G. Field Minstrel Show, he was received with audience enthusiasm and avid reviews in Lost Cause publications.[41]

From the early years of southern college football, "Dixie" was thought to bear elemental affective powers in athletic contexts, especially at intersectional games. In 1902, the University of Missouri band played the song in a parade after defeating Iowa State.[42] In 1905, the University of Michigan band played "Dixie" as a courtesy to their opponent,

Vanderbilt.[43] A 1908 report highlighted the song's affective power in that year's Michigan-Vanderbilt game:

> The band played "Dixie," and the Michigan students gave the Vanderbilt yell . . . "Holler 'Dixie' to them fellows, and they'll play our boys to a standstill"—this came from one of the Ann Arbor boys. The rebel yell was given, but on this occasion Vanderbilt failed to respond.[44]

In 1909, the University of Missouri band played "Dixie" while Missouri fans "'cut up' something scandalous."[45] Sometimes new football texts were set to "Dixie," as when the 1897 University of Georgia yearbook indicated that "Georgia Rah" should be sung to "Dixie."[46] The omission of "Dixie" by non-southern opponents could be noticeable; in this era, courtesy dictated that bands play opponents' songs. A reporter noted at the 1907 Vanderbilt-Navy game that the Marine Band "rendered popular airs, 'Dixie' excepted, throughout the struggle," an omission covered by other press.[47]

Civil War Marching Tunes in College Football

Early southern college football used other Confederate marching tunes from the Lost Cause musical matrix, mainly "Bonnie Blue Flag" and "Maryland, My Maryland."[48] As the book later shows, these tunes, along with "Dixie," were used well into the twentieth century, especially resurging at times when white southerners felt their regional racial hierarchy besieged by external political and cultural pressures. Additionally, perhaps surprisingly, the Union marching song we think of as "Battle Hymn of the Republic" became popular with white southern college students in this period. In the latter half of the nineteenth century, a tune of unknown origin was paired with the abolitionist text "John Brown's Body," then in 1861, with Julia Ward Howe's abolitionist poem "Battle Hymn of the Republic." The marriage of Howe's text with the tune yielded a marching song that became a rallying cry for Union soldiers and sympathizers, including Black Union regiments and enslaved people, with sporadic use by Confederate soldiers.[49]

Given the song's Yankee resonance, the United Daughters of the Confederacy later worked to repress southern usage of it; as late as 1932, the Georgia UDC chapter lobbied to remove "Battle Hymn" from church hymnals.[50] UDC efforts notwithstanding, in the late nineteenth century, white southern schools began using the song's refrain ("glory, glory, hallelujah") at football events. "Glory, Glory Alabama" could be heard at a 1908 College Night event in Tuscaloosa, billed as "a football song," and "Glory, Glory to Old Auburn" found its way into Auburn football culture not long afterward, where it has remained. However, the "Battle Hymn" refrain became largely identified with the University of Georgia as "Glory, Glory to Old Georgia." The association solidified very early, although the song was never designated the university's official fight song, which is "Hail to Georgia Down in Dixie." The 1897 yearbook documents an early use of "Battle Hymn" in UGA football culture with a song called "'Auburn's Colors,' to be sung to the tune of 'John Brown's Body.'" The refrain was "Glory, glory to Old Georgia."[51] By fall 1898, the Atlanta press noted UGA's use of the song.[52] A decade later, the UGA student paper could "equate the influence and effect" of the song with the affective power of iconic Ivy League fight songs "Boolah Boolah" (Yale) and "Fight for Cornell."[53] UGA music professor Hugh Hodgson arranged a band version in 1915, which the school still uses, and the song regularly appeared in UGA songbooks beginning in 1922.[54]

Michael Lanford argues that early southern football culture's use of Civil War songs—even "northern" songs such as "Battle Hymn"— indexed general sectional sentiment and military affect, thereby still vaguely perpetuating a hazy Lost Cause sensibility regardless of tune origin.[55] Certainly the "meaning" of "Battle Hymn" has been contingent and fluid in southern football contexts, as is the case with all music. A Dixieland arrangement of the song can also be heard at some UGA games and on its athletics website, recontextualizing the Union marching song in the framework of southern musical practice.[56]

Conclusion

Although blackface minstrel songs and Civil War marching tunes gave the impression of arising from the mists of a hazy, folk-like collective southern consciousness, they were mostly commercial products of the nineteenth-century sheet music market centered in urban New England. Southerners who performed and consumed these songs in football contexts, especially songs that trafficked in Lost Cause mythology, were using commercial products of mass popular culture to create an instance of Eric Hobsbawm's "invented tradition"—in this case, an invented tradition of "authentic" southern music. These songs facilitated institutional, symbolic participation in what historian Jack Carey describes as the project of "identity-inventing" at southern flagship schools. From the 1890s through the early twentieth century, these universities

> created origin stories that culturally and symbolically rooted modernizing, developing institutions in the mythologized past. Importantly, these invented traditions, which invoked the antebellum plantation as a central metaphor . . . connected the development of southern flagships directly to the promotion of white supremacy.[57]

Building a sonic regional identity shaped by nostalgic white cultural sensibilities formed part of a larger project of racialized myth-making at proto-SEC schools, which also had a gendered dimension. Trent Watts notes durable regional versions of masculinity in which white southern men historically "define themselves against models, places, and traits regarded as feminine or as black."[58] Civil War songs sonically and implicitly defined white southern masculinity against Blackness, especially Black masculinity, and the minstrel songs that musically foregrounded imagined free Black labor foreshadowed PWIs' post-integration reliance on Black football players. The musical-athletic echo highlights uncomfortable historical continuities in the white South's posture of entitlement toward Black labor.

Nonetheless, it would distort extant evidence to argue that the emerging song repertory of southern PWI football in the late nineteenth and early twentieth centuries projected a totalizing, primary, or coherent sense of regional identity or sectional sentiment. It often reflected southern white college students' investment in a nascent national college culture and avid consumption of mainstream popular music. For example, the University of Georgia's "Hail to Georgia Down in Dixie," written around 1915 by a UGA student and later adopted as the school's official fight song, used a new tune and poem which, aside from the reference to "Dixie" in its first line, sounded like the kind of peppy march ubiquitous in mainstream commercial music of the time.[59] The next chapter covers the emergence of two such southern fight songs whose reception histories neither refract nor index regional identity, instead embodying debates over competing notions of musical authorship operative in broader US commercial music in the early twentieth century.

CHAPTER 3

Who Wrote This?

Authorship and Copyright in Two Early Fight Songs

"The pigskin we can punt, the baseball we can bunt!" This clunker of a poetic line hails from "Old Vandy," one of Vanderbilt University's earliest fight songs. Written ca. 1904 by two women, Saidee S. Luff and Emma L. Ashford, "Old Vandy" was a march scored for voice and piano, printed for campus distribution but never commercially published. It spoke of outclassing athletic rival Sewanee and quoted the Vanderbilt yell "Sissss-Boommmm-Hey! Vanderbilt!"[1] The typical early twentieth-century student body created and used many such songs that never achieved the status of enduring fan favorite or official fight song. Writing fight song texts and tunes allowed students, including women, to engage with early southern football culture from the sidelines.[2] Despite the survival of many such songs and robust evidence of their cultural significance, scholars have paid scant attention to early twentieth-century college songs in any region of the US, as a campus pastime or as a music industry trend.[3] To explain this kind of historiographic gap, Elijah Wald argues that most histories of twentieth-century popular music favor exciting, unusual developments, captured on recordings and later perceived as "revolutionary," over mundane, widespread musical experiences.[4] And few categories of music were more mundane, repetitive, and ephemeral than college songs of this era. For every collegiate Tin Pan Alley hit like "Sweetheart of Sigma Chi" or the "Washington and Lee Swing," hundreds of blandly serviceable songs appeared briefly at college dances, pep rallies, and football games, then evaporated from institutional use without ever gaining wider distribution through commercial publishing or recordings.

From this morass of early college songs surfaced a few fight songs that are still in use at SEC schools, a relative rarity at these institutions until the 1920s and 1930s. This chapter covers the emergence of two such songs between ca. 1900 and 1920 with a focus on reception debates around their authorship, origins, and copyright: Georgia Tech's "Ramblin' Wreck" and the University of Florida's "We Are the Boys of Old Florida." With their scarce early printed sources and conflicting origin stories, these songs highlight the challenge of assigning copyright, authorship, and owner-ship to fight songs that used pre-existing tunes, circulated orally in stu-dent culture, and employed texts that likely developed collectively and spontaneously. These case studies are early examples of similar recurring conflicts in the history of southern college fight songs, which illuminate the competing notions of authorship operative in early twentieth-century US musical culture.

"Ramblin' Wreck from Georgia Tech":
Arrangements, Dissemination, and Copyright

A shared thread in the century-plus histories of "Ramblin' Wreck" and "Boys of Old Florida" is their use of common melodies circulating in national college culture of the early twentieth century, despite persistent student and alumni beliefs about their uniqueness. "Ramblin' Wreck from Georgia Tech," the official fight song of the Georgia Institute of Technol-ogy, uses the melody of "Son of a Gambolier," a drinking song of uncer-tain origin popular in US college culture, including early college song-books, since the nineteenth century. Tech students minimally tweaked the song's lyrics at the turn of the twentieth century, swapping "I'm the son of a, son of a, son of a, son of a, son of a gambolier" for "I'm a helluva, helluva, helluva, helluva, helluva engineer." Despite these facts, debate among Tech fans and alumni about authorship, ownership, and origins of the song and its arrangements rumbled throughout the twentieth cen-tury. The tune has been used by other universities, with likewise-nominal modifications to its liquor-sodden text. Although early Tech students recalled singing the song in the 1890s, the first extant printed reference to it in campus materials seems to be in the 1908 *Blue Print* yearbook.[5]

Despite a tune and text structure borrowed from a drinking song and circulated orally by Tech students, in 1919, voice-piano sheet music for "Ramblin' Wreck" was published claiming copyright for Georgia Tech band director Frank Roman.[6] Roman's cover for his manuscript orchestration of the song, likely post-dating the 1919 sheet music by a few years, bore the inscription "Original Orchestrations of 'Ramblin' Wreck' and Ga. Tech's alma mater written in Atlanta by Frank 'Wop' Roman/Bandmaster."[7] Neither source indicates the use of an extant tune or lyrics that circulated in student culture years prior to Roman's arrangement. Intentionally or not, these early sources implied Frank Roman's musical and lyrical authorship of "Ramblin' Wreck."

Although the Tech community later alluded to Frank Roman's copyright on "Ramblin' Wreck," Library of Congress records contain no copyrights registered by him on the song between 1906, when he was likely first affiliated with Tech, and his 1928 death.[8] Such references probably refer, then, to Roman's copyright claim printed on the 1919 voice-piano sheet music, which became the blueprint for his later band arrangement of the song. The only feature distinguishing Roman's piano and band arrangements of "Ramblin' Wreck" from a straightforward rendering of "Son of a Gambolier" is a jaunty four-bar introduction leapfrogging up and down an octave. Roman's arrangements were in Eb, the key of at least one setting of "Son of a Gambolier."[9] In 1931, the Melrose Music Corporation filed the first copyright on "Ramblin' Wreck" after buying arrangement rights from Frank Roman's widow and attributed the song's text and music to him.[10]

Frank Roman, the putative author and copyright-holder for "Ramblin' Wreck," was an Atlanta-based barber and musician deeply involved in Georgia Tech's early musical life for more than two decades. He came to campus to organize or direct a band in the early 1900s and worked there until his death in 1928.[11] Roman's geographical origin and early biography is unclear. After military duty in the Spanish-American War, he settled in Atlanta and performed in local bands, theater orchestras, and the Atlanta Symphony Orchestra.[12] A flute and piccolo player, he joined the Atlanta Federation of Musicians in 1905.[13] Roman was likely Italian-American; in addition to the ethnically stereotyped nickname "Wop," used by the city and campus press and by Roman himself, his family of origin lived in New York and Italy.[14] Roman contributed several other songs to Tech's repertoire, including the 1926 "Yellow Jacket March" and an alma mater.[15] His 1926 copyright registration for these two songs demonstrated familiarity with the process.[16] Roman also wrote the Tech song "Up With the White and Gold," published posthumously by Melrose Music.[17]

In the 1920s, as part of the contemporary craze for all things collegiate, "Ramblin' Wreck" circulated outside the Georgia Tech orbit through radio, recordings, and published music, with authorship typically attributed to Frank Roman. In the mid-1920s, Roman's Tech Rambler orchestra accompanied the school Glee Club on campus and Atlanta radio broadcasts, where they sang college songs such as "Ramblin' Wreck," light classical music, and other repertoire.[18] In 1925, Columbia recorded the Tech band and Yellow Jacket Four, a male vocal quartet, performing "Ramblin' Wreck" and other Tech songs.[19] Roman likely arranged or conducted the music for these Atlanta recording sessions, and Columbia Records listed him as composer for all songs. The campus community proudly declared it "the only phonograph record devoted to Southern college songs," an enthusiastic and possibly erroneous claim.[20] When Okeh Records released a jazz dance band recording of "Ramblin' Wreck" a few weeks later, the label credited Roman as lyricist and composer.[21] Jazz dance bands for Okeh and Victor Records recorded the song in 1929 and 1931, respectively; as with earlier records, both labels credited Roman as composer.[22]

The college song show *The Sports Revue*, seen by 30,000 people weekly in the late 1920s, used "Ramblin' Wreck" in performances across the US.[23] It was one of the few southern college songs in Thornton W. Allen's 1927 *Intercollegiate Song Book*, which reprinted Frank Roman's 1919 voice-piano arrangement complete with his copyright claim.[24] The song's dissemination beyond campus and football contexts continued into mid-century. In 1941, "Ramblin' Wreck" was the theme song of the Broadway show *My Sister Eileen*, used to mark stage entrances of the main character, an ex-Tech football player. In 1942, bandleader Fred Waring, whose act and public image was built on collegiate tropes, played "Ramblin' Wreck" on his popular national radio show. Georgia Tech Glee Club tours spread the song in the 1950s; when Nikita Kruschev and Richard Nixon met in Moscow in 1959, they sang "Ramblin' Wreck," which Kruschev knew from the Tech Glee Club's 1953 *Ed Sullivan Show* appearance. From the 1930s through 1950s, the song was recorded several more times by dance orchestras.

Because of the song's national profile, by the early 1940s, debates about its origins, authorship, arrangements, and ownership began to simmer in the Georgia Tech community. In 1943, the Tech alumni magazine expressed what became a recurring and quixotic desire to pinpoint "exactly when the words originated . . . in addition to the early and final arrangements of the music."[25] The article interviewed Michael Greenblatt, Georgia Tech band director ca. 1910–1913 and Frank Roman's predecessor, and questioned Roman's claims to musical originality on the grounds that Greenblatt's arrangement came "first" and was therefore authoritative:

> Without detracting from the fame of Frank or "Wop" Roman . . . who copyrighted "Ramblin' Wreck" with his variations as they stand today. . . . Mike Greenblatt . . . created the first band arrangement and score of the song—a handwritten manuscript—little thinking that one day it would become . . . nationally recognized.[26]

In 1945, in a burst of purported clarity on the song's textual origins, a Tech alumnus claimed that a member of the school's first graduating class was responsible for the lyrics.[27] Probably thanks to public statements such as this, by the late 1940s, perception of Roman as "Ramblin' Wreck" composer had shifted. Press coverage of Roman's posthumous 1949 cemetery monument scrupulously quoted the monument inscription which stated only that he had "orchestrated the present music for the famous 'Ramblin' Wreck' and wrote the original music for the Georgia Tech alma mater."[28]

With Frank Roman's musical role revised, Michael Greenblatt became the main character in the next cycle of discourse around song ownership and copyright. In 1953, he prepared a new arrangement of "Ramblin' Wreck" and publicly transferred its copyright to the university for $1.[29] The Atlanta press crowed that "Georgia Tech at last owns 'Rambling Wreck,'" a civic victory marked by the Atlanta Symphony Orchestra's performance of an "elaborate" arrangement of the song by symphony conductor Henry Sopkin.[30] Greenblatt's 1953 description of the song complicated exclusivity claims by the Tech community:

> [It was] current then in Southern college circles. The boys at Georgia [UGA] had the same tune with different words. So did the Auburn boys. I heard also they sang it around the turn of the century at Alabama and at Tennessee. It was an old Yale song called "The Son of a Gambolier."

We found two leads as to the origin of the work. One placed it as a nine-teenth century English drinking song. Another described it as a cho-rus number from a French opera. At any rate the tune was common in college circles around 1908. So we at Tech decided that "Rambling Wreck" was it. I arranged it and away we went with the current words and several other verses that have been lost in time. Other colleges around here dropped it after awhile, but Tech loved it and held on.[31]

Greenblatt allowed that Roman had arranged it "into a more modern form with lots of trumpet flourishes," a version which spread nationally through radio and in-person performances. In 1954, the Georgia Tech comptroller stated nebulously that income from Greenblatt's transferred copyright and the alma mater and "Yellow Jacket March" copyrights, which Tech renewed in 1954, benefitted students.[32]

Greenblatt desired to restore "Ramblin' Wreck" to an "authentic" nineteenth-century style with an "original hop-step tempo," the way "we played [it] as boys in 1908," which Greenblatt clarified was "the way it's supposed to be."[33] The nostalgic belief in a fixed, authentic version of "Ramblin' Wreck" echoed the 1925 Tech student council's plans to engrave it and the alma mater on copper plates for posterity, "to keep them exactly as they are now, for future days." The council's plans reflected early Tech concern over song ownership and authorship and a belief in Frank Roman's responsibility for the song's uniqueness: "At present there are only a few pencil-written copies of the alma mater as played by the Tech band and if they should be lost, or something happen to Frank Roman its composer, Tech would probably suffer the greatest misfortune of hav-ing lost forever this beautiful song."[34]

Although Greenblatt wanted his 1953 "Ramblin' Wreck" arrangement and copyright transfer to function as authoritative statements on the song's style, history, and ownership, they did not. The Atlanta press and Georgia Tech community continued to resurrect fruitless dialogue about the song's "originality," showing a durable unwillingness to conceive of it as a drinking song used by multiple schools with a text scarcely altered from the original. In 1955, the *Atlanta Constitution* described Dickinson College's 1870s use of "Son of a Gambolier" and printed Dickinson's lyr-ics, nearly identical to Tech's, with earnest commentary:

[Dickinson's] song does have the ring and swing of "Ramblin' Wreck" and might well be the papa of that famous song . . . if any stalwart son of the White and Gold wishes to take umbrage at this revelation, let him do so with me . . . [the person who passed along the information to the journalist] was not seeking to embarrass or enrage anybody [connected with Tech].[35]

An Atlanta newspaper article, ca. 1959, alluded to another iteration of the ongoing debate:

To those who called and wrote saying that Frank (Wop) Roman wrote the music for Georgia Tech's "Ramblin' Wreck" song, Mr. Roman did indeed take out the copyright on the song in 1919. Mr. Roman . . . had written an arrangement of the music soon after he took over his band job, but did not get it copyrighted until six years later.[36] The melody itself dates to an old folk ballad called "Son of a Gambolier" and the song was published in Tech's first yearbook, the *Blue Print* of 1908, some time before Mr. Roman came on the scene. "Tech never realized any monetary value from any of these copyrights," wrote [a Tech administrator], "but the public relations value of the song could not be purchased for any amount of money."[37]

These debates, which Greenblatt's gesture failed to suppress, resurfaced in the early 1980s, indicated by an Alabama attorney's note to the Tech President enclosed with a copy of "Son of a Gambolier" from an old songbook: "You might want to see this. . . . Here is your Ga Tech fight song!"[38] In 1985, Tech alumni publications tackled the problem in detail, asserting that "Son of a Gambolier" was a Scottish drinking ballad and laying out its textual similarities to "Ramblin' Wreck"—not a difficult charge, since the Tech lyrics scarcely deviated from the original.[39] The articles tried feebly to pin down textual origins using the conflicting recollections of elderly Georgia Tech alumni about the song's 1890s appearance.[40] One author tried to establish the drinking song's genealogy through reprints of early twentieth-century British primary sources.[41]

This resurgence of interest in the roots of "Ramblin' Wreck" was doubtless stimulated by an Atlanta law firm's 1984 investigation into its copyright history at the request of the Georgia Tech Alumni Association.[42] The firm communicated its findings with Tech's PR office, illustrating the high-stakes nature of the debates. The firm found that multiple arrangements of the song were copyrighted and that "Tech could compose its own version . . . and register its claim to copyright in that version." Attorney George M. Hopkins confirmed that

> Band music can be copyrighted for a particular arrangement of old songs. . . . The original version of "Rambling Wreck" [likely Frank Roman's 1919 sheet music with its opening riffs] is in the public domain and can be played by anyone without the payment of royalties. If a particular version of "Rambling Wreck," which is covered by an unexpired registration, is played, for profit, then the owner is entitled to a royalty fee.[43]

After distinguishing between a public-domain tune and distinctive arrangements of it that could be subject to copyright, Attorney George M. Hopkins advised the PR Office to inform alumni that

> the original tune is in the public domain and can be played by anyone without any payment. Various versions of this original tune have been copyrighted by various people. . . . Georgia Tech makes no payments to any of these copyright owners; however, it does have blanket licenses from ASCAP and BMI . . . to play all tunes which are in the portfolios of these companies.[44]

By the late twentieth century, the combination of a folk tune and Frank Roman's slight additions to it—a few introductory bars that became iconic to the Tech community—had generated decades of disagreement over authorship and originality. Consider a Tech alumni's 1994 letter articulating surprise that other schools used the tune with lyrics nearly identical to Georgia Tech's version. The editor wrote back reassuringly that despite the obvious similarities, "Tech made it famous. Frank Roman . . . revised 'Ramblin' Wreck,' adding many trumpet flourishes, and copyrighted it. Roman's version became a national hit. It was played by every name band, and broadcast from coast to coast."[45] The editor's response aligned with a long tradition of claiming Tech ownership of a public-domain tune via the idea of a special musical arrangement that invested "Ramblin' Wreck" with a degree of distinctiveness.

The University of Florida's
"We Are the Boys of Old Florida"

Similar debates over authorship and origins have surrounded "We Are the Boys from Old Florida," used at the University of Florida since the late 1910s, although not to the extent of "Ramblin' Wreck." [46] UF sources show that UF students borrowed from and tweaked the same potpourri of tunes and texts used at other southern PWIs in the first few decades of regional football. A 1911–1912 broadside of UF football songs and yells included "The University of Florida," sung to "Dixie" and riffing noticeably on its lyrics; a second UF text sung to the "Washington and Lee Swing"; and six nondescript yells.[47] Within a few years, two other songs joined the school's football repertory, gaining enough traction that they are now the main UF football songs: "We Are the Boys from Old Florida" and "Orange and Blue," discussed briefly in Chapter 7. As with "Ramblin' Wreck," the effort to assign clear origins or authorship to "We Are the Boys" has foundered on the commonality of its tune, used since the early twentieth century by the University of Nebraska ("Dear Old Nebraska U"), the Toledo public school system ("We Are Proud for Toledo"), and, with variation, the University of Chicago ("I'm Strong for Chicago").[48] Along with a shared tune, these songs employ the same lyrical template, constructed of stock couplets, into which schools' names can be inserted ("where the girls are the fairest, the boys are the squarest . . . in all kinds of weather, we'll stick together"). Although cross-institutional use of this tune and accompanying textual template has been noted since the 1960s, the UF community has still tried to locate individual authorship and an origin date for its version of the song.[49]

Consistent among the UF community's accounts of "We Are the Boys" is a belief that the song originated with a UF student in the late 1910s. Several accounts assign authorship to Robert Swanson, a student active in campus and town musical life. After Swanson's 1979 death, his widow stated that he wrote the song in 1919 after service in World War I.[50] Other accounts assign authorship to UF student John Icenhour, Swanson's contemporary and also active in the campus and Gainesville music scenes, or suggest that the two co-wrote the song.[51] The kinds of sources often extant for twentieth-century songs composed in notation and registered for copyright do not seem extant for "We Are the Boys." Library of Congress records show no copyright on the song between the 1910s and 1930s, and no manuscript seems extant until 1943.[52]

Instead of chasing notions of individual authorship, futile in this case, documenting Icenhour's and Swanson's participation in the World War I college music scene suggests how they, or someone like them, tweaked a broadly circulating popular tune with generic, malleable lyrics into "We Are the Boys from Old Florida." Cornetist Robert Swanson worked in the Gainesville and Jacksonville music scenes in the late 1910s, playing popular hits at minstrel shows, teaching dance, and directing the UF minstrel troupe.[53] Violinist John Icenhour co-founded the University Jazz Band in 1918 and sometimes led it.[54] The group performed at dances and minstrel entertainments, on and off campus.[55] Icenhour and Swanson participated in a collegiate scene that, like others across the US, featured a vibrant oral-print exchange of sheet music, recordings, radio broadcasts, and live shows, where popular tunes and texts circulated willy-nilly. The growing popularity of jazz, which valued improvisation on a flexible musical blueprint, and the music industry norm of publishing multiple arrangements of a song, meant that a popular tune and some stock lyrical phrases could be easily, spontaneously manipulated.

The earliest print references to "We Are the Boys" date from Swanson's and Icenhour's student years; in January 1921, a Pensacola newspaper printed UF songs, labeling "We Are the Boys of Old Florida" "A Minstrel Song of 1920."[56] The association with minstrelsy supports the notion that someone like Robert Swanson or John Icenhour, involved in campus and civic minstrelsy, adapted the tune's standard lyrics for UF use. In 1923, "We Are the Boys of Old Florida" first appeared in the university yearbook.[57] The song circulated via recordings and radio the rest of the decade, with a university quartet first recording it in the early 1920s.[58] A 1924 radio show representing US colleges, broadcast on Tampa's WDAE, featured UF students singing "We Are the Boys" among other football cheers and songs.[59] WDAE broadcast the song again in 1930, and likely on other occasions.[60]

By 1928, a University of Florida publication could describe "We Are the Boys" and "Orange and Blue" as the school's two "official" songs.[61]

Nonetheless, lack of clarity about the song's origins and status surfaced in the 1930s. When the *Tampa Tribune* printed its lyrics in 1930, it attributed them neither to Icenhour or Swanson, but to a W. R. Frazier.[62] UF students bemoaned the lack of an "official school anthem" in the early 1930s and proposed that four songs, including "We Are the Boys" and "Orange and Blue," be considered for this status.[63] Out of the UF song repertory, these two seemed most popular in the 1930s, when they often bookended UF glee club performances and appeared with other songs and cheers in campus materials—with firm injunctions for freshmen to learn them.[64]

The first copyright filed for "We Are the Boys" seems to have been by Thornton W. Allen, a prolific college song publisher we will meet in the next chapter, who in December 1940 copyrighted a mixed-voice arrangement of it for a University of Florida songbook.[65] Notably, Allen, perpetually cautious about attributions, did not designate a lyricist in his registration, suggesting he was unaware of a credible claim on the role.[66] A music industry veteran by 1940, Allen would have known the song used a common tune. Allen's songbook may have marked the first commercial publication of "We Are the Boys." A 1943 handwritten manuscript SATB arrangement seemingly by Robert Swanson—the manuscript bears the inscription "Bob Swanson, Author"—is also extant, suggesting that at this point in UF history, some institutional effort may have been made to determine the song's precise "authorship."[67]

Conceptual Flexibility for New Times

Later in the twentieth century, changing social contexts at SEC schools re-activated the flexible, communal concept of authorship that under-girded the early creation of "Ramblin' Wreck" and "Boys of Old Florida." Although UF and Georgia Tech were all-male schools when these fight songs emerged, they have long been coeducational, resulting in fresh scrutiny of old traditions. In the early 1990s, roughly fifty years after UF admitted women, revisionist efforts targeted the male-centric text of "We Are the Boys of Old Florida," with the ensuing controversy receiving media coverage. In 1992, UF's Committee on Sexism and Homophobia recommended revision of the song to university administration, with students offering substitutions of "Gators," "strong," or "persons" for "boys."[68] The UF student newspaper endorsed textual change and suggested that absent official alteration, students could still insert their preferred noun(s) when singing "We Are the Boys" at games.[69]

Those resisting textual alterations adopted various defenses. University administration expressed concern that an unspecified 1940s copyright (likely Thornton W. Allen's 1940 copyright on a mixed-voice arrangement, as discussed earlier) may have prohibited changes. UF football coach Steve Spurrier downplayed the term "boys," insisting that the song's dominant pronoun was "we."[70] A law student and president of a campus honor society stated that likeminded students would declare war on edited versions of the sacred song.[71] Other objectors, on-campus and off, marshaled a "slippery slope" defense, complaining that if "boys" was deemed offensive, the text should be reworded as "We are the politically correct, gender neutral individuals from somewhere."[72] One sportswriter wrote that altering "We Are the Boys" would stimulate revisions to other SEC fight songs.[73] Another journalist acknowledged "boys" as problematic but cited the importance of tradition and dismissed the problem as unserious enough to warrant administrative attention.[74] It seems the dispute was never resolved; the university's athletic website uses the old lyrics, and UF home game crowds still audibly sing the text as it entered campus culture around 1920.[75]

Similar issues around "Ramblin' Wreck from Georgia Tech" emerged years after Tech admitted women in 1952. Unlike fight songs which center on-field action, "Ramblin' Wreck" foregrounds the gendered identity of the student body, with lyrics such as "like all the jolly good fellows, I drink my whiskey clear" and a reference in Verse Two to the narrator's son attending Tech while his daughter only dresses up in school colors and cheers. In February 1988, a Georgia Tech diversity task force proposed updated lyrics acknowledging women, but alumni and students shouted down the idea, using some of the same objections that came up in the UF song debates.[76] At this point, songs so long in institutional use seem unlikely to be subject to significant alteration; they have become what university communities overwhelmingly consider to be fixed musical objects.

Conclusion: Clashing Notions of Musical Authorship

Disputes about originality, authorship, and ownership of early southern fight songs refracted conflicting notions of musical authorship that operated simultaneously in early twentieth-century US music culture. University communities' desire to determine singular, unique origins for their songs reflected Western European classical music's idea of a fixed musical work, notated in print and traceable to an individual source to whom authorship can securely be assigned. This "work concept" has been active in Western European classical music culture since the early nineteenth century.[77] Its gold standard of a fixed, notated, single-authored musical work has been central to US copyright law, which is "invested in Euro-American conceptions of creatorship."[78] Despite the concept's roots in European classical music, it has shaped ideas about popular music production and consumption in the United States, where even "the most banal 'formulaic' songs are eligible for copyright as long as they have not been copied.[79] However, Americans' consumption, production, and reception of popular music has historically clashed with legal reification of the work concept, leading to robust conflict over music as intellectual property in the United States. Early twentieth-century college campuses like the University of Florida and Georgia Tech reflected Jim Samson's assessment of social scenes whose "musical life as a whole can be more reasonably characterized through practices than through works."[80] In this case, collegiate practices for fight song production and performance included borrowing commonly used tunes with no identifiable authors, tweaking the accompanying lyrics, and circulating the results orally in many cases. These practices collided with the "work concept" that other members of the university community later tried to retroactively apply to earlier fight songs generated by collaborative and spontaneous practices.

College song publishers of the 1920s and 1930s also relied on the "work concept" to protect their property, with varying degrees of success. A 1938 lawsuit about a fight song, written like our two songs in the early twentieth century, graphically displayed these colliding notions of musical authorship. In 1938, "Someday My Prince Will Come" in Disney's *Snow White* aroused the ire of Yale alumni who thought the song echoed "Old Eli March," written by Wadsworth Doster ca. 1909 and acquired by Thornton W. Allen in 1936 for an *Intercollegiate Song Book*. The alumni alerted Doster, who alerted Allen, who sued Walt Disney Productions and affiliates, to much media fuss.[81] Filed in US District Court in October 1938, Allen's suit alleged 27 of 32 bars of the Disney song to be "infringeable" for sharing with "Old Eli March" the key, tempo, "unique chorus structure," "unique harmonic structure," repetition of thematic elements, intervallic content on identical pitches, and rhythm. The defense called as expert testimony notable US musical figure Deems Taylor, who asserted "the two songs were overall so entirely different in character" that Allen's stylistic bean-counting missed the musical forest for the trees. Any harmonic similarities between the songs, Taylor argued, derived from stock chord progressions pervasive in music textbooks and other music of the time. Armed with detailed charts, the defense's other experts testified to the ubiquity of compositional formulas in popular music.[82] In a June 1941 opinion, the New York district judge hearing the case ruled Thornton Allen's claims of musical similarity unimportant or inaccurate, and the case's outcome ultimately hinged on the circumstantial (im)probability of Frank Churchill's having known "Old Eli March" before writing "Some Day My Prince Will Come."[83]

Much like student and alumni beliefs around this chapter's two songs, the narrow musical criteria that Thornton Allen marshalled, and the defense's response to it, suggests a myopic musical perspective which denied that the early twentieth-century college song idiom relied on stock chord progressions, conventional melodic gestures, and template-like phrase structures pervasive in contemporary popular music. Allen's lawsuit and the reception histories traced in this chapter also highlight how the "work concept" valorized by music publishers collided with jazz-influenced, improvisational college music-making of the late-nineteenth and early twentieth centuries, in the South and elsewhere. As later chapters show, Thornton W. Allen's protectiveness of his college song catalogue exemplified this conceptual collision and forcefully shaped the SEC fight song repertory in the 1920s. And it all began with the subject of the next chapter: the 1910 "Washington and Lee Swing," the southern fight song that moved the college song into the popular music industry and upon which Allen built an entire publishing career—rightfully or not.

CHAPTER 4

The Song That Changed Everything and the Man Who Published It

Thornton W. Allen and the
"Washington and Lee Swing" (1910)

In the 1910s, a new, syncopated fight song written and published by students at Virginia's tiny Washington and Lee University swept white southern campuses. The "Washington and Lee Swing," published by student Thornton W. Allen in 1910, began popping up at regional football games, parades, pep rallies, and dances, its lyrics tweaked by various universities.[1] It soon became the first southern model for regional schools searching for distinctive fight songs, as when a North Carolina newspaper argued in 1916 that Davidson College needed a "first-class" song like Yale's "Boolah Boolah" or the "Washington and Lee Swing."[2] Although Washington and Lee University never joined the Southeastern Conference, by the 1920s, its iconic "Swing" was used as a fight song by proto-SEC schools like the University of Alabama and Tulane University. In 1924, publisher Thornton W. Allen's threatened litigation over unauthorized use of the song at these schools generated two new fight songs, which the next chapter documents. The first fight song to transcend campus culture, the "Swing" moved into the 1920s popular music industry and launched the Thornton

53

W. Allen Company, which published many fight songs, SEC and otherwise, over the next two decades.[3] The "Swing" gained traction amid a US vogue for football catalyzed partly by the military's use of football in wartime training. Mass media spread the sport, too; in the early 1920s, college football soared across fledgling radio broadcasts that conveyed game pageantry through microphones "strategically placed . . . to capture the sounds of the stadium: the fans, the songs, the cheers, the bands."[4] 1920s newspaper coverage of high school and college football doubled, brimming with inflated rhetoric and littered with superlatives.[5] Songs like the "Washington and Lee Swing" mediated the football cult off-campus, part of a broader national fascination with jazz-age college life.[6]

The "Washington and Lee Swing" emerged in the early years of the music industry's college song subgenre, when songs such as "College Yell: March Two-Step" (1908) and "Sweetheart of Sigma Chi" (1911) reported on the styles, slang, dance crazes, and amorous pursuits of college men and "coeds," a riveting new creature on the US social landscape. Trade magazine *Presto* described a college song market grown robust by 1922: "The customer never knows the extent of the line of so-called college songs until he or she inquires at the music counter of the big music stores in any city. Even college men see new numbers in the array of college songs and songs favored by college glee clubs."[7] In the 1920s, glee club arrangements of college songs were joined by voice and piano, banjo, ukulele, banjulele, and dance band versions using the "hot" sound, a vague term denoting the danceable, jazz-inflected music that soundtracked 1920s campus life. By facilitating college social activities, commodifying college culture, and circulating college trends, these songs supplied meta-commentary on the emergent "youth" marketing category while helping create it.[8] As the 1920s went on, performers with "star texts" built on collegiate tropes amplified the college song fad.[9] Pop sensations Fred Waring and the Pennsylvanians and Rudy Vallée and the Yale Collegians crooned college songs, including the "Washington and Lee Swing," in varsity sweaters and posed for publicity photos holding cheerleading megaphones.

While the music industry circulated collegiate tropes, 1920s US college campuses brimmed with phonograph parties, variety shows, sheet music, songbooks, records, dance crazes, radio shows, glee clubs, dance bands, and banjo, ukulele, and mandolin groups. Town-and-gown musical hubs flourished as students patronized music stores, movie theaters, and hotels and supper clubs with dance bands. Southern students continued to take trains or cars to "away" football games, partying in host cities to hot dance-band music. College students' keen interest in peers at other schools coalesced in the 1920s into a national collegiate monoculture, with athletic pageantry a key point of intra-campus exchange.[10] These students were forming a "new network of socialization" via "campus peer groups," with music a primary and unexamined mode of this formation.[11] This chapter explores white southern college peer groups' musical practices through the early histories of the "Washington and Lee Swing" and its publisher, both of which heavily shaped the broader college song industry and the SEC fight song repertory.

The "Washington and Lee Swing" (1910)

By the time Washington and Lee University students published a voice-piano version of the "Swing" through Thornton Allen's nascent company in 1910, the song had already circulated to other southern schools.[12] The "Swing" kept spreading in regional football contexts post-publication through events such as a 1912 football parade in Lexington, Virginia, when Washington and Lee students marched behind the school's band singing the "Swing" with Virginia Tech fans and students present.[13] The song's verse-refrain structure and stock musical phrases and harmonic progressions, ripe for jazz improvisation, worked well for dance bands, who disseminated it through the South in the 1910s.[14] At a 1914 Tampa, Florida dance, the song "was introduced [locally] . . . for the first time and made a great hit."[15] The next year, the "Swing" was played as a one-step at a cotillion in Austin, Texas, alongside foxtrots and hesitations, another popular dance of the time.[16] A 1916 Shreveport, Louisiana event featured a dance orchestra playing ragtime numbers, including the "Swing."[17] A 1920 tea for "college boys" in Tampa ended with couples dancing to southern college songs: Georgia Tech's "Ramblin' Wreck," the University of Georgia's "Glory, Glory to Old Georgia," and the "Washington and Lee Swing."[18]

How the "Swing" moved into the popular music industry in the 1920s is more mysterious, but its title probably helped by signifying flexibly, perhaps coding as patriotic to consumers who thought it referred directly to

George Washington and Robert E. Lee, not to a tiny school named after them. Lee's surname may have spurred regional interest within and outside of the South; the "Swing" was more heavily marketed in the region, and there was at the time a national vogue for southern-themed songs.[19] In addition to "Swing" sheet music re-printed by Thornton W. Allen in 1920, hot dance bands recorded the song in the 1920s. Some recordings were instrumental, foregrounding improvisation as testament to the song's jazz potential, such as an exuberant Dixieland version recorded in 1928 for Victor by southern college dance band Snooks Friedman and the Memphis Stompers. Some, like Columbia's 1923 recording by the Columbians Dance Orchestra De Luxe, featured a male vocal quartet backed by a dance band. The Hal Kemp Orchestra's 1928 Brunswick recording of the "Swing" included two takes, a dance band version with and without male vocal quartet.[20] And as the next chapter documents, Okeh Records released the song in 1924 as the "Tulane Swing," sparking Thornton Allen's litigious ire. In September 1930, pop star Rudy Vallée recorded it for Victor. Clearly, whoever could claim authorship, ownership, and copyright of the "Swing" had a hit on their hands.

Confirming such claims, however, has proved tricky; although no manuscript sources for its tune, text, or early arrangements seem extant, "Swing" origin stories have abounded.[21] In the 1920s and 1930s, Washington and Lee alumni, including Thornton W. Allen, recounted conflicting tales about the song's roots, agreeing and diverging at key points. The accounts concurred that between 1905 and 1910, Washington and Lee students created music and words for the "Swing," arranged it for university ensembles, then copyrighted and published it. Non-Allen recollections also concurred that the "Swing" circulated orally at Washington and Lee before Allen published and copyrighted it in 1910.[22] Where the origin stories conflicted was over precise roles in the song's creation and, therefore, over authorship claims.[23] Aside from Thornton W. Allen's accounts, these stories credited student Mark Sheafe with picking out the song's chorus on a mandolin, maybe as early as 1905, and teaching it orally to the university mandolin orchestra. All accounts attributed chorus text to Clarence Robbins, which made the "Swing" into a football song. Accounts (other than Thornton Allen's) held that Allen got involved only *after* the chorus's melody and text appeared, *may* have written the verse's melody (with text by Robbins), *definitely* arranged the song for the university band, and *certainly* copyrighted and published it in 1910.

Sources dating from the period of the song's creation substantiate some of these claims. Newspaper evidence shows that by late 1908 or early 1909, the tune's refrain was circulating on campus, credited to Mark Sheafe, and soon acquired text by Clarence Robbins.[24] Sources also confirm that the university band under Thornton Allen's directorship debuted the "Swing" in a reasonably polished incarnation (likely meaning it had acquired verses) in February 1910.[25] US copyright records show that in May 1910, Mark W. Sheafe, Thornton Whitney Allen, and Clarence A. Robbins copyrighted the "Swing" and published it through Allen's "company," which probably consisted of Allen's arranging for printing and filing for copyright.[26] When the copyright came up for renewal in 1920, Washington and Lee campus rumors swirled that Allen was selling the song's rights.[27] The sale fell through, and Allen re-published the "Swing" in 1920 with a partner who printed and distributed several thousand copies of it; Allen later claimed to have spent a hefty sum publishing and advertising this edition.[28] Thornton W. Allen's company re-published the "Swing" in many keys, time signatures, instrumentations, and arrangements over the next two decades.[29]

Despite consensus among other alumni that Thornton Allen midwifed the "Swing" through arranging and conducting rather than composing, by the mid-1920s, he claimed the lion's share of the song's credit, legacy, and profit.[30] In the absence of extant business records, it is unclear how much Allen profited from the song, although his protectiveness of it in the 1920s and 1930s, documented in the next chapter, suggests his belief in its commercial potential. Allen's most robust extant claim to "Swing" authorship came in his November 1924 article for the Washington and Lee alumni magazine, doubtless stimulated by Okeh Records' release of the song as the "Tulane Swing" earlier that year.[31] Allen's article boasted of the national reach of the "Washington and Lee Swing" through records, sheet music, and player piano rolls, stating that "over fifty of the best universities and schools have adopted it." He also credited Mark Sheafe only for "the title and a few bars of the music," adding boldly that "The 'Swing' as it is played and sung today is largely my own work" and that Clarence Robbins "came up with words for my new melody." To justify why he was only now promoting the song and defending its copyright nearly fifteen years after its initial publication, Allen averred that scarce time and money had prevented him from maximizing its commercial potential in the 1910s.[32]

As the song's popularity in the commercial music industry expanded in the early 1930s through performances and recordings by stars such as Rudy Vallée, hard feelings surfaced in the Washington and Lee community over Allen's territorialism. In November 1934, the student paper complained that Sheafe and Robbins "never received a cent from [their] labors, despite the wide sale of sheet music and recording rights."[33] The same month, the alumni magazine credited an entirely different student, Walter Bootay, for the song's melody.[34] Neither article mentioned Thornton Allen, but their publication in close temporal proximity suggests a 1934 alumni dust-up over the song. Confusingly, after years of covering "Swing" authorship controversies, the alumni magazine in 1941 unequivocally labeled Allen the song's composer.[35] As late as 1978, the debate resurfaced when an alumnus argued that Allen had only functioned as song arranger.[36] The alumnus stated boldly that although "many leading universities credit Allen with composition of their official marching and victory song," Mark Sheafe deserved primary credit.[37]

Complicating these debates was the fact that early twentieth-century popular song drew heavily on stock musical conventions, meaning songs of the era could sound much alike. The "Swing" chorus resembled, for instance, the opening of the early 1890s "Zacatecas March" by Mexican composer Genaro Codina, which circulated in piano, band, and mandolin sheet music, recordings, and performances in the early twentieth-century US. The march was performed in Richmond, Virginia, around the time the "Swing" emerged at Washington and Lee; it is possible a "Swing" co-writer heard and retained it.[38] Equally likely, however, is that the two works' similarities reflect their deployment of common harmonic progressions and melodic gestures ubiquitous in popular music of the period.

Thornton W. Allen's Early Career

Who was Thornton Whitney Allen (1890–1944), the man at the center of the "Washington and Lee Swing" authorship storm? Although now obscure, Allen was in his own time well-known in US music publishing.

His writing, arranging, acquisition, publication, and promotion of college songs, southern and otherwise, helped create a market for them from the 1920s through the early 1940s.[39] Before this, from the early 1910s to the 1920s, Allen built a career in New England's classical music scene as an entrepreneur and impresario, an evangelist for "good" music keen to capitalize on the commercial potential of classical programming and bring worthy music to the masses. After childhood musical instruction, the New Jersey native attended Washington and Lee University ca. 1910–1913 where he founded and directed the band and worked with other students to copyright and publish the "Washington and Lee Swing."[40] While in college, he also worked as a *New York Herald* correspondent.[41] After leaving university, Allen launched a barrage of musical organizing and promoting in New England, undergirded by his belief that large-scale classical music events could function not only as "a source of entertainment and education, but also as a business venture."[42] In 1915, Allen organized the Newark Music Festival.[43] In 1916, while president of his own Newark Musicians' Club, Allen started the New Jersey State Federation of Musicians, with the vague aim "to bolster up the musical conditions in this state."[44] That year he also launched subscription concerts, described as "high class almost to the extreme," at New York's Robert Treat Hotel, where exclusive clientele such as Metropolitan Opera stars ate fancy refreshments and danced to popular orchestra fare.[45] In 1917, Allen organized a Newark series that featured classical music stars Fritz Kreisler and Josef Hofman.[46] He also wrote for classical publications, working ca. 1915–1916 for the *Musical Courier*, although he exaggerated or misrepresented his editorial role.[47] By 1917, he called himself a "musical manager, self-employed."[48] In late 1919 or 1920, he returned to the *Musical Courier*.[49] Although the described activity level suggests indefatigable energy, Allen claimed a health exemption from the World War I draft.[50]

Although Thornton Allen's "company" put out only a handful of pieces aside from the "Swing" in the 1910s and early 1920s, his entrepreneurial wheels kept turning.[51] Allen's classical music activities of this period may have led him to consider the economic potential of the collegiate music consumer. In 1915, his *Musical Courier* travelogue, "Virginia and the South," asserted that musical instruction at Virginia colleges would create a large audience primed to consume "music in its higher forms."[52] Although this vision most immediately reflected Allen's interest in an untapped classical music sector, it may have given him the idea of catering to the southern university student market through college songs. The 1915 travelogue also documented early instances of Allen's focus on profit, arguing that southerners' desire for concert music was ripe for harvesting by northern investors.[53] His career-long concern for maximizing profit later expressed itself through persistent anxiety over authorship and copyright of his college song catalogue.

What Counts as "Good Music" and Who Counts as Collegiate?

In 1927, Thornton W. Allen published his first college songbook. Containing songs from more than one hundred colleges and universities, including a few southern schools, it marked his professional turn toward the genre. Allen's preface framed college songs as "good music," a product of elite cultural associations, informing readers that the book contained the "principal" songs of the "foremost schools," by "authors, composers, and arrangers well known in musical and literary fields."[54] Along with other sources from Allen's early career, the 1927 preface illuminates a conceptual foundation of his publishing work: a Eurocentric notion of "good" music, which determined what kind of compositions merited copyright protection. Although nebulous, "good music" in US musical discourse of the time indexed the styles and ideologies of Western European classical music and defined itself against novelty songs and Black-derived ragtime and jazz, which by the early 1920s saturated popular music.[55] The resulting campaign of "cultural uplift," waged by music critics, publishers, and record companies, mapped moral and educational value onto aesthetic hierarchies.[56]

Allen's 1915 *Musical Courier* travelogue made explicit the racialized dimensions of his hierarchy of musical value, which participated in this broader discourse. Its essentialist commentary framed southern Black Americans as innately and primitively musical, creators of an open repository of folk materials available for whites to freely consume: "In the South . . . the darkey loves to play and sing and the white people love to dance to his melodies. And to hear the darkey sing, accompanying himself on the banjo or guitar, is a treat no Southerner would miss."[57] Allen also credited Black "mammies" for shaping white southern children's musical sensibilities by singing "old songs" to them.[58] Allen's belief in Black musical expression as timeless supported his view of it as an archive for white consumption, in contrast to cultural expressions he trafficked in which (he thought) were produced at specific, knowable, copyrightable times. Allen wrote that he and his friends "dance[d] to the tune of the *old* darkies' banjos and guitars" and "stretch[ed] ourselves out on the lawn and listen[ed] to an *old* mammie tell us the funny *old* darkey stories, of which her supply seemed unlimited."[59] Despite his nostalgic embrace of Black music, Allen did not label it "good," stating that "whether the darkey knows or appreciates good music or not, there is born within him a great love for things melodic."[60] Paternalistically, Allen suggested giving "the negro" formal music education, including Black-only sections in concert halls, to "help to educate him along these lines."[61]

Conclusion

On the strength of the "Washington and Lee Swing" and his early career in classical circles, Thornton W. Allen became the dominant US college song publisher in the 1930s and early 1940s. Along with other collegiate products in popular culture, his songs implicitly asked and answered the question, "Who counts as collegiate?" As John Thelin notes, early twentieth-century "artifacts and symbols of college life, although sometimes seemingly frivolous, were in fact symptomatic of serious issues about social mobility and obtaining prestige in American life."[62] The college ideal portrayed in US media and purveyed by popular culture in the first half of the twentieth century, including Allen's college songs, centered first on the white male collegian and secondarily, as a romantic object, the white female student.[63] Songbooks like Thornton Allen's 1927 edition reified this exclusive vision of the college life by using only white schools' songs.[64]

Not only did Allen promote a whitewashed, male-centric version of the US college experience, he sometimes drew on Black musical culture to do so. As his travelogue indicated, he regarded Black musical labor and expression as a font of consumption and inspiration for white spectators, existing outside the protections of copyright, royalties, and compensation. This belief aligned with US intellectual property and copyright law that has historically "marked whites as producers/consumers of intellectual property in a system of racial capitalism and people of color as objects of production/consumption."[65] Privileged by silent, racialized aesthetic hierarchies of copyright law that valorized constructed notions of individual "originality," this notion of musical authorship was reified in the 1909 Copyright Act.[66] The US copyright system has therefore enabled white performers, composers, and audiences to replicate, profit from, and consume Black musical aesthetics and Black "intellectual performance property."[67] Thornton W. Allen profited from Black aesthetics and intellectual property when he published the "Metropolitan Rag" in 1917, two years after excoriating ragtime in the *Musical Courier*.[68] As Chapter 6 discusses, the University of Alabama fight song "Yea Alabama," which Allen published and promoted, was also ragtime-inflected, and the "Washington and Lee Swing" traded on the cachet of the term "swing," which at the time of the song's 1910 publication likely indexed Black musical and expressive culture.[69]

But as influential as Allen was becoming in the college song subgenre, and as loudly as southern male students were singing male-centric football texts and roaming southern city streets in pajama-clad post-game frenzies, theirs were not the only voices in the southern football soundscape. The next chapter documents how women enrolled at or associated with SEC schools used football songs to participate in pre–World War II campus life and carve out a space for themselves in southern college football culture.

CHAPTER 5

Where Are All the Ladies At?

The 1943 Paramount war propaganda film *We've Never Been Licked*, filmed at Texas A&M University with a soundtrack built from the school's fight songs, embeds a romance within a wartime storyline. In the film, a love triangle unfolds between two student-soldiers and Nina, the daughter of an A&M professor. Since Texas A&M didn't admit women until 1963, and then only in a limited capacity, Nina occupies a liminal social space in the film. Despite her key social role, she can engage with campus rituals and university life only by proxy, through relationships with men who are formally part of the institution. Nina represents many such women in the pre–World War II South, who although excluded from all-male schools, or occupying a marginal position at coeducational schools, found ways to participate in campus life. According to Amy Thompson McCandless,

> few schools in the South offered the same opportunities to women as to men in the years between 1890 and 1940. Most opened their doors to women only out of fiscal pressures or legislative demands. Even then, administrators, faculty, and students tried to discourage women from taking advantage of these opportunities. Women were denied facilities for housing and socializing and then advised to stay away because these facilities were lacking. They were told they could not compete with men in the classroom and then were blamed for taking a man's place at the university. If women persevered despite these impediments, they were subject to admissions quotas and residence restrictions.[1]

By 1930, the Southeast's "distinctive" gendered collegiate norms constituted a "dual educational program": although regional college enrollment was equal across genders, twice as many men as women attended
coeducational schools, a category that included nearly all universities that
formed the Southeastern Conference in 1932.[2] As this chapter shows, fight
song composing, performing, and consumption offered women ways to
participate at the margins of male-centric football sports culture in the
US South before World War II. After a primary case study of women
and football songs at Texas A&M University, an all-male, militaristic institution for much of the twentieth century, this chapter briefly explores
women's pre–World War II musical involvement in football culture at
several other proto-SEC schools.

By documenting these musical activities, this chapter highlights an
overlooked phenomenon in research on early college football, which has
focused on women as cheerleaders, sponsors, or spectators, especially
at southern schools.[3] In the most comprehensive treatment of women
and college football, Gerald Gems describes 1880 to 1920 as a period of
masculine retrenchment against feminism in US higher education, with
football a bulwark against "encroaching females."[4] Gems argues that
women's participation in football culture was thus limited to the "traditional Victorian functions for female spectators," reinscribed by "male-
dominated media."[5] Aside from isolated examples of women's engagement with college football in this period, Gems concludes that in general,
"women served as recipients or the audience for male sports."[6] In reality,
such assessments oversimplify women's pre–World War II roles in white
southern college football culture, which included shaping and consuming the sport's musical pageantry.

The "Aggie War Hymn"

Texas A&M's "Aggie War Hymn" was rooted in a martial masculinity
shaped by the general context of the school's militaristic institutional
life and by the specific circumstances of World War I. College football
culture, already vested with martial symbolism, ramped up its connection to US military enterprises during World War I.[7] The US government
used football in training exercises, and wartime pageantry and discourse
around college football made explicit the sports-military link. In April

1917, two days after the US entered the war, the University of Georgia Redcoats band marched in a patriotic parade in Athens, Georgia; other football bands displayed similarly martial spirit.[8] Militaristic discourse permeated white college football culture and press coverage of it, including at southern schools. At Vanderbilt, the yearbook framed the 1918 season as a martial endeavor, labeling games "battles" and players "the battery" or "machine-gunners," while the Nashville press trumpeted coaches' and players' military duties.[9] From such wartime amplification of college football's martial tendencies emerged the "Aggie War Hymn," written by a Texas A&M student soldier during World War I.[10] In early November 1918, James Vernon "Pinky" Wilson, private in the 6th Marine regiment, began writing the "War Hymn" on the back of a letter from home in a trench in the Argonne Forest and completed it during his unit's post-Armistice march into Germany.[11] Throughout its history, the song has retained this martial resonance, forming a key part of annual Musters, a longtime Texas A&M ritual celebrating the Battle of San Jacinto and military exploits of alumni. Paramount's 1943 film *We've Never Been Licked* bolstered the school's hypermasculine, militaristic public profile, mediated partly in song through footage of cadets singing and playing the "Aggie War Hymn."

The earliest versions of the "War Hymn" were also shaped by Wilson's barbershop quartet background, which stretched back to childhood.[12] Wilson's 1920 A&M yearbook biography stated that his "favorite pastime is supplying minors in the best quartette on campus"—probably the popular Cast Iron Quartet—and he was a member of the Glee Club from 1916 to 1920.[13] Wilson later said that he conceived of the "War Hymn" as a quartet number, with its opening "Hullabaloo-caneck-caneck" from an early twentieth-century university yell functioning as the "tune-up" that precedes a barbershop quartet performance.[14] During the march into Germany, Wilson organized a quartet to practice the song, which they kept doing as they occupied Kaiser Wilhelm's abandoned summer palace on the Rhine River.[15] When Wilson returned to Texas A&M post-war, he formed a new quartet which introduced the song to the campus and the town of Bryan, Texas. The quartet entertained at local theaters during reel changes; during one such performance, A&M cheerleaders overheard the group sing the "Aggie War Hymn" in a slow, "ballad" style. The cheerleaders liked the song but felt it needed "jazzing up" to function as a pep song.[16] Wilson recalled that the song's "popularity as a quartet number led the band to playing it" for football events in fall 1921.[17] As with other southern fight songs of the 1920s, the "War Hymn" was spread off-campus by glee club, quartet, and dance orchestra performances and recordings, such as the Colonial Club Orchestra's 1928 "hot" version of the song with male vocal trio for Brunswick Records.[18]

In these early reception examples, performers were men, and the barbershop quartet tradition was overwhelmingly male. What room was there for women to participate in football culture at schools like this, male-only in the first half of the twentieth century and with campus cultures made of male-dominated musical traditions? Fan studies frameworks help us find and interpret evidence of women's engagement with football culture, elusive but present in such contexts. As Erin C. Tarver writes, "Fans' relationships to teams and individual players are venues through which fans form, transmit, and reproduce their own sense of regional, gender, and racial identity."[19] Scattered sources suggest how women used A&M songs such as "Aggie War Hymn" to "form, transmit, and reproduce" their identity as football fans and participants at the edges of a hypermasculine college culture, outside the formal parameters of university and enrollment. After A&M adopted "Aggie War Hymn" for football use in the early 1920s, dance band and other arrangements moved the song into social and media spaces where women could hear it, learn it, and dance to it. Civic and school bands began playing the "War Hymn" at civic and educational events across Texas; some ensembles, especially high school bands, included young women instrumentalists. "Hot" bands played the song at dances where A&M students mingled with local women, such as at the mid-1920s A&M Corps Dances attended by women from the Bryan community.[20] At A&M Corps summer training in Post, Texas, the Post Orchestra played "that old familiar war hymn" at dances attended by local women.[21] The "Aggie War Hymn" traveled beyond Texas and even beyond the US in the 1920s, starting with the A&M marching band's first radio performance in 1923. This broadcast, which included the "War Hymn," reached Canada, Mexico, Cuba, and crosscountry to Pennsylvania and New Jersey, allowing listeners outside the campus orbit to hear the song.[22]

In the 1930s and 1940s, the relationship between Texas State College for Women (TSCW, now Texas Women's University) and Texas A&M unfolded around football, with music a prime mediator of the gendered institutional interactions. In October 1939, Texas A&M took its notorious yell practice (pep rally) to the TSCW campus in Denton, where TSCW students heard the "Aggie War Hymn" and A&M cheers and yells.[23] During these years, TSCW students played recordings of A&M songs in their dorm rooms and decorated their rooms with Aggie colors.[24] Occasionally TSCW women performed A&M songs publicly: when Texas A&M held parades in Denton, TSCW students marched with the male cadets, singing A&M songs.[25] In 1944, the fledgling TSCW band programmed the "Aggie War Hymn" at one of their earliest concerts.[26]

Women relatives of Texas A&M students also musically engaged with the school's football culture in the first half of the twentieth century through social organizations and events such as A&M Mothers Clubs, formed in cities across Texas. Like other women's social and civic groups of the time, they convened monthly luncheons with musical and rhetorical entertainments; these allowed women to participate in A&M's college culture, mediated through their sons' enrollment. At Mothers Club meetings, members sang the "Aggie War Hymn," "Spirit of Aggieland," and other school songs around the piano, reported on their sons' academic progress, and read articles aloud from the A&M student newspaper.[27] One 1950 bridal shower in Shiner, Texas, hosted and attended by women, featured the bride entering the room to the strains of the "Aggie War Hymn."[28]

Beyond listening to, dancing to, and singing the "War Hymn," women in the Texas A&M orbit wrote their own fight songs for this school that they could not attend. As discussed in a later chapter, in December 1938 and January 1939, the Texas A&M community was roiled by rumors that composer "Pinky" Wilson's sale of the "Aggie War Hymn" copyright to Thornton W. Allen meant the song could no longer be used at A&M pep rallies and football games. In response, A&M fans from across Texas composed and sent fight songs to the school's band director; out of nine songs received, two were by women.[29] Even after the copyright confusion was cleared up, band director Richard J. Dunn convened a committee to assess all nine songs, indicating that musical contributions by women to

A&M's football culture were acceptable. Three years later, in 1942, Mrs. Ford Munnerlyn (described in the press by her husband's name, customary journalistic practice at the time) wrote "The Twelfth Man," which became a popular fight song still used by the school.[30]

Other Examples

Sources suggest that similar patterns of gendered engagement unfolded at other white southern schools between the late nineteenth century and World War II, including all-male and coeducational schools. Early in the twentieth century, women wrote Georgia Tech songs despite their inability to enroll there. In 1905, Frances Brownie and Winnifred Hudson wrote "The Georgia Tech March and Two-Step," dedicating it to Tech students.[31] Daisy Chotas and Nick Chotas co-wrote "Yellow Jacket Girl" in 1929, a song which became popular on the Tech campus and which enshrined the social significance of women as a totem or mascot in the school's football culture.[32] An earlier song by the same title was written by Harold Atteridge and Jean Schwarz, the latter a female collaborator.[33]

In the 1890s and early 1900s, women involved with Vanderbilt University—coeducational since its early years—composed songs centered on campus culture, including football songs, mentioned in an earlier chapter. In 1922 or 1923, Nashville composer Emma Ashford collaborated with noted Nashville sportswriter and Vanderbilt alumnus Grantland Rice on the football song "Come On, You Commodores." Scored for voice and piano, the song was printed in a campus publication but was likely not published commercially, with lyrics written to celebrate the school's new football stadium.[34] Less clear is the collaborative process whereby Emma Ashford supplied music, which was supposed to have been written by composer Frank Crumit, with whom Rice later wrote two comedic golf songs.[35] The local press enthused over the song, hoping it allayed the concerns of "many who have thought for some time that there was too little of either musical variety or quality to harmonize with Commodore athletic teams of the last several years."[36] "Come On, You Commodores" was present in campus life over the next few years, appearing in the 1923, 1924, and 1926 Vanderbilt yearbooks.[37] Nonetheless, it never fully caught on with the student body, perhaps because of its square musical style at a time when "hot" music was the fashion in college circles. In an October 1923 account mentioning songs sung by Vanderbilt students as they cheered the departing Vanderbilt team at the train station, "Come On, You Commodores" is not listed.[38] The 1923 Vanderbilt-Sewanee game likewise featured both schools' alma maters, but "Come On, You Commodores" was either unused or omitted in press accounts.[39] Although the song did not last in Vanderbilt's institutional life beyond the 1920s, it is notable for the partnership between a woman and a well-known male sportswriter.

By the time Mississippi State University students got serious about finding a fight song, culminating in a song contest in Fall 1936, the school had admitted women for some time. Although women were involved in several capacities with the song contest held by the campus magazine *Mis-A-Sip*, public framing of the contest and its results erased women's presence and agency in campus life. This illuminates the difficult position of women on co-ed southern campuses in this period: one of nominal inclusion and erasure from the rhetoric and symbols that created public-facing institutional identities. In February 1937, a group of finalist song entries, selected by judges from the pool of submissions, were performed for the coeducational student body for voting. Mitt Evans and his Collegians, a participating ensemble, was fronted by Elise Buford, a female singer who "smilingly vocalized" for the otherwise-male instrumentalist group.[40] The Director of the men's glee club that performed contest entries for student judgment was Mrs. H. M. McKay, who had also been initially slated to serve as a judge in the song contest.[41] The second-place entry, "Marching Song," was written by a woman student (Betsy Stark, lyricist) and a male student (Theodore Russell).[42]

Despite women's involvement in the song search, discourse framed the lack of a fight song as an affliction peculiar to the Mississippi State "man": "Where the college is represented off the campus, State-men have hitherto been forced to remain silent while other students sang their college marching songs."[43] The October 1936 call for a pep song was accompanied by plans to raise prize money from "organizations . . . and men who want to see the Maroon and White uphold the place it has on the athletic fields."[44] A popular Mississippi sports columnist spread the word across the state that the "boys up at Starkville" wanted a new pep song.[45] The lyrics of the finalists' songs also used exclusively male terminology to describe the coeducational student body. The first edition of the winning entry, "Hail State," contained second and third verses (perhaps added by publisher Thornton W. Allen) with masculinized phrases: "in whatever we do, thy sons shall always strive anew" and "when the Men of State go marching by."[46] "Maroon and White," a runner-up entry, contained multiple references to the "sons" of Mississippi State.[47] Runner-up "Mississippi State Fight Song" stated "we'll stand like men whether we lose or win."[48] In fact, the title of the prizewinning song, originally called by its composer "Hail Dear Old State," was changed by Thornton W. Allen to "Men of State" with the subtitle "Hail, Mississippi State."[49]

Conclusion

Noah Cohan writes, "As with any cultural text, then, the power structures that permeate sports can greatly affect, but not ultimately determine, the potential meanings made by their readership."[50] Although the universities in this chapter were all-male or male-centric for much of the twentieth century, women in the schools' fandoms used fight songs to participate in campus life and sports pageantry, creating meanings outside the bounds of those generated by official "power structures." Cohan's reading of fans' "consumptive, receptive, and appropriative behaviors" as "acts of narrative interpretation and (re)-creation" describes how women in the orbit of these schools wrote themselves into the stories of institutional life via musical engagement with football.[51] Through the writing, performance, arrangement, and consumption of fight songs, women scripted themselves into the narratives of college football, even when the songs themselves seemed, at face value, to leave no rhetorical room for women's involvement. This re-scripting took on additional significance in the US South, where as Trent Watts argues, a durable form of white masculinity has long ardently positioned itself against an imagined feminine.[52] Women's agency in college football pageantry forms a complicated social layer in the pre–World War II southern campus, in dialogue with the dominant expressions of white masculinity that characterized southern campus life at the time. These women were helping shape a southern fight song repertory that in the 1920s was becoming, as the next chapter shows, a rich, multifaceted interplay of voices—professional and amateur, male and female—who believed that unique fight songs formed an indispensable part of a university's public-facing identity and, for publishers like Thornton Allen, an untapped regional market.

CHAPTER 6

Southern Fight Songs in the Jazz Age

Before the 1920 Tulane University-University of Michigan game, Tulane students gathered at Union Station to cheer on the team with "Dixie," sung while "overflowing with sentiment" to celebrate the first time that their university's "southern squad" was to "cross the Mason & Dixon line." Donations were taken at the station to help defeat "the Northerners," and the student newspaper stated that the occasion marked the official adoption of "Dixie" into Tulane's football repertory.[1] Despite its sectional resonance, apparently newly embraced at Tulane, "Dixie" was only one of several songs used in Tulane football culture of the early 1920s, including the "Washington and Lee Swing" (under the title "Tulane Swing") and, by the end of 1925, an entirely new fight song that Tulane still uses, "The Olive and Blue" ("Roll On, Tulane").[2] By the mid-1920s, white southern college football was acquiring national media attention for the first time, accompanied by pageantry that simultaneously expressed nostalgia for a mythologized antebellum South and student investment in national collegiate culture. As the Tulane example demonstrates, this duality was articulated musically through white southern schools' continued use of minstrel and Civil War songs alongside new fight songs that were composed, published, and distributed as commodities in the jazz-age popular music marketplace. This chapter documents how national collegiate norms and pressure from the college song publishing industry combined in this decade to generate new fight songs at the University of Kentucky, Tulane University, and the University of Alabama, which coexisted in the repertory alongside older, sectional songs.

Southern Identity and College Football in the 1920s

White southern college students, alumni, and other university stakeholders felt an increasingly urgent need for new fight songs in the 1920s as the South's love affair with and institutional investment in football ballooned. In this decade, southern schools worked to close the gap between their football programs and those of other regions, resulting in increased national media focus on the region's football.[3] By the time sociologist Howard Odum published his landmark 1936 survey of southern folkways and resources, he could use the "much lamented bigtime college football of the colleges and universities" to illustrate the region's selective ability to surpass its limitations:

> When the South decided to play football it imported much of its skill in football coaches, it set up the necessary organization and means, it built its stadia, and brought teachers and pupils from wherever they were found most appropriate to the purpose. . . . The setting of a pace by a few institutions was emulated by many.[4]

Southern universities elevated their football stature through high-profile intersectional games such as the 1926 Rose Bowl, when the University of Alabama upset the University of Washington. Sports media's geographic orientation to covering college football, previously organized around an "East-West" axis, shifted accordingly. The press considered the University of Alabama the "eastern" school going into the 1926 Rose Bowl, but the Crimson Tide "impressed [California] sportswriters as a distinctively southern team," and the Associated Press report hailed the victorious Tide as "the lads from Dixie."[5] Some newspapers used the Crimson Tide as a stand-in for the region, as in the *Pensacola News Journal* headline from January 2, 1926: "South Wins West Coast Grid Classic." Sports media framed intersectional games as a symbolic continuation of North-South conflict, a new iteration of the "us vs. them" construct that has long fired the southern white psyche and proven a good way to sell newspapers. The *Birmingham News* declared the 1926 Rose Bowl "Alabama's Victory

Greatest for South Since Battle of Bull Run" and Vanderbilt coach Dan McGugin described the Crimson Tide as "our [regional] representative fighting for us against the world." Other high-profile southern victories, such as Georgia Tech's 1929 Rose Bowl win over the University of California and the University of Georgia's 1929 defeat of Yale, provoked similar rhapsodies. "Sectional comparisons and intersectional games" came to dominate national football reporting in the 1920s, with southern football earning permanent media respect.[6]

The South, meanwhile, was happy to get some good press to offset what historian James Cobb politely calls "growing perceptions of southern benightedness" in the decade, highlighted by national focus on regional problems like lynching, a resurgent Klan, and the fundamentalist-modernist religious scuffle of the 1925 Scopes Monkey Trial.[7] Southward-aimed national scorn of the 1920s, rooted in post-Reconstruction political dynamics, was a sharp inflection point in a long trend of criticism which has historically obsessed and shaped white southerners.[8] The psychological relief white southerners felt over intersectional victories therefore outstripped mere football fandom, a sentiment palpable in Nashville sportswriter Blinkey Horn's editorial after Alabama's 1926 Rose Bowl win: "The South owes to Alabama an eternal obligation for spreading the gospel of Dixie football. . . . For Alabama went as a symbol of the Southland. Its victory will stand for many a long year as a trademark of Dixie football, Dixie courage and Dixie capacity to sneer at defeat and win."[9] Influential white southerners proclaimed football strong enough to counter the region's glaring PR problem.[10] An Alabama newspaper described the University of Alabama's Rose Bowl trips in 1926, 1927, and 1931 as "advertising that is of incalculable value," usable by politicians "in the never-ending crusade to attract outside capital" to the state.[11] The Alabama governor told the victorious 1926 Crimson Tide, "I read in a western paper at the time you left . . . that the south was full of malaria. This team has demonstrated to the world that there is no hookworm in Alabama."[12] Segregationist Alabama lawyer John McQueen, who helped bankroll the 1926 Rose Bowl trip, praised the "champions of the world" for bringing honor to the South:

> The members of the University of Washington's football team and their descendants, generations after, will speak in a soft southern accent. You lived up to the traditions of the south. When the band plays

"Dixie" over our team it can whip eleven Red Granges [the University of Illinois's star player]."[13]

McQueen's "Dixie" reference highlights southern universities' ongoing use of minstrel and Civil War songs as the schools entered the national athletic stage. "Dixie" especially marked 1920s intersectional play, as seen in the chapter's introduction. Outside the South, "Dixie" functioned as sonic shorthand to signify southern football. When the Alabama band could not travel to California for the 1926 Rose Bowl, the Pasadena Elks band performed "Dixie" for the visitors, a gesture repeated for the 1927, 1931, and 1935 Rose Bowl festivities. For the 1929 Yale-Georgia game, Yale brought a fifty-piece band to Georgia, which played "Dixie" upon exiting the train and after UGA's victory—a moment the New York Times designated a top sports memory of 1929.[14] Other sectional songs continued to ring out in the 1920s, including the "Battle Hymn of the Republic" refrain at several southern schools and "My Old Kentucky Home," mostly at the University of Kentucky. A 1922 University of Georgia songbook illuminates how blackface minstrelsy continued to inform white southern university football culture in this decade.[15] The songbook included "Raise a Rukus Tonight," printed in dialect from the narrative perspective of an enslaved person and opening with a verse about "my ole mistis" (mistress). The text framed the prospect of the narrator's freedom as comic or whimsical:

> My ole mistis promised me, Gwine to raise a rukus tonite
> That when she died she'd set me free, Gwine to raise a rukus tonite.
> O come along, my children come along, while the moon am shining bright.
> Get on the boat and down the river float, Gwine to raise a rukus tonight.

Songbook editor C. T. Conyers added a second, football-centric verse:

> Can't you hear that Georgia yell, Gwine to raise a rukus tonite.
> We'll bust the line and ring the bell, Gwine to raise a rukus tonite.
> O come along, old Georgia, come along, While the Bull dogs in the fight.
> We'll get on that ball and down the field we'll rove, then we'll raise a rukus tonite.

Clearly, regional or sectional identity played a significant rhetorical and musical role in participants' and observers' impressions of white southern college football as it emerged on the national stage. Nonetheless, such songs were insufficient to musically define southern college football cultures in the 1920s. White southern college students of the decade enthusiastically embraced national collegiate culture, meaning they wanted new, unique, and peppy fight songs like those used at other schools.[16] At the University of Kentucky, the prominence of "My Old Kentucky Home" in 1910s and early 1920s football culture exemplified this dilemma: although beloved, the hymn-like minstrel song was neither sprightly nor distinctive to the school. The answer was "On, On, U of K," with a tune written ca. 1922 by music department chairman Carl A. Lampert at the request of the football coach.[17] Although the song neither attracted the attention of major publishers nor entered broader 1920s popular music through widespread recordings and performances, it became the school's permanent fight song. Neither the melody nor text of "On, On, U of K" indexed southern identity. Years later, a Black student's 1966 letter to the student paper favorably contrasted the song's neutrality with other songs used at UK sports events. After describing how her initial hopes for her undergraduate years shattered on the rocks of campus racism, the student wrote: "But I made it through my first year, UK—Confederate flag, 'Dixie,' and all." Long described the Kappa Alpha cheering section at a Kentucky game singing "Glory, Glory, Segregation! the South Shall Rise Again." She also mentioned a UK-Illinois basketball game where the band played "Dixie." Long chided the university for expressing school spirit through retrograde songs, especially when "On, On, U of K" was available yet underused.[18] Although Long didn't mention it, UK football culture also still used "My Old Kentucky Home" for many decades after the introduction of "On, On, U of K."

Fallout from the "Tulane Swing"

While UK's need for a new fight song was generated by its use of a slow minstrel song common in other musical and cultural contexts, other white southern schools were pressed to find new fight songs in the 1920s by copyright protection of the "Washington and Lee Swing" which made it increasingly off limits. Several southern schools used the "Swing" as a fight song with tweaks to its title and text, arousing the ire of publisher Thornton W. Allen. His litigious response to this wanton borrowing produced new fight songs at Tulane University and the University of Alabama, starting in 1924–1925 when he targeted a New Orleans jazz group and Tulane University for recordings and performances of the song under the title "Tulane Swing." The resulting squabble, involving New Orleans media and the Tulane and Washington and Lee communities, foregrounded key themes that situate SEC fight song histories within the broader commercial music marketplace: debates over song authorship, ownership, and origins, accompanied by tensions between tradition and commercialism in stakeholders' perspectives.[19]

On May 19, 1925, New Orleans's WMSB radio broadcast a 1924 Okeh recording by Piron's New Orleans Orchestra titled "Tulane Swing," announced as such by the disc jockey.[20] New Orleans listener and Washington and Lee University alumnus William B. Wisdom "boiled with indignation and wrath" when he heard this and wrote letters to WMSB, the New Orleans press, the Tulane University President, and Washington and Lee University alumni and administrators lamenting the "flagrant pirating" of the "Swing."[21] The Washington and Lee Alumni Association's Louisiana branch waded into the breach with indignant meetings and a furious letter-writing campaign aimed at Tulane University, which they alleged had long used the song under the title "Tulane Swing." Extant sources confirm that Tulane students used the song since at least the early 1920s, even printing it under the erroneous and offensive title in university publications.[22] The alumni group stated that Tulane could obtain permission to use the song in rightly-titled form, blasted the Okeh recording as a "jazz jumble," and asked the Tulane student paper to denounce Okeh Records for calling the song the "Tulane Swing."[23] The alumni group rained down similar fire on WMSB in a letter reprinted in the New Orleans *Times-Picayune*.[24]

Initially, the indignation campaign was carried out entirely by Washington and Lee alumni, who despite copyright registration of the "Swing" to Thornton Allen regarded the song as their communal heritage. Their anger at Tulane centered not on lost royalties, but on stolen tradition, and they erroneously described the "Swing" as the "property of Washington and Lee University"—a mistake also made by the Tulane student paper.[25] In late July 1925, publisher Thornton W. Allen entered the fray. Unfettered by misty sentiment about tradition and heritage, Allen framed the "Swing" as a commodity with market value, sending cease-and-desist legal notices to the Tulane President and music faculty. Allen's mass-produced card contained a bold-font "Warning!," a reproduction of the "Swing" chorus, and a threat to prosecute any "person, company or institution" that broadcast, recorded, or printed the song. The notice emphasized the song's copyrighted status and named offending schools wrongfully using the "Swing," including Tulane and the Universities of Florida and Alabama. The card doubled neatly as advertising, reminding recipients that Allen's company put out "Washington and Lee Swing" arrangements for voice, dance orchestra, symphonic orchestra, and marching band as well as licensed phonograph records and player piano rolls.[26] Around this time, Allen also threatened litigation against Piron's Jazz Orchestra, whose "Tulane Swing" record sparked the brawl, although he seems to have settled with them out of court.[27]

The Tulane song scandal yielded remarkable outcomes, immediately and over the next few years. When the strife began, Tulane students and alumni intensified what may have been an existing push for a new song with "pep and swing . . . adaptable for orchestration and mass singing" through a campus song contest, with alumni promising to buy and copyright the winning entry "as our own."[28] "The Olive and Blue March" won the contest and its $100 prize and was declared the official Tulane fight song in fall 1925.[29] The "March," with geographically neutral text and music by professors Martin ten Hoor and Walter Goldstein, debuted in a band arrangement at the Tulane-Missouri game halftime.[30] It likely first appeared in print in a fall 1925 football program for the Tulane-Louisiana College game, labeled the "Prize Winner in the Contest conducted by Tulane Alumni to give Greenies a War Song of their own"—an oblique reference to the "Swing" debacle. The program urged students to sing when the band played the song and exhorted "Freshies! Sophs! Let's learn the 'Olive and Blue' and strut our stuff for Missouri!"[31] In 1926, the Tulane Alumni Association published sheet music for "The Olive and the Blue," and the song is still used by the university, often under the title "Roll On, Tulane."

Thornton Allen's efforts and a new song notwithstanding, however, Tulane kept using the "Swing." In November 1929, the New Orleans press reported that the song was still known nationally under the name "Tulane

Swing" and that it outstripped the "Olive and Blue" in fame.[32] The Tulane band's prodigious use of the song generated another round of debate in early 1932, causing the band to announce that "the authorities of Washington and Lee University," likely meaning Thornton W. Allen and outspoken alumni, had at last pressured them into dropping the song.[33]

The second outcome of the controversy was that Thornton W. Allen, not content with deterring unauthorized use of the "Swing," involved himself commercially in Tulane's quest for a new song. First, he entered a song in the 1925 contest, although his entry didn't win. Campus reports also mentioned a New York publisher interested in publishing band and orchestra arrangements of the winning song—almost certainly a reference to Allen, and suggestive of the possibility that he may have had a hand in running the contest.[34] Two years later, the Tulane Alumni Association's General Manager served on the editorial board of Allen's *Intercollegiate Songbook* (1927), which contained the prizewinning "Olive and Blue."[35] Then in mid-1932, the Tulane Alumni Association ceded the "Olive and Blue" copyright to Thornton Allen, with permission to revise, in hope of gaining broader publicity for the song.[36] Allen published a sprightly band arrangement of it under the catchier title "Roll On, Tulane" and pushed for national radio exposure for the new arrangement. Once Allen obtained this copyright, he held it tightly. When a rival publisher wrote to Tulane's president in January 1933 requesting permission to include the song in a college songbook, some Tulane faculty believed such a collaboration would generate national exposure for the song and the school.[37] Allen replied huffily, ruling out cooperation without a "suitable royalty contract" and adding:

> We know from experience that arrangements like this are not satisfactory unless with a very large company and often result in our losing a great many sales. Many times such permission takes control of the song away from you entirely and with no financial gain. Several universities have suffered materially from the result of granting permissions without knowing thoroughly all about the concerns with which they were dealing.

Allen reassured the Alumni Association of his plans for publicizing the Tulane song through electrical transcriptions while reminding them of the Depression's impact on sheet music sales.[38] The Irving Berlin Company also sought permission to use the song in a 1936 college songbook, which the Tulane Alumni Association again wanted for the sake of exposure. Although there is no record of Allen's response, he almost certainly refused the request, unless there were agreed-upon royalties.[39] The Tulane community's desire for nebulous "exposure" through circulation of the song conflicted with Allen's perspective on the song as a concrete commodity that should yield solid, quantifiable income per use.

The Tulane song controversy illuminates how myths about origins, uniqueness, and authorship have often characterized alumni and student beliefs about fight songs. Some Tulane alumni claimed that the "Swing" was really an old Tulane song called "Varsity," re-arranged and wrongly claimed by Washington and Lee University.[40] Washington and Lee alumni William B. Wisdom's complaints to New Orleans media placed the same premium on uniqueness, aimed in a different direction, arguing that his school's "great college song is different from many other university songs in that it is inherently an original product."[41] During the 1924–1925 stage of the controversy, the Washington and Lee community described the "Swing" as a "sacred hymn and heritage," the singing of which had become "almost a religious rite" whereupon students stood and removed their hats.[42] Some used patriotic rhetoric, casting the "Swing" as the school's "Star-Spangled Banner."[43] One Washington and Lee alumnus invoked sectional sentiment, asking how northerners would feel if "Dixie" were played under the title of "Way Up North in the Northland" and objecting to the "greatest radio station in the South [WSMB] operating against the tradition of that secluded Southern University nestled in the mountains, two hundred miles from any broadcasting station and powerless to reply."[44] For publishers such as Thornton Allen, however, authorship became increasingly "bureaucratic in its relation to the marketplace" after the Copyright Act of 1909, meaning that "musical authors had their two cents (literally) riding on every recording, the oversight and collection of which would inspire ASCAP and other societies of authors, along with a torrent of paperwork."[45] Such myths generated tension about the market status of fight songs: were they traditions, similar to religious or national symbols, or were they commodities; and either way, who owned them?

A New Song at the University of Alabama

Like Tulane, by the early 1920s, the University of Alabama regularly used the "Washington and Lee Swing" at football events, calling it the

"Alabama Swing."[46] And like Tulane, it got them in trouble. In November 1925, a few months after Tulane's song rodeo, the Alabama student magazine *Rammer-Jammer* announced a pep song contest in response to campus "rumblings" about the fact that the "Alabama Swing" was original "neither as to words or tune. It is a take-off on the 'Washington & Lee Swing.'"[47] The contest rules ensured that the winning entry was from its inception a commercial product, meant to be marketed on and off campus and modeled on the success of "Swing." The rules stipulated that the winning song's author "relinquishes all rights to it," laying the groundwork for a publisher to acquire and distribute it.[48] The rules also emphasized that entries should be original while also sounding like a "lively march air similar to the ones now used by other colleges"—a tension that nodded to the popularity of the "Swing" and the protectiveness of its publisher. Alabama's song contest was noted gleefully by the Washington and Lee University community, which crowed in an alumni magazine shortly after the contest rules were published that "The 'Alabama Swing' Appears Doomed!"[49] The contest was promoted by the Alabama campus newspaper *Crimson White* with the backing of faculty and the athletics publicity director.[50]

Engineering student Ethelred Lundy Sykes, *Crimson White* editor and an amateur musician active in campus ensembles, won the $50 prize for his song, "Yea Alabama," chosen from over a dozen entries.[51] In late March or early April 1926, Thornton W. Allen contracted to publish one thousand copies of a piano-voice arrangement of Sykes's "Yea Alabama." Advance buzz for the song circulated in the music industry, a sign of Allen's musical midwifery, as Victor and Okeh Records and the Yale Glee Club requested pre-publication copies.[52] The campus buzzed with excitement, too; the student paper printed breathless updates quoting Allen on the song's commercial potential and anticipating sheet music sales at 0.35 cents a copy in the school bookstore.[53] These updates emphasized Allen's ties to the "Washington and Lee Swing," hitching the new song's prospects to the older hit. Broader regional excitement about the Alabama Rose Bowl victory in January 1926 meant that the school's new song merited press coverage that spring in Atlanta, Montgomery, Orlando, and Tampa.

Thornton Allen's speed in securing rights for and marketing "Yea Alabama" and the language of the *Rammer-Jammer* contest rules strongly suggest his involvement in the contest. Absent extant documentation but given other evidence, we can theorize the following: in July 1925, the University of Alabama and many other schools, including Tulane, received Thornton Allen's warning about unauthorized use of the "Swing"; Alabama was one of several southern schools directly named in the cease-and-desist communications.[54] Allen's threat stimulated Alabama to run a song contest with his input, including his agreement to publish and market the winning song in exchange for its copyright. This would account for the rules clause requiring the author to cede copyright, although the actual copyright transfer seems to have been thorny. When the *Rammer-Jammer* debuted the voice-piano score for "Yea Alabama" in May 1926, it noted that the song was "copyrighted 1926 by the *Rammer-Jammer*, University of Alabama, published exclusively by Thornton W. Allen."[55] However, by the time the song appeared in Allen's 1927 *Intercollegiate Songbook*, its copyright had traveled from the *Rammer-Jammer* to author Ethelred Sykes and to Thornton W. Allen—likely Allen's initial intent.[56] The university's seriousness about replacing the "Swing" with "Yea Alabama" also suggests it feared a legal threat in 1925–1926.[57] University of Alabama President George Denny served on the editorial board of Allen's 1927 college songbook, further implying recent song-related contact between Allen and the school.[58]

In the absence of extant records from Thornton Allen, it's unknown how or how much he promoted the song. What is clear is that, like the "Swing" before it, "Yea Alabama" first circulated largely in non-marching-band contexts. The spring 1926 voice-piano score had a "hot" ragtime sensibility that worked well in social contexts beyond football. Rests on the chorus's downbeats created a "ragged" feel, propelled by a left-hand stride bass pounding beneath close-voiced right-hand chromatic chords. Just after the song's debut in the May 1926 *Rammer-Jammer*, W. C. Polla, who had arranged the "Washington and Lee Swing" as a fox-trot for Thornton Allen, arranged "Yea Alabama" for dance orchestra.[59] The song, sometimes labeled a "fox-trot" by the press, began to appear at dances.[60] In fall 1926, campus glee clubs and vocal quartets worked to teach the song to Alabama students.[61] In September 1928, jazz bandleader Herman "Snooks" Friedman and his Memphis Stompers recorded it for Victor at the Memphis Auditorium, part of his 1928–1931 sessions that included the "Washington and Lee Swing." Friedman's recording of "Yea Alabama" was subtitled "a stomp," a 1920s dance term; likely it used Polla's arrangement as a blueprint for its Dixieland improvisations.

Although no record of their collaboration seems extant, in 1927, prolific arranger May Singhi Breen added ukulele and banjulele chords to "Yea Alabama" for Allen.[62] Ukuleles, banjos, and the hybrid banjulele—portable, quiet, playable by amateurs—were ubiquitous on 1920s campuses, thanks largely to May Breen's ukulele performances, advocacy, and arrangements for prominent publishers.[63] Breen's chord diagrams may have informed the 1928 Victor recording of "Yea Alabama" by Snooks Friedman and his Memphis Stompers, where a banjo can be heard strumming valiantly and persistently.[64] Breen also added ukulele chords to Allen's "Washington and Lee Swing." Breen worked with publishers on large compilations of arrangements of hit songs that soundtracked 1920s and 1930s collegiate life, adding ukulele and banjo chords in her signature diagram formation above voice-piano staves.[65] Sometimes these compilations included college songs, such as a 1930 Irving Berlin folio containing Breen's diagrams for "Hoosier Hop" and "Don't Get Collegiate."[66] Breen's work provided another musical avenue for college songs to be performed and consumed outside of football contexts, offering a slice of collegiate glamor to any music consumer through the twang of the ukulele.

In addition to arrangements such as May Breen's and W. C. Polla's that generated wider usage, the title "Yea Alabama" traded on the market allure of southern identity, which may have given it off-campus appeal. To the non-collegiate sheet music or record buyer, the title likely slotted the song in the same category as other 1920s songs "Alabama Moon," "Alabama Stomp," "Alabama Mamma," "Goodbye, My Alabama Baby," "Alabama Jubilee Breakdown," "Way Down in Alabama," "My Alabama Home," and "Alabama Flood." All in all, Thornton W. Allen was clearly marketing and distributing the University of Alabama's new song as a potential "hit."

In privileging the role of commercial music publishing and its concern with copyright and sales, the above analysis of the origins and early history of "Yea Alabama" contrasts with university, fan, and media accounts which largely locate the song's impetus in an organic swell of student sentiment and desire for unique tradition.[67] Despite durable fan belief that college football pageantry represents spontaneous expressions of tradition insulated from market forces, SEC schools have historically led the charge to commercialize multiple aspects of college football, starting in the early 1920s when the Southern Conference schools that later formed the SEC were already vexing the NCAA through their openness to "commercializing" football via means such as athletic scholarships. A 1939 report by *New Yorker* sports journalist and broadcaster John R. Tunis sorting college football programs according to "profit motive" placed the Southeastern Conference, formed 1932, in the most extreme category, where economic concerns were dominant.[68] The account of "Yea Alabama" documented here shows that not only athletic and administrative aspects of SEC football but also its pageantry have historically been marked by tensions between tradition and commercialism.

"Yea Alabama" also stylistically drew on musical expression emerging from African Americans, who were not admitted to the University of Alabama for another four decades and then only under duress. Ragtime grew in the late nineteenth century partly from the Black cakewalk dance, becoming a chief tributary feeding the river of early jazz. From 1896, when songs were first marketed as ragtime, the style saturated US popular music, regardless of whether or not songs were formally labeled "rags."[69] Ragtime's syncopation, jagged melodic lines, chromatic harmonies, march-like structure and groove, and stride piano bassline mark "Yea, Alabama," which like much popular music of its time was built from ragtime's four-bar phrases and sixteen-bar strains.[70] The University of Alabama wasn't the only proto-SEC school to use jazz or ragtime in 1920s football music. In that decade, Louisiana State University likely started using "Tiger Rag" at games and pep rallies, and their marching band had played ragtime at football events since the 1910s.[71] "Tiger Rag" was popularized for broader audiences through a recording by the white Dixieland Jazz Band in 1917 and 1918; recordings by many jazz artists followed. Although it is hard and often fruitless to attempt to track down singular origins of a popular melody, the roots of "Tiger Rag" predated the Dixieland Jazz Band recordings, likely lying in the early twentieth-century jazz community of New Orleans, made up largely of Black musicians.[72]

"Tiger Rag" and "Yea Alabama" highlight the complex racial and economic fabric of US popular music, animated as they were by styles that emerged from Black musical culture in the late nineteenth and early twentieth centuries. By the 1920s, these styles informed mainstream popular music, "provid[ing] the dominant culture with musical markers of so-called African American authenticity and an understanding of sonic blackness."[73] Southern white universities' use of "musical markers" that

coded "Black" in this era exemplified the "Blacksound" concept articulated by Matthew Morrison, which wrestles with "the ways in which
aesthetic and performance practices of African Americans have been
exploited and embedded in the discourses of popular music and sound."[74]
Used by schools that were light years away from admitting African Americans, these kinds of songs allowed southern PWIs to build institutional
profiles from the cultural materials of the group they marginalized and
enabled white southern students to "express themselves through the
consumption and performance of commodified black aesthetics without carrying the burden of being black."[75]

Conclusion

The white South has historically strived for a dual identity as a distinctive
region and a valued participant in national life.[76] Southern PWIs' continued use of old minstrel songs and Civil War tunes at football events
alongside newer fight songs confirms that southern flagship universities—
students, faculty, administrators, alumni—were in the early twentieth
century symbolically rooted in a mythologized past while also working
to modernize themselves.[77] In terms of new southern fight songs, this
modernization took the form of students and other university members responding to the power of the "Washington and Lee Swing" and
subsequent copyright restrictions to generate new songs, incorporating
popular music styles rooted in Black musical practices, disseminating and
consuming fight songs through "hot" dance band arrangements, and collaborating with publishers to copyright, distribute, and market football
songs as commodities in the popular music industry. While southern students and alumni framed fight songs in the 1920s in sentimental terms of
school tradition and collective ownership, publishers such as Thornton W.
Allen understood college songs as copyrighted commodities that constituted an increasingly robust category of the commercial music industry.
The next chapter explores the peak of that subgenre's popularity in the
United States, reached in the 1930s, and documents the network of publishers and national and regional performers who sustained the college
song as a fashionable commodity during the Depression.

CHAPTER 7

The Business of College Songs in the 1930s

In April 1931, Thornton W. Allen reported to the University of Maine Alumni Association on notable performances of "Hats Off to the Band," a University of Maine song he published in several arrangements for the Association. He wrote to them that "Hats Off" had been played at shows in New York and Philadelphia hotels and at a Toronto skating club, mostly by dance orchestras, with some radio simulcasting. To stimulate this broad exposure, Allen had mailed "Hats Off" orchestrations to many dance bands, including national acts Guy Lombardo and Jack Denny and amateur or semi-pro groups such as Guy French and His Collegians at Arkansas's State College.[1] As Allen's report suggests, intersecting channels of publishers and performers disseminated and popularized college songs in the 1930s, the peak of their mass appeal in US popular culture. Between the world wars, attending college became part of a US "culture of aspiration," with higher education renouncing its status as "a scarce commodity and an elite experience."[2] Football and its pageantry remained a chief vector for interest and investment in higher education, promoted by universities through athletic PR departments and collaborations with major advertising agencies.[3] Increasingly sophisticated radio broadcasts brought the sonic world of college football to listeners, transforming anyone into a "vicarious alumnus."[4] Capitalizing on the football cult, college song publishers and performers soundtracked the "collegiate" trope for 1930s consumers.[5] This chapter documents that vibrant network of college song publishers, dominated by Thornton Allen, and national and regional "collegiate" performers, laying groundwork for the next chapter on the flowering of new fight songs at Southeastern Conference schools in the 1930s.

Acquiring, Marketing, and Protecting College Songs in the 1930s

In 1938, music journalist Louis Reid accurately stated that "most college songs are published by Thornton W. Allen, A.S.C.A.P. In fact, Allen specializes in this classification. He also writes college songs on order."[6] After sparse college song copyrights in the 1920s, Allen's catalogue mushroomed in the 1930s as he worked with US universities to acquire, arrange, or write fight songs and publish them in sheet music, folio, and songbook form. In addition to songs and books for specific schools, Allen published a series compiling songs of multiple schools into regional volumes (Eastern, Southern, and Western), encompassing the Intercollegiate Band Folios and *Famous College Songs for Orchestra*. By the middle of the decade, he was copyrighting roughly ten college songs or songbooks annually.[7] In the late 1920s, when Allen got serious about college songs, southern schools represented a relatively untapped market, often lacking the established fight songs of schools with older football programs. By the end of the 1930s, Allen had changed this through publishing versions of the SEC fight songs "Vanderbilt Forever," "Ramblin' Wreck from Georgia Tech," "Hail to Georgia Down in Dixie," "Cheer for LSU," "Kentucky Fight," "Razorback Rootin' Song," "Yea Alabama," "Song of the Crimson Tide," "Roll On, Tulane," "Orange and Blue," "Alabama's Day," "Alabama's Victory Songs," and Mississippi State University's "Hail, [Men of] State."[8] Thornton Allen's work in the 1930s as the nation's dominant college song publisher provides a window into a flourishing, under-researched sector of US popular music. Since Allen left no archival collection, his publishing activities must be reconstructed through disparate sources, including records of his work with the University of Maine Alumni Association, to show how he acquired, promoted, and protected his catalogue in the 1930s, which included many SEC fight songs.

Allen built his catalogue partly by writing or co-writing new songs, working mostly with alumni and student associations to compose new university songs or re-arrange their existing ones. As the next chapter shows, 1930s southern students and alumni believed with great urgency that a new fight song, or a catchier arrangement of an old one, could form a key part of their institution's national profile. In 1932, Allen contracted with The Order of the Grail, a University of North Carolina student association, to write a school song. Allen submitted multiple melodies and texts for approval with the agreement that after satisfactory revisions to the selected song, he would print it in an Intercollegiate Songbook and place it on a national radio hook-up.[9] Allen sometimes re-arranged a southern school's existing fight song, as when the Tulane Alumni Association allowed him to create, copyright, and publish a peppier version of "The Olive and Blue," covered earlier. In 1935, Allen's new arrangement of the University of Florida's "Orange and Blue" generated considerable campus buzz, culminating in his visit to a UF game for the arrangement's halftime debut. At the show, which honored UF song composers, Allen's arrangement received special attention and an ovation; he was also honored for having written "March of the Fighting Gators."[10] Earlier in 1935, excitement rippled through the UF community when its school songs, including Allen's "March of the Fighting Gators," were performed on NBC radio by notable orchestras such as Benny Goodman's—likely a result of Allen's aggressive marketing.[11]

Allen also built his catalogue by acquiring existing song copyrights, often with permission to publish a new sheet music arrangement, or to include them in school songbooks. University of Maine Alumni Association records provide a detailed look at Allen's acquisition of existing songs. In Spring 1931, the Association ceded the copyright of Harry D. O'Neil's "Spirit of Maine" to Allen, who published it with ukulele chords.[12] Transaction records show Allen to be conversant with the complex mechanics of copyright transfer and keenly aware of marketing strategy.[13] Allen assured the Association that the copyright transferal would yield sales, although he was concerned about the similarities between "Spirit of Maine" and the University of Maine's "Stein Song," popularized by a Rudy Vallée record.[14] Allen also cautioned that publishing a college song in spring was poor timing: it missed the seasonal fall surge of interest.[15]

Records of Allen's work on a University of Maine songbook in 1931 document how he built his songbook catalogue, marked by excruciating attention to profit margins. Allen first sent samples of his earlier songbooks to the Alumni Association, inaugurating months of haggling. Ever pecunious, he reeled off variables determining production costs: page count, the existence of a usable die-cut university seal, ink printing style, paper type, front matter amount, and cloth cover style. Of paramount concern was the status of engraved song plates. Would the school furnish them? Did Allen already own them in his inventory? Costliest of all, must they be engraved anew for the project? Allen calculated these costs on the basis of a two thousand-book print run projected for September 1931.[16]

For his college song sheet music, folios, and books, Allen worked to generate royalties through printed music, record sales, and live and media performances. Allen's 1930s advertising copy highlighted his music's social flexibility: "College Music for College, [K-12] School, Parade, and Dance" announced the cover of a 1930s catalogue.[17] An *Intercollegiate Songbook* advertisement emphasized that its contents were "popular on the campus, radio, and at football games."[18] Allen never wasted interior covers, covering them with thumbnail images and incipits of his other songs, especially his prized "Washington and Lee Swing."[19] He experimented with premium-priced "limited deluxe editions" of the *Intercollegiate Songbook* containing "pictures of the foremost college stadia."[20] He harnessed radio's promotional power, giving a 1930 talk on Columbia and WABC called "Music in the American Colleges" which discussed "the influence of college songs on the tastes of music lovers" and positioned Allen as "one of the foremost authorities on college music."[21]

In fall 1932, Allen launched an ambitious publicity project, College Song Week, ostensibly to "swell the singing section at football games"—a framing that obscured his commercial goals. More than one hundred colleges participated, including Northwestern University and the University of Michigan, with campus radio stations at the Universities of Illinois and Notre Dame broadcasting college song programs.[22] College Song Week was repeated in fall 1933 with campus "sings" supplementing formal programs—part of Allen's euphemistically described effort "to familiarize the country" with college songs.[23] Media coverage of 1933 College Song Week, shaped by Allen's interviews and press releases, framed college songs as a communal repertory, a folk song corpus, thereby erasing their commodity status. Avoiding sales and marketing language, Thornton Allen lamented to the press that the public knew only a few songs from the "larger and more prominent schools," a problem that College Song Week would rectify with radio broadcasts of more obscure songs.[24]

Despite this non-commercial framing, little more than a year later, Allen privately indicated concern over low college song sales, telling the University of Maine Alumni Association in January 1935 that "things have been pretty bad, worse than most of us admit." An enclosed royalty statement confirmed that no copies of the University of Maine songbook or "Spirit of Maine" sheet music sold in 1934.[25] However altruistically Allen may have framed College Song Week to the press, it was an attempt to boost sagging sales beyond the limited boundaries of campus life during the lean early years of the Depression.

Within months of this dismal report, Allen hit on an idea to harness the commercial power of radio, sheet music, film, and recordings: the Allen Intercollegiate Clearinghouse (AIC), which would consolidate songs of many schools into a single body over which Allen would exert licensing control, receiving a fifteen percent cut of royalties per song licensed.[26] Allen explained to prospective member schools that the AIC would facilitate college song permission requests from media companies, especially after he sent those companies the AIC song inventory to stimulate demand.[27] To sway schools into joining the AIC, Allen sent a long list of schools and songs which had already joined, or would likely agree to join.[28] To the University of Maine Alumni Association, he also dangled the possibility of Ford and Chevrolet royalty checks for radio play of their schools songs on radio shows sponsored by the car companies.[29] By late June 1935, the AIC boasted over five hundred schools, including "practically the entire South."[30] Within a few months of its formation, the AIC had licensed more than one hundred college songs for recordings and eleven for movies.[31] In addition to the AIC, in the early 1940s, Allen created collective radio licensing agreements for at least fifty of his college songs, including some southern ones.[32]

Not content with large-scale marketing efforts such as the AIC, Allen micro-managed advertising on a smaller scale. When he learned in 1935 that no "Spirit of Maine" copies were on sale at the University of Maine bookstore, he chastised the Alumni Association.[33] In 1936, upon hearing that the 1937 Maine state tercentenary would feature a song commissioned from Broadway composers, he urged the Alumni Association to plug one of Allen's University of Maine songs for the state celebration. At the very least, he insisted, a "[University of] Maine man should write such a song" for the occasion.[34] Allen and his clients sometimes disagreed about respective roles in and parameters of such publicity measures. In September 1937, Allen scolded the Alumni Association for inadequate promotion of his Maine college songs, warning that competitors would fill the vacuum:

> I do not know what you are doing at Maine to move these songs, but I do know that unless they are used by the students and copies are displayed where students and alumni will see them, we cannot expect sales. We are trying to do the best we can at this end but unless the college gets behind these songs the radio stations and other possible users will continue to use the "Stein Song." It has been a very difficult task to get the radio stations to use the newer songs and we would like to get back some of the money we have put into these songs, and I know you would like to receive some income from them. Now that the new [football] season is starting may be [sic] something could be done at your end.[35]

The Association assured Allen of their efforts but emphasized that due to their "very substantial investment in the song books," they prioritized book over sheet music sales.[36] One of Allen's last extant letters to the Association, from 1942, reported no orders for Maine songs "in a long time," asking plaintively "can anything be done to increase sales at local stores or the Alumni office?"[37]

As a key component of his 1930s work, Allen lavished detailed, defensive attention on copyright matters, leveraging his knowledge of the US copyright system to preserve profit margins.[38] In August 1931, six months into songbook negotiations, the University of Maine Alumni Association informed Allen that the school had published a 1910 songbook with another publisher, introducing a host of copyright issues.[39] Allen and the Association spilled much ink over the legality of reusing contents from the 1910 book, thereby lowering production costs. Allen advised the Alumni Association Songbook Committee on researching the copyright status of songs in the 1910 book: which publishers to contact for song information, which songs and tunes were in the public domain, which arrangements were copyrighted, which musical aspects of arrangements to tweak to merit a new copyright, alternate tune names, and potential sources for "free" arrangements. Allen's vast mental reservoir of tune sources, arrangements, and their legal status meant he cross-compared tunes from memory, sometimes handwriting bars of music in letters to make his point.[40] At other times, Allen consulted Library of Congress copyright records, colleagues, and *Musical Courier* records to find copyright information on tunes and arrangements.[41]

To minimize costs, Allen brazenly asked other publishers to freely cede the kind of intellectual and artistic property that he himself refused to share. With wild overreach, he pushed the University of Maine Alumni Association to insist that the 1910 Maine songbook publisher give the Association engraved plates used in printing the book, advising the group to raise the specter of copyright infringement in the 1910 book to extract the plates.[42] In June 1931, Allen breezily told the Alumni Association that he expected prominent publisher Walter Fischer to grant use of the popular "Stein Song" for their new University of Maine songbook.[43] Fischer denied the request, pointedly asking Allen if he would let the "Washington and Lee Swing" be used for free. Allen replied in the highly disingenuous affirmative, but Fischer insisted on negotiating a royalty for the "Stein Song." After a similar rejection from another publisher, Allen advised the Alumni Association to approach publishers directly about permissions rather than through him to avoid problems of market competition.[44] Ultimately, Allen prioritized caution and cost-cutting: if song permissions and copyright statuses could not be verified or secured for free, the Alumni Association should "write some new songs and let the students learn them."[45]

To protect his song catalogue, Allen regularly denied permission requests in the 1930s, highlighting the conflict between his notion of fight songs as individually owned commodities and other stakeholders' beliefs that fight songs represented communal, non-commercial traditions. He refused to allow reprints of copyrighted Tulane songs in other companies' songbooks, documented earlier. In 1936, Allen and the University of Texas had a public blow-up when he tried to collect royalties on an arrangement of "The Eyes of Texas" from a publisher wishing to print it in a fraternity songbook. The University of Texas assembled a legal team to argue that the school owned the song's copyright, resulting in legal threats against Allen.[46] In early 1937, Allen denied the Intercollegiate Music League's request to reprint "Spirit of Maine" in a song folio, peevishly reiterating that he was "absolutely opposed" to the idea.

He framed his objections non-commercially, claiming vaguely that the League's stockholders were ignorant about the schools whose interests they claimed to serve and, without apparent irony, labeling the group "just a money-making scheme . . . a racket."[47]

These permissions denials were part of Allen's broader and paranoid protections of his intellectual property, culminating in the late 1930s in the failed lawsuit against the Walt Disney Company, documented earlier, and a public tussle with Texas A&M University over the "Aggie War Hymn." Concerns over "War Hymn" ownership emerged in late 1938 when its author J. V. "Pinky" Wilson wrote a new set of lyrics for the song and sold its copyright to Thornton Allen for what the Texas press called "a low fee."[48] According to Allen's correspondence with the Texas A&M band director, Wilson initiated the sale.[49] The A&M community panicked, believing that Allen's copyright prohibited them from using the "War Hymn" at school events without paying fees and fearing a copyright battle with Allen like the one fought by the University of Texas.[50] Texas A&M therefore ran a search for new school songs.[51] Since a volley of new A&M songs contravened Allen's purpose in acquiring the "War Song" copyright, he responded publicly to quell the alarm. In a letter to the A&M band director, partly reprinted in the school paper in early 1939, Allen clarified his goals in great and defensive detail: to distribute sheet music nationally; to make college songs available for media use; to collect royalties for authors; and to protect the songs from use without permission or rights.[52] Allen assured A&M readers that the "regular activities of the College," such as "campus sings, glee club and band concerts, and football games" were considered "educational, charitable, and religious performances," exempt from paying usage fees or securing printed rights. Only "public performances for profit by a commercial concern" would require a license. Allen's exasperation bled through as he explained that this was a standard copyright arrangement covering college songs.[53]

In Allen's telling, he benevolently acquired the Aggie "War Hymn" to facilitate national exposure through an ASCAP license that granted license-holders permission to perform any song in his catalogue. Now, he explained, "prominent radio stations from coast to coast" could program the "War Hymn" without copyright concerns. Allen appealed to A&M school pride, insinuating that the "War Hymn" was little-heard outside Texas, and assured readers he would send the song to major media outlets and companies.[54] This altruistic framing obscured the fundamentally commercial nature of copyright transferal. Despite his pacifying efforts, conflict over the A&M community's sense of ownership of the song, and Allen's treatment of it as a commodity, resurfaced the next year. In spring 1940, A&M ensembles planning to record the "War Hymn" learned they would have to pay Allen's company the ASCAP fee of two cents per record. A reporter covering the ensuing scuffle complained that collective sentiment and school spirit should have trumped "Pinky" Wilson's claims to song ownership in the first place, arguing that "the Aggies had taken it to their hearts and made it their own." The reporter was restating a common A&M community belief: the "War Hymn" belonged to them, a claim which placed the song outside the realm of commodification.[55]

Thornton Allen's acquisition, marketing, and protection of his catalogue, built on the notion of college songs as commodities, foregrounds a tension between commercialism and tradition that marked broader college song discourse in the 1930s. In a 1934 *Saturday Evening Post* feature, writer and composer Kenneth S. Clarke alluded to the economic aspect of the college football pageantry in which such songs were embedded: "Bands and colors and organized hullabaloo appeal to the general public to the tune of millions of dollars of gate receipts every year" and subsidize other collegiate sports.[56] Clarke contrasted this knowledge with the typical alumnus's naïve rationale for pageantry, labeling the two views "the sentimentalist vs. the realist." [57] Nonetheless, Clarke, who worked in music publishing, called fight songs "the living embodiment of college tradition."[58] His acknowledgment highlights the tension underwriting the college song industry of the 1930s, at the center of which stood Thornton W. Allen.

Collegiate Singing Stars of the 1930s

More than once, Thornton Allen mentioned Rudy Vallée's hit 1930 recording of the University of Maine "Stein Song" to the school's Alumni Association as a yardstick for measuring the marketability of other Maine college songs.[59] Allen knew that a star's radio, in-person, and recorded performances of a college song would boost its sheet music sales, and Rudy Vallée was the brightest star in the 1930s collegiate "crooner" firmament. When Vallée began recording college songs in 1930, the country, sliding into the worst of the Depression, was eager for reassuring and aspirational collegiate glamour, embodied by an "increasingly collegian type" of crooner: a "young, handsome . . . white male" combining intimate, microphone-hugging vocals with dance-band jazz and a celebrity image built from collegiate symbols and themes.[60] Rudy Vallée's career started in the 1920s when as a student he toured the New England college dance circuit with his "sweet jazz" band.[61] For most of his career, Vallée wore a letterman sweater in photos and at shows, was often pictured with a cheerleading megaphone, and attended Yale football games, to press delight.[62] He sang and recorded many songs that were either loosely about college life or affiliated with specific schools and starred in the 1935 college-themed film *Sweet Music*. Vallée recorded mostly romantic songs until February 1930, when his dance band version of the "Stein Song (University of Maine)" for Victor launched a burst of college song recordings including "Washington and Lee Swing," "Betty Co-Ed," "Good Night, Poor Harvard," "Harvardiana," Yale's "Eli, Eli," "Sweetheart of my Student Days," and Yale's "Whiffenpoof Song."[63] Vallée's college song output was mostly rooted in Ivy League university culture; some songs, such as the "Swing," were about football and were used as real fight songs.

Fred Waring and the Pennsylvanians also built their star text from collegiate tropes, rooted in Waring's experiences of rich 1920s campus musical life.[64] After a smash early 1920s performance at a University of Michigan dance, Waring's group earned Detroit radio spots, and in April 1925, they recorded the Broadway hit "Collegiate" for Victor Records, one of the first big college song records, followed in the late 1920s and early 1930s by "Penn State Medley," "Collegiate Blues," "University of Penn Medley," "I Love the College Girls," "Sweetheart of Sigma Chi," "Yale Blues," "Collegiana," "Anybody's College Song," and "College Medley" which included the "Washington and Lee Swing."[65] In addition to these records, Waring linked himself to campus musical culture with his act's synchronized megaphone routines, glee-club singing, and performance of college songs in the 1937 film *Varsity Show*.[66] Fred Waring created at least 238 arrangements of college songs for concerts, radio, and recordings, an association that continued into the 1960s with college song LPs, long after the popular music industry had moved on from the collegiate subgenre.[67] The 1920s and 1930s campus music scene also shaped the career and aesthetic of Bing Crosby, active in college glee clubs and a star of Universal's 1933 film *College Humor*. Crosby occasionally sang college songs, performing the University of Tennessee's "Spirit of the Hill" fight song after discussing the Tennessee-Alabama game on his NBC radio show *Kraft Music Hall* in October 1939.[68] Crosby recorded college songs, although less frequently than Waring and Vallée, and his crooning style was intertwined with 1930s college music culture.

In the 1930s, these stars worked from central popular culture locations and networks—New York, Hollywood, Broadway, the national vaude-ville circuit, and national radio, creating collegiate content that south-ern audiences eagerly consumed. Rudy Vallée's NBC and Fred Waring's CBS radio broadcasts were heard across the South in the 1930s, and their films ran in southern theaters. Victor Records advertised Vallée's records in southern newspapers; a Birmingham newspaper ad assured readers that "no matter what your Alma Mater is, you won't be able to resist the infectious swing of the University of Maine's 'Stein Song.'"[69] An Octo-ber 1930 *Birmingham News* poll showed Vallée to be Birmingham's favor-ite dance orchestra leader, edging out national acts Guy Lombardo and Wayne King.[70] Rudy Vallée toured the South, playing a two-week con-cert series in Miami in 1931 and appearing with his orchestra at a 1933 film festival in Tampa, where he returned in 1937 for a five-night gig. Vallée and his orchestra performed at Atlanta's Fox Theater in 1933, a one-day event hyped for weeks by the Atlanta press which included three perfor-mances and a late-night dance, open to many Atlanta citizens.[71] Vallée broadcast his NBC hookup *The Fleischmann Yeast Hour* from New Orleans and Dallas when he was in town for shows.[72] The southern press often foregrounded the collegiate dimensions of the crooners' radio and live shows, mentioning specific college songs that would be featured.[73] *Miami Herald* coverage of Vallée's concerts focused on his newfound appeal to male listeners with the "Stein Song" record, perceived as more masculine than his romantic ballads.[74] The *Tampa Times* enthused over Fred Waring's "Football Smoker" radio program of college songs he wrote and arranged by request: "it makes us wonder why the University of Tampa has not put in their request for a brand new college song."[75] In 1936, Vanderbilt University's glee club planned to perform Fred Waring's arrangements, surely not the only southern school to do so.[76]

This network of national star collegiate performers was augmented by regional musicians who performed similar fare rooted in their con-nections to southern campuses. For every Rudy Vallée or Fred Waring, a dozen regional dance orchestras animated the white southern 1930s college music scene, as bandleaders such as Nashville's Frances Craig (1900–1966) and North Carolina's Kay Kyser (1905–1985) toured the SEC circuit playing for dances, dinners, variety shows, and other social events—careers that grew out of their own collegiate experiences. Frances Craig's career illustrates how regional orchestras performed the same styles and repertories for southern college audiences that were made famous by national collegiate acts. The Tennessee-born composer and pianist built a steady career as a dance orchestra leader playing "sweet" music for dinner clubs, country clubs, and hotels in Nashville, Birmingham, and other southern cities. His profile remained regional except for a freak 1947 hit recording of his song "Near You," yielding a surge of radio play and national tours. Craig's career began at Vanderbilt in the early 1920s when he organized a student dance orchestra that played contemporary jazz-inflected styles and repertoire, a danceable mix of sweet and semi-hot numbers including college songs like "Sweetheart of Sigma Chi," which he recorded for Columbia and played at gigs.[77] Craig leveraged radio power early in his career, beginning a decades-long association with Nashville's WSM in October 1925 at the station's inaugural broadcast.[78] Craig's group performed live from the WSM studios and the station broadcast his daily gig at Nashville's Hermitage Hotel.[79] Even at lower wattage in the late 1920s, WSM was audible as far away as Florida; when in the 1930s it began to broadcast at higher wattage, it cemented Craig's southeastern reputation.[80] Craig's radio work also included national hookups.[81] After his college years, Craig's orchestra remained intertwined with the college set, playing a key social role in Vanderbilt's "late-thirties, libidinous, dance-crazy, pre-war" social scene.[82] In the 1930s, Craig's group performed pre-football-game shows from the Hermitage Hotel, broadcast on WSM radio, that included college songs such as Craig's "Dynamite," a Vanderbilt fight song he wrote in 1938.[83] In the 1930s, Craig's group toured to Sewanee, the University of Alabama, the University of Tennessee, the University of North Carolina, North Carolina State, Auburn University (then Alabama Polytechnical Institute), the University of Georgia, and Georgia Tech.[84] Frances Craig was a successful southern version of the big-time collegiate crooners. Lesser-known southern dance orchestras such as the hot jazz band Snooks Friedman and his Memphis Stompers and the Louisiana Ramblers also played campus gigs and recorded dance-band versions of southern college fight songs.[85]

Conclusion: College Songs and 1930s Collegiate Identity

As college became a reality for more Americans, the middle-class identities and "middlebrow" song repertory of star collegiate crooners connected with 1930s consumers.[86] College songs and the stars who performed them traded on and contributed to the "idealized college boy" trope, defined in the US imagination as a "Hollywood crooner type . . . usually the star quarterback, whose masculine credentials were not compromised by a little sweet singing to win the girl."[87] This trope captivated 1930s consumers, sketching a reassuring social world animated by the agency of white, middle-class young men with college women functioning as romantic partners.[88] In signifying a gendered, racialized, and classed "collegiate" identity, 1930s college songs support David Brackett's argument that genre formation in US popular music was built on identity categories that articulated social difference.[89] If, as Brackett also argues, popular music genres emerge from a dynamic interplay of style characteristics and consumer and creator identity, college songs can be considered a distinct identity-based genre or subgenre of 1930s popular music, one overlooked in the historiography of twentieth-century US popular music.[90] Southerners along with people in the rest of the US avidly consumed and contributed to this subgenre, confirming Karl Hagstrom Miller's argument that a "history attuned to continuities across regions stands a better chance of accurately chronicling the development of American popular music."[91] A network of college song publishers and national and regional performers made collegiate cachet available to consumers of any social identity, inviting listeners to vicariously interface with the college mystique and granting them a sonic connection to an aspirational ideal at a time when the US sorely needed it. The next chapter documents the 1930s apex of SEC schools' search for unique fight songs that would allow them to participate in this category of the commercial music industry and solidify their football pageantry in a relatively new quest to define their public-facing institutional profiles.

CHAPTER 8

Make It Hot

Pushing for Pep in the 1930s

In 1936, the American Society of Composers, Authors, and Publishers (ASCAP) reported Yale's "Boola Boola" to be the year's most-performed college song, with 2,152 documented performances. A second Yale song topped the ASCAP list, which included only one southern fight song.[1] Kenneth Clarke, Princeton alumni and fight song composer, compiled a similarly New-England-centric list of the best college songs for a 1938 *Saturday Evening Post* feature, granting southern songs only two of twenty-two spots.[2] Crooners' college song records, their performers' star texts, and many college-themed movies and stage shows were likewise rooted in New England collegiate culture in the 1930s. Despite being sidelined in the national "collegiate" craze, however, more enduring SEC fight songs were created in the 1930s than in any decade before or since. Against the backdrop of the popular music industry's college song niche and the formation of the Southeastern Conference, lasting fight songs emerged in the 1930s at the University of Arkansas, Mississippi State University, Vanderbilt University, the University of Mississippi, and Louisiana State University.

In the South, New Deal money improved white flagship universities, including football stadiums.[3] By the mid-1930s, southern college football gate receipts had rebounded from an early-Depression low point, and southern powerbrokers launched high-profile bowl games to boost tourism in southern cities.[4] The Associated Press began its college football poll, creating the first nationalized team rankings, and in December 1932, the Southeastern Conference formed in Atlanta, largely made of former

Southern Conference schools.[5] The fledgling SEC—cheerfully amenable to commercialization—scandalized the rest of higher education, which strained to preserve the fiction of amateurism in college football.[6] By the mid-1930s, these developments motivated white southern universities to crystallize their football pageantry into effective marketing and public relations tools. It was a bad time not to have a good fight song.

A Song Lost and Found at the University of Arkansas

The strange story of "Arkansas Fight," buried for two decades, began between 1910 and 1913 when engineering student William Edwin Douglass wrote the song and music professor Henry Tovey arranged it. Douglass, a clarinetist active in campus and town music, enjoyed a close and opaque relationship with the colorful, eccentric Tovey, acquiring the nickname "Tovey's pet."[7] An extant musical manuscript for "Arkansas Fight" from Douglass's student days bears both their names and Douglass's graduation year, although it is unclear in whose hand.[8] After Douglass and Tovey worked on "Arkansas Fight," also called "Field Song," the song lay fallow and unpublished for several decades, leaving little trace in University of Arkansas yearbooks and newspapers of the 1910s and 1920s.[9] Unusually well-documented pride in the university's alma mater, written by Henry Tovey and used at pep rallies and football games in the 1910s, may have precluded embrace of the Tovey-Douglass song.[10] By the early 1920s, "hot" music dominated the school's student life, including football culture.[11] Pep rallies featured the Arkansas Travelers campus dance orchestra playing "their peppiest pieces," and university marching band members played in local jazz groups.[12] In this climate, Arkansas students and alumni voiced growing concern over the lack of a peppy fight song. A 1921 student editorial called the alma mater, still the only institutional song, a "relic":

> The University is desperately in need of a new school song that will grip the hearts of the students . . . [with] unsurpassed enthusiasm and . . . impress upon the mind of every student an uncontrollable urge to be up and doing [sic] for the university of Arkansas. . . . To call [the Alma Mater] our school song and publish it as such is doing an irretrievable injury to the prominence and reputation which school songs have in general attained.[13]

The editorial called for a songwriting contest with a $200 prize, a suggestion echoed in a 1922 letter to the student paper that described the alma mater as "too lofty and dignified" to work as a pep song. Such complaints showed students' awareness of national college song culture; some lamented that the University of Texas had "The Eyes of Texas" while Arkansas was songless and called for a pep club like the Southern Methodist University Mustangs or the University of Texas Cowboys, which would "be of especial use in putting our school song over."[14] New songs popped up, but none stuck. In 1923, a professor presented a song at an Arkansas Boosters Club meeting, and although a "decided hit" at that week's pep rally, it made no discernible impact on school culture.[15] In 1924, William M. Paisley (class of 1925), wrote "Arkansas Pep Song," the first fight song to generate excitement on campus, at least through the late 1920s. Nonetheless, in 1925, students bewailed the band's lack of new songs and funding, describing the ensemble's "few popular songs [and] marches" as a "standing joke."[16]

Song fever climaxed in 1928 and 1929, likely due in part to the school's growing presence on campus radio station KUOA, which had broadcast Arkansas football games since 1924.[17] By September 1929, KUOA aired near-daily university broadcasts: football games, student programs, women's and family programs, agricultural and musical programs, and campus interest show "Razorback Ramblings," all of which generated coverage in alumni and student publications.[18] KUOA reached nearly thirty states and parts of Canada and often featured university music groups and booster organizations whose studio presence would have highlighted the school's lack of a signature fight song.[19]

In October 1928, a women's campus booster group launched a "Know Your Pep Song" campaign, likely referring to William Paisley's 1924 "Arkansas Pep Song," also called "Razorback Pep Song."[20] Despite this campaign, the next month, the Pi Kappa Journalism Society sponsored a pep song contest seeking a single stanza of text, eight "short, snappy lines . . . with a simple rhyme scheme [that is] peppy, meaningful, and easy to sing." Music faculty would compose music and score the resulting song for orchestra and band. The student paper assured readers that the song would not supplant the beloved alma mater.[21] Alumni also announced a pep song contest with rules echoing those of the student contest, suggesting coordination. The announcement emphasized the need for "a

new spirited football song," a "peppy march" with a "lively tune."[22] Both
the student and alumni contest announcements emphasized the need for
a song livelier than the alma mater, which they assured readers was not
endangered. The article provided song models, quoting fight song lyrics from midwestern universities.[23] University of Arkansas alumni didn't
only want to hear a pep song at games or on radio; alumni clubs in New
York City, Pittsburgh, Chicago, Tulsa, Memphis, and Little Rock sang
school songs at their meetings.[24] In December, with no suitable submissions, students extended their contest to March 1929, where it seems to
have petered out, with no finalists selected.[25] At last, the June 1929 *Arkansas Alumnus* printed its winning entry, a voice-piano manuscript for "Victory," with text by Bryan L. Milburn and music by a professor.[26] Although
arranged by band director F. J. Foutz and used at Fall 1929 Homecoming,
"Victory" didn't excite students.[27] Its text seems to have been plucked uni-
laterally from contest entries by Lawrence Powell, a British music professor with a classical choral background, rather than chosen by the student body. The piano arrangement of "Victory" printed in the alumni
magazine was frumpy and outdated, with an Alberti bass better suited
to an eighteenth-century keyboard sonata.[28] It likely was only printed in
campus publications, not published commercially.[29]

These factors would have helped the 1931 "Razorback Rootin,'" published by Thornton W. Allen, to supersede "Victory." "Razorback Rootin'" was written by three alumni; two women supplied the words and
William M. Paisley, composer of the 1924 "Razorback Pep Song," wrote
the music. Allen published the song with ukulele chords as sheet music
and in his 1931 *Intercollegiate Songbook*. Radio dissemination of "Razorback Rootin'" generated excitement in Arkansas campus publications,
which earnestly and hyperbolically described it as a "national hit," point-
ing to its radio play on national hookups *Bayuk Stag Party* and *Parade of
the States*, and by Vincent Lopez's orchestra. NBC musical director Keith
McLeod programmed "Razorback Rootin'" on New York's WEAF, sung
by a men's glee club.[30] The song's distribution via national media and publishing was likely thanks to William Paisley, who post-graduation moved
to New York to study music and work at NBC Radio.[31] Arkansas alumni
crowed about "Razorback Rootin'" and students began using it: surely
this was the long-awaited song.[32] In early 1932, campus radio KUOA made
it the station's theme song, and station director W. S. Gregson organized
a recording of it.[33]

Despite this promising start, "Razorback Rootin'" was overtaken in popularity when in May 1932, the *Arkansas Alumnus* announced band director F. J. Foutz's discovery of William Edwin Douglass's circa-1913 "Field Song," stating vaguely that Foutz "secured a copy of it this year and it came into immediate popularity."[34] The *Alumnus* article suggests that the "Field Song" was used several months prior to May 1932, at the same time that "Razorback Rootin'" was making a splash. It is not clear why the "Field Song" won out over "Razorback Rootin'"; it is possible, given Thornton Allen's contemporary tussles with other schools around song copyrights, that the University of Arkansas wanted a pep song unfettered by legal concerns, and the "Field Song" fit the bill. "Razorback Rootin'" may also have been associated more with basketball than football.[35] Although "Field Song" / "Arkansas Fight" is now the school's official fight song and attained some student popularity after its rediscovery, it was by no means the clear favorite in the 1930s, when it was only one song in a broad and varied football repertory. On a 1936 postgame national radio broadcast, the University of Arkansas band played the "Field Song," "Cruiser Harvard March," "Arkansas Traveler," and "Darktown Strutters' Ball."[36] The broadcast exemplified the band's colorful 1930s repertory of marches, novelty songs, swinging arrangements of pop hits such as "Blue Skies" and "Remember," and hillbilly songs.[37] Inexplicably, the university trotted out "Victory," winner of the 1928–1929 alumni song contest, as its official fight song for 1934 Homecoming.[38] When Arkansas native and baritone Ross Graham performed on an NBC program celebrating the Arkansas state centennial in April 1936, he sang the "Razorback pep song" [sic] by Bill Paisley, although it's unclear whether this referred to Paisley's 1924 song of that title or to his 1931 "Razorback Rootin.'"[39]

In the 1940s, school sources began to refer more frequently to an "Arkansas Fight Song," likely meaning Douglass's "Field Song," although it was still embedded within a repertory that encompassed newer and older songs, including those signifying regional or sectional identity.[40] At the University of Arkansas, this matrix included "Dixie," "Arkansas Traveler," and the alma mater.[41] Calls for new spirit-boosting football songs and cheers still emerged in the 1940s alongside criticism of the band for overplaying certain choruses and marches, worry over students not knowing or singing the alma mater at games, and handwringing over the general "lack of pep [that] is a chronic Arkansas condition."[42] As late as 1948,

"Razorback Rhythm" was the theme song of a University of Arkansas radio program, but by the mid-1950s, "Arkansas Fight" solidified into the school's fight song.[43] In 1954, the band recorded it under the title "Arkansas Fight Song" for the campus radio show, and the song, along with the alma mater, was printed and distributed for homecoming, accompanied by campus press coverage of its unusual decades-long dormancy.[44] University music faculty arranged the song several times over the next few decades, often accompanied by uncertainty over its origins—confusion rectified in 1993 when William Douglass's children produced sources documenting their father's musical life at the university eight decades earlier.[45] Although "Field Song" dated from the early 1910s, its unusual chronology of adoption accords with song-related urgency that surged across the Southeastern Conference in the 1930s.

Thornton W. Allen's Imprint on a Mississippi State University Song Contest

In 1937, Thornton W. Allen published a *Mississippi State College Songs* folio containing four songs for Mississippi State University: "Men of State" ("Hail State"), "Marching Song," "Maroon and White" ("Alma Mater"), and "Mississippi State Fight Song." Except the alma mater, the folio's contents were generated by a 1936–1937 campus songwriting contest, a typical result of student and alumni constituencies trying to develop unique fight songs and a sign of Allen's capitalizing on their efforts. In October 1936, student magazine *Mis-A-Sip* ran a song contest notice highlighting students' longtime and pained awareness of the dearth of a unique fight song. The announcement listed schools with notable songs—the Citadel, the University of Alabama, Georgia Tech—and recalled Mississippi State's public humiliation by a dance band that, for want of something better, cheekily performed "Turkey in the Straw" as the school's college song.[46]

Various football songs had circulated on campus since the school's earliest days of playing the sport. A typed set of lyrics (ca. 1915–1916) by a veterinary medicine professor attested to early faculty efforts to provide the school with football songs. These included an alma mater text sung to "America," a football poem paired with "Hot Time in the Old Town Tonight" (a minstrel tune popular in early twentieth-century college culture), and football texts set to the tunes "Tipperary" and "Our

Director March."[47] Short-lived 1920s examples of songs used in Mississippi State football culture included "Our Alma Mater" (a football poem sung to "Madelon"), "Roll on Aggies," and "Fite Boys," with the latter two sung to unknown tunes. Mississippi State also used the "Washington and Lee Swing" with the text "Put 'Em Beneath the Sod."[48] These songs largely used pre-existing tunes circulating broadly in college culture, making them unattractive as enduring song candidates. Like other student bodies, Mississippi State in the 1930s valued sonic expressions of "pep" in football culture. Freshmen received "M" books of cheers and yells and were required to attend pep rallies, sit together at games, learn football cheers and yells, and master the alma mater within a week of arriving on campus.[49] In this atmosphere, the absence of a snappy fight song was sorely felt, especially because the only song reliably identified with Mississippi State football was the school's hymn-like alma mater.

The 1936 *Mis-A-Sip* contest generated robust communications and feature articles, providing a window into campus songwriting contests of the time.[50] In these, the winning song was framed as a commodity by multiple stakeholders, subject to copyright, pregnant with economic value, and worthy of financial investment. The $10 prize money initially offered by the *Mis-A-Sip* rose to $55 through Alumni Association, campus newspaper, and university administrator contributions.[51] While prize money typified such contests, more atypical was the contest's unequivocal framing of the money as recompense for ceding copyright:

> The winning entry will be turned over to the Mississippi State Student Association to be copyrighted and to become the exclusive property of the student body. The prize money, of course, will be considered as payment for the song submitted. Should more than one song be turned in that will be suitable . . . more than one may be purchased.[52]

Mis-A-Sip coverage foregrounded the song's commercial value by quoting a faculty member's nebulous estimate that its public relations worth to the university could exceed $10,000.[53] The *Mis-A-Sip* emphasized that professional songwriters could enter the contest, stipulating that if suitable lyrics were received, the student body would raise funds to pay a professional composer for a tune.[54]

Dance bands figured prominently in the contest, demonstrating the mechanics of 1930s fight song reception and dissemination. The Mississippi State Glee Club and Mitt Evans and the Collegians, a campus dance band, performed contest entries for students to vote on, meaning the songs needed to be "hot," or at least arrangeable to sound like it.[55] Contest rules reinforced this, emphasizing the undesirability of square, staid songs: the winning entry should be "a snappy tune" with "plenty of 'swing.'"[56] Lyrics could be flexible; swinging musical style counted more.[57] The winning song, "Hail Dear Old State" ("Hail State"), by Joseph Burleson Peavey, was announced in the school newspaper with text printed later in the *Mis-A-Sip*. It received only half of the 1244 student votes cast, with remaining votes split between other songs.[58] Peavey, owner of a Meridian, Mississippi, music store, never attended Mississippi State, later stating that Meridian native and Collegians bandleader Mitt Evans alerted him to the contest a few months beforehand. Evans promised that if Peavey wrote and arranged a good song for dance band, the Collegians would "plug" it at school dances prior to judging. Peavey admitted that this gave "Hail State" a "jump" on other song entries.[59] Peavey's recollections, postdated by roughly thirty years, are both refuted and substantiated by the February 1937 contest results announcement, which indicated that "Hail State" predated the contest, but by three years—not a few months as Peavey stated.[60] Mitt's Collegians likely played "Hail State" at campus dances before the 1937 contest, familiarizing students with it.

Thornton Allen published the folio of prizewinning and runner-up songs in 1937, the year of the contest results, and in fact likely had precontest contact with Joseph Peavey. According to the February 1937 contest results announcement,

> "Hail, Dear Old State" is not a new song. It was written about three years ago, and was given to a publisher of college songs, who hesitated to publish it without some school behind it. Since the students of this school have shown how well they do like it, it will be published and will be available in the near future.[61]

Surely the unnamed publisher was Thornton W. Allen, given his concern with profit, his prodigious work to generate or acquire college songs, and his 1937 publication of the Mississippi State folio. In running his Meridian music store, Joseph Peavey would have known publisher niches, with Allen the top college song publisher at the time. It is also possible that the Mississippi State Student Association had contact with Thornton Allen that shaped song contest rules: their laser focus on copyright echoes language in the University of Alabama's 1925 song contest rules, which also likely bore Allen's imprint. Allen's copyrighting of runner-up songs, a clever provision built into contest rules which further argues for his involvement, enabled him to sell a Mississippi State folio rather than sheet music of a single song. Out of twenty-one song contest entries, three songs—including Peavey's "Hail State"—were presented to Mississippi State students in dance band and orchestra arrangements in February 1937.[62] All three entries plus the alma mater ended up in Allen's folio. A few weeks after the school narrowly voted "Hail State" its fight song, Mitt Evans and his Collegians embarked on a spring break tour north to Oxford, Mississippi, and south to the state's coast, with residencies at supper clubs, casinos, and hotels.[63] Fronted by vocalist Elsie Buford, the otherwise all-male band likely used the tour to spread the new "Hail State."[64]

A Dance Band Leader Writes a Vanderbilt Song

With 1933's "Vanderbilt Forever," noted sportswriter and Vanderbilt alumnus Grantland Rice added another fight song to the pile the school had tried and discarded since the early twentieth century. He wrote the text and Thornton W. Allen wrote the music and published the song.[65] The Nashville press heralded "Vanderbilt Forever," including Rice himself in a self-serving editorial: "What Vanderbilt has needed for some years . . . is an improvement in the doleful and unchanging program presented by the college band. . . . For the first time in years, Vanderbilt will have something original in the way of martial music."[66] Vanderbilt began using the song at games, the alumni office organized sheet music sales, Thornton Allen mailed copies of it to radio stations, and Francis Craig's orchestra played it on WSM.[67] The Vanderbilt glee club performed "Vanderbilt Forever" and the 1934 *Commodore* yearbook printed its text. In May 1937, when Vanderbilt broadcast a high-profile show in NBC's Pontiac Variety Show Night series, its ensembles played and sang "Vanderbilt Forever."[68] Despite this sporadic student use of the song in its early years, it did not take root.[69] The Alumni Association displayed mild interest in it, and Grantland Rice certainly had strong ties to the group.[70] However, alumni seem not to have performed it often. When Vanderbilt alumni gathered in New York in 1935, they sang the alma mater followed with a spiritual sung by Nashville tenor James Melton, broadcast over WSM.[71] Accounts of 1936 alumni gatherings mention singing "songs" and "old songs," but do not name "Vanderbilt Forever."[72]

The Vanderbilt community's periodic calls for better football music intensified in fall 1936 for several converging reasons. Since Vanderbilt's football pageantry unfolded off-campus, with street parades and "take-overs" of theaters and hotels, and—increasingly—on radio, students were conscious of public perception of their football pageantry.[73] Nashville's WSM boosted its Vanderbilt coverage in the early 1930s with glee club performances and regular football broadcasts.[74] Vanderbilt band airtime grew with features like a 1938 "battle of the bands" with the University of Mississippi, broadcast from Nashville's War Memorial Auditorium.[75] In Fall 1936, the band received new uniforms and halftime "stunts" and a remade organizational scheme and constitution.[76] That fall, to counteract upperclassmen's posture of sophisticated boredom, Vanderbilt instituted a freshman cheering section with prompt cards and new yells.[77] In 1937, the push for pep advanced with the formation of the Vanderbilt Junior Athletic Association, which optimized the football soundscape through a new public address system, sound truck, and "short [and] snappy" band music; pep events; and improved cheerleading.[78]

In this context, Frances Craig's "Dynamite" emerged in 1938, ultimately although not immediately dislodging "Vanderbilt Forever." Thornton Allen's Sousa-like "Vanderbilt Forever" march likely sounded "square" to Vanderbilt students, who in the mid-1930s listened to Fats Waller and Bing Crosby records, hired Tommy Dorsey's band for campus dances, and attended Fletcher Henderson and Duke Ellington shows in Knoxville and Nashville.[79] In the dance-saturated context of 1930s SEC football culture, with dances on campus or at local clubs and hotels a gameday centerpiece, "Vanderbilt Forever" probably didn't swing hard enough.[80] Francis Craig and his orchestra, at the heart of campus dance culture, knew student tastes and could easily popularize a new Vanderbilt song.[81] The diaries of student and fraternity member Ben Austin documented Craig's musical role in Vanderbilt's late-1930s student life.[82] Austin described a vertiginous

campus scene brimming with parties, dances, dinners, and theater out-
ings in which Francis Craig featured prominently as a figure intimately
involved in student life. Craig hobnobbed with students at dances, pre-
dicting football scores, placing bets, and playing songs for specific couples.[83] Ben Austin and Craig often consulted on dance repertoire, with
Austin steering Craig toward slow pieces and sentimental waltzes for
amorous purposes.[84] Craig's place in Vanderbilt culture was exemplified
by his pregame WSM broadcasts from the Hermitage Hotel, where in the
late 1930s he talked football and played fight songs with his orchestra.[85]

The week of the November 12, 1938, Vanderbilt-Tennessee game, Francis Craig wrote "Dynamite" and premiered it on his Friday night WSM
show.[86] The song was quickly printed as a broadside sponsored by a gas
station to circulate to students.[87] The Vanderbilt band played the song
at halftime in Knoxville the next day and Craig's orchestra performed it
again that night on the radio, meaning it was already arranged for dance
orchestra and marching band.[88] Positive press coverage ensued in the
Tennessean and the campus paper, including a student editorial praising
Craig for addressing "Vanderbilt's long-standing need for an individual
school song."[89] Nonetheless, "Dynamite" did not soon become the university's only or main song.[90] It also did not remediate the band's "consistent sordid performance" and ineffectual "antics," nor boost a perceived
lack of football spirit, which the student body continued to bemoan for
the next decade.[91] So feeble was Vanderbilt's pageantry in Fall 1941 that a
mandate of unclear origins insisted that freshmen march with the band
to Dudley Field for home games to amplify school spirit.[92] Underfunding
and administrative disarray, exacerbated by wartime measures, plagued
the band. Although band membership opened to women in late fall 1943,
who soon constituted one-fourth of the group, the wartime band played
at only one or two games over the next couple of years, returning to
functionality only in 1945.[93]

It is therefore hard to reconstruct how "Dynamite" became the
school's fight song, although some inflection points are discernible.
In 1941, Edwin Morris published "Dynamite," Fred Waring played it
on national radio, and Francis Craig conducted it at a football game.[94]
The surge of exposure was likely due to ASCAP's war with radio stations, resulting in a radio ban of ASCAP songs "Vanderbilt Forever" and
another Vanderbilt song, "Cheer for the Gold and Black."[95] By the late

1940s, Vanderbilt football programs typically printed "Dynamite," an indication that it was regarded as the school's chief song.[96] Another inflection point in the song's reception history was the resolution of longtime band problems. The ensemble's woes climaxed when Vanderbilt created a band committee in 1949 to improve management and repertoire, resulting in a student coup.[97] University administration intervened and hired the school's first full-time band director, James H. Parnell, in fall 1952.[98] Parnell shaped up the band and premiered a new "Dynamite" arrangement for hundreds of alumni within months of his arrival.[99] "Dynamite" had filtered into student usage by this time; an account described drunken students singing its chorus around a piano in the wee hours after the 1948 Vanderbilt-University of Mississippi game.[100] Parnell's hiring and new "Dynamite" arrangement helped cement the song's institutional usage, although Parnell reminded the public that "we are always interested in receiving new fight songs."[101]

Building on Confederate Identity:
The University of Mississippi's "Forward Rebels"

Alone out of new SEC fight songs in the 1930s, the University of Mississippi's "Forward Rebels" ("Rebels March") evoked sectional sentiment, written as part of the school's 1936 neo-Confederate rebranding. Like other contemporary SEC fight songs, "Forward Rebels" emerged from the crucible of mid-1930s campus concern around the lack thereof. Before "Forward Rebels," the University of Mississippi used many pep songs, with efforts to find a unique one simmering in the late 1920s and climaxing in 1936 amidst the anxieties about school spirit then endemic to SEC schools.[102] A 1931 campus fight song contest had failed, despite offering $100 in prizes, granting a six-week extension, and receiving entries from around the US.[103] In 1932, a joke even circulated about the university marching band playing at a funeral to ensure sadness.[104] The university's 1934 Homecoming festivities illustrate how the lack of a fight song would have been keenly felt by students, alumni, and visitors, because the festivities included so many opportunities to hear school songs: at a Friday night pep rally, a Saturday morning band parade, an alumni association meeting, the game itself, and an evening dance.[105] In 1935, band director Roy Coats wrote a new alma mater tune for the school, which also likely highlighted the absence of a fight song.[106] In fall 1936, the student paper agitated for a new fight song, using its weekly "Band Rhythm" column to urge new band director R. N. Whitfield to secure and arrange one. The paper suggested adopting the "Ole Miss March," recently written by Aileen Tyre (likely a student or alumna), citing its recent radio play and urging the band to make a "snappy arrangement" of it.[107] It seems the paper pressured Whitfield into acquiring and evaluating potential fight songs, although not in time to debut one during the 1936 season.[108]

Instead, the university band premiered a new march called "Forward Rebels" for the student body in February 1937 to vote on adopting it as the school's fight song. By the time the band left on spring tour a few weeks later, planning to play "Forward Rebels" ("Fighting Rebels," as it was first called) for audiences around the state, the song had been well-received on campus.[109] The new march was a collaboration between student Egbert Francis "Sleepy" Yerby, who wrote the tune; Simon Kooyman, a Clarksdale, Mississippi, band director who arranged it; and Mrs. R. N. Whitfield Jr., wife of the band director and author of the lyrics.[110] Her text was standard pep song fare, sprinkled with references to Rebels, the Southland, and the school's nickname, "Ole Miss." Despite the song's rear-facing title, Yerby's tune was contemporary—catchy, syncopated, and "hot," testifying to his embeddedness in 1930s collegiate musical life. Like other student fight song writers of the decade, Yerby was active on campus; he was a Sigma Chi pledge, YMCA member, and President of the Ole Miss Musical Club who played saxophone and clarinet in the Mississippians campus dance orchestra.[111] Yerby was also student director of the marching band, placing him in regular contact with its director and his wife.[112] Like Mississippi State University's Mitt Evans and the Collegians, the Mississippians toured the state with the glee club.[113] Yerby's song fit with University of Mississippi students' desire for peppier football music in general, reflective of contemporary collegiate tastes, resulting in a fall 1939 marching band "policy that will streamline the type of music played at games . . . instead of marches of the past, popular tunes and novelties will be featured henceforth."[114] When Yerby enrolled ca. 1933–1934, the university had not embarked on its rebranding mission, and had only recently officially organized the marching band.[115]

The school's new "Rebels" identity, complete with the Colonel Reb mascot, debuted in Fall 1936, accompanied by new "Rebel Yells" and augmented in early 1937 by the debut of "Forward Rebels."[116] The "Rebels" theme was chosen through a well-publicized contest pushed by southern sports media that yielded over six hundred name suggestions, culled to five finalists by a small group of alumni, students, and Athletic Association members. The group sent five sectionally themed suggestions—"Rebels," "Confederates," "Raiders," "Stonewalls," and "Ole Miss"—to twenty-one southern sports journalists, and eighteen of them voted for "Rebels." A small group of alumni given final judgment in the matter ratified the choice.[117] University of Mississippi alumnus Ben Guider, who submitted the winning entry, wrote that "Rebels" was "short, musical, inspiring, simple for publication purposes," and eye-catching for sports media and fans. It also, he added, "calls to mind the glories of the Old South and that historic struggle of the Civil War in which the State of Mississippi took so noble and outstanding a part, and for which every Mississippian should feel proud."[118] Student and alumni cooperation in the rebranding typified intensifying collaborative efforts among SEC stakeholders in the 1930s to crystallize their schools' public-facing identities, although some administrators and Mississippi journalists had misgivings about the new Rebels identity.[119] Even before the rebranding, Confederate symbols and Lost Cause mythology figured into the school's public image. The nickname "Ole Miss," thought of by a woman student in 1892, came from a supposed reference by enslaved people to a plantation's mistress. As historian Jack Carey notes, the "Rebels" marketing initiative coincided with the receipt of federal money for University of Mississippi football stadium and the school's pursuit of an "ambitious football schedule." By pairing Confederate symbols with elements of "modernity and contemporary culture," the school self-consciously positioned itself relative to the Old South in an "attempt to shroud [itself] in a mystique which transcended time and enlisted the authority of tradition in the promotion of the institution." It was an instance, Carey argues, of the southern white supremacist embrace of the New Deal "as a mechanism to build up white democracy" in the region.[120]

The new "Forward Rebels," performed by the renamed marching band—described as "the nucleus of the Rebel spirit"—became an audible component of the Confederate rebranding and was printed in university publications going forward.[121] As with other SEC schools of the time, the new fight song, which turned out to be the enduring and official one, was not at first used consistently, and was still augmented by a matrix of other school favorites.[122] After the Dixiecrat movement erupted at the 1948 Democratic Convention, with frenzied University of Mississippi students carrying a Confederate battle flag, "Dixie" and the flag experienced a broad resurgence in southern culture, including in University of Mississippi football culture. After 1948, "Dixie" was often sung at the school alongside "Forward Rebels," linking a modern song and an older song to project sectional intransigence that spanned the decades.[123] These symbols weren't a spontaneous afterthought; incoming freshmen were advised in 1949 that

> you will need to know all verses of "Dixie" . . . and be able to sing it with gusto; we are proud Southerners and want people to know it. . . . You will see a huge Confederate Flag unfurled that will cover the Football field. This doesn't mean that we are not citizens of the Union; it simply means we don't want anybody to run over us—anywhere, anytime.[124]

The school hung onto "Dixie" long after other universities gave it up. Like other schools of the time, however, there was still openness to other fight songs; in December 1940, Fred Waring promised to write a new University of Mississippi fight song and perform it on the radio if enough students signed a campus petition.[125]

Conclusion

The bulk of the Southeastern Conference fight songs that have been officially adopted by member schools or have achieved enduring institutional usage were written in the 1930s. The composition, publication, distribution, and performance of new SEC fight songs in the 1930s rested on the bedrock of the college song industry documented in Chapter 7, consisting of an intricate network of specialized publishers and regional and national "collegiate" performers. These new songs emerged from southern campus musical cultures marked by the national heyday of the dance band; their composition and early reception histories are marked by student emphasis on having a "hot," danceable football song to use at multiple social occasions, in the years before college fight songs became the domain of the marching band. The micro-histories of these songs also show that across the SEC in the 1930s, students, alumni, and sometimes administrators worked in aggregate to create or locate fight songs that would enhance institutional public image and solidify student and alumni ties, to one another and to their respective schools. Collaborating with college song publishers to move their songs into the commercial market-place, or simply to facilitate easier campus distribution, was a key part of this work: students and alumni of the 1930s could reasonably expect a new fight song to gain off-campus interest through voice-piano and dance-band arrangements in the "college song" niche, thereby enhancing a school's public profile. The next chapter examines a hyperbolic case study of this regional trend: Louisiana politician Huey P. Long's musical involvement with Louisiana State University's marching band and football program.

CHAPTER 9

Huey Long's Band Plays His Songs

In Louisiana in the 1930s, the outsized personality of populist politician Huey P. Long collided with the push by Southeastern Conference schools to crystallize their football pageantry. From 1930 to his September 1935 assassination, Huey Long—as Louisiana governor, US Senator, and presidential candidate—enmeshed himself in the affairs of Louisiana State University (LSU), largely through appointing as president the compliant Dr. James Monroe Smith, whom *Time* magazine called an "ideal academic puppet."[1] On top of manhandling LSU's administrative, physical plant, and financial matters, Long micromanaged its marching band. He hired and fired band directors; gave halftime speeches; traveled with the band; led them in parades; interfered in ensemble repertory, instrumentation, and size; and co-wrote football songs, one of which, "Touchdown for LSU," is still used. Huey Long's involvement with the LSU band and his broader use of music in his political career was noted by contemporary university, state, and national media and has since been recounted by journalists, scholars, and enthusiasts of Louisiana lore. These accounts mostly frame Long's musical activities at LSU as a string of disjunct anecdotes attributable to his colossal personality, unmoored from broader historical context.[2]

But ahistorical observations centering Long's personality can't fully account for his involvement with the LSU band, writing of college songs, and broader use of collegiate music as a political tool. As this chapter shows, Long's LSU musical activities were not merely refracted through

his hyperbolic persona, but also linked to key 1930s regional phenomena documented in the two previous chapters: southern embrace of
the "collegiate" trope ubiquitous in national popular culture, including
college songs, and SEC schools' ambitious expansion and robust public
relations initiatives, with football culture a vector for the latter. In a 1962
letter about Huey Long, Robert Penn Warren wrote that the "son-of-a-
bitch" displayed a pragmatic "streak of genius" for publicity measures
that reinforced his power.[3] For a few brief but memorable years, Long
used the LSU marching band and the songs he wrote with its director
to mediate this grasp on power, giving voice to his political aspirations
while indelibly imprinting LSU's football pageantry and Louisiana public
memory. This chapter shows how the son-of-a-bitch did it.[4]

Huey Long as the Band's Human Resources Manager

Huey Long's musical activities at LSU fit within his wider political use
of musical pageantry and sonic spectacle in his campaigns for Louisiana governor (1924 and 1928), US Senate (1930), and president (1935) and
his time in office. His political events were known for fiery speeches,
recorded and live music, and brass band parades across Louisiana.[5] One
of the first Louisiana politicians to broadcast radio speeches, Long gave
radio talks in his home state—more informal than those he broadcast
as senator in Washington, DC—that ran for hours, punctuated by brass
band performances.[6] Long sang in church choirs on the campaign trail
and played his childhood Jew's harp at events.[7] He treated New Orleans's
dance bands as his own personal orchestras, often staying at suites at New
Orleans's Heidelberg and Roosevelt Hotels to enjoy the city's nightlife.
The Roosevelt's Blue Room Night Club became Long's "court" where
he watched prize fights, dance bands, and shows by stars Phil Harris and
Sophie Tucker.[8] In hotels and restaurants, Long requested songs, then
clambered onstage to "direct" the band in performing the numbers.[9]
Extant footage of Long with entertainers such as Ina Ray Hutton and her
All-Girls Orchestra shows a man enamored of popular music, waving his
hands with a beatific expression and making complimentary remarks to
performers.[10] Castro Carazo, whom Long hired to lead the LSU band in
1934, recalled Long's avid if clumsy bandleading, his gratitude for being
allowed to "conduct," and his particular love of the 1930s hit "Smoke
Gets in Your Eyes."[11]

Within this context, 1930s collegiate music soundtracked Huey Long's imagined and real political persona, even apart from his involvement with LSU's band. Long never attended his beloved LSU and enrolled only briefly at Tulane University, later stating he lacked time for college in his youth.[12] College music expressed Long's infatuation with the campus life he never got to live, which he described as "a glamorous land of make-believe."[13] In his short speculative book *My First Days in the White House*, Long fantasized about a brass band leading a "happy throng" up the White House steps on his inauguration day where they "serenade[d]" the crowd as young people unfurled a banner emblazoned "On Our Way to College."[14] An early adopter of sound trucks, Long used them to amplify his speeches and preview his appearances at upcoming campaign stops, playing music and announcements to stir excitement. To launch Long's campaign for senate, on August 22, 1930, sound trucks paraded through St. Martinville, Louisiana, blasting Rudy Vallée's hit college song "Maine Stein Song."[15] The song's aspirational affect evoked the optimism that Long wanted poor Louisiana voters—hit hard early in the Depression, like residents of other cotton states—to associate with him.

However, Long's main use of college music to build his political persona and promote the state's flagship university came through managing LSU's band leadership, co-writing songs with its director, and shaping its public spectacles, although lack of extant documentation, or opacity in what does survive, makes it hard to reconstruct his involvement.[16] For example, in 1933, Huey Long wrote to an LSU student who sought his help in securing a band scholarship that "contrary to general belief, I have no influence in this respect." Huey Long then told the student to take his request to President James Monroe Smith—a Long appointee later jailed for fraud and embezzlement. Such documentation illuminates little about Long's role in the band program![17] Enough sources do survive to clarify some aspects of Long's involvement with the LSU band, starting with his management of its personnel. Twice he selected LSU's band directors, first in 1930 when he ousted Frank T. Guilbeau and replaced him with Alfred W. Wickboldt, musical director at New Orleans's Orpheum Theater.[18] Drafts of an LSU press release obliquely acknowledged Long's personnel shuffling, crowing "Governor Long has a band" and quoting Long's jokes about owning the group, which he promised to "hand over" to Wickboldt. Upon hiring Wickboldt, Long pushed for bold new purple

and gold band uniforms with fancy details, expanded ensemble instrumentation with oboes and bassoons, and acquired improved instruments
for the whole group.[19] In 1931, Wickboldt composed "The Governor Long
March" for his patron, incorporating a tune he heard Long hum on a
hunting trip.[20] This tribute notwithstanding, in December 1934, Long pressured Wickboldt to resign and hired Castro Carazo, as the *Tennessean* put
it, to "direct Huey Long's L.S.U. Band."[21] The *New York Times* reported
that Long hired Carazo—a veteran bandleader with a classical and jazz
background and broadcast experience—to launch a massive band radio
presence, a scheme that never materialized but which suggests Long's
belief in the band's PR potential.[22] Long spontaneously hired Carazo away
from his job as Roosevelt Hotel orchestra director, sending a car to whisk
him from the hotel to Baton Rouge for a meeting with Long and university personnel, whom Long ordered to support Carazo—authority the
new director used to purchase instruments, uniforms, and likely, music.[23]

No English-language scholarship exists on Castro Carazo, despite his
importance in US marching band history—evidence of a public profile
swallowed by Huey Long's shadow. Compounding this omission is mis-
information that circulated in Carazo's lifetime, such as the paternalistic
and doubly inaccurate assertion that Long "brought" Carazo to Louisiana from Cuba.[24] Castro Carazo (1895–1981), native of Costa Rica, was
active in US and international musical life before, during, and after his
work at LSU.[25] After attending San Jose's Santa Cecilia School of Music
and the Barcelona Conservatory, he led dance orchestras in New York and
toured South America with operatic and orchestral groups. Carazo came
to New Orleans ca. 1922 as the Strand Theater's music director, becoming music director at the city's new Saenger Theater in 1927.[26] Carazo
briefly returned to Costa Rica in the early 1930s to direct its military bands,
yielding the title "Colonel," which the US press used for him, and a life-
long habit of wearing a military uniform. Soon Carazo came back to
Louisiana permanently, first to lead the dance orchestra at the Roosevelt
Hotel's Blue Room, where he met Huey Long.[27] Carazo's compositions
and arrangements for instrumental and vocal soloists, chamber ensembles, and larger groups were published in the US and Spanish-speaking
countries; some were recorded by Victor in 1933.[28] US military ensembles played Carazo's marches at government events, a source of modest
fame later in his life.[29] Carazo's career began in an era when professional

musicians attained fluidity in a range of musical idioms, and he moved freely as composer, conductor, and arranger through the porous boundaries between classical, light classical, dance orchestra, and marching and symphonic band music.[30] Carazo outlasted Huey Long at LSU by almost five years until a reformist board removed him in 1940 and thereafter led a robust musical life in Louisiana as a teacher, clinician, adjudicator, and composer until his death in 1981.[31]

With Carazo as director, Huey Long funded expenses that amplified the band's and the university's public profile, such as travel to away games.[32] Extant photographs of Long handing dollar bills to LSU band members imply micro-involvement in the ensemble's finances.[33] At Long's behest, Carazo enlarged the band to over two hundred members and upped its showmanship quotient. The two brainstormed ideas for enlivened pageantry; Carazo even suggested the group play on horseback at a New York parade with LSU colors woven into the animals' tails—an idea Long vetoed only on the grounds of students' lack of equestrian experience. Carazo, with his dance orchestra background, expanded band repertoire to include Dixieland arrangements and 1930s popular music, making the group sound "swinging."[34] In one of his first halftime shows, the LSU band performed the popular waltz "Dancing to the Moon" instead of the marches and military drill routines that LSU fans had come to expect.[35] Although the LSU band played jazz and ragtime before the Long-Carazo years, popular memory credited the duo with reshaping the band's repertory, showmanship, and public image.[36] In later years, LSU honored Carazo through halftime shows dedicated to his legacy, such as at the 1972 Auburn-LSU game, when a band tribute resulted in media praise of Carazo for "transforming a sedate, military band into a strutting, rollicking collection of brasses, reeds and drums" and creating the vibrant halftime show tradition for which LSU became known.[37]

The perception that Carazo reshaped the band was not merely retroactive; it was voiced during his time at LSU by on- and off-campus media who touted the band's "latest syncopated formations."[38] In fact, 1930s student publications largely credited Castro Carazo for molding the band, with very little reference to Long's relationship with or influence on the ensemble.[39] Student paper coverage of Carazo's hiring interviewed the new director about his goals for the ensemble, making no mention of Huey Long, whose name was also missing from the student paper's coverage of the forced resignation of director Wickboldt.[40] Similarly, the *Gumbo* yearbook attributed the band's numerical growth and new uniforms solely to Castro Carazo.[41] Regardless of whether student publications accurately described the distribution of agency between the two men, many observers regarded the LSU band as Long's pet project and Castro Carazo as "Huey's man" or "Huey's composer," even decades after Long's assassination.[42]

Songwriting with Castro Carazo

In addition to selecting LSU band directors, Huey Long co-wrote campaign and football songs with Castro Carazo that were performed by the LSU band in the 1930s and, in some cases, well afterward. Soon after meeting Carazo at the Roosevelt, where Carazo allowed Long to "conduct" his orchestra, Long asked him to co-write a campaign song in late 1934 or early 1935.[43] The result was "Every Man a King," its title a slogan drawn from the rhetoric of earlier Democratic presidential candidate William Jennings Bryan ("every man a king, but no one wears a crown"). Although no evidence documenting their musical collaborations seems extant, Carazo recalled that songwriting with Long unfolded spontaneously, starting with "Every Man a King."[44] As Carazo was about to take the Roosevelt Hotel bandstand, he received an urgent call from Huey Long alerting him that a chauffeur would ferry him to Long's Baton Rouge hotel suite. There, equipped with neither music paper nor piano, Carazo drew staff lines on hotel stationary and wrote down a tune in verse-chorus structure with chord symbols while a pajama'd Long reclined on his bed, reading newspapers. Twenty minutes later, Carazo whistled the tune to Long, who pronounced it "damn good."[45] Carazo next whistled one phrase at a time so that Long could scribble down lyrics, yielding a text that sketched a cartoonish populist platform promising castles and millionaire status (for men, at any rate). Carazo, Long, and a small entourage trooped up to the eleventh floor to try "Every Man a King" on the piano, and the song was apparently broadcast on radio that night. It may have been broadcast by Carazo at a piano since his orchestra was back in New Orleans, or there may have been an orchestra at the Baton Rouge hotel to play it. "Every Man a King" was built on harmonic conventions common to popular song at the time, and any professional musician could have played its chord changes after one hearing, even without a written arrangement.[46]

"Every Man a King" functioned as a fight song for Long's fleeting presidential campaign, a sonic signature that created buzz and conveyed bites of information. It is easy to imagine that Long thought of "Every Man a King" this way: he sometimes refracted his political experiences through a football lens, comparing his navigation of political crowds to running interference and joking that LSU players could learn from him.[47] Long's campaign certainly used it like a fight song, mailing voters records of the song with a Huey speech on the B-side, and the LSU band performed it at campus events, including football games and pep rallies.[48] During one spirited radio speech, the senator paused four times for a band to play "Every Man a King" in the studio, punctuating his oratory as a band would punctuate a football game.[49] Extant footage shows Long at a political rally singing "Every Man a King" accompanied by one of his beloved brass bands.[50] It also sounded like a fight song: its first two phrases hewed closely to opening phrases of the "Washington and Lee Swing" chorus, testifying to the stock melodic gestures and chord progressions of pre-war popular song. Despite Carazo's publishing history, which presumably connected him to established music publishers and printers, "Every Man A King" was published by the National Book Company in New Orleans, a vanity press Huey Long's associates launched to publish his autobiography in 1933.[51] Printed as a march for piano and voice in Bb, the bare-bones edition used handwritten rather than typeset music notation, and the score started at the bottom of the cover page, saving the expense of a separate cover. M. Witmark and Sons of New York also published "Every Man a King" in 1935, retaining the key and instrumentation but using typeset instead of handwritten notation, an altered piano accompaniment, and banjo and ukulele tablature. In the absence of records from either publisher, it is unknown how many copies were printed by either one.

After "Every Man a King," Long and Carazo wrote two LSU songs, "Touchdown for LSU" and "Darling of LSU," published by the National Book Company in the 1935 voice and piano folio *Two L.S.U. Songs*.[52] The folio's purple-and-gold cover pictured an LSU campus tower framed by photographs of Long and Carazo flanking an LSU pennant. Like "Every Man a King," these songs were printed using handwritten, not typeset, notation. Although "Touchdown for LSU" was later arranged for marching band, its first edition foregrounded the common 1930s dissemination of fight songs via voice-piano sheet music. The piano arrangement in B♭ major, labeled a March, opens with a four-bar introduction whose first two bars imitate a trumpet fanfare. Its lyrics consist of phrases common to fight songs ("hold that ball, throw that ball, let's run through the line" and "give them hell and a little bit more") with mentions of Tigers and LSU colors. Its form comprises a chorus, a dramatic middle section of short motifs sequenced over harmonic modulations, and another statement of the chorus. Repeats of the chorus could replace the middle section, unusual for a fight song, in a football context. The other song, "Darling of LSU," a sentimental song about a woman student, echoed popular ballads of the 1930s, with a melodic contour, harmonic language, and romantic lyrics strongly reminiscent of Long's favorite song "Smoke Gets in Your Eyes."

The National Book Company likely published the two songs in summer 1935.[53] By late October 1935, M. Witmark and Sons purchased their copyrights and arranged for a New York orchestra to record the songs for Decca.[54] The Witmark editions maintained the National Book Company's key and instrumentation but refined both songs with typeset notation, detailed dynamics, enriched piano parts, and guitar, ukulele, and banjo chords. In "Touchdown for LSU," enhanced harmonies sounded snappier, with sevenths added to triads in the middle section, as did extra "rah rahs." The middle section was now labeled "Interlude," sensible in a voice-piano context. "Darling of LSU" received new chord voicings, redistribution of content between the pianist's hands, and rewritten rhythmic values effecting a smoother melodic line. Photographs of Carazo and Long disappeared from the cover, leaving the LSU tower haloed with golden light against purple haze and framed by a Spanish moss tree—a common southern signifier in US music publishing.

Although no early sources seem extant for either song, shreds of evidence hint that "Darling of LSU" traveled a circuitous path to publication. In early April 1935, the LSU student paper announced that Castro Carazo had written a new melody, a "dreamy fox-trot . . . strictly sentimental," for which a campus contest would generate lyrics. Contest guidelines left the lyric's subject open and promised the winner a shared copyright with Carazo and half the song's proceeds.[55] Carazo's knowledge of popular song conventions shaped contest rules, which stipulated that the lyric's last line must work as the song's title and provided sample lyrics with tips about rhyme scheme and metrical accent.[56] On April 5, the *Reveille* printed Carazo's melody for those interested in writing lyrics for it.[57] Contest judges were Carazo, an English professor, and the *Reveille* editor.[58] In early May, the deadline was extended, suggesting either no suitable entries or none at all.[59] A few weeks later, the *Reveille* named the first-place winner, Frank V. Cardenia—a senior and clarinetist in the LSU band—and printed his lyrics.[60] Titled "It Must Be Spring," Cardenia's poem combined a meditation on springtime with generic lines about romance, and no mention of college life. What happened next is unclear, but by the time the song was published by the National Book Company and M. Witmark and Sons, Cardenia's text was gone, the song was titled "Darling of LSU," and Huey Long was credited as author of the lyrics, which were now about an LSU woman student. Perhaps when Long discovered "his" composer had written a new melody, he overrode contest results to supply the text himself. The LSU band often performed Long's and Carazo's other songs at the time of the contest, and Long may have seen Carazo's ballad as another chance to write himself into the LSU repertory and community.[61]

"Darling of LSU" was not the only romantic college ballad that Long wrote (or co-wrote). In 1935, the National Book Company published "Miss Vandy," dedicated "to the Co-Eds of Vanderbilt University," with a cover sporting Vanderbilt black and gold and a photograph of a Vanderbilt administrator's daughter. The cover credits only Huey Long for the whole song, although interior copy states that the song was written and copyrighted by Huey P. Long and arranged by Castro Carazo. It seems likely that Carazo wrote the melody and harmony, too, although it is unclear why he was not credited as composer. The "slow waltz," scored for voice and piano and printed from handwritten notation, referenced college life, opening with the phrase "the campus lights are gleaming bright at dear old Vanderbilt tonight"; later the narrator sees "the co-ed of my dreams." The sheet music also contained a foxtrot version of the "Miss Vandy" chorus, morphing the waltz into 4/4 time with corresponding shifts in melodic rhythm, harmonic support, and accompaniment patterns. Both versions—waltz and foxtrot—were dance-centric.

With typically grandiose rhetoric, Huey Long described these songs as "just sweet ditties"; his *real* goal was to write opera, although he sang "Touchdown for LSU" for reporters and proudly discussed his songs with them.[62] Despite mild press buzz, Long's college songs seem not to have generated significant campus interest or usage immediately after their publication. In the mid-to-late 1930s they appeared in neither the *Gumbo* yearbook nor the *L-Books*, a guidebook for incoming students containing football cheers, yells, and songs, and the LSU alumni magazine did not mention the songs.[63] The 1935–1939 *L Books* contained only the LSU alma mater, with no fight songs at all, including "Touchdown for LSU." By contrast, the 1931–1934 *L-Books* contained numerous fight songs; like other SEC schools, LSU used many football songs in the years before the Long-Carazo songs, although no single song was dominant in the mid-1930s.[64] In 1937, Carazo co-wrote "Fight for LSU," published by Thornton W. Allen in a three-song LSU folio that included a new song by Allen. The folio's publication so soon after the appearance of the Long-Carazo songs, and its omission of them, suggests that they were not embraced at LSU.[65] Thornton Allen, ever attuned to marketability, surely would have tried to obtain the Long-Carazo LSU songs if he thought them viable. The Long-Carazo songs received some attention outside the LSU community, mostly in the wake of Long's September 1935 assassination. In October 1935, Nashville's WSM and a New York station aired "Darling of LSU," "Every Man a King," and "Touchdown for LSU," and the Louisiana Ramblers recorded all four of the Long-Carazo collaborations for Decca.[66]

Band Spectacles and The Voice of the State

Not content with hiring band directors and writing songs about college life, Huey Long inserted himself in the middle of it.[67] When Long traveled with the LSU band to football games, he marched with the ensemble through host cities and gave speeches in football stadiums in a stunning elision of his political power with the public image of Louisiana's flagship university.[68] Long's October 1934 trip to Nashville for the LSU-Vanderbilt game illuminates how he enmeshed his political persona and goals with university football pageantry. The trip was documented in detail by a Nashville press corps that drooled over an entourage of nearly five thousand LSU fans, students, and personnel presided over by Huey Long. Before the trip started, Long called the traffic manager of the Illinois Central Railroad and told him he would pay $6 per person to transport the LSU student body to Nashville—a rate he locked in by threatening the ICR President with increased taxes on rail bridges in Louisiana.[69] Then Long sent sound trucks to Nashville as a sonic vanguard to anticipate his arrival. The trucks parked inside Vanderbilt's Dudley Stadium, awaiting Long's halftime speech.[70] With rail cars painted "Hurray for Huey," the caravan set off.[71] Huey Long had selected from the LSU band a "personal orchestra" to travel in his car; after hearing the small group, he summoned an additional piccolo and two clarinets.[72] Passage from Louisiana through Mississippi to Tennessee generated more shenanigans. Long's staff telegraphed the Vicksburg mayor for a banjo, two fiddlers, and a singer, all of whom boarded the train. Now pleased with his ensemble, Long requested they play "River, Stay Away from My Door."[73] When Tennessee officials rejected the notion of a large Louisiana police force crossing state lines, Long called the Tennessee State Game Warden to request an emergency deputation of Louisiana police as Tennessee game wardens to guard "wildlife" on the train. Thus deputized, they crossed the state line unhindered.[74]

The LSU parade route started with the Louisiana contingent's arrival at Union Station, wound through downtown Nashville, and culminated in a performance on the steps of the War Memorial Auditorium, followed by one within the venue. The press speculated that Long might conduct the outdoor concert, although it's unclear whether he did.[75] Before the Saturday afternoon game, Senator Huey P. Long, Vanderbilt coach Dan McGugin, and Nashville mayor Hilary E. Howse led the 125-piece LSU band in a second parade through downtown Nashville.[76] Over the stadium PA system, McGugin introduced Long to the crowd as the "All-American football rooter of all time."[77] Long may also have led a male vocal quartet at a stadium microphone.[78] Footage of Long at LSU football games shows that the "All-American football rooter" vigorously cheered and sang, waving his arms, moving his body, and attracting stares from spectators.[79] Advance publicity rumored that Long would announce his presidential campaign at halftime of the LSU-Vanderbilt game. He did not: the referee limited him to a two-minute speech in front of the 20,000-person crowd after the LSU band took up most of halftime.[80]

The anticipation of Long's campaign announcement, the sight of politicians leading a band through downtown Nashville, Long's political machinations on the train trip, and dramatic press coverage demonstrate how Huey Long used LSU's marching band to build his political persona and brand.[81] Long's outdoor band-driven spectacles also enacted broader "potentialities for [civic] membership and exclusion," despite his populist rhetoric.[82] Conducted in southern urban spaces—"sites where interactions and expressions helped shape relationships of power"—and backed by the white male marching band of Louisiana's flagship university, these events made concrete the gendered, racialized, and classed hierarchies of 1930s southern society.[83] As Marina Peterson writes, "urban public space is a key site for the expression and negotiation of citizenship in cities."[84] These events reminded participants and spectators that full citizenship and participation in southern society belonged to the demographic marching noisily through downtown streets, loudly reasserting ownership over public space that had never been seriously contested. In addition to appearing with the LSU band at football events, Long used the ensemble for political and campaign events, marching with it in Mardi Gras parades and having it play an outdoor concert at a May 1930 open house for the new governor's mansion.[85] Used like this, Long's LSU band and the songs he co-wrote with its director projected the voice of the state—the voice of male-centric, middle- and upper-class white southern democracy, which southern flagship universities worked to uphold in this period.[86]

Although this voice echoed a regional world structured by gendered and racialized hierarchies, in the 1930s, women's college enrollment grew, including in the South. Within a decade of Long's assassination, women outnumbered men at LSU, and during World War II, they finally joined the marching band.[87] Huey Long's "Sweetheart of Vandy" and "Darling of LSU" may have limited women's role in campus life to passive reception of romantic adoration, but since their 1906 admission to LSU, women had contributed actively to university culture. Like Huey Long, they even wrote football songs: before Long became involved with the LSU band, student Doralice Fontane Cessano (class of 1928) wrote the fight song "Tigers," printed in *L Books* for several years and likely sung on campus.[88] The omission of women from Long's musical-political rhetoric was noted in his own time. A 1935 performance by Ina Ray Hutton and her All Girl Orchestra of Long's "Every Man a King" with Huey Long standing by was prefaced by Senator Long drawling to Hutton, "Aren't you gonna sing it, since we changed that last line to mean 'every girl a queen'?"

Hutton sang the song with her orchestra, inserting the new line "every girl a queen" after each statement of the phrase "every man a king."[89]

Black people figured into Huey Long's musical projections of his imagined society at the margins, in the silent, subservient position southern whites expected them to occupy.[90] A little-known Long campaign song published in 1935 by the National Book Company, "Follow Long," featured bucolic cover art of a rural road fading into the sunset, cutting its way through tilled fields presided over by a white columned house. For Black Louisianans in the 1930s, this image would have not, perhaps, evoked a hopeful future, but a continuation of the sharecropping system or white nostalgia for the antebellum plantation South.[91] The image indexes the strain of backward-looking white southern thought expressed in the 1930s by the Nashville Agrarians, who as a regional intellectual movement "were leading the retreat from reality, pining for an agrarian utopia that was built on the backs of a cheap, inexhaustible supply of black labor."[92] Long's vision of collegiate life, projected in his musical activities with the school, excluded Black students. They were not admitted to LSU until the 1950s, and white southern higher education in the 1930s was generally marked by "an unspoken code of self-censorship" in which "it was clearly understood that any questioning of the racial status quo would probably bring dismissal."[93] Nonetheless, LSU, like other SEC schools, used Black cultural products—including musical repertoire and styles—and Black human mascots to build their football pageantry in the 1930s.[94] They capitalized on Black culture without engaging Black citizens as equal participants in the educational endeavor—a manifestation of the paternalistic "racial dream world" white southerners lived out in the 1930s in which "the institutionalization of physical and social separation was accompanied by the 'total escape of black people from the white mind.'"[95]

Conclusion

Although Huey Long's college songs and his appearances with the LSU marching band projected an idealized version of white southern collegiate life, they obscured real-life conflict between the politician and the LSU student body. In a 1934 tussle with the student newspaper that attracted the attention of national media and the American Association of University

Professors, Huey Long tried to muzzle the *Reveille* after it printed an anti-Long letter, complaining to the press that "this damn journalism school is turning out newspaper men to write against me!" Long's handpicked university president, James Monroe Smith, ordered the *Reveille* student editorial board to submit to faculty censorship or be closed, so the board resigned *en masse* and agitated for editorial independence from the upper administration. President Smith responded with twenty-six student suspensions and a handful of expulsions.[96] Amid such naked corruption, Long still used the LSU band and his songs with Carazo to construct a fantasy campus world and propel his political ambitions. Although Long's urge to generate publicity and spectacle was personality-driven, it also channeled the 1930s popularity of the "collegiate" trope and exemplified SEC schools' trend of crystallizing their football music as administrators, alumni, and students self-consciously sensed that they were, or wanted to be, part of the national higher education landscape—context that newly sharpens our historical understanding of Long's musical activities at LSU. By the end of the decade, Huey Long was long gone, and most SEC schools had introduced what would eventually become their official fight songs. As the next chapter shows, the final few additions to the SEC fight song canon came not from within institutional ranks, but from external, often professional musical sources, reflective of college football's increasing postwar professionalization and television-driven media reach.

CHAPTER 10

Three Postwar Fight Songs

After the 1930s burst of fight songs, the Southeastern Conference repertory seemed stable, at least in terms of singular, official fight songs. Then, between 1955 and 1972, new fight songs emerged at Auburn University, the University of South Carolina, and the University of Tennessee, eventually displacing songs long used at the schools to join and close the SEC "canon." Developed and adopted much differently than earlier SEC fight songs, these three appeared in the wake of postwar changes that swept the US South, including higher education, where the economic and cultural importance of SEC football mushroomed.[1] In the early 1940s, tradition-minded SEC alumni and leaders who favored economic and practical restraints on football tussled with newer leadership empathetic to national trends of collegiate athletic bureaucratization and expansion.[2] By the end of World War II, Tulane University and Sewanee, realizing the SEC's inevitable trajectory, left the conference over this ideological split. NCAA regulations tried to limit football's role in college life, but SEC schools evaded or defied the 1948 NCAA "sanity code" to engage in a national football "arms race."[3] By the late 1940s, the SEC was recruiting with athletic scholarships, exploring TV broadcasting, enlarging athletic budgets and PR departments, and launching bowl games with southern business and civic leaders.[4] SEC teams began air travel, and public funding for southern university football stadiums boomed, albeit inequitably distributed between PWIs and HBCUs.[5] The SEC upped its promotional game by working with university athletic PR departments to produce

an annual *Press and Radio Dope Book*.[6] These books complemented football media guides, written by noted sports journalists and sponsored by
advertisers, that flourished between the 1930s and 1950s and shaped a
more educated football consumer.[7] In this supercharged, commercial-
ized postwar atmosphere, the veneer of college football's "amateur ideal"
wore laughably thin.

Television's lucrative promise encouraged increasingly sophisticated
college football pageantry.[8] In response, postwar SEC marching bands
became large, glossy groups with full-time directors and support from
university administrators and boosters who recognized a band's unique
role in crafting the "highly entertaining marketable [football] spectacle"
sought by TV networks.[9] Polished halftime shows developed around
cohesive themes, as at the 1956 University of Alabama-Auburn game,
where Auburn's band performed a New South booster tribute to Alabama's industries, forming an oil well, rocket, naval docks, and tractor
to accompany their playing of "That Old Black Magic," "How High the
Moon," "Mobile," and "Down Yonder." The University of Alabama band
performed a Broadway routine with hits from *Carousel, Oklahoma, South
Pacific*, and *The King and I*.[10] In the 1960s and 1970s, SEC bands drew from
a richer range of musical idioms, incorporating classical music such as
Verdi arias, Stravinsky's *Firebird* suite, and Richard Strauss's *Also sprach
Zarathustra*.[11] Contemporary popular music figured prominently, as with
Vanderbilt's 1967 halftime show of that year's Billboard hits and the University of South Carolina band's 1976 Elton John medley.[12] Broadway
musicals and film scores became common at SEC halftime shows; favorites were excerpts from *Dr. Zhivago, Music Man*, and *Fiddler on the Roof*.[13]

Postwar campus musical cultures shifted in other ways, too: the
importance of dance bands—once a chief vector for the dissemination
of football songs—dwindled as the 1940s went on, as did the popularity of
the ukulele and banjo, for which many fight songs were arranged before
World War II. The vogue for syrupy, earnest "collegiate"-themed crooners and songs waned in the commercial music industry, the dreams they
peddled punctured by the realities of war and by changing musical tastes.
Emerging in these contexts, the three new SEC fight songs written and
adopted between 1955 and 1972 demonstrate how marching bands and
directors, powerful boosters, and external music professionals shaped
postwar SEC football pageantry. In these conditions, fight songs, while
still important, were only one dimension of a rich and varied football

soundscape that grew ever more complex as the stadium public address system's capabilities to pipe in sound effects and popular music matured in the 1970s.

Auburn Gets a New Song Whether It Wants One or Not

When Auburn University got a new fight song in 1955, it wasn't because the school lacked one. For decades, Auburn students had played and sung "Glory, Glory to Old Auburn," "Tiger Rag," "Dixie," and the "Auburn Victory March" at games and pep rallies.[14] "Auburn Victory March"—unlike the other three songs, unique to the school—was written by music professor A. W. Traxler in 1933 during that decade's surge in SEC fight songs. The march was received gladly on campus, where copies of it were distributed to a student body proud that it had already been broadcast on Nashville's famed WSM radio.[15] In 1936, Thornton W. Allen published Traxler's march in an Auburn song folio, noted by the Alabama press.[16] Various artists recorded "Auburn Victory March" for RCA Victor and other labels in the early 1950s.[17] These years also saw Auburn students print books of yells and songs, like those at other schools, for freshmen.[18] The mid-century Auburn community seemed satisfied with this repertory: there is no evidence that it was agitating for a new song. The student paper's detailed coverage of football pageantry in the early 1950s contained no complaints about fight songs, nor did contemporary yearbooks.[19]

A notable exception to this state of happy contentment was Georgia textile magnate Roy Sewell, who rarely embraced the status quo at Auburn University—especially where football was concerned. In his mid-century roles as booster, donor, and Alumni Club member and officer, Sewell tweaked everything about Auburn football that he could get his hands on.[20] Despite describing himself to head coach Ralph Jordan as "not knowing very much about football," Roy Sewell sent bold, detailed critiques of game strategy and administrative processes to coaches.[21] In contact with Auburn personnel, including President Ralph Brown Draughon, Sewell acted as recruiter, even advocating for the admission of academically underqualified athletes.[22] Through an incessant stream of letters, telephone calls, and visits, Sewell addressed coach Ralph Jordan's physical, religious, and psychological health in copious and invasive detail. He shipped the coach Christian devotional literature, fretted over his weight gain, recommended to him the work of self-help gurus Dale

Carnegie and Norman Vincent Peale, and—in a fit of concern over the coach's mental state—flew Jordan to New York to meet with Peale.[23] For Sewell, Auburn boosterism was a form of civil religion; he expressed to coach Jordan that together they could "accomplish our goal of making Auburn greater and more serviceable, not only to the State but to the whole United States. . . . I pray that you will be blessed and guided in your work."[24] Sewell peppered his letters to Jordan with religious, spiritual, and motivational mottoes, some of which Sewell had typed and sewn into his own hatbands.[25] At public events, Sewell's relationship with Auburn was characterized by this quasi-religious rhetoric; in 1963, President Draughon described him as a "symbol of hard work and Christian endeavor," a comment that Sewell answered by declaiming a personal Auburn creed: "The Auburn spirit will be an eternal asset to me. When everything goes against you and you feel you can't hold out any longer, the Auburn spirit teaches you that things will change with time. It helps me through the day. . . . I believe in Auburn and all it stands for."[26]

His fervor expressed itself through a one-man economy of reciprocity in gifts of pheasants and new suits for Auburn staff who in turn gave Sewell permission to visit practices, access athletic records, visit coaches, and retain game-day parking privileges.[27] Sewell openly summarized this dynamic in a July 1957 letter to coach Ralph Jordan: "As you know, I have helped you acquire many football players during the last few years. I now wish to ask you a favor." Sewell then requested that Jordan release an Auburn player to work at his textile company.[28]

In this philanthropic context, Roy Sewell gave Auburn what turned out to be his most enduring gift, and one that nobody asked for: a new fight song. Thin extant sources suggest that Sewell drove the song acquisition scheme; his song plans were noted only briefly in his voluminous correspondence with coach Ralph Jordan, who replied with polite detachment "I sincerely hope that something wonderful will come out of the proposed song," and equally briefly in his correspondence with President Ralph Draughon.[29] Sewell first approached well-known songwriter Dick Manning in early 1955, wooing him and lyricist Harry Goodman for a potential Auburn song commission by hosting them at New York's swanky Stork Club.[30] Manning submitted several songs to Sewell, none of which passed muster.[31] By July, Sewell turned to a pair of Radio City Music Hall songwriters, lyricist Al Stillman and composer

Robert Allen. The Stillman-Allen team wrote songs used in midcentury radio and television and recorded by stars such as Johnny Matthis.[32] The pair sent multiple submissions to Sewell, who convened a committee that included the chair of the Auburn music department to assess the songs.[33] Sewell "filled in" Al Stillman on aspects of Auburn institutional life to inform his lyric-writing and paid the team $2500.00 for the committee's selection, "War Eagle."[34] The title used a beloved Auburn yell of the same name.[35]

"War Eagle" was published in fall 1955 as a voice-piano score with a bright orange cover bearing a squawking, flapping eagle. A photograph of the Auburn stadium press box and the words to the school's alma mater filled the back cover.[36] The southern press covered and printed "War Eagle" weeks before the Auburn band debuted it, suggesting that the university or Roy Sewell, or both, guided its advance publicity.[37] Sewell bought the song copyright for the Auburn Alumni Association and presented the group with sheet music and a recording of the song.[38] "War Eagle" was meant to debut at the September 24, 1955 season opener against the University of Tennessee-Chattanooga, announced in the Auburn student paper which printed the new song's lyrics.[39] Music department head Hubert Liverman, member of the song selection committee, arranged it for band and previewed it for president Draughon and other Auburn staff at the piano.[40] However, Auburn's band was temporarily director-less, so "War Eagle" was premiered by another school's band, its melody printed in that day's football program under the heading "Auburn's new fight song!"[41] By the time Auburn played the University of Kentucky a few weeks later, its band—now with a director—played a pregame show with the new song, alongside minstrel song "My Old Kentucky Home."[42] The campus showed signs of embracing the song within the week; the men's octet taught it to the student body and the band announced that halftime shows would now start with "War Eagle."[43] Despite a few murmurs of dislike, in late October 1955, the Auburn paper stated that "War Eagle" had "swept through the student body," ascribing to the song a surge of spirit at a low point in a game. The paper credited its popularity to the band director's "policy of playing [it] at every opportunity."[44] The next fall, when Roy Sewell was elected Auburn Alumni Association president, he was saluted by the band at halftime with a performance of "War Eagle."[45] The song was not Sewell's final contribution to Auburn football pageantry; in 1957, he sent his textile company's designer to New York to select fabric and styles for new band uniforms.[46]

Early off-campus reception of "War Eagle" showed that new fight songs were still big news in the mid-1950s. In covering the song's fall 1955 release, the southern press often foregrounded the songwriting team's geographic affiliation and work in national entertainment, labeling them "New York" or "Tin Pan Alley" songwriters.[47] Sectional sentiment undergirded some regional critiques of the song; the *Montgomery Advertiser* described its "driveling lines" as "insipid," "anemic," "suited to the Ladies' Aid Society," and unfit to express the "defiant cacophony" and "undaunted spirit" of the titular War Eagle yell, which the author called the "Rebel Yell in modern dress."[48] Nonetheless, by the following year, southern radio stations were playing recordings of "War Eagle."[49] In 1958, Roy Sewell hired Ray Ellis to direct an orchestra for Capitol Records in a new recording of the song, which the Alumni Association distributed free of cost.[50] "War Eagle" had wormed its way into Auburn's song repertory.

When Roy Sewell spoke to the media about "War Eagle" in the mid-1950s, he maintained that its impetus was Auburn's lack of distinctive songs, noting the school's reliance on "Tiger Rag" and "Glory Glory," songs used at other schools. Sewell conveniently omitted A. W. Traxler's published, recorded, and much-used "Auburn Victory March," which he surely knew.[51] Sewell's selective assessment of Auburn's song repertory suggests that his near-religious desire to contribute to the school's pageantry and history, rather than institutional need, drove his song acquisition. Sewell's song saga exemplifies how individual philanthropy in higher education functions as a "social relationship, fueled by a range of motivations and with a range of outcomes," able to powerfully shape institutional life.[52] As Sewell's memoir memorably put it: "listed alphabetically, his philanthropy has been devoted to Auburn University and Baptist churches and causes."[53] In later years, Auburn often memorialized Sewell's contributions, including on-field recognition of him at the 1983 Homecoming halftime show, where the band spelled out "Mr. Roy" and played "War Eagle."[54]

Broadway Comes to the University of South Carolina

In the late 1960s, the University of South Carolina (USC) also looked outside its institutional sphere for a new fight song, a reflection of the growing professionalization of SEC marching band culture. As was the case at

Auburn, the late-1960s efforts of one or two powerful individuals yielded a new fight song, in contrast to collective student or alumni actions that generated earlier SEC fight songs. Even more than Auburn, USC had by the late 1960s accumulated many fight songs, some of which were still used. Unusually exhaustive archival sources document USC's rich fight song history stretching back to 1914, when the English department head wrote and published "Carolina's Day," a pep song referencing early football foes Clemson University and the University of Charleston.[55] Although used sporadically for years, the song never became dominant.[56] Part of a second song published in the late 1910s and used at many schools, the "NC-4 March," formed the basis of USC's first significant fight song, initially played by 1920s dance orchestras and used by the marching band into the 1960s.[57] The 1920s saw the writing of one or two more USC fight songs, although it is unclear whether they were used. The 1925 "Carolina Hail!" was arranged from the tune "Santa Lucia," paired with USC lyrics, and published by the USC Dean's office in a folio with "America" and "Dixie."[58] The "Carolina Football Song" of the late 1920s or early 1930s survives more informally as scraps of USC text pasted over the lyrics of another school's song in Thornton W. Allen's 1927 *Intercollegiate Songbook*.[59] 1920s USC students also used other fight songs for which musical scores seem not to be extant.[60] These examples confirm USC's participation in early national college song trends of using common tunes and circulating songs on campus via piano-voice and dance orchestra scores published and printed by small or non-commercial publishers.

USC's 1930s fight songs also aligned with SEC trends, with the school's most enduring fight song until the late 1960s emerging in that decade from a campus song contest. In the mid-1930s, student M. Carrére Salley wrote text and music for "Carolina Fight Song," later called "The Old Fight Song" or "Carolina Let Your Voices Ring," for a fraternity-sponsored contest bearing the hefty prize of $500, never fully paid.[61] USC used the song only sporadically until band director James Pritchard revived it in the late 1950s and 1960s with new arrangements and modifications.[62] Like other schools in the late 1930s and early 1940s, USC appeared on Fred Waring's college song radio program, *Chesterfield Pleasure Time*. Waring, who composed a song for each week's featured institution, wrote "The Gamecocks of SCU [sic]" for USC in 1940. The USC symphonic band performed Waring's 6/8 march, although it is unclear whether the marching band played it as a fight song at games.[63]

Band director James Pritchard, at USC in various capacities from the 1960s through the 1980s, expanded school repertory by reviving older fight songs and adding new ones, with his late-1960s adaptation of the Broadway song "Step to the Rear" eventually becoming USC's main fight song.[64] Pritchard's formal, scrupulous process for legally acquiring and using the song contrasted with the wanton scavenging of tunes common in earlier SEC football culture. In 1968, Pritchard heard Elmer Bernstein's "Step to the Rear" from the show *How Now, Dow Jones*, copyrighted in 1967 by Carwin Music, and began to direct the USC band in playing an arrangement of it published by Edwin Morris at football games.[65] In a mid-season meeting called for the purpose, head coach Paul Dietzel expressed enthusiasm for "Step to the Rear" and requested that Pritchard wholly replace the 1936 "Carolina Fight Song" with the new Broadway song.[66] The two agreed that Dietzel would write new text for the song, a fact first kept quiet on campus, and Pritchard obtained rights to pair Dietzel's text with the Edwin Morris band arrangement under the title "Fighting Gamecocks Lead the Way."[67] Through copious communications, Pritchard informed Edwin Morris of his plans to change the arrangement's key from A♭ to E♭ "to make it practical for singing with a band," shared Dietzel's lyrics, and requested television, radio, and high school band permissions. Pritchard's legwork ensured that USC could print lyrics for pep rallies, circulate recordings of the song on campus and throughout the state, and retain record sale profits for the band.[68] Edwin Morris granted Pritchard expedited song permissions to facilitate use during football season, and USC groups premiered "Fighting Gamecocks Lead the Way" on WIS-TV on November 10, 1968, and at USC's annual band day on November 16.[69] By fall 1969, the band played it as the main fight song, and Pritchard finalized recording rights on the song for the band and concert choir.[70]

Late-1960s dissatisfaction with available USC fight songs partly stemmed from stylistic problems with M. Carrére Salley's 1936 "Carolina Fight Song," which Pritchard had used intermittently. The song's wide range, long duration, clunky lyrics, and resulting lack of student enthusiasm were delicately discussed in a spurt of awkward correspondence between Salley, Pritchard, and coach Dietzel.[71] For once in this book, aesthetics trumped money: USC paid royalties to Edwin Morris to use "Step to the Rear" / "Fighting Gamecocks Lead the Way" even though Salley granted USC the right to freely record and perform "Carolina Fight Song" in perpetuity.[72] For Salley, writing a USC song was a matter of pride; he told Dietzel in 1968 that "for over twenty-five years, I have been trying to come up with a successful Fight Song for the University"—a sentiment he made good on by writing "a set of optional words" for "Fighting Gamecocks Lead the Way" a month after the new song's debut! These included such memorable lines as "we'll make a monkey out of you," and Dietzel and Pritchard predictably retained Dietzel's text.[73] Despite Pritchard's shift toward using "Fighting Gamecocks Lead the Way" at football games, he didn't jettison Salley's "Carolina Fight Song"; the USC band and choir recorded it in 1969 for a *Songs of Carolina* album.[74]

"Fighting Gamecocks Lead the Way" found a quick foothold with the band due to the uncommonly granular involvement in football pageantry of Paul Dietzel while coaching USC football from 1966 to 1974. Out of the songs and schools surveyed in this book, "Fighting Gamecocks Leads the Way" represents the only documented case of an SEC coach's explicit shaping of football music. This was characteristic for Dietzel, who wrote words to the fight song "Hey, Look Me Over" while coaching at LSU from 1955 to 1961 and wrote a poem on football's masculinizing effects that he trotted out at athletic banquets in the 1960s.[75] While coaching at USC, Dietzel penned a weekly column for the student paper urging greater spirit, admonishing students to "learn the cheers. And cheer and scream! Not this polite little yea team jazz [*sic*]. I mean, yell your guts out."[76] Dietzel's 1968 work with Pritchard on the new song was part of their broader collaboration on USC football music during their overlapping tenures, from 1966 to 1969. In Dietzel's first season, the USC band dedicated a halftime show to him, playing his LSU fight song and spelling out "Paul" on-field.[77] Pritchard communicated with Dietzel about budgetary needs such as better amplification with controls in the band area of the football stands.[78] When Pritchard announced his resignation in June 1969, he thanked Dietzel for helping him "build a better band."[79]

Although the top-down intervention that introduced "Fighting Gamecocks Lead the Way" into USC repertoire is well-documented, less clear is immediate student reception of the song. Although the student paper of the late 1960s covered some aspects of football pageantry, it published no notable coverage of the new song in fall 1968, nor in the months afterward. Like other SEC student papers of the time, the late-1960s *Gamecock* focused less on the minutia of football pageantry that dominated earlier

SEC student papers and more on social issues, political controversies, and campus activism. The new song was also not mentioned in the *Garnet and Black* yearbook in the late 1960s and early 1970s. As with the other fight songs in this chapter, "Fighting Gamecocks" represented a new era when additions and refinements to SEC football pageantry often no longer emerged from student bodies relatively united in school spirit. By this time, student interests had expanded beyond and diverged from the 1920s and 1930s southern campus monocultures centered on football games, parades, dances, and pageantry. Although "Fighting Gamecocks Lead the Way" was not the final fight song introduced by USC band directors, it has remained the school's main fight song.[80]

"A Little Town in Big Orange Country"

Like Auburn and USC, by the second half of the twentieth century, the University of Tennessee (UT) had accumulated a constellation of fight songs and only acquired a new one at the late date of 1972 because of one person's actions. As was the case at USC, UT's adoption of a new fight song was entirely band-driven. Earlier in the twentieth century, UT students used football songs set to folk tunes such as the German melody "The Watch on the Rhine" and popular tunes such as "College Life," "Oh, Who Will Smoke My Meerschaum Pipe," "In Your Eyes," "Linger Awhile," and "She Wouldn't Do, Do, Do---."[81] By the mid-1920s, two lasting songs emerged: "Down the Field" ("Here's to Old U. of T.") and "Spirit of the Hill," both often printed in 1920s football programs.[82] Late in the decade, UT students solidified and disseminated their football song stock, partnering with alumni to publish a 1929 songbook which contained the above two songs and a handful of others that later passed out of usage.[83] In 1938 and 1939, the UT fight song repertory grew when the school's highly ranked football team received national coverage, expanded its athletic publicity, and figured prominently in the Broadway musical *Too Many Girls*.[84] In late 1938, Thornton W. Allen published the UT song "Fight, Vols, Fight," written with Gwen and Milo Sweet, professionals who worked with him on other college songs.[85] Allen may have noted an opening for a new, unique UT fight song since "Down the Field" borrowed a Yale melody, although it remains the school's official fight song.[86] Major southern papers covered publication of the song, which UT premiered at the January 1939 Orange Bowl.[87] Students began to use "Fight, Vols,

Fight!" alongside "Down the Field" and "Spirit of the Hill."[88]

Thirty years later, the UT marching band still played these three songs in its pregame and halftime shows, along with "Tennessee Waltz," which director Jay Julian added to the repertory in the 1960s.[89] Together with the alma mater, by the 1970s, this group of songs was regularly heard at UT football games. Then, in 1972, buried in the middle of a halftime show, the UT band played a country music medley that included the Osborne Brothers' bluegrass hit of a few years earlier, "Rocky Top." An SEC band playing contemporary or traditional country music in halftime shows was not unusual at the time—in 1971, the Vanderbilt band performed a similar halftime medley—but UT's eventual repeated use of this bluegrass or country song as a fight song was atypical.[90] Over the next few decades, "Rocky Top" joined the UT fight song canon, the second instance—after USC's adaptation of a Broadway song—of a popular song morphing into a lasting SEC fight song. Noted country songwriters Boudleaux and Felice Bryant wrote "Rocky Top" in December 1967 at a Gatlinburg hotel while composing songs for Archie Campbell's proposed "old folks" album—retrospective, moribund material which Felice found depressing. After she suggested an up-tempo, mood-elevating break from this content, her annoyed husband began "beating the guitar" in frustration with riffs that turned into "Rocky Top."[91] Within a few minutes, the Bryants later enjoyed claiming, they hammered out the song's lyrics, melody, and chords, although the original manuscript shows evidence of refining.[92] In his younger days, Boudleaux had, in addition to classical training, acquired considerable fiddle chops, and "Rocky Top" shows his conversance with the "hillbilly music" and "old fiddle hoedowns" he once played with string bands on Atlanta's WSB radio.[93] A few weeks later, Grand Ole Opry bluegrass act the Osborne Brothers requested material from the Bryants for an upcoming Decca session, and Felice suggested "that bluegrass thing" written in Gatlinburg.[94] The Osborne Brothers released "Rocky Top" as a B-side on December 25, 1967. Popular radio host Ralph Emery kept spinning it on his country show, and the song attained a modest spot on Billboard's country charts.[95]

On October 21, 1972, at a Knoxville game with the University of Alabama, the UT halftime show opened, as was customary in those years, with school songs ("Vol Fanfare," "Down the Field," and "March On, Mighty Vols"), followed by the "Emblem of Unity" march and "Autumn Leaves."[96] After this, the MC intoned:

October has been proclaimed National Country Music Month. To a new drill of circles, hexagons, stars, and spirals, the Tennessee Band salutes one of our state's great industries with a country music medley starting with "The Columbus Stockade Blues," "Wabash Cannonball," and a little town in Big Orange Country called "Rocky Top" Tennessee.[97]

Out of these three songs, "Rocky Top" was the only modern commercial number, but due to the Osborne Brothers' high-octane bluegrass version of it and its proximity to older songs in the medley, fans may have thought it traditional.[98] They may also have heard the MC's comments as a factual geographical observation, although at the time there was no Tennessee town called "Rocky Top." The song and its initial framing in UT pageantry were masterpieces of artifice denoting a mythic construction of Appalachian authenticity that UT later cashed in on. By fall 1978, "Rocky Top" was entrenched enough at UT to warrant a halftime show honoring the Bryants, but it is hard to reconstruct how it became thus enshrined.[99] Throughout the 1970s, the marching band never added "Rocky Top" to its relatively fixed pregame repertoire nor to the group of songs that framed its halftime shows.[100] The band also did not often play "Rocky Top" during 1970s halftime shows, aside from re-using the country medley containing the song at a December 1972 bowl game.[101]

Where the UT band *did* play "Rocky Top" was during games, a fact noted by fans upset enough about its perceived overuse to complain to Jay Julian, UT band director from 1961 to 1993. In fall 1977, one fan politely asked that the band play UT's "fight song" (likely "Fight, Vols, Fight" or "Down the Field") more often, adding "I'm happy to be identified with 'Rocky Top' and 'Tennessee Waltz,' but when this other song is played, my blood really runs orange."[102] A less diplomatic fan griped in 1979 that the UT band played "Rocky Top" nine times to feeble effect during a disastrous game against Mississippi State University: not only did MSU's team play better, charged the irate letter-writer, its band performed a wider selection. The fan urged Julian to "dig into your vast repertoire" and play "something besides 'Rocky Top'" at the upcoming Notre Dame game.[103] Scattered complaints notwithstanding, fans likely demonstrated sufficient enthusiasm for the song during games, or presumably Julian would have dropped it.

However, no extant print evidence suggests that "Rocky Top" became meaningful outside of football contexts to alumni or students in the 1970s, in contrast to its later saturation of UT iconography, lore, and merchandise. *Volunteer* yearbooks were silent on the song until 1979, then only printing a tiny photograph of the fall 1978 halftime show honoring the Bryants.[104] The *Tennessee Alumnus* never mentioned the song in the 1970s, focusing instead on fundraising and institutional progress. The *UT Daily Beacon* also gave "Rocky Top" little to no attention in the 1970s, having by this point shifted away from details of football pageantry toward social issues such as feminism, women's studies, rape, gay rights, abortion, the Nixon scandal, and Black student activism.[105] A rare exception to the *Beacon*'s silence on 1970s football pageantry surrounded the November 18, 1972, UT-University of Mississippi game, which indexed broader social issues. The visiting Mississippi band was expected to play "Dixie," a song some UT students by that time regarded with distaste.[106] Concern over whether the visiting band would or should play "Dixie" garnered more student press coverage than "Rocky Top," which received none.

Although UT later embraced the Appalachian caricatures of "Rocky Top" as an institutional symbol, the song's tropes did not resonate with 1970s student culture.[107] 1970s *Beacon* and yearbook issues suggest that UT students largely consumed mainstream national entertainment by stars such as Dionne Warwick, Eric Clapton, and the Harlem Globetrotters—not country music. The homecoming theme in 1972, the year the UT band debuted "Rocky Top," was "Nostalgia, Past and Present," with noted fiddler John Hartford playing at a campus hoedown. Campus coverage of the festivities shows that students treated the theme as ironic, cartoonish, and unrepresentative of modern cultural aesthetics. The mountaineering culture spoofed in "Rocky Top" and represented in aspects of 1972 homecoming festivities was a world apart from the undercurrents of social changes, activism, and national mass culture that animated 1970s campus life.[108] Ten days after the band's premiere of "Rocky Top," the *UT Daily Beacon* ran an unflattering photographic spread called "This is Knoxville Now . . . What Will Knoxville Be Tomorrow?" The spread contained images of a Klan cross-burning captioned "Culture," a decrepit wooden building captioned "Housing," piles of street rubbish captioned "Fire Safety," and men lolling outside a defunct upholstery store labeled "Recreation."[109] These pictures of Knoxville's abjection, rather than the cheery strains of "Rocky Top," more incisively indexed how 1970s UT students regarded Appalachian tropes and myths.

Although no sources describing band director Jay Julian's early perspective on "Rocky Top" seem extant, he likely didn't anticipate its eventual popularity in UT football culture. The song was only one example of his broader 1970s effort to highlight Tennessee's country music industry through programming country repertoire and guest artists. In December 1972, saxophonist Boots Randolph—a key contributor to the "Nashville sound" that defined contemporary commercial country—performed at a UT bowl game halftime show.[110] Julian also invited country music icon Roy Acuff to perform in the Fall 1979 Homecoming halftime show, an invitation he accepted after first declining.[111] UT's 1970s halftime shows included contemporary and classic country songs such as Hank Williams's "Hey, Good Looking," the Western swing song "Steel Guitar Rag," the 1971 John Denver hit "Take Me Home, Country Roads," and Tanya Tucker's 1972 "Delta Dawn," among others.[112] Country fare represented only a slice of the UT band's versatile stylistic range in its 1970s halftime shows, which encompassed rock (Three Dog Night's "Joy to the World"), Elvis nostalgia, Duke Ellington works, and classical music (J. S. Bach's *Art of the Fugue* and Richard Strauss's *Also sprach Zarathustra*).[113]

Where Is Rocky Top?

UT's institutional earworm, written and adopted during great and lasting social change in the South, bemoans the plagues of smog, urban density, and new technology over the sounds of bluegrass, long associated with "traditional" cultural and political values. In the song, urban modernity plays the role of enemy in an iteration of the us-vs.-them dynamic that has long fired the white southern psyche, and the song's narrator finds half-comical refuge from the woes of "cramped-up city life" atop a mythic mountain populated by wild women and moonshiners—in other words, hillbillies. In the 1960s, media representations of the southern hillbilly reflected social, landscape, and economic transformations rocking the region and the nation. When the Bryants wrote "Rocky Top" in 1967, the hillbilly was experiencing a popular culture resurgence, "uniquely positioned as a white 'other'" that refracted Americans' "widespread questioning of the price of 'progress'" and their desire to "reconcile the past and present."[114] In 1973, the year after the UT band first played "Rocky

Top," the new Carnegie Classification system designated the University of Tennessee a tier-one research institution. The eventual adoption of a bluegrass song as a sonic icon for an institution chasing modern progress reflected the "ambiguity" of "hillbilly music," which also experienced a resurgence in the disorienting 1960s and 1970s. [115] Although historically "promoted as 'white' folk music . . . by and for predominantly rural and small-town southerners who looked back nostalgically to a simpler agrarian life," hillbilly music, encompassing country and bluegrass, was in fact a "product of modern industrial capitalism and cutting-edge technology."[116]

In the years since "Rocky Top" entered UT football culture, as T. R. C. Hutton writes, "whatever associations [the song] had with the 'hillbilly' concept" have morphed into "an object of fun (and profitable!) derision urban and suburban Tennesseans wanted to appropriate for themselves rather than disparage in others."[117] UT has effectively leveraged the song's comic and nostalgic ambiguity, in 2005 contracting with the House of Bryant, licensing and copyright holder for the Bryant song catalogue, to use "Rocky Top" on UT merchandise and in conjunction with a UT "product development" lab, the Rocky Top Institute. The Institute trains students in retail, hospitality, and tourism management, with proceeds flowing back to the institute, the House of Bryant, and UT band scholarships.[118] "Rocky Top" lyrics festoon a glossy mural at UT's main library and adorn school shirts and mugs as a powerful "neolocalism" that uses "local commodities, experiences or traditions" to index a vaguely Appalachian "idea of rootedness or sense of belonging."[119] The bluegrass hit has become an ironic avatar for UT, a cultural symbol ventriloquizing this modern institution's allegiance to a mythic, commodified construction of Appalachia as a "region engaged in a centuries-long struggle to the death with modernity."[120] The song's long arm has reached beyond the school, too. In 2014, after a legal battle with the House of Bryant, the tiny town of Lake City, Tennessee, changed its name to Rocky Top, trading on a mass commercial product to forge what we could call an "imagined neolocalism."

Conclusion

The last three major fight songs to join the SEC repertory demonstrate how after World War II, SEC football music became more professionalized, shaped "top-down" by powerful stakeholders with access to high-profile composers and the professional knowledge and cultural capital to negotiate sophisticated copyright and licensing issues. No longer emerging like earlier SEC fight songs from the grassroots efforts of student bodies and alumni and disseminated via hot dance bands or ukulele arrangements, these three songs testify to the marching band's postwar importance and to the power of individual boosters or donors to shape college football pageantry. They also index changes in campus culture, collegiate taste, and the commercial music industry, representing an era when college songs no longer formed a significant category in mainstream popular music or occupied students' energies and attention. In the early 1970s, SEC fight songs such as "Rocky Top" still could generate a powerful sense of regionalized, although not necessarily sectional, identity, while the other two songs covered in the chapter did not signify melodically or textually on southern identity markers. The final chapter explores similar thematic expressions of continuity and change in the SEC fight song repertory across the century chronicled in this book.

CHAPTER 11

What Fades and
What Remains

In late 1955, controversy swept the South over Georgia Tech's invitation to play the University of Pittsburgh, with its lone Black player, in New Orleans's January 1956 Sugar Bowl. SEC schools had quietly played integrated teams before, but never in a high-profile game on southern turf. Georgia governor Marv Griffin intervened, sending a well-publicized telegram to Tech coach Bobby Dodd warning him against precipitating a regional "Armageddon" by accepting the invitation. Angry Tech students' march on the governor's mansion and regional campus protests changed Griffin's public stance; for these young southern whites, participation in national football culture trumped the maintenance of stringent segregationist norms.[1] The incident highlighted how college football evoked multiple meanings for postwar southerners, signifying participation in national culture along with the potential for some nebulous sense of regional vindication.[2] It also foreshadowed the inevitable integration of SEC sports, which finally began at the University of Kentucky in the late 1960s, years after SEC schools began sporadically admitting Black students.[3] By 1980, thirty-three percent of SEC football players were Black.[4] Before that tectonic change, in the 1950s and much of the 1960s, the SEC resisted integration, making a last stand in the form of sectional football pageantry that projected a new postwar "consciousness of being *Southern*."[5]

This pageantry surged at key inflection points when white southerners reacted to external attacks on the region's racial hierarchy, including in 1948, when southern "Dixiecrats" split from the national Democratic party over its integrationist agenda; in 1954, when rage over *Brown vs. Board of Education* boiled over; and from 1961 to 1965, with the celebration of Civil War centennials. And in the late 1960s, this sectional football pageantry finally began to fade from SEC practice, crumpling under the forces of integration and campus activism. Tracking the post-integration disappearance of "Dixie" in SEC football and examining a case study of popular song piped into the contemporary SEC football stadium lets us panoramically assess continuity and change in the SEC fight song repertory as it relates to the book's major analytical themes, unfolding across the timeframe and trajectories the book has outlined.

Resurgent midcentury sectional football pageantry included Old-South-themed halftime shows, minstrel and Civil War songs covered earlier in the book, and widespread use of the Confederate battle flag.[6] Old South halftime shows abounded across the conference; at the University of Mississippi, these routines included Civil War and minstrel songs played by a band dressed in Confederate gray, a sixty-by-ninety-foot Confederate battle flag, and a large wooden magnolia from which women students emerged and in which they sometimes got stuck—an avatar for the constricting orthodoxies around white southern womanhood.[7] Sons of the Confederate Veterans and students in antebellum costume appeared in SEC Old South halftime shows, as in a 1958 Mississippi State University show.[8] Minstrel songs and tropes were prominent; in 1949, the University of Tennessee band wore blackface makeup as it performed minstrel songs and dances.[9] Entire halftime shows were built around minstrelsy: Auburn University's 1952 "old time minstrel show" featured an interlocutor, the Mister Bones character, and majorettes dancing a "minstrel shuffle."[10] A 1953 University of Arkansas Stephen Foster halftime show aired on NBC's *Pigskin Panorama* in the school's first national television broadcast.[11] By 1957, the NAACP was urging media networks to ban or edit Foster's minstrel songs such as "My Old Kentucky Home," a campaign that attracted the ire of powerful white southerners.[12] Nonetheless, SEC football culture continued to use Foster's songs in the 1950s and 1960s, retaining the racist terms against which the NAACP lobbied.[13] Other midcentury southern football pageantry nested symbols of state identity within sectional or national identity. The 1952 University of Florida homecoming celebrating the state centennial included "Dixie," a Confederate flag formation, and signs urging fans to "vote, vote, vote" in that year's US presidential election.[14] A 1962 University of South Carolina halftime show incorporated "Dixie," state songs "Carolina Moon" and "Carolina in the Morning," and US patriotic songs.[15]

The University of South Carolina 1961 halftime show "Songs of the Confederacy," extolling the centennial of the Civil War's start, distilled these trends into a sonic concentrate.[16] Performed on USC's band day, the show included numerous South Carolina high school bands. Although the stadium MC boomed that the show was "dedicated to the one hundredth anniversary of the terrible war," the repertoire and the crowd's responses to it were far from dejected. While spelling out "DIXIE" on-field—a formation retained throughout the show—the massed bands launched into what the MC called a "rollicking minstrel song of the 60s, the 'Yellow Rose of Texas.'" This was followed by "Maryland, My Maryland" (one of several songs to which the crowd sang along lustily) and "Goober Peas," a Confederate song about southerners' limited wartime diet. When the MC reminded the crowd that "Carolina was first" (to secede), they went wild. Cheering greeted the Confederate marching tune "Bonnie Blue Flag," the MC's mention of Robert E. Lee, and a song called "General Lee's Grand March." The show concluded with "Dixie," over which scattered rebel yells can be heard in extant footage.[17]

This pageantry emblematized "the rhetoric of regional pride and institutional autonomy . . . served up to [white] Southern alumni during the 1950s and 1960s."[18] By the late 1960s, however, such rhetoric and symbols were no longer uniformly accepted in SEC football culture. "Dixie" especially became a lightning rod for protests in the SEC, part of a regional and national wave of campus activism around race-related social issues.[19] The "Dixie" controversies that rippled across the conference in the late 1960s signaled a shift in the focus of campus race debates away from legal battles toward "institutional practices and cultural climate."[20] By the early 1970s, many SEC schools had stopped playing "Dixie" at games.[21] Where the song's fate was undecided, it generated student debate. In fall 1972, some University of Tennessee students didn't want the visiting University of Mississippi band to play "Dixie" at a Knoxville game, discussed in the previous chapter. In 1968, the University of Arkansas's Southern Student Organizing Committee sought a ban on "Dixie." Arkansas band director Richard Worthington countered that the band would play it at homecoming, describing it as a "pep song which draws the same response" as the Arkansas fight song.'"[22] The following fall, Black University of Arkansas students lay down on-field while the band played "Dixie" at a University of Texas game—with President Nixon and evangelist Billy Graham in attendance.[23]

The University of Georgia's "Dixie" problem, stretching from 1969 to the mid-1970s and well-documented in archival materials, highlights how the song debates indexed broader regional sentiments for white stakeholders on and off campus that often unfolded around battle lines of class and respectability. In February 1969, the UGA Black Student Union submitted to the president "A Moratorium on White Racism," a list of demands including the recruitment of Black athletes and a ban on "Dixie."[24] Two years later, after a brief halt, UGA again played "Dixie" at football events, prompting a Black Student Union letter to the president comparing the song to a swastika, promising a "determined, physical backlash" in the face of its usage, and reminding the administration that "Dixie is dead and you can't revive it."[25] In 1970 and 1971, the controversy intensified: fans injured a Black UGA marching band member in a violent demand to "play 'Dixie,' ni****," while more SEC schools dropped the song. In November 1971, UGA band director Roger Dancz stated publicly that the band would forego "Dixie" and removed the word from the ensemble's name.[26] The issue lay dormant until 1974, when a UGA student launched the Union of American Peoples (UAP), an organization whose platform included the restoration of "Dixie" to university athletic life.[27] Driven by UAP agitation, UGA's student government held a Fall 1974 referendum in which five thousand students voted by a margin of 3:1 to retain "Dixie." Director Dancz restated his reasons for suppressing the song, now backed by UGA president Fred Davison, who framed the issue as one of academic freedom: music faculty had the right to choose ensemble repertoire.[28] National coverage of the controversy ensured broad exposure, and UGA alumni and fans from eleven states wrote letters to university administration, most of them irate and some threatening to withhold donations if UGA did not resurrect "Dixie."[29]

Over the next two years, the Georgia press ran editorials and letters largely defending "Dixie."[30] Dancz's refusal to program the song earned his family ominous and obscene communications and a banner calling for his firing, hung in downtown Athens during 1975 homecoming.[31] By fall 1976, the problem was so inflamed that William Tate, longtime Dean of Men and respected figure in the UGA community, wrote an editorial for an Athens newspaper advocating for dropping the song.[32] Tate's piece generated another round of alumni and fan correspondence to university administrators, much of it still pro-"Dixie" yet interspersed with grudging acknowledgment of the logic of Tate's arguments.[33] In a sign of raging sectional sentiment, the pro-"Dixie" faction took to describing the Redcoat band as the "Turn-Coat" band.[34]

Both the song's champions and its detractors refracted their arguments through the lens of class affiliation and respectability. An internal UGA memo regarding the controversy sniffed out this dynamic, stating that "Dixie" communications to the university were coming from two camps: "professional people, 'solid citizens'" and a "small and unrepresentative group of 'redneck-thinking partisans.'"[35] As the South eased out of the Civil Rights era, Confederate symbols such as "Dixie" became linked with reactionary working-class white southern sentiment, mediated prominently in popular culture through, i.e., the visual and sonic symbolism of southern rock band Lynyrd Skynyrd. Many "Dixie" defenders contended with this cultural baggage by invoking educational, community, and professional credentials and affiliations to shroud sectional sentiment in middle-class respectability. When Phil Jones, Sons of Confederate Veterans (SCV) member and UGA alumnus, wrote to UGA administrators in defense of "Dixie," he emphasized his status as a Rotary Club member and a Presbyterian. Jones condemned Roger Dancz's remarks about "Dixie" stirring up "a bunch of drunks at football games" and listed pillar-of-the-community SCV members in his Florida chapter (bank officers, managers of major utilities companies, "attorneys, ministers, doctors") to dissociate "Dixie" lovers from the putative drunks.[36]

Similarly, those advocating for dropping "Dixie" argued not that the song was immoral or racist, but that it looked backward and smacked of emotional extremism, arguments which indexed classist concerns. John C. Stephens Jr., Dean of UGA's Franklin College of Arts and Sciences, cautiously allowed that "emotionalism has its place, I suppose, but [UGA needs] reasonable solutions," writing to William Tate that he agreed UGA should drop the song.[37] Tate's 1976 editorial emphasized that most other SEC schools had jettisoned "Dixie"; retaining it would put UGA out of step with modern conference trends.[38] Those in favor of removing "Dixie" also employed pragmatic arguments: the song under-mined recruitment of Black athletes, a necessary demographic in mod-ern college sports.[39] A minstrel song voicing the imagined perspective of a Black person yearning for the Old South and its plantation system built on forced Black labor was unwelcome in this new era of SEC universities' efforts to recruit Black athletes to provide unpaid labor in unwelcoming institutional contexts.

By the early 1970s, "Dixie" was considered by white SEC powerbrokers not unethical, but *tacky*, and dissonant with institutional goals. As SEC administrators and many alumni sought to align their institutions' images with middle-class US aesthetics and values, the reactionary, working-class associations accumulated by "Dixie" projected a "regional white identity that remained in constant conflict with the American national image."[40] The SEC "Dixie" controversies illustrate the mutability of white southern ideas about and expressions of regional identity refracted in post-Civil-Rights football pageantry. In this period, Andrew Doyle argues, middle-class white southerners, desperate for national approval, saw SEC football as a public relations symbol—an apologetic for a nebulous white "south-ern way of life."[41] When "Dixie" ceased to represent common aesthetic and cultural ground for white SEC powerbrokers due to its shifting class associations, it no longer functioned as a viable apologetic. Like black-face minstrelsy more broadly, "Dixie" had traversed a long and twisting road from working-class entertainment to respectable middle-class fare and occasional symbol of elite white southern institutions, then back to symbolizing working-class culture and politics again.

The disappearance of the SEC's pan-conference fight song marked the end of a long era of unambiguously sectional songs, although other songs indexing regional identity have endured in SEC football culture. Although no lasting fight songs played by marching bands joined the SEC canon after "Rocky Top" in 1972, an unofficial one did, and it demon-strates continuity with SEC fight song reception histories that refract themes of race, gender, and regional identity across the century spanned in the book. At the same time that "Dixie" faded from SEC usage, an iconic white southern working-class cultural product emerged that later wove itself into the sonic quilt of SEC football pageantry: Lynyrd Sky-nyrd's 1974 "Sweet Home Alabama," which the University of Alabama began piping into its stadium in the late 1990s.[42] In the two-plus decades between the song's production and its introduction into Alabama football, college football's soundscape had expanded to encompass sound effects, musical riffs, commercial jingles, and popular songs piped through the PA system before, during, and after games.[43] High-tech PA stadium systems and sophisticated licensing agreements created by university legal departments have given recorded popular music a more prominent role in the football soundscape, allowing songs such as "Sweet Home Alabama" to function as informal or unofficial fight songs. Although musical reception is not static across time, Lynyrd Skynyrd's 1970s associations with southern white working-class masculinity were arguably so powerful that they resonate down to the present. As Zachary J. Lechner writes, the social and political unrest of those years prompted white Americans to draw on cultural expressions of "white, working-class, rural, masculine, and anachronistic" southern-ness as a "malleable . . . narrative concept" used to address the national problem of "rootlessness."[44] As the "soundtrack of the second New South urbanization and modernization," southern rock helped white Americans navigate a destabilizing phase of regional and national life.[45]

Southern rock also contributed to the 1970s "redneck pride" phenomenon, which elevated white working-class tastes and attitudes in defiance of middle-class aesthetics and norms.[46] Skynyrd's unreconstructed, macho, Confederate-inflected "star text" and songs like "Sweet Home Alabama" made the band a potent symbol of white southern insurgence, regardless of their offstage political beliefs or their session collaborations with Black instrumentalists and singers.[47] Merry Clayton, one of three Black women who sang backup on "Sweet Home Alabama," initially didn't want to participate in the session, believing the song projected reactionary white southern political sentiment. Clayton changed her mind when her husband suggested that Black singers could provide an important affective counterpoint to the song's problematic racial and political sensibilities, later stating of herself and her two Black female colleagues that "There was nothing sweet about Alabama. You can hear our anger."[48]

Fast-forward several decades: when "Sweet Home Alabama" blares through Bryant-Denny Stadium's PA system, it morphs the venue into a sizzling cauldron of noise and light, hypermasculine guitar riffs thundering while wraparound screens and a massive Jumbotron flash crimson and white. A mostly white crowd yells along to the white southern working-class anthem, now linked to the collective student identity of a relatively elite university that exists partly to facilitate class mobility, delivering students from a working-class future. Enlivened by Black women backup singers, the song rocks the stadium during a break in a violent athletic spectacle played by what is, in the University of Alabama's case, an overwhelmingly Black football roster performing unpaid, difficult, and dangerous labor. The interlude's social dynamics exemplify Erin C. Tarver's argument that "the racialization of contemporary sports fandom" is inextricably linked to "the instrumentalization of people of color as symbols of power in the creation and reproduction of racial whiteness."[49]

Of course, white SEC football players and Black SEC fans exist, and Nell Irvin Painter cautions against monolithic readings of southern experience, reminding us that "race, class, and gender constitute three essential but blunt tools of analysis" and that "beyond even the most finely tuned categories lives . . . individual subjectivity."[50] Even allowing for degrees of individual subjectivity, in this football context, the song projects durable southern orthodoxies around race and masculinity, evidence that "broadly shared or at least broadly recognized notions of white southern manhood" still powerfully inform southern culture.[51] In continuity with rowdy turn-of-the-century football parades documented in Chapter 1, "Sweet Home Alabama" reminds us that white southern college football's public or semi-public spaces have always echoed with sonic projections of rambunctious white masculinity.

As Christopher Cooper and H. Gibbs Knotts write, "the South and the southern experience are defined in part by many factors, principally historical forces and the lasting presence of uniquely southern cultural symbols."[52] "Sweet Home Alabama" is not "Dixie"; it is neither a minstrel song nor a Confederate marching tune. Still, it echoes earlier SEC usage of "uniquely southern cultural symbols," including products of the popular music marketplace, to sonically amplify a white-framed regional identity and demarcate the southern college football stadium as a place of white authority and power, especially white male authority and power. The University of Alabama's identification with the song has generated iconic footage which evokes the athletic dominance of the South in modern college football and circulates frequently in sports television and on social media. "Sweet Home Alabama" also pops up at University of Alabama alumni social events such as wedding receptions, where DJs play it while attendees interpolate—just as they do in the stadium—a rowdy "Roll Tide Roll" between Lynyrd Skynyrd's phrases. Both women and men participate enthusiastically in such contexts, a reminder that while the SEC fight song repertory centers on a hypermasculine and violent sport, women have historically found great meaning and a source of identity in SEC fandom, contributing to and participating in the SEC soundscape through various modes of musical expression, consumption, and creation.

The continuities and changes explored in the analysis of these two songs, separated by a century in their adoption into SEC musical practice, raises the question of southern exceptionalism: is the SEC fight song repertory musically, culturally, or historically unique in big-time college football?[53] The conference wants you to believe—is economically invested in your belief—that SEC football resonates with some mystical quality, some heightened sense of meaning, summarized in its recent branding tagline "The SEC: it just means more." Although the SEC's earlier use of Civil War and minstrel songs that refracted themes of race and sectional identity are distinctive in college football history, other aspects of SEC music aren't. Contemporary PWI use of popular music that primarily "codes white" during football games is not exclusive to the SEC, as John Michael McCluskey has shown.[54] When seen this way, the University of Alabama's use of "Sweet Home Alabama" becomes a regionalized instance of a national trend McCluskey identifies in which "the soundscapes of [Power Five college] football are constructed . . . to only allow for token celebrations of blackness in specific moments while using white sonic icons as the primary sounds associated with the sport's portrayals of power and victory."[55] As Matthew D. Lassiter and Joseph Crespino caution, although we must "historicize the idea of Southern distinctiveness as a cultural, political, and legal construction that has been very real in its consequences," placing too much analytical weight on the concept of southern exceptionalism skews historical evidence and obscures how SEC music, in its past and present incarnations, exemplifies broader national patterns and values.[56]

Regarding southern musical consumption and production, Karl Hagstrom Miller warns against historiographic over-investment in exceptionalism, calling for a richer and more accurate version of US music history "attuned to continuities across regions."[57] In answering his call, this book shows that a through-line in a century of SEC fight song production and reception is white southerners' avid embrace of mainstream popular music and their participation in national collegiate culture, especially prior to World War II. Although the SEC fight song repertory has at times included unmistakably regional or sectional songs, it also has encompassed many that are not, and the whole repertory has always been embedded within and participated in larger commercial music trends and practices. When SEC schools used fight songs that drew on Black musical styles while actively excluding African Americans from admission, they were part of a widespread historic pattern of white US institutions and powerbrokers profiting from Black cultural products. When southern students, alumni, musicians, and public figures such as Huey P. Long avidly consumed and contributed to the 1930s apex of college songs as a commercial music category and popular culture phenomenon, they were participating in mainstream musical fads and practices. Additionally, SEC fight song reception has been shaped by broader debates and discourses in US commercial music history around copyright, authorship, and origins, manifesting in tensions between publishers who treat fight songs as individually owned commodities and stakeholders who regard them as the collective heritage of a university community.

The belief among college football fans in the Orphic power of this collective musical heritage, a conviction that the right song at the right time can materially sway game outcome, is also not specific to the South, although here it has at times hitched itself to sectional sentiment. This belief has been pervasive and durable in national college football culture since the late nineteenth century, undergirding every complaint about impotent fight songs, every fight song contest, and every student or alumni effort to find or write a new song. In the metaphysics of football fandom, people speak of their team as federal representatives in some invisible and cosmic democracy: "WE won this weekend," crows a football fan who sat on the couch, remote control in hand. College fight songs of all regions invite fans to embodied communal participation in this mystic transaction—singing, swaying, humming with others—shared rituals and gestures that obscure the commodity status of fight songs. This phenomenological disconnect is not unique to the Southeastern Conference. Across the United States, fight songs' affective power forge powerful communal bonds among fans, students, and alumni that seemingly transcend the commercial marketplace in which college songs are historically embedded. In the South, this affective power has generated additional sedimentary layers of meaning related to race, gender, and regional identity, showing us the power of even the simplest vernacular and commercial music to create, shape, and reflect identity along social axes. Natalie Ring writes that regions are both "symbolic and material entities."[58] As long as the Southeastern Conference dominates US college football, its pageantry invites us to hear how the symbolic entity of the modern US South is defined through a complex web of commodified musical traditions—one long and tangled in the making.

Overtime

In October 2011, a sports journalist voiced a common geographic complaint about the University of Missouri's impending move to the Southeastern Conference: the school does "not fit in the SEC" because "Missouri is neither in the South nor the East."[1] Nonetheless, in 2012, the SEC formally admitted Texas A&M University and the University of Missouri, and in 2025, the conference's elastic conceptual boundaries will stretch to enfold the Universities of Texas and Oklahoma, inaugurating more discourse about the material constitution of the South. Unlike Deep South states, Texas and Missouri can claim geographical affinity with regions of the US besides the South through cultural practices and historical-political trajectories that at times have aligned them elsewhere. As Charles Reagan Wilson wryly observed of Missouri's place in broader schemas of the South's material composition,

> Defining the South itself must take into account the varieties of southern experience. "The South" appears at times, for example, as a historical term—the eleven states of the former Confederacy. But Kentucky and Missouri were slave states in 1861, shared many customs and attitudes with people farther south, and, hey, we play them in athletics because they are in the SEC.[2]

The University of Missouri's fight song history certainly evinces "customs and attitudes" common to the Southeastern Conference. The school used "Dixie" at football events well into the twentieth century, along with other sectional songs such as the 1929 "When the Varsity Band Plays Dixie."[3] The school's earlier, gendered expressions of football pageantry likewise fit those of other SEC or proto-SEC schools. "Every True Son," sung to the tune of "It's a Long Way to Tipperary," has been one of its chief football songs since the early twentieth century. In the past two decades, the university inserted an optional "Daughter" in the title, so that university materials now print the song as "Every True Son/Daughter." As at other SEC schools, the song's gendered language obscured the presence and agency of women at the University of Missouri, where they have been admitted since 1867. University of Missouri women contributed to the same football music that at times erased their presence; the Young Women's Christian Association sponsored the publication of early college football songbooks.[4] The school's pattern of fight song acquisition also roughly fits with the SEC fight song trajectory outlined in the book. Missouri began playing intercollegiate football in 1890, the decade in which other proto-SEC schools adopted the sport. Early in its football history, Missouri borrowed tunes of schools with established football programs, such as a melody copyrighted by Cornell University for which a University of Missouri alumnus paid $1400 for the university to use.[5] Missouri students and alumni busied themselves in the first half of the twentieth century in finding a unique fight song through song contests and, like other schools, cycled through many football songs.[6] The school identified its fight song, "Fight, Tiger," with original text and tune, in 1946, a slightly later date compared to most SEC schools.[7] Would you map the state of Missouri in the South? Maybe, and maybe not: but if you judge the question purely by the history of University of Missouri fight songs, the school fits into the larger story of Southeastern Conference football music—a last reminder that these simple little songs have much to tell us if we know how to hear them.

College Songs Published, Written, or Copyrighted by Thornton W. Allen

TITLE	TEXT AUTHOR(S)	MUSIC COMPOSER(S) AND/OR ARRANGER(S)
"Washington and Lee Swing"	C. A. Robbins	T. W. Allen & Mark Sheafe
"Washington and Lee Swing"	C. A. Robbins	T. W. Allen & Mark Sheafe
"Maroon Victory"	George J. Stelljes Jr.	George J. Stelljes Jr.
"Yea Alabama"	Ethelred Lundy Sykes	Ethelred Lundy Sykes
"All Hail, Arizona! Alma Mater Song"	E. C. Monroe	Dorothy H. Monroe
"Here's to the Colors of Crimson-White"	Vincent Hardy Bell	J. B. Ludebuehl, arr. T. Garner for male voices
"Victory Song"	T. W. Allen	T. W. Allen
"Old S.U."	E. Edwin Sheldon	E. Edwin Sheldon
"Memories of Connecticut"	George Warrek	Oscar D'Esope, arr. A. S. Davis
"Football Blues"	T. W. Allen	T. W. Allen
"University of Dayton Flyer's March"	J .B. Meiler	J. B. Meiler, arr. Maurice R. Reichard; orch. Pts, with words
"Washington and Lee Swing"	C. A. Robbins	T. W. Allen and M. W. Sheafe; with ukulele, banjo and guitar arr. Roy Smeck, and C melody, E flat alto and B flat tenor sax arr. W. C. Polla
"Fight! Wildcats! Fight!"	Douglas Holsclaw	T. W. Allen and D. Holsclaw, with uke arr. Roy Smeck
"Pal of My College Days; Smoky Dreams"	T. W. Allen	T. W. Allen with uke arr. Roy Smeck
"Spirit of Maine"	Harry D. O'Neil	Harry D. O'Neil with uke arr. Roy Smeck
"March of Triumph" (march foxtrot)	Gabriel Jacoby	Gabriel Jacoby, arr. T. W. Allen with uke, tenor banjo, and Hawaiian guitar arr. Roy Smeck, arr. for sax and other C, E♭, and B♭ instruments W. C. Polla and male quartet, unaccomp., arr. Carl F. Price
"March of the Fighting Gators"	T. W. Allen	T. W. Allen, uke arr. Roy Smeck

COPYRIGHT DATE/NUMBER	SOURCE *Catalogue of Copyright Entries*, LoC Copyright Office (Washington: US Govt Printing Office)	COPYRIGHT NOTES (all copyrights held solely by T. W. Allen and/ or his company unless otherwise noted here)
05/17/1910 (15491)	New Series Vol. 5 Nos. 1–26, Part 1, Jan-June 1910, 884	T. W. Allen & Robert G. Thach, Lexington, VA
12/26/1920 (31493)	New Series Vol. 15 No. 8, 1920, 1927	Thornton W. Allen Co./T. W. Allen & Robert G. Thach, New York ("copyright is claimed on new matter")
05/01/1923 (6767)	New Series Vol. 18 No. 1, 1923, 419	
04/22/1926 (8652)	New Series Vol. 22 for the Year 1927, Nos. 1–12, 1928, 435	*Rammer Jammer*, U of AL, Tuscaloosa
10/30/1926 (18580)	New Series Vol. 21, Part 2, Last Half of 1926, Nos. 7–12, 1927, 956	U of AZ Student Body, Tucson
04/08/1927 (7649)	New Series Vol. 22 for the Year 1927, Nos. 1–12, 1928, 398	Tom Garner, Tuscaloosa, AL
08/08/1928 (20223)	New Series Vol. 23 Part 2, Last Half of 1928, Nos. 7–12, 1929, 1047	Student Assembly, U of MD, College Park, MD
10/29/1928 (24254)	New Series Vol. 23 Part 2, Last Half of 1928, Nos. 7–12, 1929, 1252	E. Edwin Sheldon, Sellinsgrove, PA
12/20/1928 (26354)	New Series Vol. 23 Part 2, Last Half of 1928, Nos. 7–12, 1929, 1369	Connecticut Ag College, Storrs, CT. In *Connecticut Agriculture College, Four Songs.*
10/14/1929 (22538)	New Series Vol. 24, No. 7, 1929, 1194	
06/02/1930 (17825)	New Series Vol. 25, 1930, 914	U of Dayton
09/26/1930 (25498)	New Series Vol. 25, 1930, 1301	
10/29/1930 (26357)	New Series Vol. 25, 1930, 1344	
10/22/1930 (27430)	New Series Vol. 25, 1930, 1393	
03/12/1931 (7960)	New Series Vol. 26 for the year 1931 Nos. 1–12, 1932, 392	
03/28/1931 (9981)	New Series Vol. 26 for the year 1931 Nos. 1–12, 1932, 499	
08/26/1931 (20109)	New Series Vol. 26 for the year 1931 Nos. 1–12, 1932, 1036	

TITLE	TEXT AUTHOR(S)	MUSIC COMPOSER(S) AND/OR ARRANGER(S)
"Indian Warriors Song, Wa-hoo" (Victory Song of William & Mary College)	Barrett Roberts	T. W. Allen, uke arr. Roy Smeck
Intercollegiate Songbook		Compiled by Allen, ed. by Carl F. Price, uke & guitar arr. Roy Smeck
"When the Big State Team Goes Tearing Along" (?)	T. W. Allen (presumably)	T. W. Allen (presumably)
"Phi Delta Theta on Parade"	T. W. Allen (presumably)	T. W. Allen (presumably)
"March On, Cincinnati"	T. W. Allen	T. W. Allen, uke arr. May Singhi Breen
"Vanderbilt Forever"	T. W. Allen with Grantland Rice	
Rudy Vallée, *Collection of Vagabond Songs*		Compiled and ed. T. W. Allen, arr. Stan Tucker
"Alabama Victory Song"	T. W. Allen	T. W. Allen
"Alabama's Day"	T. W. Allen	T. W. Allen
"My Phi Delta Theta Sweetheart"	T. W. Allen	T. W. Allen
"The Orange and Blue"	George Hamilton & T. W. Allen	T. W. Allen
"Princeton Tiger Gridiron March"	Paul Dickey	Paul Dickey
"Yellow Jacket Girl"	Daisy Chotas	Nick Chotas
"On, Wisconsin"	Carl Beck	W. T. Purdy, new piano arr. T. W. Allen
"Alma Mater: Blair Academy Song"	Malcolm F. Joy	T. W. Allen
College Songs Folio A	Arr. with and without words, T. W. Allen	Arr. with and without words, T. W. Allen
Intercollegiate Song Book	Compiled and edited, T. W. Allen	Compiled and edited, T. W. Allen
"Sorority Memories"	T. W. Allen(?)	T. W. Allen(?)
Cornell Songs	Arr. T. W. Allen	Arr. T. W. Allen

COPYRIGHT DATE/NUMBER	SOURCE *Catalogue of Copyright Entries*, LoC Copyright Office (Washington: US Govt Printing Office)	COPYRIGHT NOTES (all copyrights held solely by T. W. Allen and/ or his company unless otherwise noted here)
09/28/1931 (22145)	New Series Vol. 26 No. 9, 1931, 1137	
Popular ed. 09/19/1931 (27082)	New Series Vol. 26 No. 9, 1931, 1382)	Intercollegiate Song Book, Inc.
05/05/1932 (12702)	New Series Vol. 27 for the year 1932, Nos. 1–12, 1933, 569)	
11/08/1932 (25513)	New Series Vol. 27, Part 2, Last Half of 1932, Nos. 9–12, 1933, 1066	
09/14/1933 (18702)	New Series Vol. 28 Part 1, First Half of 1933 Nos. 1–9, 1934, 775	
09/14/1933 (19450)	New Series Vol. 28 Part 1, First Half of 1933 Nos. 1–9, 1934, 801	
02/10/1934 (4346)	New Series Vol. 29, First Half of 1934, Nos. 1–12, 1935, 172	
12/13/1934 (25767)	New Series Vol. 29 Part 2, Last Half of 1934, Nos. 9–12, 1935, 1114	Unpublished
12/13/1934 (25768)	New Series Vol. 29 Part 2, Last Half of 1934, Nos. 9–12, 1935, 1114	Unpublished
10/25/1935 (26218)	New Series Vol. 30 Part 2, Last Half of 1935, Nos. 10–12, 1936, 1180	arr. for uke; no arranger listed
11/02/1935 (16403)	New Series Vol. 30 Part 2, Last Half of 1935, Nos. 10–12, 1936, 1187	
10/25/1935 (26488)	New Series Vol. 30 Part 2, Last Half of 1935, Nos. 10–12, 1936, 1190	
10/25/1935 (27256)	New Series Vol. 30 Part 2, Last Half of 1935, Nos. 10–12, 1936, 1219	
11/12/1935 (2058)	New Series Vol. 31 Part 1, First Half of 1936, Nos. 1–8, 1937, 77	Arr. for uke; no arranger listed
01/13/1936 (14)	New Series Vol. 31 Part 1, First Half of 1936, Nos. 1–8, 1937, 123)	
04/04/1936 (13181)	New Series Vol. 31 Part 1, First Half of 1936, Nos. 1–8, 1937, 598)	
10/06/1936 (12164–12166)	New Series Vol. 31 Part 1, First Half of 1936, Nos. 1–8, 1937, 571	Arr. for uke; no arranger listed
05/03/1937 (13368)	New Series Vol. 31 Part 1, First Half of 1936, Nos. 1–8, 1937, 617	Arr. for piano, T. W. Allen; unpublished
05/28/1937 (14420)	New Series Vol. 32, for the year 1937, Nos. 1–12, 1938, 672	

TITLE	TEXT AUTHOR(S)	MUSIC COMPOSER(S) AND/OR ARRANGER(S)
"Drink A Highball" and "Alma Mater"	Isaac Hampshur Jones	T. W. Allen, arr. male voices; uke arr. for "Drink A Highball"
"Men of State: Hail Mississippi State"	T. W. Allen	J. W. Peavey & T. W. Allen
"The Blue and White"	F. E. Wilber	Set to tune "Amici," arr. T. W. Allen, male voices
"Fight for LSU"	W. G. "Hickey" Higginbotham	Castro Carazo
"Washington & Lee Swing"	C. A. Robbins	T. W. Allen and M. W. Sheafe
Bowdoin Songs		New arr., T. W. Allen
Songs of Lehigh University		Composed and arr. T. W. Allen and others, compiled and ed. A. E. Buchanana Jr.
"Flying Cardinals: Marching Song"	Paul D. H. Loman	Paul D. H. Loman
"Orange O"	E. T. Reed	Neil Reed, arr. T. W. Allen
Williams Songs	Arr. T. W. Allen	
"Knute Rockne of Notre Dame"	Tom Lysaght	Tom Lysaght
"Old Eli March"	Wadsworth Doster	Wadsworth Doster
"We're Mustangs" and "Hail! S.M.U."	Paul Matthews	Etta Frances Fairs
Folio of Popular College Songs	Compiled & arr. T. W. Allen	
"Stand Up for the Blue and Gold"	Gwen Sweet	Milo Sweet
"Let's Go Trojan"	Gwen Sweet	Milo Sweet
"OH and IO"	Frank Crumit	Frank Crumit

COPYRIGHT DATE/NUMBER	SOURCE *Catalogue of Copyright Entries*, LoC Copyright Office (Washington: US Govt Printing Office)	COPYRIGHT NOTES (all copyrights held solely by T. W. Allen and/ or his company unless otherwise noted here)
12/08/1936 (14573)	New Series Vol. 32, for the year 1937, Nos. 1–12, 1938, 678	
06/11/1937 (18241)	New Series Vol. 32, for the year 1937, Nos. 1–12, 1938, 860	
06/11/1937 (25071)	(New Series Vol. 32 Part 2, Last Half of 1937, Nos. 10–12, 1938, 1183	In *Pennsylvania State College, Four Songs*
06/11/1937	New Series Vol. 32 Part 2, Last Half of 1937, Nos. 10–12, 1938, 1194	In *Louisiana State University Songs*
10/07/1937 (355)	New Series Vol. 32 Part 2, Last Half of 1937, Nos. 10–12, 1938, 364	Renewal: copyright by Mark W. Sheafe, Watertown SD as one of the authors of music
11/05/1937 (27137)	New Series Vol. 32 Part 2, Last Half of 1937, Nos. 10–12, 1938, 1280	
11/20/1937 (1513)	New Series Vol. 32 Part 2, Last Half of 1937, Nos. 10–12, 1938, 57	Copyright Lehigh University; 2 of these Lehigh songs entered separately in this copyright catalogue (p. 141)
04/22/1938 (14816)	New Series Vol. 33 Part I, First Half of 1938, Nos. 1–9, 1939, 648	
04/22/1938 (1635)	New Series Vol. 33 Part I, First Half of 1938, Nos. 1–9, 1939, 690	
04/22/1938 (16955)	(New Series Vol. 33 Part I, First Half of 1938, Nos. 1–9, 1939, 722)	
07/19/1938 (21310)	(New Series Vol. 33 Part I, First Half of 1938, Nos. 1–9, 1939, 905)	
10/06/1936 [*sic*] (21865)	(New Series Vol. 33 Part I, First Half of 1938, Nos. 1–9, 1939, 925)	
07/19/1938 (22688)	(New Series Vol. 33 Part I, First Half of 1938, Nos. 1–9, 1939, 954)	
09/02/1938 (25999)	(New Series Vol. 33 Part 2, Last Half of 1938, Nos. 10–12, 1939, 1100)	
10/31/1938 (31927)	(New Series Vol. 33 Part 2, Last Half of 1938, Nos. 10–12, 1939, 1334)	
11/19/1938 (34924)	(New Series Vol. 33 Part 2, Last Half of 1938, Nos. 10–12, 1939, 1465)	
09/02/1938 (35770)	(New Series Vol. 33 Part 2, Last Half of 1938, Nos. 10–12, 1939, 1495)	

TITLE	TEXT AUTHOR(S)	MUSIC COMPOSER(S) AND/OR ARRANGER(S)
"Fight, Vols, Fight"	Gwen Sweet	Milo Sweet
"Aggie War Hymn"	"Pinky" Wilson	"Pinky" Wilson, arr. T. W. Allen 4 male voices, unaccomp.
"California Forever"	(unclear if there are lyrics)	T. W. Allen, melody w/piano accomp.
"California Loyalty"	(unclear if there are lyrics)	T. W. Allen, melody w/piano accomp.
"Salute to the Golden Bear"	(unclear if there are lyrics)	T. W. Allen
"Alma Mater"	W. St. Clair	C. D. Coppes, arr. H. E. Pike
"Cherry and White Wins the Day"	Benny Davis	Benny Davis, arr. T. W. Allen (pf)
"Fight, Temple, Fight"	Maurice E. Swerdlow	Maurice E. Swerdlow, arr. T. W. Allen (pf)
Football Song Hits for Orchestra; Allen Intercollegiate Medley Nos. 3, 4		Arr. T. W. Allen
"Give Three Cheers"	R. Helen Warford	R. Helen Warford, pf
"Indiana Victory"	Russell P. Harker	Russell P. Harker
"Let's Cheer Again for Temple"	Bertram Bennett	David Zoob
"Oskee-Wow-Wow"	Howard R. Green	H. V. Hill, arr. T. W. Allen
Songs of Michigan State College		Arr. Thomas W. Allen [sic] & Emerson Oelen
"Washington and Lee Swing"	By T. W. Allen and M. W. Sheafe	T. W. Allen and M. W. Sheafe; arr. Paul Yoder—military band parts w/conductor
"Washington and Lee Swing"	By T. W. Allen and M. W. Sheafe	T. W. Allen and M. W. Sheafe; arr. Charles Magnanate, pf accordion
"Chant"	H. C. Scott	C. S. Harris, arr. T. W. Allen satbttbb
"On, Wisconsin: March"	Carl Beck	W. T. Purdy, arr. Anthony Gallarini, pf accordion

COPYRIGHT DATE/NUMBER	SOURCE *Catalogue of Copyright Entries*, LoC Copyright Office (Washington: US Govt Printing Office)	COPYRIGHT NOTES (all copyrights held solely by T. W. Allen and/ or his company unless otherwise noted here)
12/18/1938 (589)	(1939 New Series, Vol. 31 No. 1, 1939, 21)	
12/08/1938 (2986)	(1939 New Series, Vol. 31 No. 1, 1939, 125)	
03/07/1939 (9448)	(1939 New Series, Vol. 31 No. 1, 1939, 422)	Unpublished
03/07/1939 (9448)	(1939 New Series, Vol. 31 No. 1, 1939, 422)	Unpublished
02/25/1939 (11650)	(1939 New Series, Vol. 31 No. 1, 1939, 502)	Unpublished
11/09/1938 (21792)	(1939 New Series, Vol. 34, No. 8, 1939, 961)	
11/09/1938 (22172)	(1939 New Series, Vol. 34, No. 8, 1939, 974)	
11/09/1938 (22575)	(1939 New Series, Vol. 34, No. 8, 1939, 989)	
07/27/1939 (22607, 22608)	(1939 New Series, Vol. 34, No. 8, 1939, 990)	
11/09/1938 (22710)	(1939 New Series, Vol. 34, No. 8, 1939, 994)	
06/12/1939 (23262)	(1939 New Series, Vol. 34, No. 8, 1939, 1013)	Also copyrighted by T. W. Allen Co. that year in military band arrangement, p. 304
11/09/1938 (23554)	(1939 New Series, Vol. 34, No. 8, 1939, 1024)	
06/12/1939 (24355)	(1939 New Series, Vol. 34, No. 8, 1939, 1053)	
11/21/1938 (24918)	(1939 New Series, Vol. 34, No. 8, 1939, 1073)	
06/29/1939 (25470)	(1939 New Series, Vol. 34, No. 8, 1939, 1093)	
08/22/1939 (28640)	(1939 New Series, Vol. 34, No. 8, 1939, 1221)	
10/10/1939 (33605)	(1939 New Series, Vol. 34, No. 8, 1939, 1434)	
09/27/1939 (35250)	(1939 New Series, Vol. 34, No. 8, 1939, 1494)	

TITLE	TEXT AUTHOR(S)	MUSIC COMPOSER(S) AND/OR ARRANGER(S)
"V.M.I. Spirit"	B. Bowering	B. Bowering, arr. Geo. Briegel, band pts
"Fight! Vols, Fight"	T. W. Allen & Milo Sweet	T. W. Allen & Milo Sweet, arr. Charles Fielder, military band pts
"Fight! Oregon"	C. H. Keeney	T. W. Allen & Milo Sweet
"Let's Fight! For Texas Christian"	Gwen Sweet	Milo Sweet
Bennett Songs: Songs of Bennett College	Carol Cotton, Mrs. Guy Lambert, & others	Edith Player Brown, R. Nathaniel Dett, & T. W. Allen
Bicentennial Songs of the University of Pennsylvania	Edward Foley & Thornton Oakley	Robert Doone & Robert Elmore
"Fight! For Texas Christian"	Milo Sweet & T. W. Allen	Milo Sweet & T. W. Allen
"Fight On for Oregon"	Leslie Irvin	Leslie Irvin
"Men of Nebraska"	Royale Schoen, T. W. Allen & Milo Sweet	Royale Schoen, T. W. Allen & Milo Sweet
"Oregon Battle Song"	C. H. Keeney	T. W. Allen & Milo Sweet
"Hail! Florida"	W. R. Frazier	L. Y. Dyrenforth, pf
"We Are the Boys from Old Florida"		Arr. mixed voices, T. W. Allen
"Fight Down the Field for Stanford"	Ferdinand Mendenhall, T. W. Allen & Milo Sweet	Ferdinand Mendenhall, T. W. Allen & Milo Sweet
"Alumni Song"	George Archer Ferguson	Carroll Ragan
"Salute to the Generals"	T. W. Allen	T. W. Allen
"Carry Me Back to Old Virginny" (James Bland), "Swanee River" (Stephen Foster), & "Dixie" (Dan Emmett)		Arr. T. W. Allen, male voices
"Salute to the Generals"	T. W. Allen	T. W. Allen, arr. Dick Kent, military band pts

COPYRIGHT DATE/NUMBER	SOURCE *Catalogue of Copyright Entries*, LoC Copyright Office (Washington: US Govt Printing Office)	COPYRIGHT NOTES (all copyrights held solely by T. W. Allen and/ or his company unless otherwise noted here)
10/30/1939 (39145)	(1939 New Series, Vol. 34, No. 8, 1939, 1643)	
12/21/1939 (687)	(New Series Vol. 35 Pt 1, First Half of 1940, Nos. 1–5, 1941, 25)	
02/23/1940 (8291)	(New Series Vol. 35 Pt 1, First Half of 1940, Nos. 1–5, 1941, 334)	
04/01/1940 (9426)	(New Series Vol. 35 Pt 1, First Half of 1940, Nos. 1–5, 1941, 375)	
05/14/1940 (19581)	(New Series Vol. 35 Pt 1, First Half of 1940, Nos. 1–5, 1941, 840)	
06/17/1940 (19595)	(New Series Vol. 35 Pt 2, Last Half of 1940, Nos. 6–12, 1941, 841)	
11/08/1940 (36268)	(New Series Vol. 35 Pt 2, Last Half of 1940, Nos. 6–12, 1941, 1524)	
10/18/1940 (36269)	(New Series Vol. 35 Pt 2, Last Half of 1940, Nos. 6–12, 1941, 1524)	
11/08/1940 (40521)	(New Series Vol. 35 Pt 2, Last Half of 1940, Nos. 6–12, 1941, 1697)	
10/18/1940 (37760)	(New Series Vol. 35 Pt 2, Last Half of 1940, Nos. 6–12, 1941, 1577)	
12/14/1940 (963)	(New Series Vol. 36, Part 1, First Half of 1941, Nos. 1–4 [n.d.], 34)	
12/14/1940 (3597)	(New Series Vol. 36, Part 1, First Half of 1941, Nos. 1–4 [n.d.], 126)	
11/29/1940 (10440)	(New Series Vol. 36, Part 1, First Half of 1941, Nos. 1–4 [n.d.], 405)	
07/25/1940 (15994)	(New Series Vol. 36, Part 1, First Half of 1941, Nos. 1–4 [n.d.], 622)	
05/05/1941 (25175)	(1941 New Series Vol. 36 No. 5 1941, 988)	
05/19/1941 (27187)	(1941 New Series Vol. 36 No. 5 1941, 1092)	Although not strictly college songs, these minstrel songs were used at southern PWI football games.
06/02/1941 (19328)	(1941 New Series Vol. 36 No. 5 1941, 1168)	

TITLE	TEXT AUTHOR(S)	MUSIC COMPOSER(S) AND/OR ARRANGER(S)
"Salute to the Generals" (Fox-trot)	T. W. Allen	T. W. Allen, arr. Dick Kent, orchestra pts
College Classics: Famous Songs		Arr. T. W. Allen for voice & pf, or male chorus
College Classics: Famous Songs, Medleys 1–6		Compiled T. W. Allen, Arr. Dick Kent, orchestra parts
"Fight! Fight! Fight!"	Richard M. Skidmore	Richard M. Skidmore, arr. T. W. Allen
"Fighting Spartans"	Keith McKellop	Keith McKellop, arr. T. W. Allen
"Go! O-hi-o"	T. W. Allen	T. W. Allen
"Hail! Stanford Hail!"	Albert W. Smith	Mary Roberts Coolidge, arr. T. W. Allen men's voices
"Hail Purdue"	J. Morrison	E. J. Wotawa, arr. T. W. Allen mixed chorus & men's chorus
"Alma Mater"	R. E. Holch	A. E. Holch, arr. T. W. Allen
"Fly, Navy, Fly"	T. W. Allen & Milo Sweet	T. W. Allen & Milo Sweet, pf & treble
"Sans Souci"	Percy Fridenburg	Anon., arr. Guy Whitney [pseud of Th. W. Allen]
"Battle Cry"	Clifford L. Waite	Clifford L. Waite, arr. T. W. Allen
"Bengal Swing"	Elisabeth K. MacMillan McHugh	Elisabeth K. MacMillan McHugh
"Cheer for the Beavers"	Edwin T. Reed	Lillian McElroy Hunt & Neil Reed, arr. T. W. Allen
"For Chicago"	Donald R. Richberg	T. W. Allen, music & arr.
"Fly Navy Fly"	T. W. Allen & Milo Sweet	T. W. Allen & Milo Sweet, arr. Freeman High for mixed voices
"Fly Navy Fly"	T. W. Allen & Milo Sweet	T. W. Allen & Milo Sweet, arr. Helmy Kresa for orchestra
"Roll Along, San Diego State"	T. W. Allen & Given [sic] Sweet	T. W. Allen & Milo Sweet, melody (unpublished)
"Wyoming Battle Song"	T. W. Allen & Gwen Sweet	T. W. Allen & Milo Sweet

COPYRIGHT DATE/NUMBER	SOURCE *Catalogue of Copyright Entries*, LoC Copyright Office (Washington: US Govt Printing Office)	COPYRIGHT NOTES (all copyrights held solely by T. W. Allen and/ or his company unless otherwise noted here)
06/02/1941 (19329)	(1941 New Series Vol. 36 No. 5 1941, 1168)	
09/23/1941 (41535)	(1941 New Series Vol. 36 No. 5 1941, 1676)	Allen Intercollegiate Music
09/23/1941 (41536–41541)	(1941 New Series Vol. 36 No. 5 1941, 1676)	Allen Intercollegiate Music
10/07/1941 (41794)	(1941 New Series Vol. 36 No. 5 1941, 1685)	
10/07/1941 (41796)	(1941 New Series Vol. 36 No. 5 1941, 1685)	
09/23/1941 (1268)	(1942 New Series Vol. 37 No. 1, 35)	
10/25/1941 (6255) © AIC, not T. W. Allen Co.	(1942 New Series Vol. 37 No. 1, 204)	Allen Intercollegiate Music
10/05/1942 (42993)	(New Series Vol. 37 No. 2, 1942, 1577)	
11/26/1943 [*sic*] (50878)	(New Series Vol. 37 No. 2, 1942, 1868)	
12/04/1942 (47859)	(New Series Vol. 37 No. 2, 1942, 1767)	
11/06/1942 (52785)	(New Series Vol. 37 No. 2, 1942, 1921)	This tune was used for many alma maters.
11/06/1942 (51016)	(New Series Vol. 37 No. 2, 1942, 1872)	
11/16/1942 (51038), © AIC	(New Series Vol. 37 No. 2, 1942, 1872)	Allen Intercollegiate Music
10/05/1942 (42206), © AIC	(New Series Vol. 37 No. 2, 1942, 1548)	Allen Intercollegiate Music
10/05/1942 (42787), © AIC	(New Series Vol. 37 No. 2, 1942, 1569)	Allen Intercollegiate Music
03/19/1943 (10968)	(New Series Vol. 38 No. 1, 1943, 364)	
03/19/1943 (10969)	(New Series Vol. 38 No. 1, 1943, 364)	
02/10/1943 (5871)	(New Series Vol. 38 No. 1, 1943, 185)	
03/01/1943 (7071)	(New Series Vol. 38 No. 1, 1943, 220)	

TITLE	TEXT AUTHOR(S)	MUSIC COMPOSER(S) AND/OR ARRANGER(S)
"On! Sooners"	T. W. Allen & Gwen Sweet	T. W. Allen & Milo Sweet
*wrote a number of WW2 songs in these years (not recorded in this table)		
"Roll Along, Maryland"	T. W. Allen	T. W. Allen, pf
Beloit College Song Book		Arr. T. W. Allen & others for mixed voices
"Eagles on Parade"		T. W. Allen, melody w/pf accomp.
"For the Glory of Wisconsin"		T. W. Allen, pf
"March on, Southwestern"		T. W. Allen, pf
"Salute to Wisconsin"		T. W. Allen, pf
"Sweep Down the Field"		T. W. Allen, pf
"Take Her Down"	T. W. Allen & Milo Sweet	T. W. Allen & Milo Sweet, pf
"Wisconsin Forever"	T. W. Allen	T. W. Allen
"I Want to Go Back to Old Beloit"		Arr. T. W. Allen
"In the Bond of Sigma Pi"	Arthur Sidnell	Tune, The Palisades, arr. T. W. Allen, mixed voices
"Fight On for Texas Tech"	T. W. Allen	T. W. Allen
"Texas Tech Has Got to Win"	T. W. Allen	T. W. Allen
"Let's Go, Texas Tech"	T. W. Allen	T. W. Allen
"Let's Go, Texas Tech"	T. W. Allen	T. W. Allen
"Texas Tech Has Got to Win"	T. W. Allen	T. W. Allen

COPYRIGHT DATE/NUMBER	SOURCE *Catalogue of Copyright Entries*, LoC Copyright Office (Washington: US Govt Printing Office)	COPYRIGHT NOTES (all copyrights held solely by T. W. Allen and/ or his company unless otherwise noted here)
03/01/1943 (8758)	(New Series Vol. 38 No. 1, 1943, 280)	
12/30/1943 (46525), unpubl.	New Series Vol. 38, No. 7, Second Half of 1943, 1519	
11/19/1943 (43394)	New Series Vol. 38, No. 7, Second Half of 1943, 1431	
12/30/1943 (44025), unpubl.	New Series Vol. 38, No. 7, Second Half of 1943, 1449	
12/20/1943 (44300), unpubl.	New Series Vol. 38, No. 7, Second Half of 1943, 1453	
12/20/1943 (45678), unpubl.	New Series Vol. 38, No. 7, Second Half of 1943, 1495	
12/20/1943 (46581), unpubl.	New Series Vol. 38, No. 7, Second Half of 1943, 1520	
12/30/1943 (47064), unpubl.	New Series Vol. 38, No. 7, Second Half of 1943, 1534	
12/20/1943 (47116), unpubl.	New Series Vol. 38, No. 7, Second Half of 1943, 1536	
12/20/1943 (48106), unpubl.	New Series Vol. 38, No. 7, Second Half of 1943, 1564	
11/19/1943 (44746), AIC	New Series Vol. 38, No. 7, Second Half of 1943, 1469	
11/19/1943 (45021)	New Series Vol. 38, No. 7, Second Half of 1943, 1477	
03/29/1944 (11307), unpubl.	New Series Vol. 39, No. 1, First Part of 1944, 380	
03/29/1944 (13642), unpubl.	New Series Vol. 39, No. 1, First Part of 1944, 445	
03/29/1944 (17461), unpubl.	New Series Vol. 39, No. 1, First Part of 1944, 591	
09/20/1944 (48880)	New Series Vol. 39 Part 2, Last Half of 1944, Nos. 7–12, 1707	
09/20/1944 (50489)	New Series Vol. 39 Part 2, Last Half of 1944, Nos. 7–12, 1752	

TITLE	TEXT AUTHOR(S)	MUSIC COMPOSER(S) AND/OR ARRANGER(S)
"O College Mother, Beautiful"	Paul W. Horn	Samuel A. Ward, pf
"On, Men of Clemson"	T. W. Allen	T. W. Allen
"Fight On for Texas Tech" and "Texas Tech Has Got to Win"	T. W. Allen	T. W. Allen, arr. Frank A. Panella, band parts
"Bulldog Rally Song"	Gwen Sweet	Milo Sweet
"Hurricane Fight Song"	Milo Sweet	Milo Sweet
"Nevada, We Salute You"	Milo Sweet	Milo Sweet
Auburn Songs ("Auburn Alma Mater"/"Auburn Victory March"/"Fight 'Em, Tigers")	William T. Wood/A. Traxler/Joseph Marino & William Sykes	William T. Wood/A. Traxler/Joseph Marino & William Sykes, arr. T. W. Allen
"Score, Stanford, Score"	T. W. Allen	T. W. Allen
Westminster College Songs (4)	(see © entry for author info—mostly other authors)	(see © entry for author info—mostly other authors)
"Army Blue" & "Alma Mater"	Paul S. Reinecke	Ferd Kucken, arr. T. W. Allen male voices
"Fight Song"	F. I. Lankey	F. I. Lankey, arr. Leonard Falcone, band parts w/conductor score
Stanford Songs		
"I Lift My Glass as the Years Pass By"	Grantland Rice	Henderson E. Van Surdam & Ted Eastwood, male quartet
Intercollegiate Band Folio No. 1		Arr. George F. Briegel, military band parts
"Sesquicentennial Song"	Robert Hood Bowers	Robert Hood Bowers
ALLEN'S COPYRIGHTS FOUND THROUGH OTHER SOURCES		
"Razorback Rootin' Song"	Jewell Hughes (class of '15) & Catharine Walker (class of '30)	William M. Paisley (class of '26), uke arr. Roy Smeck

COPYRIGHT DATE/NUMBER	SOURCE *Catalogue of Copyright Entries*, LoC Copyright Office (Washington: US Govt Printing Office)	COPYRIGHT NOTES (all copyrights held solely by T. W. Allen and/or his company unless otherwise noted here)
09/20/1944 (44680)	New Series Vol. 39 Part 2, Last Half of 1944, Nos. 7–12, 1569)	
10/25/1941 [*sic*] (15363)	New Series Vol. 40 Part 1, First Half of 1945, Nos. 1–9, 480	
04/26/1945 (23044)	New Series Vol. 40 Part 1, First Half of 1945, Nos. 1–9, 732	
04/10/1945 (17401)	New Series Vol. 40 Part 1, First Half of 1945, Nos. 1–9, 550	
04/10/1945 (18471)	New Series Vol. 40 Part 1, First Half of 1945, Nos. 1–9, 581)	
04/10/1945 (20079)	New Series Vol. 40 Part 1, First Half of 1945, Nos. 1–9, 627	
11/04/1936 [*sic*] (55386)	New Series Vol. 40 Part 2, Last Half of 1945, Nos. 10–12, 1843	
10/10/1945 (61411)	New Series Vol. 40 Part 2, Last Half of 1945, Nos. 10–12, 2014	
10/06/1945 (63119)	New Series Vol. 40 Part 2, Last Half of 1945, Nos. 10–12, 2062	
09/23/1941 [*sic*] (55312)	New Series Vol. 40 Part 2, Last Half of 1945, Nos. 10–12, 1841	
10/10/1945 (56951)	New Series Vol. 40 Part 2, Last Half of 1945, Nos. 10–12, 1888	
10/10/1945 (61945)	New Series Vol. 40 Part 2, Last Half of 1945, Nos. 10–12, 2029	Song Book compiled by a committee appointed by the Associated Students of Stanford University
06/11/1945 (57937)	New Series Vol. 40 Part 2, Last Half of 1945, Nos. 10–12, 1916	
10/26/1936 [*sic*]	New Series Vol. 40 Part 2, Last Half of 1945, Nos. 10–12, 1934	
10/10/1939 [*sic*] (61472)	New Series Vol. 40 Part 2, Last Half of 1945, Nos. 10–12, 2016	
1931		Footnote explaining what a Razorback is

NOTES

Introduction

1. This paragraph reprinted with permission from Carrie Allen Tipton, "Battle Sounds," *Deep South Magazine*, September 2, 2015, https://deepsouthmag.com/2015/09/02/battle-sounds.

2. Patrick B. Miller, "The Manly, the Moral, and the Proficient: College Sport in the New South," in *Sporting World of the Modern South*, ed. Patrick B. Miller (Urbana: University of Illinois Press, 2002), 30.

3. Flannery O'Connor called the South "Christ-haunted" in "Some Aspects of the Grotesque in Southern Fiction," *Mystery and Manners: Occasional Prose* (New York: MacMillan, 1969), 44. Eric Bain-Selbo, *Game Day and God: Football, Faith, and Politics in the American South* (Macon, GA: Mercer University Press, 2018). Charles Reagan Wilson describes the "Sports South myth, which views sports as central to the modern southern identity," in "Bryant, Paul W. 'Bear,'" *New Encyclopedia of Southern Culture*, vol. 16, *Sports and Recreation* (Chapel Hill: University of North Carolina Press, 2011), 264–65.

4. In "Music as Narrative in American College Football" (PhD diss., University of Kentucky, 2016), ethnomusicologist John Michael McCluskey uses ethnographic methodology to assess stadium music, marching band music, and sound effects in Power Five college football—currently the only book-length study of music in college football. Fight songs are briefly mentioned in John Sayle Watterson, *College Football: History, Spectacle, Controversy* (Baltimore, MD: Johns Hopkins University Press, 2000); Michael Oriard, *King Football: Sport and Spectacle in the Golden Age of Radio and Newsreels, Movies and Magazines, the Weekly and the Daily Press* (Chapel Hill: University of North Carolina Press, 2001) and *Bowled Over: Big-Time College Football from the Sixties to the BCS Era* (Chapel Hill: University of North Carolina Press, 2009); and Brian M. Ingrassia, *The Rise of Gridiron University: Higher Education's Uneasy Alliance with Big-Time Football* (Lawrence: University Press of Kansas, 2012).

5. Simon J. Bronner, *Campus Traditions: Folklore from the Old-Time College to the Modern Mega-University* (Jackson: University Press of Mississippi, 2012).

6. Mark Bernstein, *Football: The Ivy League Origins of an American Obsession* (Philadelphia: University of Pennsylvania Press, 2001), 97.

7. Scholarship on southern college football includes Andrew Doyle, "Causes Won, Not Lost: Football and Southern Culture, 1892–1983" (PhD diss., Emory University, 1998); Bain-Selbo, *Game Day and God*; and Andrew McIlwaine Bell, *The Origins of Southern College Football: How an Ivy League Game Became a Southern Tradition* (Baton Rouge: Louisiana State University Press, 2020); of these, Doyle and Bain-Selbo briefly address music. Journalistic books on southern football largely adopt a hagiographic stance, including Warren St. John, *Rammer Jammer Yellow Hammer: A Journey into the Heart of Fan Mania* (New York: Broadway Books, 2004); Clay Travis, *Dixieland Delight: A Football Season on the Road in the Southeastern Conference* (New York: Harper Entertainment, 2007); Ray Glier, *How the SEC Became Goliath: The Making of College Football's Most Dominant Conference* (New York: Howard Books, 2012); and Paul Finebaum, *My Conference Can Beat Your Conference: Why the SEC Still Rules College Football* (New York: Harper, 2014). They glorify SEC football achievements of the late twentieth and early twenty-first centuries through a focus on colorful characters, lively anecdotes, and hyperbolic fan behavior. Sources are mostly interviews, autobiographical reflections, and observations of fan rituals. Exceptions include Christopher J. Walsh's *Where Football Is King* (Lanham, MD: Taylor Trade Publishing, 2006) and the *ESPN Encyclopedia: Southeastern Conference Football*, ed. Michael MacCambridge (New York: Ballantine, 2009), which contain SEC statistics and historical data. Traditions, rituals, and fight songs are mentioned but not historicized in the journalistic books.
8. Robert F. O'Brien, ed., *School Songs of America's Colleges and Universities: A Directory* (Westport, CT: Greenwood Press, 1991); William Studwell and Bruce Schueneman, eds., *College Fight Songs: An Annotated Anthology* (New York: Routledge, 2011) and *College Fight Songs II: A Supplementary Anthology* (New York: Routledge, 2013).
9. Wald writes of scholars' tendency to minimize the contributions of more pedestrian jazz musicians such as bandleaders Paul Whiteman and Guy Lombardo in favor of highlighting the comparatively small recording catalogue of innovators such as Louis Armstrong and his Hot Five. This approach, derived from scholars' preferred aesthetics, obscures the historical reality of Whiteman's and Lombardo's popularity and dominance of average consumer preferences, partly through sheer volume of recorded output, in their own time—much more so than artists such as Armstrong. See Wald's Introduction to *How the Beatles Destroyed Rock 'n' Roll: An Alternative History of American Popular Music* (Oxford: Oxford University Press, 2011).
10. Karl Hagstrom Miller, *Segregating Sound: Inventing Folk and Pop Music in the Age of Jim Crow* (Durham, NC: Duke University Press, 2010).
11. Ken McLeod, *We Are the Champions: The Politics of Sports and Popular Music* (New York: Routledge, 2011), x.
12. Doyle, "Causes Won, Not Lost,"; Bain-Selbo, *Game Day and God*; Michael Lanford, "'When the Band Plays Dixie over Our Team, It Can Whip Eleven Red Granges': The Origin of Civil War Melodies in College Fight Songs" (paper presented at the Thirty-Sixth Annual Conference of the Society for

American Music, Ottawa, Ontario, March 21, 2010); Christian McWhirter, *Battle Hymns: The Power and Popularity of Music in the Civil War* (Chapel Hill: University of North Carolina Press, 2012); Derrick E. White, "Race, Football, and 'Dixie' at the University of Florida," *Florida Historical Quarterly* 88, no. 4 (Spring 2010): 469–96. For application of this idea to the University of Texas's "Eyes of Texas" fight song controversy, see Tipton, "Minstrel Songs."

13. Matthew Morrison, "Race, Blacksound, and the (Re)Making of Musicological Discourse," *Journal of the American Musicological Society*, 72 no. 3 (Fall 2019): 781–823; Morrison, "Blacksound" in *The Oxford Handbook of Western Music and Philosophy*, ed. Tomás McAuley, Nanette Nielson, Jerrold Levinson, and Ariana Phillips-Hutton (Oxford: Oxford University Press, 2021), e-book.

14. Ingrid Monson, *Saying Something: Jazz Improvisation and Expression* (Chicago, IL: University of Chicago Press, 1996), 103.

15. Gerald R. Gems, *For Pride, Profit, and Patriarchy: Football and the Incorporation of American Cultural Values* (Lanham, MD: Rowman and Littlefield, 2000), 50.

16. Gems, *For Pride, Profit, and Patriarchy*, 51.

17. Gems, *For Pride, Profit, and Patriarchy*, 51.

18. Doyle, "Causes Won, Not Lost," discusses the role of young women as "sponsors" at early white southern college football games, allowing college men to cosplay the gallant southern "Cavalier" ideal upheld in the game's early pageantry. Doyle also describes white southern women attending early games, and para-football activities such as gameday dances, for social purposes. Patrick B. Miller states that the presence of women in early southern college football culture dignified the sport. Miller, *Sporting World*, 33.

19. Hazel V. Carby, foreword to *Silencing the Past: The Power and Production of History* by Michel-Rolph Trouillot, 20th anniversary ed., (Boston: Beacon Press, 2015), xii.

20. "For the Glory of T.C.U" (Dallas, TX: C. Andrade III, 1938), voice and piano score of a football text that Rice co-wrote with other authors, Grantland Rice Papers, MSS.0364, Box 8, Folder 15, Vanderbilt University Special Collections and University Archives.

21. Dee Baily, "College Songs" (*Grove Music Online/Oxford Music Online*, 2012); see also historicization of the changing nature of this term between the 1850s and 1930s in Chapter 1.

22. Elijah Wald's *How the Beatles Destroyed Rock 'n' Roll* and Lloyd Winstead's *When Colleges Sang: The Story of Singing in American College Life* (Tuscaloosa: University of Alabama Press, 2013) briefly discuss college songs in the context of early twentieth-century collegiate music culture and practice. Neither delves into college song composition, publication, marketing, and reception. In *America's Musical Life* (New York: Norton, 2001), 717, Richard Crawford touches on the musical culture of 1920s college campuses and mentions the college song publishing niche, with a focus on the link between 1920s jazz, rebellion, and youth culture. Dee Baily wrote a short 2012 entry on the college song for *Grove Music Online/Oxford Music Online*. Alison McCracken's *Real Men Don't Sing: Crooning in American Culture* (Durham, NC: Duke

University Press, 2015) discusses how the 1930s pop culture vogue for all things collegiate was driven partly by crooners Rudy Vallée and Bing Crosby, rooted in college songs and campus glee clubs. McCracken's focus is on the performers' star texts and vocal style, not on the repertoire.

23. Watterson, *College Football*, 46.

24. Donald Gruensfelder documents how the "commercialization of college football, influence of professional sports, violation of the amateur spirit, [and] recruiting and subsidizing of athletes" concerned members of the Southern Conference (forerunner of the Southeastern Conference) as early as the 1920s in "A History of The Origin and Development of the Southeastern Conference" (MS thesis, University of Illinois, 1964), 40. Chapter 1 addresses more literature on this topic.

25. Jack Carey, *Jim Crow U: White Authority and the Idea of the Southern University* (unpublished manuscript, 2020). Many thanks to Carey for generously sharing his developing book materials.

26. Kolan Thomas Morelock, *Taking the Town: Collegiate and Community Culture in the Bluegrass, 1880–1917* (Lexington: University of Kentucky Press, 2008), 10.

27. Official SEC records were not available during this project due to their digitization in Texas A&M University's archives. Charlie Hussey, Association Commissioner of the Southeastern Conference, email to author, November 2019.

28. Work on the history and cultural significance of HBCU football music includes Frederick McKindra, "The Rich, Black, Southern Heritage of Hip-Hop Majorettes," BuzzfeedNews, May 7, 2019, https://www.buzzfeednews.com/article/frederickmckindra/marching-bands-hip-hop-majorettes-jsettes-prancing-elites; Robert H. Clark, "A Narrative History of African American Marching Band: Toward a Historicultural Understanding," *Journal of Historical Research in Music Education* 41, no. 1 (October 2019): 5–32; Antron D. Mahoney, "Reclaiming the Beat: The Sweet Subversive Sounds of HBCU Marching Bands," *Southern Cultures* 27, no. 4 (Winter 2021): 78–97.

29. Walker Percy, Introduction to William Alexander Percy, *Lanterns on the Levee: Recollections of a Planter's Son* [1941] (Baton Rouge: Louisiana State University Press, 1973), ix.

30. Carolin Duttlinger, "Walter Benjamin: Fragments, Salvage, and Detours," *Times Literary Supplement*, August 2019, https://www.the-tls.co.uk/articles/walter-benjamin-fragments-salvage-detours.

Chapter 1

1. "Tech Students Celebrate Their Clemson Victory," *Atlanta Constitution*, November 26, 1909.

2. "Tech Students Celebrate."

3. R. Murray Schafer popularized the concept of the soundscape as encompassing a given environment's sonic phenomena; see *The Soundscape: Our Sonic Environment and the Tuning of the World* (Rochester, VT: Destiny Books, 1994). John Michael McCluskey has applied this concept to the wide range of

sounds heard in modern college football stadiums; see "Music as Narrative in American College Football" (PhD diss., University of Kentucky, 2016) and "'Rough! Tough! Real Stuff!': Music, Militarism, and Masculinity in American College Football," *American Music* 37 no. 1 (2019): 29–57.

4. In 1869, Princeton and Rutgers University, under slightly different names, played the first significant intercollegiate game; in 1876, Columbia, Harvard, Princeton, and Yale formed the Intercollegiate Football Association; see John Grasso, *Historical Dictionary of Football* (Lanham, MD: Scarecrow Press, 2013). Andrew McIlwaine Bell's evidence of an earlier proto-football game scheduled and canceled between Washington and Lee University and the Virginia Military Institute a month before the Princeton-Rutgers match does not significantly alter the established understanding of the historical trajectory of the sport's adoption in the South in the early 1890s. Andrew McIlwaine Bell, *The Origins of Southern College Football: How an Ivy League Game Became a Southern Tradition* (Baton Rouge: Louisiana State University Press, 2020), 5–6. On college football's early years, see chapters 1, 2, and 3 of John Sayle Watterson, *College Football: History, Spectacle, Controversy* (Baltimore, MD: Johns Hopkins Press, 2000); the introduction of Michael Oriard, *Bowled Over*; chapter 1 of Lane Demas, *Integrating the Gridiron: Black Civil Rights and American College Football* (New Brunswick, NJ: Rutgers University Press, 2011); and chapter 1 of Winton U. Solberg, *Creating the Big Ten: Courage, Corruption, and Commercialization* (Urbana: University of Illinois Press, 2018).

5. Nicholas Syrett, *The Company He Keeps: A History of White College Fraternities* (Chapel Hill: University of North Carolina Press, 2009), 81; Brian Ingrassia, *The Rise of Gridiron University: Higher Education's Uneasy Alliance with Big-Time Football* (Lawrence: University of Kansas Press, 2012), 3–6; and chapters 1, 2, and 3 of Solberg, *Creating the Big Ten*.

6. Andrew Zimbalist documents the economics of college football in the 1880s in chapter 1 of *Unpaid Professionals: Commercialism and Conflict in Big-Time College Sports* (Princeton, NJ: Princeton University Press, 2001). Zimbalist also describes how the NCAA's 1905 founding "articulated a philosophy of amateurism, but [without] pretensions to coordinate the economic policies of its membership" (90). For more on early debates around amateurism in college football, see chapter 3 of Solberg, *Creating the Big Ten*, and parts 1 and 2 of Watterson, *College Football*.

7. See introduction and chapter 1 of Mark Dyreson, *Making the American Team: Sport, Culture, and the Olympic Experience* (Urbana: University of Illinois Press, 1998).

8. Syrett, *The Company He Keeps*, 43–44.

9. Morelock, *Taking the Town:* 71, 109–15, 120–21, 124–25, 135, and chapter 3.

10. Chapter 4 of J. Lloyd Winstead, *When Colleges Sang: The Story of Singing in American College Life* (Athens: University of Georgia Press, 2013). It wasn't until the mid-twentieth century that "college songs" had come to mean "songs about college life" or "songs of a specific institution" and included pep songs or football songs, which we now call fight songs.

11. Extant period college songbooks include *Songs of Yale* (New Haven, CT: T. H. Pease, 1855); Charles Wistar Stevens, ed., *College Songbook: A Collection of American College Songs with Piano-forte Accompaniment* (Boston, MA: Russell and Tolman, 1860); Henry Randall Waite, ed., *College Songs: A Collection of New and Popular Songs of the American Colleges* (New York: Oliver Ditson, 1880); and Thomas G. Shepard, ed., *College Songs and Glees: Including the Most Admired Songs, New and Old, Used in the Colleges of America* (Cincinnati, OH: John Church, 1896).

12. "Now It's a College 'Rooters' Meeting; How Athletic Teams Are Cheered to Victory . . . Some of the Old Songs That Are Sung," *Topeka Daily Herald*, December 7, 1901. "Marching Through Georgia" was a Union marching song celebrating General William T. Sherman's incendiary path to the sea through that state, composed by popular songwriter George F. Root.

13. John Thelin, *A History of American Higher Education,* 3rd ed. (Baltimore, MD: Johns Hopkins University Press, 2019), 156.

14. This phenomenon was part of a broader set of exchanges and perspectives regarding the South's economic, social, political, and educational flaws and prospects relative to the rest of the US or to "the North." See Natalie Ring, *The Problem South: Region, Empire, and the New Liberal State, 1880–1930* (Athens: University of Georgia Press, 2012) and Angie Maxwell, *The Indicted South: Public Criticism, Southern Inferiority, and the Politics of Whiteness* (Chapel Hill: University of North Carolina Press, 2014). John Thelin notes that no southern schools made "the historical lists of great universities in the early 1900s" (*History of American Higher Education*, 140).

15. Syrett, *The Company He Keeps*, 70.

16. Andrew Doyle, "Causes Won, Not Lost."

17. "Princeton Beaten by Sons of Old Eli," *Atlanta Constitution*, November 19, 1905.

18. "Princeton Beaten."

19. "Jing Dah-Dah, Boom! Football and Brass Bands Will Rule Today," *Atlanta Constitution*, February 20, 1892. The *Atlanta Constitution*, which historian Andrew Doyle describes as "the unofficial house organ of New South boosters," blurred the boundaries between reporting and promotion in the 1890s through deals with university and civic leaders which gave them shares of gate receipts from football games played in Atlanta (Doyle, "Causes Won, Not Lost," 4, 5–6).

20. Miller, *Sporting World*, 30. The Universities of Alabama and Georgia, Auburn University (then called Alabama Polytechnic Institute), Sewanee University, the Georgia Institute of Technology, and Vanderbilt University were the first proto-Southeastern Conference Schools to adopt football in the early 1890s, so the chapter relies on sources from them. By ca. 1910, other proto-SEC schools also had football programs.

21. Coach A. L. Bondurant, "Mississippi's First Football Team," *Mississippian*, November 12, 1913, facsimile of typed transcription in Billy Watkins, *University of Mississippi Football Vault: The History of the Rebels* (Atlanta, GA: Whitman Publishing, 2009), 20–21.

22. *Sewanee '95*, 1895, UA2 University of the South Athletics Records, Box 17, Folder 2, William R. Laurie University Archives and Special Collections, Sewanee University; football program, University of Tennessee vs. Sewanee, October 18, 1913, "Sewanee Marching Songs and Yells" (n.p.) contains "Yale Marching Song," "Princeton Cannon March," Yale's "Boola Boola," "Princeton Cannon March," and "Strike Up the Band," University of Tennessee Football Programs, Digital Collections, University of Tennessee Libraries.

23. Miller, *Sporting World*, 31.

24. "Jolly College Men," *Atlanta Constitution*, November 19, 1892.

25. Thomas Walter Reed, *History of the University of Georgia* (unpublished manuscript, ca. 1949), 3426–27, Hargrett Rare Book and Manuscript Library, University of Georgia.

26. "To-Day's Foot Ball Game," *Nashville American*, November 30, 1893.

27. In his introduction to *Hearing History: A Reader*, Mark M. Smith writes of the methodological challenge of reconstructing historical sounds and soundscapes, which requires scholars to "tease perceptions of sound from printed evidence" (Athens: University of Georgia Press, 2004), x.

28. "Techs 12, Mercer 12," *Atlanta Constitution*, November 22, 1896.

29. "Line Up, Boys!" *Atlanta Constitution*, November 18, 1893.

30. An early account of the cheer appears in Samuel R. Williamson, *Sewanee Sesquicentennial History: The Making of the University of the South* (Sewanee, TN: University of the South, 2008), 245. Later versions of the cheer ran "Rip 'em up, tear 'em up, leave 'em in the lurch! Down with the heathens, up with the church!" See also the many cheers and songs related to Vanderbilt in an untitled Sewanee football song booklet, 1895, UA2 University of the South Athletics Records, Box 17, Folder 2, William R. Laurie University Archives and Special Collections, Sewanee University.

31. See, for example, the 1892 Sewanee vs. Louisville Athletic Club football program. In the game's early days, printed programs like this oriented fans to the new sport by listing rules, printing team colors, and including texts of yells and cheers. This program, probably from Sewanee's first football season, printed the Sewanee cheer as "Rah! Rah! Ree! Var-si-ty! Hey! Yep! Hey! Yep! Se-wa-nee!" UA2 University of the South Athletics Records, Box 17, Folder 2, William R. Laurie University Archives and Special Collections, Sewanee University.

32. "Enthusiasm Is Aroused," *Nashville American*, October 22, 1909.

33. Grantland Rice, "Great Crowd Coming," *Nashville Tennessean*, October 29, 1907.

34. Grantland Rice, "Rousing Welcome for Wolverines," *Nashville American*, November 2, 1907.

35. Andrew Doyle writes of "football's triumph over oratory" and Nicholas Syrett describes football's displacement of rhetorical and literary societies on the late nineteenth-century campus. Doyle, "Causes Won, Not Lost," 88; Syrett, *The Company He Keeps*.

36. "The Weapons of Georgia's Lung Brigade," *Pandora* (Athens, GA: Fraternities of the University of Georgia, 1897), 189–90.

37. "Narratio Tristis Quaedam," *Corolla* (University of Alabama, 1893), 132–33.
38. "Jing Dah-Dah, Boom! Football and Brass Bands Will Rule Today," *Atlanta Constitution*, February 20, 1892. Beyond the headline, the article includes no information about the bands; judging from other reports within the next decade, the bands referenced in the headline were probably civic or regimental, not university-sponsored. During the 1904 Georgia-Georgia Tech game, the Sixteenth Infantry Band played. "Tech Team Captures State Championship," *Atlanta Constitution*, November 13, 1904. See also an 1892 account stating that "the Georgia boys made a very strong impression on the streets. Behind the Fifth regiment band they marched from the Kimball to Piedmont Park, making the air vibrate with college yells as they went." "College Boys Take Atlanta," *Atlanta Constitution*, November 28, 1892.
39. "Rivals of Long Standing Meet on Gridiron Today," *Atlanta Constitution*, November 28, 1901.
40. Robin J. Richards, *The University of Georgia Redcoat Marching Band: 1905–2005* (Charleston, SC: Arcadia Press, 2004).
41. "Tech Rooters to Have Band: Preparations Are Made to Offset Georgia's Great Rooting Proclivities," *Atlanta Constitution*, November 9, 1906.
42. *Kentuckian*, University of Kentucky, 1908, 122.
43. "Vanderbilt Brass Band," *Nashville American*, December 22, 1909.
44. "Great Tech-Georgia Game at Ponce de Leon Today," *Atlanta Constitution*, November 19, 1910.
45. "Techs 12, Mercer 12," *Atlanta Constitution*, November 22, 1896.
46. "Rivals of Long Standing Meet on Gridiron Today," *Atlanta Constitution*, November 28, 1901.
47. "Tech Students Celebrate Their Clemson Victory," *Atlanta Constitution*, November 26, 1909.
48. By contrast, some schools in other regions with established football traditions had dedicated stadiums or fields by the time southern schools adopted football. New Haven's Yale Field was used from 1884 to 1914 for football, at some point in that period accommodating 33,000 spectators. Harvard built a football stadium in 1903 with similar capacity.
49. Ingrassia, *The Rise of Gridiron University*, 9.
50. After the Supreme Court's *Plessy v. Ferguson* ruling about separate-but-equal facilities, African Americans in the South could not use hotels and trains as freely as could white students. Although these spaces were theoretically public, they were fully accessible only for the privileged.
51. In the Nashville press, sports journalists Claude "Blinkey" Horn and Vanderbilt alumnus Grantland Rice published prolific descriptions of college football pageantry.
52. For the history of Nashville and Atlanta in this period, see Don H. Doyle, *New Men, New Cities, New South: Atlanta, Nashville, Charleston, Mobile, 1860–1910* (Chapel Hill: University of North Carolina Press, 1990); Ronald H. Bayor, *Race and the Shaping of Twentieth Century Atlanta* (Chapel Hill: University of North Carolina Press, 2000); Louis Kyriakoudes, *The Social Origins of the*

Urban South: Race, Gender, and Migration in Nashville and Middle Tennessee, 1890–1930 (Chapel Hill: University of North Carolina Press, 2003); and Reiko Hillyer, chapter 5, *Designing Dixie: Tourism, Memory, and Urban Space in the New South* (Charlottesville: University of Virginia Press, 2014). For historiography of the Gilded-Age and Progressive-Era urban South, see Don Doyle, introduction of *New Men, New Cities*; David Goldfield, preface, *Region, Race, and Cities: Interpreting the Urban South* (Baton Rouge: Louisiana State University Press, 1997); Thomas Hatchett, "Race Shapes the New South City," *Journal of Urban History* 26, no. 2 (January 2000): 259–66; Kenneth A. Scherzer, "Southern Cities—How Exceptional?" *Journal of Urban History* 26, no. 5 (July 2000): 692–706; and Jeffrey Strickland, "Race and Ethnicity in Mobile, Alabama," *Journal of Urban History* 33, no. 1 (November 2006): 130–39.

53. Train receipts showed that 1,100 Auburn and University of Georgia students descended on Atlanta in November 1892 for the schools' first game ("College Boys Take Atlanta; College Colors, Yells, and Songs Were the Order of the Day Yesterday," *Atlanta Constitution*, November 28, 1892).

54. "Line Up, Boys!" *Atlanta Constitution*, November 18, 1893.

55. "Commodores Off for Yale Game," *Tennessean*, October 20, 1910, 7; "Vanderbilt Hopes to Hold Down Yale Score," *Tennessean*, October 20, 1910.

56. "Sewanee Tiger, Siss Boom Ah!" and "Parade the Streets and Yell Themselves Hoarse," *Tennessean*, November 6, 1909.

57. Map of Nashville, Tennessee (Marshall and Bruce Co., 1896), Map 1368, Tennessee State Library and Archives Map Collection. The Tulane Hotel was initially called the Nicholson Hotel, which is how it is designated on this 1896 map.

58. "'Old Alabam,'" *Atlanta Constitution*, February 21, 1892.

59. A play in the 1910 University of Kentucky yearbook written by students to dramatize the University of Kentucky-University of Illinois game indicates that Kentucky fans learned via telegram of their team's victory over the University of Illinois in fall 1909, then met them at the train station with a brass band to sing and cheer (*Kentuckian*, 1910, 272–75).

60. "Tech Students Celebrate Their Clemson Victory," *Atlanta Constitution*, November 26, 1909.

61. Doyle, "Causes Won, Not Lost," 134.

62. "Great Eleven," *Nashville American*, October 13, 1907.

63. Multiple articles, joint Sunday morning edition, *Nashville American* and *Nashville Tennessean*, October 23, 1910.

64. "Great Eleven Will Get Royal Welcome Home," *Nashville American*, October 13, 1907.

65. "Line Up Boys!," *Atlanta Constitution*, November 18, 1893.

66. "Tech Students Celebrate Their Clemson Victory," *Atlanta Constitution*, November 26, 1909. A 1907 Nashville rally held to welcome the victorious Vanderbilt team after an intersectional game included Tennessee governor Malcolm Patterson and Samuel Douglas, President of the Nashville Board of Trade. At the meeting, Governor Patterson stated, "the eyes of the whole

South were on you boys when you played . . . the whole South is proud of you . . . *in order to show you what you have done by your magnificent victory of last Saturday, I issue you a blanket pardon for anything you may do within the next two or three days.*" Emphasis mine; "Commodores Are Welcomed Home," *Nashville American,* October 16, 1907.

67. Untitled Sewanee football song booklet, 1895, UA2 University of the South Athletics Records, Box 17, Folder 2, William R. Laurie University Archives and Special Collections, Sewanee University. The text was set to the tune of George F. Root's Civil War song "Marching Through Georgia."

68. Marina Peterson, *Sound, Space and the City: Civic Performance in Downtown Los Angeles* (Philadelphia: University of Pennsylvania Press, 2012), 9. On sound studies literature that engages notions of sound, power, politics and public space, see Introduction of *Music, Sound and Space: Transformations of Public and Private Experience,* ed. Georgina Born (New York: Cambridge University Press, 2013); Michael Bull and Les Back, eds., *The Auditory Culture Reader,* 2nd ed (London: Bloomsbury Academic, 2016); and Kaleb Goldschmitt's review of *Music, Sound and Space: Transformations of Public and Private Experience* in *Ethnomusicology Forum* 24, no. 3 (2015), 485.

69. Mark A. Johnson, *Rough Tactics: Black Performance in Political Spectacles, 1877–1932* (Jackson: University Press of Mississippi, 2021).

70. Mark A. Johnson writes of political spectacles in this period of US history as embodying "political implications [that] influence the way that people understand and interact with the people and world around them and sensationalize society's norms, mores, and values." Johnson, *Rough Tactics,* 8.

71. Mark M. Smith, chapter 2 of *Listening to Nineteenth Century America* (Chapel Hill: University of North Carolina Press, 2001); Raymond W. Smilor, "American Noise," in *Hearing History: A Reader,* ed. Mark M. Smith (Athens: University of Georgia Press, 2004).

72. J. A. Anderson, City Attorney, "Peace, Good Order, and Morals," *Code of the City of Atlanta, Adopted by the Mayor and General Council, September 4, 1899, and Approved the Same Day* (Atlanta, GA: Byrd Printing Co., 1899), sections 1803–1806 and 1848, 414–15; 438. In Atlanta city records, these noise-governing codes were stable for years preceding and following the period covered in this section.

73. J. C. Bradford, *Charter of the City of Nashville and Other Acts of Assembly Relating Thereto, Published by the Authority of the Mayor and City Council* (Nashville, TN, 1885), 10; 216.

74. Edwin A. Price, city attorney, and K. T. McConnico, asst. city attorney, Part III, Municipal Regulations, Title II: Regulations to Secure Order, Decency, and Good Morals, *Digest of the Ordinances of the City of Nashville* (Nashville, TN: Boylin Printing Co., 1901), 497, 500–501, 518.

75. Trent Watts, ed., *White Masculinity in the Recent South* (Baton Rouge: Louisiana State University Press, 2008), 8.

76. Elizabeth W. Biggs, "Everyone Play: Sound, Public Space, and the (Re)Making of Place" (PhD diss., Princeton University, 2009), 16–18.

77. Thorstein Veblen, *The Theory of the Leisure Class*, reprint of 1st ed. (London: Taylor and Francis, 1992 [1899]).

78. Watts, *White Masculinity*, 15.

79. Andrew Doyle documents some opposition to football among university administrators and clergy based on the sport's violence and frivolous, wanton revelry in "Foolish and Useless Sport: The Southern Evangelical Crusade against Intercollegiate Football," *Journal of Sport History* 24, no. 3 (Fall 1997), 317–40.

80. Doyle, "Causes Won, Not Lost," 136.

81. Watterson, *College Football: History, Spectacle, Controversy*, 44.

82. James Connolly, "Bringing the City Back In: Space and Place in the Urban History of the Gilded Age and Progressive Era," *Journal of the Gilded Age and Progressive Era* 1 no. 3 (July 2002), 278.

83. Ted Ownby, *Subduing Satan: Religion, Recreation, and Manhood in the Rural South, 1865–1920* (Chapel Hill: University of North Carolina Press, 2014), ix.

84. Miller, *Sporting World*, 22.

85. Jack Carey, *Jim Crow U.*

Chapter 2

1. *Kentuckian* (University of Kentucky, 1910), 272–75.

2. This chapter reprints portions from Carrie Allen Tipton, "Minstrel Songs Like 'The Eyes of Texas' Were Once Common on Football Saturdays in the South," *The Andscape* [formerly *The Undefeated*], November 24, 2021, https://andscape.com/features/minstrel-songs-like-the-eyes-of-texas-were-once-common-on-college-football-saturdays-in-the-south. Copyright ESPN, reprinted courtesy of *The Andscape*.

3. Since southern PWIs often drew from a similar and fluid repertory of football songs ca. 1890–1910, the chapter uses sources from several schools.

4. Research exists on Lost Cause myths and symbols in early white southern college football, although it doesn't discuss music beyond noting the use of "Dixie." See Andrew Doyle, "Causes Won, Not Lost;" Patrick Miller, "The Manly, the Moral, and the Proficient: College Sport in the New South," in Miller, *Sporting World*; Andrew McIlwaine Bell, *The Origins of Southern College Football*; and J. Hardin Hobson, "Football Culture at New South Universities: Lost Cause and Old South Memory, Modernity, and Martial Manhood," in *The History of American College Football: Institutional Policy, Culture, and Reform*, ed. Christian Anderson and Amber Fallucca (London: Routledge Press, 2021). For an overview of the Lost Cause's roots and reach in southern and US culture, politics, and society, see Charles Reagan Wilson, *Baptized in Blood: The Religion of the Lost Cause, 1865–1920*, 2nd ed. (Athens: University of Georgia Press, 2009); Karen Cox, *Dixie's Daughters: The United Daughters of the Confederacy and the Preservation of Confederate Culture*, 2nd ed. (Gainesville: University of Florida Press, 2019); Adam Domby, *The False Cause: Fraud, Fabrication, and White Supremacy in Confederate Memory* (Charlottesville:

University of Virginia Press, 2020); and Edward R. Crowther's Introduction to *The Enduring Lost Cause: Afterlives of a Redeemer Nation* (Knoxville: University of Tennessee Press, 2020).

5. Cox, *Dixie's Daughters*; Wilson, *Baptized in Blood*.

6. Scholars have noted Confederate memorial events' use of these songs without connecting them to contemporaneous college football culture. Christian McWhirter documents Civil War and Stephen Foster songs in cultural expressions of the Lost Cause myth in *Battle Hymns* and Charles Reagan Wilson briefly discusses hymns and hymn *contrafacta* at Lost Cause events in chapter 1 of *Baptized in Blood*.

7. McWhirter, *Battle Hymns*, 205.

8. McWhirter, *Battle Hymns*, 205.

9. "The Public Schools: Exercises Conducted Yesterday in Honor of Gen. Robt. E. Lee's Birthday," *Wilmington Morning Star*, January 20, 1900.

10. "Kentucky Welcome," *Owensboro Messenger*, May 31, 1900.

11. "Toast the Old Flag," *Times-Democrat* (New Orleans, LA), May 23, 1903.

12. "Veterans of the Lost Cause Spend a Glorious Day," *Courier-Journal* (Louisville, KY), September 11, 1904.

13. Matthew Morrison, "Blacksound," in *Oxford Handbook of Western Music and Philosophy*, ed. Tomás McAuley, Nanette Nielsen, Jerrold Levinson, and Ariana Phillips-Hutton (Oxford: Oxford University Press, 2021), 557.

14. Morrison, "Blacksound," 570; 557.

15. Morrison, "Blacksound," 562.

16. Minstrel song composers were typically white, although their songs likely evinced white-Black cultural and musical exchanges that are impossible to unspool. Christopher Smith emphasizes Stephen Foster's late-1840s shipping clerk work on the Cincinnati waterfront as a key site of Black-white cultural exchanges. Smith, *The Creolization of American Culture: William Sidney Mount and the Roots of Blackface Minstrelsy* (Urbana: University of Illinois Press, 2013). Of these interfaces and their impact on popular culture, Smith writes that "dominant mainstream culture tends to appropriate from subordinate minority culture . . . as with its ambiguous and sometimes equally exploitative cousin 'representation,' appropriation is the heart of the process by which popular culture is born, transmitted, and transmuted" (21–22).

17. William Mahar, *Behind the Burnt Cork Mask: Early Blackface Minstrelsy and Antebellum American Popular Culture* (Urbana: University of Illinois Press, 1999), 1. A rich scholarly literature encompasses a range of interpretive stances on issues of agency, race, power, appropriation, and representation in minstrelsy, including Christopher Smith, *Creolization of American Culture*; Katrina Dyonne Thompson, *Ring Shout, Wheel About: The Racial Politics of Music and Dance in North American Slavery* (Urbana: University of Illinois Press, 2014); Brian Roberts, *Blackface Nation: Race, Reform, and Identity in American Popular Music, 1812–1925* (Chicago: University of Chicago Press, 2017); and Morrison, "Blacksound." In 1999, William Mahar described two "poles" of minstrel

research perspectives: scholarship that perceives "connections and mutually beneficial exchanges between white and black forms of cultural production in antebellum popular culture," and research that "emphasizes minstrelsy's debt to white fancy and its legitimation of racial domination" (*Behind the Burnt Cork*, 6). This still seems an accurate historiographic assessment. For a more recent historiographic overview of minstrel literature, see Karl Hagstrom Miller's essay on the twentieth anniversary of Eric Lott's landmark *Love and Theft: Blackface Minstrelsy and the American Working Class*, "Revisiting Minstrelsy: *Love and Theft* at Twenty," *American Music* 33, no. 2 (Summer 2015): 274–80.

18. Rae Lynn Barnes, "Yes, Politicians Wore Blackface; It Used to Be All-American 'Fun,'" *Washington Post*, February 8, 2019, https://www.washingtonpost.com/outlook/yes-politicians-wore-blackface-it-used-to-be-all-american-fun/2019/02/08/821b268c-2b0d-11e9-b011-d8500644dc98_story.html.

19. Mahar, *Behind the Burnt Cork*, 8.

20. Sandra Graham, *Spirituals and the Birth of the Black Entertainment Industry* (Urbana: University of Illinois Press, 2018), xi; 113; 126; 250–51.

21. Roberts, *Blackface Nation*, 182.

22. *Kentuckian* (University of Kentucky, 1907), n.p.

23. *Kentuckian* (University of Kentucky, 1903), 116.

24. *Kentuckian* (University of Kentucky, 1913), 165; "Louisville Cardinals Mourn to the Music of 20 to 0," *The Idea* 6, no. 11 (November 27, 1913).

25. "Alumni Celebration Is Feature of Week," *Kentucky Kernel*, December 2, 1915.

26. "Wildcat Band Receives Praise from Southern Newspapers, Citizens," *Kentucky Kernel*, November 23, 1923. Reinforcing arguments made elsewhere in this chapter, the *Kernel* account quipped that the Kentucky band and team went "Marching through Georgia," citing the Civil War song celebrating Union general William T. Sherman's incendiary march to the sea. The account also mentioned a minstrel show band fundraiser.

27. Gene Moore, "University Band Adds Lustre [*sic*] to the Triumphant Football Finish," *Kentucky Kernel*, December 5, 1924.

28. John H. Cowan, "Tribute to the Composer of 'My Old Kentucky Home,'" *The Idea* 6, no. 17 (January 22, 1914).

29. In his essay "Unveiling Black Labor," Steven Knepper describes how the southern plantation myth "focused on leisure in an idealized countryside, [and] offered a pastoral vision of the antebellum South," which could only be sustained by "veil[ing] the economics of the plantation and . . . the exploited black labor upon which it depended. . . . While some [white literary and artistic] depictions hid black labor altogether, most . . . naturalized it, aestheticized it, or refigured it as leisure," in *Reassessing the 1930s South*, ed. Karen Cox and Sarah Gardner (Baton Rouge: Louisiana State University Press, 2018), 13.

30. Despite interpretations of Foster's later minstrel songs as empathetic to enslaved people, many white Americans in the late nineteenth and early twentieth centuries likely heard "My Old Kentucky Home" as a sentimental

paean to a lost, romanticized South. This perspective was articulated in an anonymous feature in the September 23, 1897, *Valentine (NE) Democrat* that described "My Old Kentucky Home" as "one of Foster's "soul-stirring Southern melodies . . . characterized by melancholy presentiment that the days of slavery were numbered" and inspired by pastoral beauty that included "negroes performing their duties [and] lazy little darkies in the cabins." Of course, the song could function nostalgically only by its obscuring the violent reality of Black plantation labor.

31. *Florida Alumni Songs* (Gainesville, FL: University of Florida Alumni Association), undated songbook [likely early twentieth century], Digital Collections, University of Florida Archives.

32. "UF Songs and Yells," undated broadside, Digital Collections, University of Florida Libraries. Interestingly, "Old Folks at Home" did not appear in a sample of University of Florida *F Books* (annual booklets orienting freshmen to campus life) from the 1920s through the early 1960s. *F Books* from these years contained songs written for the University of Florida along with some tunes in the public domain: "We Are the Boys from Old Florida," "Orange and Blue," "March of the Fighting Gators," "Cheer for the Orange and Blue," "Cheer for Florida," "March On, Florida," and the alma mater (Powell Majors, editor-in-chief, *The "F" Book of the University of Florida, 1926–1927*, vol. II. no. 1, 17–19; Bob Matthews, editor-in-chief, *F Book 1935–1936 University of Florida*, 41–43; Bob MacLeish, ed., *The "F" Book of the University of Florida, 1946–1947*, vol. 19, 176–77; Don Bacon, ed., *The F Book: Official University of Florida Student Handbook, 1955–1956*, vol. 28, 116–17; *F Book 1960–1961*, vol. 32, 127), University of Florida Libraries, University Archives. University of Florida yearbooks and the student newspaper from the late nineteenth through mid-twentieth centuries contained few or no references to "Old Folks at Home."

33. Other southern PWIs used "Old Folks at Home." Michael Lanford cites a January 2, 1931, *Los Angeles Times* report ("Synthetic Southerners Aid Authentic Variety"), stating that the Pasadena Elks Band played "Dixie," "Swanee River" ["Old Folks at Home"] and "Maryland, My Maryland" in honor of University of Alabama fans at that year's Rose Bowl ("When the Band Plays 'Dixie'"). In addition to university usage, both songs were adopted by the respective states in which they are narratively set; in the late twentieth century, Kentucky and Florida legislators scrubbed the songs of racist epithets.

34. Tipton, "Minstrel Songs Were Once Common."

35. Knepper, "Unveiling Black Labor," 13.

36. Black man "Blind Jim" Ivy was involved in an unclear capacity with University of Mississippi football from the 1890s until 1955, traveling with the team and attending games. Recent fan literature framed him as an "enthusiastic supporter" who "encouraged and entertained fans"; extant photographs show him at games in a suit (Billy Watkins, *University of Mississippi Football Vault: The History of the Rebels* [Atlanta, GA: Whitman Publishing], 10). In this period the University of Georgia also used or employed a young Black man as a mascot figure, as did Louisiana State University in the 1930s.

37. William Rhoden, *Forty Million Dollar Slaves: The Rise, Fall, and Redemption of the Black Athlete* (New York: Crown Publishers, 2006) and Billy Hawkins, *The New Plantation* (Basingstoke: Palgrave Macmillan, 2010).

38. Michael Lanford and Christian McWhirter note the use of "Dixie" and "Battle Hymn of the Republic" at white southern college football games from the 1890s onward. Lanford, "When the Band Plays"; McWhirter, *Battle Hymns*. In "From Desegregation to Integration: Race, Football, and 'Dixie' at the University of Florida," *Florida Historical Quarterly* 88, no. 4: 469–96, Derrick White covers the use of Dixie in 1950s and 60s SEC football.

39. Reflective of minstrelsy's tangled compositional roots, the origins of "Dixie" are debatable, with recent scholarship arguing for acknowledgement of Emmett's "extensive tune-collecting from the free-black Snowden family of musicians, near whom he retired, in Knox Co., Ohio" (Christopher Smith, *Creolization of American Culture*, 31).

40. McWhirter, *Battle Hymns*, 66.

41. McWhirter, *Battle Hymns*, 195–204.

42. "Nothing So Good for College Discipline as Football," *St. Louis Post-Dispatch*, November 9, 1902.

43. "Commodores Give Yost Hard Fight," *Minneapolis Journal*, October 15, 1905.

44. "University of Michigan Defeats Vanderbilt by a Score of 24 to 6," *Tennessean*, November 1, 1908.

45. Untitled report, *Kansas City Times*, November 26, 1909.

46. F. K. B., "Georgia Rah," *Pandora* (Athens, GA: Fraternities of the University of Georgia, 1897), 189.

47. "Commodores Play Middies to a Standstill," *Nashville American*, October 13, 1907.

48. Andrew Doyle briefly notes the occasional use of songs like "Bonnie Blue Flag" ("Causes Won, Not Lost") in early college football as does Michael Lanford ("When the Band Plays"). To give only one example of primary source evidence for this, an 1895 booklet of Sewanee football songs set new football texts to Civil War tunes "Marching through Georgia" and "Bonnie Blue Flag (*Sewanee '95*, 1895), 11, 13, UA2 University of the South Athletics Records, Box 17, Folder 2, William R. Laurie University Archives and Special Collections, Sewanee University. These are only a few examples of what seems to have been a common trend in early proto-SEC football.

49. Steven Cornelius, *Music of the Civil War Era* (Westport, CT: Greenwood Press, 2004); Johari Jabir, *Conjuring Freedom: Music and Masculinity in the Civil War's Gospel Army* (Columbus: Ohio State University Press, 2017).

50. McWhirter, *Battle Hymns*, 206.

51. "Auburn's Colors," *Pandora* (Athens, GA: Fraternities of the University of Georgia, 1897), 190.

52. "Georgia Ready, Auburn Confident," *Atlanta Constitution*, November 22, 1898.

53. Untitled editorial, *Red and Black*, October 5, 1908, n.p., cited in Lanford, "When the Band Plays 'Dixie.'"

54. Robin J. Richards, *University of Georgia Redcoats Band: 1905–2005* (Charleston, SC: Arcadia Publishing, 2004), 12; C. T. Conyers, ed., *Georgia Songs and Airs* (Athens, GA: Georgia Glee and Mandolin Clubs), 1922.
55. Lanford, "When the Band Plays 'Dixie.'"
56. "Songs of the Georgia Bulldogs," University of Georgia Athletics, accessed April 27, 2020, https://georgiadogs.com/sports/2017/6/16/songs.aspx.
57. Jack Carey, *Jim Crow U*, chapter 1, "Origin Stories," 7.
58. Trent Watts, *White Masculinity*, 3. Although the Black-white binary is socially and historically constructed, it has operated powerfully in the South. As Jennifer Lynn Stoever writes, "Despite copious amounts of scholarship documenting the complexities of the US racial spectrum, the black/white binary still retains an enormous amount of symbolic weight and material consequence," *The Sonic Color Line* (New York: New York University Press, 2016), 21.
59. "Hail to U-G-A," words and music by Gaines W. Walter, appears on a lyric sheet of UGA songs from the UGA student days of Senator Richard B. Russell, Jr., torn from an unknown publication, ca. 1915. The song is now called "Hail to Georgia." In Richard B. Russell, Jr. Papers, RBRL/001/RBR, Richard B. Russell Library for Political Research and Studies, Special Collections Libraries, University of Georgia. Also printed as the second song after "Glory to Old Georgia" in Conyers, *Georgia Songs and Airs*.

Chapter 3

1. Although extant copies of "Old Vandy" are undated, Saidee S. Luff was in the Vanderbilt Class of 1904 and likely co-wrote the song during her student years. Saidee S. Luff and Emma L. Ashford, "Old Vandy," ca. 1904, Emma L. Ashford Papers, MSS.0027, Vanderbilt University Special Collections and University Archives.
2. See Chapter 5 for historical context on women's engagement with campus culture at white southern universities from the late nineteenth century to World War II.
3. Elijah Wald's *How the Beatles Destroyed Rock 'n' Roll* and J. Lloyd Winstead's *When Colleges Sang* briefly discuss college songs in the context of early twentieth-century collegiate music culture, although they provide little detail on styles, themes, composition, publication, dissemination, promotion, and reception. In *America's Musical Life: A History*, Richard Crawford briefly links 1920s college songs with jazz, rebellion, and youth culture (London: W.W. Norton, 2001). See also Dee Baily, "College Songs," *Grove Music Online/Oxford Music Online* (2012) and the introduction of Robert F. O'Brien's compilation *School Songs of America's Colleges and Universities: A Directory*. The latter does not historicize the college song phenomenon and contains factual errors.
4. Wald, *How the Beatles Destroyed Rock 'n' Roll*, 10–11, 62, 65, 84–85.
5. "A Bag of Wind: What Causes Whitlock to Blush," *The Blue Print* (Atlanta, GA: Students of the Georgia Institute of Technology), 1908, 138.

6. Frank Roman, "Ramblin' Wreck," (Atlanta, GA: no publisher), 1919, voice-piano sheet music, "Songs of Georgia Tech" vertical file, Georgia Tech Library, Archives and Special Collections.

7. Frank Roman, "Ramblin' Wreck," 192[?], unpublished manuscript orchestration, "Songs of Georgia Tech" vertical file, Georgia Tech Library, Archives and Special Collections. The orchestration likely dates from the early- to mid-1920s, when Roman led campus ensembles in recording and performing "Ramblin' Wreck."

8. The 1919 "Ramblin' Wreck" sheet music listed no publisher; along with the lack of a registered copyright, this suggests that Frank Roman worked directly with a printer without the intermediary of a publisher who might have filed, or encouraged Roman to file, a copyright.

9. Copy of "Son of a Gambolier" from unnamed songbook, enclosed with correspondence from Henry B. Welch, Attorney, to President's Office, Georgia Tech, December 1983, "Ramblin' Wreck" vertical file, Georgia Tech Library, Archives and Special Collections.

10. "Ramblin' Wreck from Georgia Tech," Copyright No. 4654, Library of Congress Copyright Office, *Catalogue of Copyright Entries* New Series, vol. 26 for the year 1931, nos. 1–12, 226–227. According to 1984 research by Atlanta law firm Newton, Hopkins and Ormsby, Melrose Music renewed its 1931 copyright in 1958 (Library of Congress correspondence with George M. Hopkins, April 1984, "Songs of Georgia Tech" vertical file, Georgia Tech Library, Archives and Special Collections). It is unclear which arrangement(s) Frank Roman's widow sold to Melrose.

11. A 1925 source gives 1902 as the date of Roman's arrival on campus ("Frank Roman, Director of the Band, Came to Tech 23 Years Ago," *Technique*, November 27, 1925, "Frank Roman" vertical file, Georgia Tech Library, Archives and Special Collections) while another source dated his campus arrival to 1911 ("'Wop' Roman, Tech Band Leader, Dies," *Atlanta Constitution*, December 20, 1928, "Frank Roman" vertical file, Georgia Tech Library, Archives and Special Collections). Both sources assert that Roman founded the Tech band, but later sources state that Michael Greenblatt directed the band from 1910 to 1913 and recruited Roman to take over ("When Did Ramblin' Wreck Start?" *The Georgia Tech Alumnus* Sept-Oct 1943, 9. "Ramblin' Wreck" vertical file, Georgia Tech Library, Archives and Special Collections).

12. "Frank Roman Dies Suddenly," untitled Georgia Tech publication, Vol. 7 No. 5, 1928, n.p., "Frank Roman" vertical file, Georgia Tech Library, Archives and Special Collections.

13. "'Wop' Roman, Tech Band Leader, Dies," *Atlanta Constitution*, December 20, 1928, "Frank Roman" vertical file, Georgia Tech Library, Archives and Special Collections.

14. O. B. Keeler, "Frank Roman," *Atlanta Journal*, December 20, 1928, and "Roman," *Atlanta Journal*, December 20, 1928, "Frank Roman" vertical file, Georgia Tech Library, Archives and Special Collections.

15. "Frank Roman Has Composed New Tech March, But Has No Words; Who Will Write Them?" *Technique*, March 26, 1926, "Frank Roman" vertical file, Georgia Tech Library, Archives and Special Collections.

16. Library of Congress Copyright Office, *Catalogue of Copyright Entries* Vol. 21 No. 1, 1926, 551 and Vol. 21 No. 2, 1926, 1654.

17. Frank Roman, "Up with the White and Gold" (Melrose Music, n.d.), photocopy of sheet music, "Ramblin' Wreck" vertical file, Georgia Tech Library, Archives and Special Collections.

18. "Radio News, Station WGST, Georgia Tech," *Technique*, November 20, 1925; "Frank Roman Has Composed"; "Director Frank Roman and Band Score Over WGST," *Technique*, March 25, 1927, "Frank Roman" vertical file, Georgia Tech Library, Archives and Special Collections.

19. Columbia Records W141072 and W141073, October 1, 1925 (*Discography of American Historical Recordings*, s.v. "Columbia matrix W141072. Ramblin' wreck / Georgia Tech Band," accessed January 31, 2022, https://adp.library. ucsb.edu/index.php/matrix/detail/2000030837/W141072-Ramblin_wreck and "Columbia matrix W141073. Ramblin' wreck / Yellow Jacket Four of 1925," accessed January 31, 2022, https://adp.library.ucsb.edu/index.php/ matrix/detail/2000030838/W141073-Ramblin_wreck); "Tech First College in South to Have School Songs Put On Record," *Technique*, November 6, 1925; "Send the Latest Columbia Record Home" (advertisement for "Ramblin' Wreck" record), *Technique*, November 20, 1925, "Ramblin' Wreck" vertical file, Georgia Tech Library, Archives and Special Collections.

20. "First Records of 'Ramblin' Wreck' On Sale November 9," *Technique*, November 6, 1925, "Ramblin' Wreck" vertical file, Georgia Tech Library, Archives and Special Collections.

21. *Discography of American Historical Recordings*, s.v. "Okeh matrix 73749. Rambling wreck from Georgia Tech / Jazz Pilots ; Johnny Marvin," accessed January 31, 2022, https://adp.library.ucsb.edu/index.php/matrix/ detail/2000205913/73749-Rambling_wreck_from_Georgia_Tech.

22. *Discography of American Historical Recordings*, s.v. "Okeh matrix W401493. Rambling wreck from Georgia Tech / Goofus Five Orchestra," accessed January 31, 2022, https://adp.library.ucsb.edu/index.php/matrix/ detail/2000210317/W401493-Rambling_wreck_from_Georgia_Tech.

23. The revue, directed by Charlie Calvert, performed in St. Louis, Dallas, New Orleans, Kansas City, and other cities, including a week-long residency at Atlanta's Howard Theater in October 1927 ("'Ramblin' Wreck' to be Featured in Sports Review; Opens in Howard," *Technique*, September 30, 1927, "Ramblin' Wreck" vertical file, Georgia Tech Library, Archives and Special Collections).

24. Roman, Frank, "Rambling [*sic*] Wreck from Georgia Tech," *Intercollegiate Song Book* (New York: Thornton W. Allen, 1927), 78–79.

25. "When Did Ramblin' Wreck Start?" *Georgia Tech Alumnus*, Sept–Oct 1943, 9, "Ramblin' Wreck" vertical file, Georgia Tech Library, Archives and Special Collections.

26. It is unclear whether the article refers to the 1919 sheet music marked "copyright Frank Roman" or to a band arrangement; either way, it repeats the

Tech community's common misperception that Roman filed a copyright on "Ramblin' Wreck." "When Did Ramblin' Wreck Start?"

27. Howard Cutter, 1945 letter to *Atlanta Constitution* quoted in John Dunn, "Ballad of the Rambling Wreck," *Tech Topics,* October 1985, 7B, "Ramblin' Wreck" vertical file, Georgia Tech Library, Archives and Special Collections.

28. "Monument for Tech Bandleader to be Unveiled," *Atlanta Constitution,* May 8, 1949; photograph of Frank Roman monument in Greenwood Cemetery (Atlanta Georgia, undated), "Frank Roman" vertical file, Georgia Tech Library, Archives and Special Collections.

29. Ed Danforth, "Georgia Tech Now Owns Its Famous Song . . . 'Rambling Wreck'" *Atlanta Journal and Constitution Magazine,* March 29, 1953, "Ramblin' Wreck" vertical file, Georgia Tech Library, Archives and Special Collections. Michael Greenblatt, "Ramblin' Wreck," typeset musical score in Georgia Tech Songs Collection, U318, Box 1, Folder 13, Georgia Tech Library, Archives and Special Collections. The score bears the typed note "as originally arranged by Mike Greenblatt" with a handwritten "1911." Although the archival inventory lists the score's date as 1911, it is probably Greenblatt's 1953 arrangement. If the 1911 version were extant, Greenblatt likely wouldn't have written a new one in 1953 to re-capture the sound of the song's early versions. The inscription on the copy, "To Louise and Dan MacIntyre, from Mike Greenblatt, 8/15/56," suggests 1953 would be a more likely date. Further, the score's copyright seal, "Registration Ep. 67254," uses an "EP" classification not employed by the US Copyright Catalogue until ca. 1950 (see https://www. copyright.gov/historic-records/admin-classification.pdf). "1911" may have been Greenblatt's indication that he first arranged the song *in this fashion* in 1911. I have been unable to locate the entry for EP 67254 in the 1911 or in the 1953 copyright catalogs (in the case of the 1953 catalogues, in the published, unpublished, or renewal sections), which would clarify the score's date.

30. Danforth, "Georgia Tech Now Owns Its Famous Song." The Atlanta Symphony Orchestra performed the "Ramblin' Reck [*sic*] Overture" on the Tech campus in January 1954.

31. Danforth, "Georgia Tech Now Owns Its Famous Song."

32. "Tech Renews Rights to Its Famed Songs," *Atlanta Journal,* April 8, 1954, "Songs of Georgia Tech" vertical file, Georgia Tech Library, Archives and Special Collections. In the absence of extant records, it is unclear how and when Georgia Tech acquired the copyright to "Alma Mater" and "Yellow Jacket March."

33. Danforth, "Georgia Tech Now Owns Its Famous Song."

34. "College Songs To Be Recorded on Copper Plates," *Technique,* December 18, 1925, "Ramblin' Wreck" vertical file, Georgia Tech Library, Archives and Special Collections.

35. Harold Martin, "No Offense Meant to Georgia Tech!" *Atlanta Constitution,* December 3, 1995, "Georgia Tech Songs" vertical file, Georgia Tech Library, Archives and Special Collections.

36. See earlier footnote about discrepancies regarding when Roman began directing the Tech band; note also the persistent belief in Roman's filing of copyright on "Ramblin' Wreck."

37. Untitled clipping, undated, "Ramblin' Wreck" vertical file, Georgia Tech Library, Archives and Special Collections. The clipping's reference to Nikita Kruschev and Richard Nixon singing the song at a meeting in Russia dates it to no earlier than 1959; it seems to be from an Atlanta newspaper.
38. Henry B. Welch, Attorney, to President's Office, Georgia Tech, December 1983, "Ramblin' Wreck" vertical file, Georgia Tech Library, Archives and Special Collections.
39. John Dunn, "Ballad of a Great Fight Song," *Georgia Tech Alumni Magazine* 60, no. 2 (Spring 1985), 19, "Ramblin' Wreck" vertical file, Georgia Tech Library, Archives and Special Collections.
40. Dunn, "Ballad of a Great Fight Song," and "Ballad of the Rambling Wreck," *Tech Topics*, October 1985, "Ramblin' Wreck" vertical file, Georgia Tech Library, Archives and Special Collections.
41. Dunn, "Ballad of the Rambling Wreck."
42. George M. Hopkins to John Culver (Assistant Vice President of Public Relations and Development, Georgia Tech), May 10, 1984, 2, "Ramblin' Wreck" vertical file, Georgia Tech Library, Archives and Special Collections.
43. Hopkins to Culver, May 10, 1984.
44. Hopkins to Culver, May 10, 1984. ASCAP is the American Society of Composers, Authors, and Publishers, and BMI refers to Broadcast Music, Inc.
45. Melvin Kranzberg and Editor, "Miners Sing Kindred Song," *Tech Topics*, Spring 1994, 2–3, "Ramblin' Wreck" vertical file, Georgia Tech Library, Archives and Special Collections.
46. UF grew from several Floridian higher education institutions of the latter nineteenth century; in the early twentieth century, the Gainesville campus became the most prominent of this network and assumed the University of Florida name. With this centralization of institutional power came a football program.
47. "Florida Yells 1911–12," UF Songs and Yells, University of Florida George A. Smathers Libraries, University Archives.
48. Gary Kirkland, "F-L-O-R-I-D-A, Or Is It T-O-L-E-D-O?," *Gainesville Sun*, October 9, 2005, https://www.gainesville.com/news/20051009/f-l-o-r-i-d-a-or-is-it-t-o-l-e-d-o. Searches of Library of Congress Copyright Catalogues for these three titles from 1906 through 1924 (1906 is the earliest year Kirkland's article stated that the song may have been "written" by someone) did not yield a copyright registered for any of the three titles in the article.
49. Miller Davis, "Our Orange Bowl: Color It Red," *Miami News*, January 2, 1964; Patrick Pinak's 2020 article lists possible "authors" and timeframes for the song's origins ("UF's 'We Are the Boys' Tradition Gives Gator Fans Chills," *Fan Buzz*, April 1, 2020, https://fanbuzz.com/college-football/sec/florida/we-are-the-boys-tradition.
50. Alan Ginsburg, "UF Fight Song Lives On After Author's Death," *The Alligator*, March 26, 1979.
51. Kirkland, "F-L-O-R-I-D-A."
52. The UF archives own a manuscript arrangement of "We Are the Boys" (SATB) by Bob Swanson (presumably Robert Swanson), which they date to

1943 (UF Songs and Yells, University of Florida George A. Smathers Libraries, University Archives). Neither Swanson nor anyone else registered this arrangement in the 1943 Library of Congress *Catalogue of Copyright Entries*.

53. "Program, The University of Florida Greater Minstrels, Season 1915," *Florida Alligator*, May 28, 1915; "Learn to Dance" advertisement, *Florida Alligator*, November 21, 1916; "Minstrel Makes Big Hit With Two Shows in Jax," *Florida Alligator*, May 7, 1920.

54. *The Seminole* (Gainesville: The Junior Class of the University of Florida, 1919), 201.

55. "Florida Minstrel Promises Comedy," *Florida Alligator*, March 12, 1920; "K. A. Easter Ball," *Florida Alligator*, April 23, 1920.

56. "University of Florida Songs," *Pensacola News Journal*, January 9, 1921.

57. "Yells and Songs," *The Seminole* (Gainesville: The Junior Class of the University of Florida, 1923), 191.

58. "James Melton, Famed Alumnus, Here Next Week," *Florida Alligator*, April 27, 1945.

59. "Students Harmonize Air in Jazzy, Radio Program," *Tampa Daily Times*, August 29, 1924.

60. "WDAE Plans to Broadcast New Features," *Tampa Times*, April 18, 1930.

61. "Florida's Official Songs to Be Sung at Chapel Exercises," *Orange and Blue Daily Bulletin (Summer School News)*, June 22, 1928.

62. "At 'Em Gators," Wilson Sporting Goods advertisement, *Tampa Tribune*, October 4, 1930. W. R. Frazier was the lyricist for UF song "Hail Florida," copyrighted in 1940 by Thornton W. Allen (Library of Congress, *Catalogue of Copyright Entries*, New Series, vol. 36, Part 1, First Half of 1941, nos. 1–4, 34). The *Tampa Tribune* article is the only source I've found linking Frazier to "We Are the Boys."

63. "Peek and Pokes," *Florida Alligator*, November 19, 1932.

64. "Final Program Is Rendered by Glee Club," *Florida Alligator*, May 22, 1932; "Stand Up and Cheer," *The Florida Alligator*, September 29, 1935.

65. Library of Congress, *Catalogue of Copyright Entries*, New Series, vol. 36, Part 1, First Half of 1941, nos. 1-4, 126. Allen's copyright applied to the arrangement, not to the tune and text.

66. *University of Florida Songs* (New York: Thornton W. Allen Co., 1940). The songbook contains six University of Florida songs and Stephen Foster's "Old Folks at Home," long associated with Florida and UF.

67. Bob Swanson, "We Are the Boys of Old Florida" (SATB), 1943, unpublished manuscript, UF Songs and Yells, University of Florida George A. Smathers Libraries, University Archives.

68. Jon Glass, "Committee Suggests Revisions to 'Sexist' Fight Song," *Alligator*, November 4, 1992.

69. Editorial staff, "Traditions," *Alligator*, November 18, 1992.

70. Jon Glass, "Committee Suggests Revisions to 'Sexist' Fight Song," *Alligator*, November 4, 1992.

71. Jack Wheat, "Decades-Old Song May Be Outdated," *Miami Herald*, November 1, 1992.

72. Mark A. Hoffman, Letter to the Editor, *Alligator*, November 9, 1992.

73. David Climer, "Some Fight Songs Are Out of Tune," *Tennessean*, October 29, 1992.

74. Bob Morris, "The Fun Is in the Sway at My Old F-L-O-R-I-D-A," *Orlando Sentinel*, November 27, 1992.

75. University of Florida, "Gator Traditions," https://floridagators.com/sports/2015/12/10/_traditions_.aspx, accessed June 28, 2020.

76. Scott Lange, "'To Hell' With It: Diversity Movement Talks of Change in Georgia Tech Song," *Technique*, February 6, 1988; Steve Faris, "Alum Pronounces Verdict on Fight Song Changes," *Technique*, February 13, 1988; Josh Daws, "Apology to the Diversity Task Force," *Technique*, February 27, 1988; Anthony Godfrey, "Does Task Force Represent Students?," *Technique*, February 27, 1988; Mindy Wiggins, "Ray: Changing Song Low on List of Priorities," February 13, 1988.

77. Lydia Goehr historicizes and theorizes the "work concept" in *The Imaginary Museum of Musical Works: An Essay in the Philosophy of Music*, rev. ed. (New York: Oxford University Press, 2007). Stephen Rose explains that the conceptual complexities of musical authorship in the European classical tradition, which informed understanding of copyright and authorship in early US popular music, arise from "music's dual existence in writing and in performance," adding that the idea of the notated musical work is linked in this tradition to the idea of an author, in *Musical Authorship from Schütz to Bach* (Cambridge: Cambridge University Press, 2021), 4.

78. Anjali Vats, *The Color of Creatorship: Intellectual Property, Race, and the Making of Americans* (Palo Alto, CA: Stanford University Press, 2020), 21. As Susan Scafidi writes in *Who Owns Culture?: Appropriation and Authenticity in American Law*, the US copyright system therefore "struggles to assign rights" outside the Enlightenment-derived, solitary-genius construct, leaving it unequipped to confer legal recognition on "group authorship" (New Brunswick: Rutgers University Press, 2005), 11.

79. Simon Frith and Lee Marshall concur that "the prominence of the [Western] idea of originality within copyright discourse" leaves no room for "the continuing process of re-creation" that marks much music-making, in *Music and Copyright*, 2nd ed., ed. Simon Frith and Lee Marshall (New York: Routledge and Edinburgh Univ. Press, 2004), 11.

80. Jim Samson, "The Musical Work and Nineteenth-Century History," in *The Cambridge History of Nineteenth-Century Music* ed. Jim Samson, (Cambridge: Cambridge University Press, 2002), 24. Samson is referring to "musical life" in Western Europe prior to the emergence of the work concept in the nineteenth century, but his statement applies here. On copyright in early twentieth-century US popular music, see Jane Mathieu, "'The Injustice of the Thing': Negotiating the Song Market in the U.S. Copyright Debates of 1906–1910," *Popular Music* 44, no. 3 (2021), 292–305.

81. "Man Claims Snow White Air as His Own," *Pittsburgh Post-Gazette*, May 27, 1938; syndicated untitled notice in *Great Falls Tribune* (Great Falls, MT), October 22, 1938, and *Daily Oklahoman*, October 24, 1938; David Felts, "Second Thoughts" column, *Decatur Herald* (Decatur, IL), October 25, 1938.

82. Court proceedings, *Allen v. Walt Disney Productions, Ltd. et al.*, 41 F. Supp. 134 (Southern District New York, 1941), June 27, 1941.

83. Court proceedings, *Allen v. Walt Disney Productions, Ltd. et al.*, 41 F. Supp. 134 (Southern District New York, 1941), June 27, 1941.

Chapter 4

1. Among other examples, the broadside "Florida Yells 1911–12" contained the "Washington and Lee Swing" (UF Yells and Songs, George A. Smathers Libraries, University of Florida Special Collections and Archives).

2. "Davidson Offers a Prize for Best Song," *Concord Daily Tribune* (Concord, NC), October 21, 1916.

3. See the appendix for a list of Thornton W. Allen's college song copyrights.

4. Winstead, *When Colleges Sang*, 161.

5. Oriard, *King Football*, 11, 28–29. John Sayle Watterson documents college football's professionalization, increased game attendance, and new stadiums amid growing college enrollment ca. 1919–1925 in chapter 8, *College Football*. Raymond Schmidt's preface to *Shaping American Football: The Transformation of an American Sport, 1919–1930* describes the 1920s as a foundational era in establishing college football as a US pastime as the media glamorized and nationalized it (Syracuse, NY: Syracuse University Press, 2007).

6. Thelin, *A History of American Higher Education*, 157. In 1927, Thornton W. Allen attributed increased demand for college songs to the football craze in the Preface of his *Intercollegiate Song Book: Alma Mater and Football Songs* (New York: Thornton W. Allen Company, 1927).

7. "Interest in College Songs: Spirited Demand for That Variety of Sheet Music Explained by Announcement of Contest," *Presto*, December 1922, 24.

8. Wald, *How the Beatles Destroyed Rock 'n' Roll*, 64. On college-driven youth culture of the 1920s and its foundational contributions to US ideas about leisure, conformity, family, and other sociological aspects, see Paula Fass, *The Damned and the Beautiful: American Youth in the 1920s* (Oxford: Oxford University Press, 1977).

9. Richard J. Dyer, *Stars*, 3rd ed. (London: BFI Publishing, 1979).

10. Fass, *The Damned and the Beautiful*, 126–28, 230–31.

11. Fass, *The Damned and the Beautiful*, 369.

12. "'Washington and Lee Swing' Being Published," *Ring-Tum Phi*, May 11, 1910.

13. "College Spirit Runs Riot at Lexington," *Newport News* (Newport, VA), November 9, 1912.

14. Thornton Allen encouraged this flexibility in the 1930s by publishing a "College Edition" (2/4 time march) and "Popular Edition" (lilting 6/8 version) of the song.

15. "Pleasant Dance," *Tampa Times*, August 1, 1914.

16. Myrtle Garrett Kiley, ed., "Society," *Austin American-Statesman*, November 25, 1915.

17. Advertisement, *Times* (Shreveport, LA), December 16, 1916.

18. "Leap-Year Tea Dance Final Social Affair of Holidays," *Tampa Times*, January 5, 1920.

19. "Swing to be Published Soon," *Ring-Tum Phi*, April 27, 1920. This article quoted a letter from New York's Fifth Avenue Publishing Company about their plans to buy "Swing" rights from Thornton Allen and distribute the song "all over the South," ensuring it was "widely advertised" in the region. The letter cited orders received from "across the South and North" for the song's 1920 edition. On Tin Pan Alley's southern song trend, see chapter 1 in Karen Cox, *Dreaming of Dixie*.

20. *Discography of American Historical Recordings*, s.v. "Allen, Thornton W.," accessed August 26, 2022, https://adp.library.ucsb.edu/names/109451.

21. In lieu of extant Thornton W. Allen Company records from this period, the song's early publication history must be pieced together with sheet music, US copyright records, and coverage in Washington and Lee University student and alumni publications.

22. "'Washington and Lee Swing' Being Published," *Ring-Tum Phi*, May 11, 1910. This article states it was being published "by a New York house." This may have referred to the location of the music printer, or Thornton Allen may have obtained a New York postal address for his publishing company.

23. "'Washington and Lee Swing' Production of Three Students," *Ring-Tum Phi*, February 18, 1919; "The Washington and Lee Swing," *Alumni Magazine*, July 1927, 21–22; "From W. T. Riviere, '12," *Alumni Magazine*, November 1927, 26; "'And We Will Roll Virginia' . . . Author of 'Swing' to See Game," *Ring-Tum Phi*, November 9, 1934.

24. Untitled notice re. new text for Mark Sheafe's "Washington and Lee Swing," *Ring-Tum Phi*, October 26, 1908; "General Words for 'Washington and Lee Swing,'" *Ring-Tum Phi*, January 25, 1909.

25. "The University Band Appears," *Ring-Tum Phi*, February 2, 1910.

26. Library of Congress Copyright Office, *Catalogue of Copyright Entries Part Three*, New Series, vol. 5, Part I, Jan-June, 1910, nos. 1-26, 884. The 1910 "Swing" entry assigned textual copyright to Robbins and musical copyright to Allen and Sheafe. It also complicates the question of authorship by mentioning another Washington and Lee student not named in accounts of the song's history cited in this chapter, noting that on May 19, Thornton Allen and Robert G. Thach filed a joint copyright for the music. Thach's name appears on early sheet music versions, although later versions indicate the copyright for music and words was transferred to Allen in 1930. Robert Thach was a significant campus figure, active as football team manager, president of the Washington and Lee spring ball, and in musical organizations and fraternities (*Calyx* yearbook, 1910–1913; "Virginia Zeta, Washington and Lee University," *Phi Delta Theta Scroll*, vol. XXXV, September/November 1910, 67, 228, 351).

27. "Swing to Be Published Soon," *Ring-Tum Phi*, April 27, 1920.

28. "Copies of Swing to be Here by 22nd," *Ring-Tum Phi*, May 11, 1920; Thornton W. Allen, "The 'Washington and Lee Swing,'" *Alumni Magazine*, November 1924, 13, 26.

29. Some versions hinted at the song's confusing origins. The cover of Allen's 1930s "College Edition" indicated that the "Swing" music was by Thornton Allen and Mark Sheafe with text by Allen and Clarence Robbins, but the interior stated "Music by Thornton W. Allen, suggested by M. W. Sheafe."

30. See Allen's earliest known comments about copyright infringement of the "Swing" in Thornton W. Allen, "The 'Washington and Lee Swing,'" *Alumni Magazine*, November 1924, 13, 26; and his comments regarding ownership in "'Swing' Plagiarized by Other Students," *Ring-Tum Phi*, November 18, 1925, printed fully in "Continued Abuse of the 'Swing,'" *Alumni Magazine*, October 1925, 22. In a 1931 scuffle with Rudy Vallée over misattribution of the "Swing" to Tulane University, Allen did not correct Vallée when the singer referred to him publicly as the sole "composer" of the "Swing" ("Band Leader Writes Story about Swing," *Ring-Tum Phi*, March 3, 1931).

31. The scant extant documentation of this lawsuit appears in the next chapter.

32. Thornton W. Allen, "The 'Washington and Lee Swing,'" *Alumni Magazine*, November 1924, 13, 26.

33. "'And We Will Roll Virginia.'"

34. "He Wrote the Words to the Immortal Swing," *Alumni Magazine*, November 1934, 14.

35. "A New Washington and Lee Songbook," *Alumni Magazine*, May 1941, 4.

36. Robert Bleakley James Jr., "The Ubiquitous Swing," *Alumni Magazine of Washington and Lee*, July 1978, 9–10.

37. James, "The Ubiquitous Swing," 10.

38. By 1895, the popularity of the "Zacatecas March" in the US had merited a third edition of the piano score from San Francisco's Armstrong and Bacon (Lester S. Levy Sheet Music Collection, Johns Hopkins University Sheridan Libraries and Museums); other companies published editions of it, including Chicago's National Music Company (Historic American Sheet Music Collection, Duke University Repository Collections and Archives). Early twentieth-century recordings were made by Banda de Zapadores (1905, Victor Records' "Spanish Music" line; *Discography of American Historical Recordings*, s.v. "Victor matrix 112-Z. Zacatecas / Banda de Zapadores," accessed April 12, 2021, https://adp.library.ucsb.edu/index.php/matrix/detail/600000126/112-Z-Zacatecas) and Banda Espanola (Columbia Records, 1906) ("New Columbia Records: June 1906" advertisement, *The Chat* [Brooklyn, NY], May 26, 1906). For documentation of "Zacatecas March" US performances in this era, see "Mexican Band," *Brownsville (TX) Herald*, July 6, 1896; "Successful Recital," *Dayton (OH) Herald*, August 31, 1898; "Music," *Los Angeles Evening Express*, February 25, 1899; "Commencement Exercises at Pettsgrove," *Miltonian* (Milton, PA), June 16, 1899; "President Diaz' Day," *Arizona Republic*, September 16, 1903; "Tuesday Marks Fair Opening: Music in Auditorium," *Bangor (ME) Daily News*, August 28, 1906. The "Zacatecas March" was performed in Richmond, Virginia, in 1906; see Untitled Concert Notice, March misattributed to G. W. Niles, *Times-Dispatch* (Richmond, VA), February 17, 1906.

39. Thornton. W. Allen Obituary, "The Final Curtain," *Billboard*, August
    12, 1944, 31; "Allen, Thornton W.," Daniel McNamara, ed., *The ASCAP
    Biographical Dictionary of Composers, Authors, and Publishers*, 2nd ed. (New
    York: Thomas Y. Crowell Company, 1952). Despite Allen's importance
    in US music history and his national reputation in his own time as a
    composer, arranger, publisher, critic, and impresario, no scholarship exists
    on him. This chapter triangulates information about Allen's life and career
    from newspapers, music trade journals, Washington and Lee University
    student and alumni publications, and scattered correspondence with
    Allen's company clients extant in archives. No single archival collection
    of Thornton W. Allen's papers seems to exist. Some sources contain
    errors, such as the ASCAP biographical entry cited, which attributes the
    composition of the "Washington and Lee Swing" exclusively to Allen when
    the reality was murkier, as this chapter shows.
40. "Allen, Thornton Whitney," Cesar Saerchinger, ed., *International Who's Who
    in Music and Musical Gazetteer* (New York: Current Literature Publishing Co.,
    1918), 18–19. For Allen's college musical activities, see Washington and Lee
    University *Calyx* yearbooks, 1910–1913.
41. "Virginia Zeta, Washington and Lee University," *Phi Delta Theta Scroll* vol.
    XXXV, September/November 1910, 228.
42. Allen boasted expansively that large music festivals would generate revenues
    for local instrument sellers, publishers, sheet music stores, Victrola dealers,
    street cars, taxicabs, carriages, trains, cafes, department stores, tailors, shoe-
    sales, milliners, and more (Thornton W. Allen, "Music Festivals," *News and
    Observer* (Raleigh NC), April 30, 1916.
43. Untitled notice, *Morning Call* (Paterson, NJ), May 29, 1915.
44. Untitled notice, *Morning Call* (Paterson NJ), January 25, 1916.
45. "The Newark Musical Receptions," *Newarker*, Sept-Oct 1916, 330-331.
46. "Great Series of Concerts: Homer, Martinelli, Kreisler and Others to Appear
    in Newark This Season," *Montclair Times* (Montclair, NJ), November 3, 1917.
47. 1915 census records listed Allen's occupation as "Editor, *Musical Courier*";
    this was likely inaccurate ("New Jersey State Census, 1915," database with
    images, *FamilySearch* (https://familysearch.org/ark:/61903/1:1:QV9Q-3VY4
    : 23 February 2021), Thornton W. Allen in household of Lyman W Allen,
    Newark, 9 ward, 12 district, Essex, New Jersey, United States; citing sheet #2B,
    household 38, line #68, New Jersey State Library, Trenton; FHL microfilm
    1,465,520). Allen's name appeared neither on the *Courier* masthead nor in
    its list of associate editors. A brief untitled notice in the December 2, 1916,
    Musical Courier stated that Allen had been a "Newark representative" of the
    Courier but that he was "no longer connected with this paper. Mr. Allen is
    devoting all of his time to the Hotel Robert Treat (Newark) concerts and
    other interests, musical and mercantile."
48. "United States World War I Draft Registration Cards, 1917–1918," database
    with images, *FamilySearch* (https://familysearch.org/ark:/61903/3:1:33S7-8BTQ-
    KP6?cc=1968530&wc=9FHJ-FM9%3A928311801%2C928835101 : 22 October

2019), New Jersey > Newark City no 4; A-B > image 71 of 1000; citing NARA microfilm publication M1509 (Washington, DC: National Archives and Records Administration, n.d.).

49. "'Swing' to be Published Soon," *Ring-Tum Phi*, April 27, 1920.

50. "United States World War I Draft Registration Cards, 1917–1918. Allen may have served in World War I, but likely not in active combat due to the health exemption cited earlier; I have been unable to find government records confirming this ("'Swing' to be Published Soon.")

51. See Appendix.

52. Thornton W. Allen, "Virginia and the South: Part Four," *Musical Courier*, June 30, 1915, 31-32.

53. Allen was using a known economic tactic wherein southern boosters tried to attract northern capital to invest in the US South by boasting of untapped resources, opportunities, and labor and consumer sectors in the region; see Hillyer, *Designing Dixie*.

54. Allen, preface, *Intercollegiate Song Book*.

55. Joshua Gailey, "Beginning Bands: Progressive Reform and the Birth of the American School Band Industry, 1907–1940" (PhD diss., Yale University, 2019), 25–29; footnotes 14–15 provide a historiographic overview of "good music" discourse in early twentieth-century US music.

56. See chapter 5 of Miller, *Segregating Sound*.

57. Thornton W. Allen, "Virginia and the South: Part Seven," *Musical Courier*, July 21, 1915, 18. These kinds of descriptions reflected "enlightenment conceptions of colonial subjects as barbarous, childlike, innocent, and without higher intellectual capacity" which shaped white Americans' ideas about people of color as creators of intellectual and artistic property, in Vats, *The Color of Creatorship*, 195.

58. Thornton W. Allen, "Virginia and the South: Part One," *Musical Courier*, June 2, 1915, 38. Allen referred to the "mammy" figure as a source of musical nurturing later in the series: "The Southerner owes a great deal to the old negro mammie—the same old mammie who nursed him, taught him to walk, and gave him his first musical training, his first lesson in real negro music" (Part Six, July 14, 1915, 31).

59. Thornton W. Allen, "Virginia and the South: Part Three," *Musical Courier*, June 23, 1915, 39. Emphasis added.

60. Thornton W. Allen, "Virginia and the South: Part Seven," *Musical Courier*, July 21, 1915, 18.

61. Thornton W. Allen, "Virginia and the South: Part Seven," *Musical Courier*, July 21, 1915, 18.

62. Thelin, *A History of American Higher Education*, 168.

63. Thelin, *A History of American Higher Education*, 169; 186.

64. Thelin, *A History of American Higher Education*, 186.

65. Anjali Vats, *The Color of Creatorship*, 29.

66. Jane Mathieu, "The Injustice of the Thing," 292–305.

67. Morrison, "Blacksound."

68. Anna Case's "Metropolitan Rag" for piano was copyrighted by the Thornton W. Allen Company on March 21, 1917 (*Catalogue of Copyright Entries* New Series, vol. 12, Annual Index for 1917, nos. 1–9, 301).

69. In 1903, Black composer Will Marion Cook wrote the ragtime-inflected "Swing Along" for the show *In Dahomey*, which toured the US from 1903 to 1907. In 1912, Cook published sheet music for "Swing Along," further spreading the syncopated song. Richard Crawford, *America's Musical Life: A History* (New York: Norton, 2001), 535–36. By the time the "Washington and Lee Swing" was published in 1910, "swing" would have likely evoked the cultural cachet of Black popular music, rhythm, and dance through, e.g., Arthur Collins's and Byron Harlan's recording of "Swingin' in de Sky" (Victor B-9037, 1910) and recordings of the spiritual "Swing Low, Sweet Chariot," such as a 1909 Victor record by the Fisk Jubilee Singers (Victor B-8420).

Chapter 5

1. Amy Thompson McCandless, "Maintaining the Spirit and Tone of Robust Manliness: The Battle against Coeducation at Southern Colleges and Universities, 1890–1940," *NWSA Journal* 2, no. 2 (Spring 1990): 211.

2. Howard Odum, *Southern Regions of the United States* (Chapel Hill: University of North Carolina Press, 1936), 114–15.

3. Andrew Doyle, "Causes Won, Not Lost," discusses the role of young women (students and otherwise) as "sponsors" of early southern college football games, allowing male participants to inhabit the role of the gallant southern "Cavalier" ideal upheld in the game's early pageantry and ritual. Doyle also describes gameday rituals surrounding early southern football at which women attended games, and para-football activities such as gameday dances, for social purposes. Patrick B. Miller states that the presence of women in early southern college football culture dignified the sport; they engaged in it only as a social event, in Miller, *Sporting World*, 33. In assessing women's participation in football culture at the national level, Historian John Sayle Watterson states that "in the early days . . . women played a highly visible role in big-time football," which he nebulously describes as meaning that they "embraced the spectacle" and demonstrated a "grasp of the game," but only as "part of the colorful backdrop" of the sport in the late nineteenth century. Watterson's only concrete examples of women's engagement with early college football fall in the "minor yet identifiable niche" of shaping "policy through marriage to coaches and presidents." Watterson attributes some of this to Progressive-era gender segregation in football: "as cheering and singing at games became more organized, women were seen as a distraction. No longer were co-eds or off-campus female admirers encouraged to attend cheer practice," and there were pushes for all-male cheering sections and gender-segregated stadium seating, in Watterson, *College Football*, 99–100. In explaining the lack of roles for women in college football culture immediately

post–World War I, Brian Ingrassia argues that male students of the time were "alarmed at women's increased interest in sports, or were trying to reclaim space from female students," in *The Rise of Gridiron University: Higher Education's Uneasy Alliance with Big-Time Football* (Lawrence: University of Kansas Press, 2012), 146.

4. Gerald R. Gems, *For Pride, Profit, and Patriarchy: Football and the Incorporation of American Cultural Values* (Lanham, MD: Rowman and Littlefield, 2000), 50.

5. Gems, *For Pride, Profit, and Patriarchy*, 51.

6. Gems, *For Pride, Profit, and Patriarchy*, 58.

7. On martial, hypermasculine elements in the college football soundscape, see McCluskey, "'Rough! Tough!,'" 29–57.

8. Robin J. Richards, *University of Georgia Redcoats Band*, 14.

9. Vanderbilt football player and World War I casualty Irby Rice Kirby was lauded for his sacrifice for years afterward in Nashville papers and Vanderbilt publications, which linked his bravery with football heroics and training, in Fred Russell and Maxwell E. Benson, eds., *Fifty Years of Vanderbilt Football* (Nashville, TN: Russell and Benson, 1938), 36–38. Flowery rhetoric coupling southern football players' World War I bravery with sports-honed physical prowess and mental grit was common in wartime discourse and in later retrospection; see Fuzzy Woodruff's reminiscences of wartime football heroes in his *History of Southern Football, 1890–1928* (Atlanta, GA: Walter W. Brown, 1928), 49.

10. "Aggie Traditions: Aggie Songs," Texas A&M University, accessed August 31, 2020, https://www.tamu.edu/traditions/gameday/aggie-songs/index.html.

11. George Carmack, "'Aggie War Hymn' is Greatest of All," *San Antonio Express-News*, March 1, 1975, "Pinky Wilson" biographical/vertical file, Cushing Memorial Library and Archives, Texas A&M University.

12. Carmack, "'Aggie War Hymn.'"

13. "Class of 1920," *The Longhorn* (R. H. Harris, K. J. Edwards, and the Senior Class of the Agricultural & Mechanical College of Texas: College Station, TX, 1920), 138. "Wilson" (no first name) is mentioned as a member of the Cast Iron Quartet in "Big Noise Minstrel Was Great Success," *Battalion*, February 26, 1920; this corresponds with his time at A&M.

14. Carmack, "'Aggie War Hymn.'"

15. Carmack, "'Aggie War Hymn.'"

16. Becky Swanson, "'War Hymn' Author Pinky Wilson Dead," *Battalion*, September 1, 1980, "Pinky Wilson" biographical/vertical file, Cushing Memorial Library and Archives, Texas A&M University.

17. "'Aggie War Hymn'"; Hymn Author Celebrates Birthday," *Eagle* (Bryan, TX), n.d., "Pinky Wilson" biographical/vertical file, Cushing Memorial Library and Archives, Texas A&M University. The song was first introduced at a Fall 1920 Texas A&M yell practice, then officially adopted for university use in Fall 1921 (Becky Swanson, "'War Hymn' Author Pinky Wilson Dead," *Battalion*, September 1, 1980, "Pinky Wilson" biographical/vertical file, Cushing Memorial Library and Archives, Texas A&M University).

18. *Discography of American Historical Recordings*, s.v. "Colonial Club Orchestra," accessed September 1, 2020, https://adp.library.ucsb.edu/names/114863.

19. Erin C. Tarver, *The I in Team: Sports Fandom and the Reproduction of Identity* (Chicago: University of Chicago Press, 2017), 2.

20. "Corps Dances," *The Longhorn* (Texas A&M College: D. B. Baxt, T. R. Black, Victor LeMay, and the Senior Class, 1925), 265.

21. "Signal Corps Summer Camp," *The Longhorn* (Texas A&M College: A. J. Longley, G. E. Garrett, G. E. Christensen, and the Senior Class, 1926), 170.

22. Donald B. and Mary Jo Powell, *The Fightin' Texas Aggies Band* (College Station: Texas A&M University Press, 1994), 7–8.

23. "'Ag War Hymn' to Ring Out Over TSCW Campus," *Fort Worth Star-Telegram*, October 20, 1939.

24. Dorothy Trant, "TSCW Campus Chatter," *Eagle* (Bryan, TX), November 19, 1940; "Corps Trips and Redbud Festival Circled Dates on Calendar for Tessies," *Denton Record-Chronicle*, August 20, 1948.

25. "Annual Corps Trip is the Top November Date for Tessies," *Denton Record-Chronicle*, August 28, 1946.

26. "T.S.C.W. Band Program Friday," *Denton Record-Chronicle*, March 2, 1944.

27. "Mothers' Club Gives Luncheon for A&M Students, Parents," *Abilene Reporter-News*, December 31, 1952; "A&M Mothers Club Hosted by Duo," *Abilene Reporter-News*, November 24, 1954; "A&M Mothers Have Meeting," *The Marshall News Messenger*, January 16, 1955.

28. "Future Bride Feted with Shower Sunday," *Shiner Gazette*, November 23, 1950.

29. "Many Songs Are Submitted for Use By Aggies; Need for More Felt By Cadet Corps," *Eagle* (Bryan TX), January 11, 1939; "Committee to Work on School Song Problem Appointed by Bob Adams," *Battalion*, January 10, 1939.

30. Lorraine Barnes, "Battle of Music is Big Part of Texan-A&M Game," *Austin American Statesman*, November 25, 1952.

31. Georgia Tech Songs Collection, UA318, Box 1, Folder 7, Archives and Special Collections, Georgia Institute of Technology.

32. Georgia Tech Songs Collection, UA318, Box 1, Folder 20, Archives and Special Collections, Georgia Institute of Technology.

33. Georgia Tech Songs Collection, UA318, Box 1, Folder 8, Archives and Special Collections, Georgia Institute of Technology.

34. "Grantland Rice, Inspired by Stadium, Writes New Song," *Commodore* (Vanderbilt University, 1923), 22 digital. The *Commodore* feature included the text of Rice's song but no printed music.

35. Rice's text was discussed in "Long-Sought Vanderbilt Student Song Is Written by Grantland Rice," *Tennessean*, January 7, 1923, which stated that the composer was not Emma Ashford, but Frank Crumit. The January 1923 *Vanderbilt Alumnus* announced that "in response to a persistent demand for such a song," Rice would write a football song with "his friend Frank Crumit, a well known [*sic*] music composer. The song was sung by Mrs. Thomas H. Malone, Jr., at a meeting in December [1922]. . . . It has not been published, but it is expected that steps will be taken to add this to the collection of

Vanderbilt cheering songs" ("Grantland Rice Writes Song," n.p.). However, by the time the alumni magazine printed the finished song in October 1923, its tune was credited to Emma Ashford. Crumit and Rice did eventually collaborate on sports songs; in 1930, Leo Feist published two golf songs by the pair (Grantland Rice Papers, MSS.0364, Box 8, Folder 15, Vanderbilt University Special Collections and Archives). No evidence of Rice's song collaborations with Emma Ashford or Frank Crumit survives in the Grantland Rice Papers or the Emma Ashford Collection in the Vanderbilt University Special Collections and Archives.

36. "Long-Sought Vanderbilt Student Song."

37. "Come On, You Commodores," with Emma Ashford's music, was sung at a freshman event ("Young Students at Vanderbilt Are Club's Honor Guests," *Tennessean*, October 9, 1924). The song's text also appeared in the 1923 *Commodore* yearbook. In 1924, sheet music, with musical attribution to Emma Ashford, was printed in the yearbook—unusual for yearbooks of this period (*Commodore* [Vanderbilt University, 1924], 19 digital). In 1926, a truncated version of "Come On, You Commodores" was printed in the yearbook, with no lyricist or composer attributions (*Commodore* [Vanderbilt University: 1926], 115, digital).

38. "Vandy Team Cheered by Boys Left Behind," *Tennessean*, October 12, 1923.

39. "Stadium Crowd Proves Sewanee Game Still Best," *Tennessean*, November 30, 1923.

40. "Students to Vote on Leading Songs at Benefit Dance," *Reflector*, Feb. 3, 1937; "Collegians Plan Vacation Tour," *Reflector*, March 10, 1937; *Reveille* (Mississippi State University, 1936), 238; *Reveille* (Mississippi State University, 1937), 223; *Reveille* (Mississippi State University, 1938), 264. In 1936, the band also had a male vocalist in addition to Elise Buford.

41. "Deadline on Song Contest Reset," *Mis-A-Sip*, January 1937; "Pep Songs to Get Final Test Friday at Special Chapel," *Reflector*, February 10, 1937.

42. "Marching Song," music by Theodore Russell and words by Betsy Stark, *Mississippi State College Songs* (New York: Thornton W. Allen Company, 1937), 5; "Students Decide on Outstanding Song in Contest," *Reflector*, February 17, 1937.

43. "Interest in Pep Song Increases," *Mis-A-Sip*, November 1936, 10.

44. "We Want a New Pep Song," *Mis-A-Sip*, October 1937, 11.

45. Pursuer Hewitt, "Hew-itt to the Line, Let the Chips Fall Where They May," *Clarion-Ledger* (Jackson MS), October 10, 1936.

46. "Men of State," music and words by J. B. Peavey and Thornton W. Allen, *Mississippi State College Songs* (New York: Thornton W. Allen Company, 1937), 3, 4.

47. "Maroon and White (Alma Mater)," music by Henry E. Wamsley and words by T. Paul Haney Jr., *Mississippi State College Songs* (New York: Thornton W. Allen Company, 1937), 6–7.

48. "Mississippi State Fight Song," James Harvey, *Mississippi State College Songs* (New York: Thornton W. Allen Company, 1937), 8.

49. "Men of State," Peavey and Allen. Peavey recalled Allen obtaining his permission to change the title (Virginia Nash, "'Hail State, Born in the '30s, Still Thrilling MSU Fight Song," *Starkville Daily News*, November 26, 1969, "MSU Songs" vertical file, Mississippi State University Libraries Archives and Special Collections). Peavey's original title, "Hail Dear Old State," appeared in the February 1937 *Reflector* article discussing the winning entries and in typed lyrics from contest entries that the *Mis-A-Sip* staff prepared for judges ("MSU Songs" vertical file, Mississippi State University Libraries Archives and Special Collections).

50. Noah Cohan, *We Average Unbeautiful Watchers: Fan Narratives and the Reading of American Sports* (Lincoln: University of Nebraska Press, 2019), 3.

51. Cohan, *We Average Unbeautiful Watchers*, 2.

52. Watts, introduction to *White Masculinity*.

Chapter 6

1. "Tulane Team Falls in For Michigan," *Hullabaloo*, October 29, 1920.

2. "Tulane Swing" appeared in sources such as "Football Songs," Tulane University Student Handbook, 1920–1921, "Tulane Songs" vertical file, University Archives, Tulane University Special Collections, New Orleans, LA, and "The Tulane Swing," football program, Tulane vs. University of Tennessee, November 15, 1924, 13.

3. Football stadiums were built in the 1920s at the University of Tennessee (1921), Vanderbilt (1922), Louisiana State University (1924), and the University of Georgia (1929). Ingrassia, *Rise of Gridiron University*, 168.

4. Odum, *Southern Regions of the United States*, 509.

5. Oriard, *King Football*, 65; January 1926 Associated Press Rose Bowl report cited in Lanford, "When the Band Plays 'Dixie.'"

6. Oriard, *King Football*, 65.

7. James Cobb, *Away Down South: A History of Southern Identity* (Oxford: Oxford University Press, 2005), 109.

8. Ring, *The Problem South*; Maxwell, *The Indicted South*.

9. Blinkey Horn, "First Title Torpedo Will be Fied [*sic*] Tonight as Vandy Battles Terrors," *Tennessean*, January 2, 1926.

10. As early as 1912, University of Alabama President George Denny believed football to be "a tool for building enrollment and gaining notoriety," in Walsh, *Where Football Is King*, 134.

11. Oriard, *King Football*, 85.

12. Quoted in Lanford, "When the Band Plays 'Dixie.'"

13. Quoted in Lanford, "When the Band Plays 'Dixie.'"

14. Lanford, "When the Band Plays 'Dixie.'"

15. C. T. Conyers, ed. and Assistant Leader of the Georgia Glee Club, *Georgia Songs: Songs and Airs That Are Associated with the Life of the Student Body of University of Georgia* (Athens, GA: University of Georgia Glee and Mandolin Clubs, 1922), 8.

16. Lisa Lindquist Dorr, "Fifty Percent Moonshine and Fifty Percent Moonshine: Social Life and College Youth Culture in Alabama, 1913–1933," in Ted Ownby, ed., *Manners and Southern History* (Jackson: University Press of Mississippi, 2007), 45–46. On US students' self-conscious participation in national college culture in the 1920s, see Fass, *Damned and the Beautiful.*

17. Carl Lampert, "On! On! U of K," original manuscript, 1922, J-60, 2001 UA065, flat file case 1, drawer 7, folder 5, Special Collections, University of Kentucky Libraries. Accounts printed in later campus materials such as yearbooks attributed the new song to the coach's request.

18. Ann K. Long, "Message to UK From One 'Unable to Belong,'" letter to the editor, *Kentucky Kernel*, December 13, 1966.

19. Allen's refusal to accept "subsequent acts of reception lying far beyond authorial reach" as legitimate musical products highlighted his investment in the Western European classical conception of musical authorship and ownership outlined in the previous chapter; see Chris May, "Jurisprudence v Musicology: Riffs from the Land Down Under," *Music and Letters* 97, no. 4 (Nov 2016): 628.

20. Ok 40189 and Pa 40189, S-72320-B.

21. William B. Wisdom to Tulane President Albert Dinwiddie and WMSB radio, May 20, 1925; "Radio Carries 'Tulane Swing' to Washington and Lee Hearer, Who Protests Song Was Stolen," *Hullabaloo*, May 1925; "W.&L. Alumni Say 'Swing' Was Misused," *Hullabaloo*, May 29, 1925; William B. Wisdom to WSMB radio, May 20, 1925, reprinted in *Hullabaloo*; "Radio Carries 'Tulane Swing' to Washington and Lee Hearer, Who Protests Song Was Stolen," *Hullabaloo*, May 1925. All items, Presidents Record Group, Series 6: Dinwiddie, Albert Bledsoe: Songs, 1925-1936, University Archives, Tulane University Special Collections, New Orleans, LA.

22. For example, "Tulane Swing" appeared in "Football Songs," Tulane University Student Handbook, 1920-1921, "Tulane Songs" vertical file, University Archives, Tulane University Special Collections, New Orleans, LA, and "The Tulane Swing," football program, Tulane vs. University of Tennessee, November 15, 1924, 13.

23. Louisiana Washington and Lee Alumni Association to Albert Dinwiddie, May 21, 1925, Presidents Record Group, Series 6: Dinwiddie, Albert Bledsoe: Songs, 1925-1936, University Archives, Tulane University Special Collections, New Orleans, LA.

24. Louisiana Washington and Lee Alumni Association to WSMB radio, May 21, 1925; "Protests WSMB on Tulane Swing," *Times-Picayune*, May 1925, Presidents Record Group, Series 6: Dinwiddie, Albert Bledsoe: Songs, 1925-1936, University Archives, Tulane University Special Collections, New Orleans, LA.

25. Louisiana Washington and Lee Alumni Association to *Times-Picayune*, May 22, 1925; "W.&L. Alumni Say 'Swing' Was Misused," *Hullabaloo*, May 29, 1925; Presidents Record Group, Series 6: Dinwiddie, Albert Bledsoe: Songs, 1925–1936, University Archives, Tulane University Special Collections, New Orleans, LA.

26. Mass-produced postcards, Thornton W. Allen Company to President and Leader of Musical Clubs, Tulane University, postmarked July 27, 1925, Presidents Record Group, Series 6: Dinwiddie, Albert Bledsoe: Songs, 1925-1936, University Archives, Tulane University Special Collections, New Orleans, LA.

27. Johnny DeDroit, Interview, December 4, 1969, in *Oral History Files*, edited by Betty B. Rankin, Richard B. Allen, and Keith V. Abramson, New Orleans: William Ransom Hogan Jazz Archive, Tulane University. On copyright and recordings in early twentieth-century US popular music, see Lisa Gitelman, "Recorded Sound, Recording Race, Recording Property," in *Hearing History: A Reader*, ed. Mark M. Smith (Athens: University of Georgia Press, 2004). Allen's reaction to the Okeh jazz recording highlights conflicting models of musical authorship operative in 1920s jazz and in 1920s music publishing, with the latter's notion of authorship backed up by US copyright law. Unlike the Western European classical music model of authorship that informed the work of publishers like Thornton Allen, jazz privileges communal authorship; see Gabriel Solis, "'A Unique Chunk of Jazz Reality': Authorship, Musical Work Concepts, and Thelonious Monk's Live Recordings from the Five Spot, 1958," *Ethnomusicology* 48, no. 3 (Fall 2004): 315–47.

28. "Football Fight Song Is Wanted by T.U. Alumni," *Hullabaloo*, May 29, 1925; "'Olive and Blue' Replaces Old 'Swing,'" *Hullabaloo*, October 2, 1925; Presidents Record Group, Series 6: Dinwiddie, Albert Bledsoe: Songs, 1925–1936, University Archives, Tulane University Special Collections, New Orleans, LA.

29. "Football Fight Song Is Wanted"; "'Olive and Blue' Replaces Old 'Swing.'"

30. "Tulane New Fight Song Makes Hit," *Hullabaloo*, October 2, 1925, Presidents Record Group, Series 6: Dinwiddie, Albert Bledsoe: Songs, 1925–1936, University Archives, Tulane University Special Collections, New Orleans, LA.

31. Souvenir Program, Tulane vs. Louisiana College, September 26, 1925, University Archives, Tulane University Special Collections, New Orleans, LA.

32. "Ah, A Song," *Times-Picayune*, November 23, 1929, 13, Presidents Record Group, Series 6: Dinwiddie, Albert Bledsoe: Songs, 1925–1936, University Archives, Tulane University Special Collections, New Orleans, LA.

33. "'Swing' Dropped by Tulane Band after Criticism," *Hullabaloo*, January 22, 1932, Presidents Record Group, Series 6: Dinwiddie, Albert Bledsoe: Songs, 1925-1936, University Archives, Tulane University Special Collections, New Orleans, LA.

34. "'Olive and Blue' Replaces Old 'Swing.'"

35. Allen, *Intercollegiate Songbook*, front matter.

36. "Revised Copy of 'Olive and Blue' Is Now on Sale," *Hullabaloo*, May 27, 1932; general manager of Tulane Alumni Association Ike Armstrong to Charles Edward Thomas, editor, *The Delta* (Sigma Nu Fraternity), August 25, 1932, Presidents Record Group, Series 6: Dinwiddie, Albert Bledsoe: Songs, 1925-1936, University Archives, Tulane University Special Collections, New Orleans, LA.

37. Ellis B. Hall to president [Albert Dinwiddie] of Tulane University, January 13, 1933; Dinwiddie to Hall, January 21, 1933; handwritten note enclosed states,

"Dr. Hard [Tulane faculty?] thinks it will be an advantage and he hopes that the Alumni Association can get permission from the owner of the copyright," Presidents Record Group, Series 6: Dinwiddie, Albert Bledsoe: Songs, 1925–1936, University Archives, Tulane University Special Collections, New Orleans, LA.

38. Thornton W. Allen to Ike Armstrong, Tulane Alumni Association, February 14, 1933, Presidents Record Group, Series 6: Dinwiddie, Albert Bledsoe: Songs, 1925–1936, University Archives, Tulane University Special Collections, New Orleans, LA.
39. General Manager of Tulane Alumni Association Charlie Rucker to Dean Douglas Anderson, Acting President, Tulane University, January 16, 1936; Rucker to Irving Berlin, Inc., January 16, 1936, Presidents Record Group, Series 6: Dinwiddie, Albert Bledsoe: Songs, 1925–1936, University Archives, Tulane University Special Collections, New Orleans, LA.
40. William B. Wisdom, "The 'Tulane Swing,'" Letter to Editor, *Times-Picayune*, May 24, 1925; "The 'Swing,'" *Hullabaloo*, May 29, 1925, Presidents Record Group, Series 6: Dinwiddie, Albert Bledsoe: Songs, 1925–1936, University Archives, Tulane University Special Collections, New Orleans, LA.
41. "Render Unto Caesar," William B. Wisdom, May 19, 1925, copy enclosed with Wisdom letter to President Albert Dinwiddie, Tulane University, May 20, 1925, Presidents Record Group, Series 6: Dinwiddie, Albert Bledsoe: Songs, 1925-1936, University Archives, Tulane University Special Collections, New Orleans, LA.
42. "Radio Carries 'Tulane Swing' to Washington and Lee Hearer, Who Protests Song Was Stolen," *Hullabaloo*, May 1925; "Render Unto Caesar," William B. Wisdom, May 19, 1925, copy enclosed with Wisdom letter to President A. B. Dinwiddie, Tulane University, May 20, 1925, Presidents Record Group, Series 6: Dinwiddie, Albert Bledsoe: Songs, 1925-1936, University Archives, Tulane University Special Collections, New Orleans, LA.
43. Louisiana Washington and Lee Alumni Association to *Times-Picayune*, May 22, 1925 and to President Albert Dinwdiddie, Tulane University, May 21, 1925, Presidents Record Group, Series 6: Dinwiddie, Albert Bledsoe: Songs, 1925-1936, University Archives, Tulane University Special Collections, New Orleans, LA.
44. "Render Unto Caesar," William B. Wisdom, May 19, 1925, copy enclosed with Wisdom letter to President A. B. Dinwiddie, Tulane University, May 20, 1925, Presidents Record Group, Series 6: Dinwiddie, Albert Bledsoe: Songs, 1925-1936, University Archives, Tulane University Special Collections, New Orleans, LA.
45. Gitelman, "Recorded Sound," 292.
46. Jeff Coleman, University of Alabama Class of 1925, to University of Alabama Assistant Athletic Director Steve Townsend (1989–1997), undated; "Alabama Swing," University of Alabama student handbook (1921–1922), 77–78, "Songs and Music" vertical file, University Libraries Special Collections, University of Alabama.
47. "Of a New Song," *Rammer-Jammer*, November 1925, 39.
48. "Of a New Song."

49. "The 'Alabama Swing' Appears Doomed!" *Alumni Magazine* (Washington and Lee University), January 1926, 14.

50. "The 'Alabama Swing' Appears Doomed!"; "Days Are Numbered for Alabama Swing," *Montgomery Advertiser*, February 24, 1926.

51. "Of Our New Song," *Rammer-Jammer*, April 1926, 138; Arthur MacLean, "Sykes, Song Composer," *Rammer-Jammer*, May 1926, 159–62.

52. "'Yea Alabama' to Appear in April" and "'Yea Alabama!' to Appear This Month," *Crimson White*, April 1926; "Receive New Song 900 Copies Ready," *Crimson White*, May 1926; "Songs and Music" vertical file, University Libraries Special Collections, University of Alabama.

53. "'Yea Alabama' to Appear in April"; "'Yea Alabama!' to Appear This Month"; "Receive New Song 900 Copies Ready."

54. Mass-produced postcards, Thornton W. Allen Company to President and Leader of Musical Clubs, Tulane University, postmarked July 27, 1925, Presidents Record Group, Series 6: Dinwiddie, Albert Bledsoe: Songs, 1925–1936, University Archives, Tulane University Special Collections, New Orleans, LA. No communications from Thornton W. Allen are extant in the University of Alabama's George Denny Presidential Papers or university legal correspondence files (author's email communications with staff, University Archives, University of Alabama, October 4, 2019, and Paul Pruitt, Bounds Law Library, University of Alabama, October 8, 2019).

55. MacLean, "Sykes, Song Composer."

56. Allen, *Intercollegiate Song Book*, 2.

57. Press coverage of the "Yea Alabama" marching band arrangement created for the 1926 football season stated that it was to replace the "Washington and Lee Swing" ("'Yea Alabama' Is New War Tune at Capstone College, *Montgomery Advertiser*, March 18, 1926). The *Rammer-Jammer*'s first printing of "Yea Alabama" in May 1926 also reiterated that it was meant "to replace the 'Swing' which belongs to Washington & Lee" (MacLean, "Sykes, Song Composer").

58. Allen, *Intercollegiate Songbook*, front matter.

59. Ethelred Lundy Sykes and W. C. Polla, arr., "Yea Alabama: Arranged for Orchestra" (New York: Thornton W. Allen, 1926. "Songs" vertical file, University Libraries Special Collections, University of Alabama.

60. The University of Kansas Glee Club Director told a newspaper reporter that "it is a new thing to hear a fox-trot college song" but conceded that it did reflect popular collegiate taste ("'Bama's New Song Making Big Hit," *Montgomery Advertiser*, September 21, 1926). Dances began to feature the song, such as a Montgomery, Alabama, cotillion event with a dance orchestra playing "Yea Alabama" and, incidentally and ecumenically, "Glory, Glory to Ole Auburn." ("Cotillion Team Dance Takes Place," *Montgomery Advertiser*, December 24, 1927).

61. "All University Turns Out to Attend College Night Under Auspices of Y," *Montgomery Advertiser*, September 24, 1926.

62. Ethelred Lundy Sykes, composer, May Singhi Breen, ukulele/banjulele arr., "Yea Alabama" (New York: Thornton W. Allen), ca. 1927.

63. Breen popularized the ukulele among young US music consumers through her radio performances, chord diagram system, and method books. The piano-ukulele-vocal duo Breen formed with her composer husband Peter DeRose aired on NBC's *Sweethearts of the Air* from 1923 to 1939. Breen later joined ASCAP and worked to encourage professional US music circles to accept the ukulele as a legitimate instrument, trying for example to convince the American Federation of Musicians to allow her to join as a ukulele player. This debate highlights the wrangling over "good" music and elevated musical taste that animated US classical and popular music industries in the first half of the twentieth century. For more on Breen and the early twentieth-century popularity of the ukulele in US popular music, see Jim Tranquada, *The Ukulele: A History* (Honolulu: University of Hawaii Press, 2012); Harriet Works Corley, "May Singhi Breen," *Wireless Age*, July 1925, 14–15; Paul Harrison, "Radio Star Insists Uke Is Musical Instrument," *Dayton (OH) Daily News*, January 8, 1932; Statement of May Singhi Breen in Support of S.1106 and S.1444, *Rendition of Musical Compositions on Coin-Operated Machines*, Hearing Before the U.S. Senate Committee on the Judiciary, Oct. 26, 1953, 12; "Obituary: May Singhi Breen, Ukulele Lady of Radio in 20s and 30s, Dead," *New York Times*, December 20, 1970.
64. Snooks Friedman and his Memphis Stompers, "Yea Alabama," Victor BE-45486, October 1928.
65. Leo Feist, piano arr., and May Singhi Breen, ukulele arr., *Feist Dance Folio No. 12: Thirty of the Latest Song Hits Arranged as Fox Trots, Waltzes, Etc.* (New York: Leo Feist, 1927).
66. May Singhi Breen, ukulele arr., *Universal Dance Folio for Piano, No. 19: Selected from the Most Popular Song Hits of the Season* (New York: Irving Berlin, 1930).
67. Examples include Richard Johnson, "For 90 Years, Bama's Been Singing about Beating Washington. Now They Meet Again," *SBNation*, December 31, 2016; "How a Football Championship Gave Us 'Yea, Alabama,'" University of Alabama *News Center*, September 4, 2018, https://news.ua.edu/2018/09/how-a-football-championship-gave-us-yea-alabama; and Ken Roberts, "'Go Teach the Bulldogs
to Behave': What to Know About Alabama's Fight Song," *Tuscaloosa News*, January 7, 2022, https://www.tuscaloosanews.com/story/news/2022/01/07/alabama-crimson-tide-football-fight-song-lyrics-marching-band-georgia-uga-bulldogs/9133716002.
68. John R. Tunis, "What Price College Football?" *American Mercury* 48 (Oct. 1939), 129–42.
69. Richard Crawford, *America's Musical Life: A History* (New York: Norton, 2005), 540–41.
70. Crawford, *America's Musical Life*, 540–41.
71. Tom Continé and Faye Phillips, *The Golden Band from Tigerland: A History of LSU's Marching Band* (Baton Rouge: Louisiana State University Press, 2016).
72. Ted Gioia, "Tiger Rag," in Ted Gioia, ed., *Jazz Standards: A Guide to the Repertoire* (Oxford: Oxford University Press, 2012), 434–36.

73. Naomi Andre and Denise Von Glahn, "Colloquy: Shadow Culture Narratives: Race, Gender, and American Music Historiography," *Journal of the American Musicological Society* 73, no. 3 (Fall 2020): 714.
74. Matthew Morrison, "Race, Blacksound," 791.
75. Morrison, "Race, Blacksound," 791.
76. Cobb, *Away Down South.*
77. Carey, *Jim Crow U.*

Chapter 7

1. Thornton W. Allen to Charles Crossland, April 30, 1931, University of Maine Alumni Association Records, 1872–1988, UA RG 0013.001, Box 5, Folder 3, University of Maine Special Collections.
2. John Thelin, *History of American Higher Education*, 205; David O. Levine, *The American College and the Culture of Aspiration, 1915–1940* (Ithaca, NY: Cornell University Press, 1986).
3. Thelin, *History of American Higher Education*, 210; David Turpie, "From Broadway to Hollywood: The Image of the 1939 University of Tennessee Football Team and the Americanization of the South," *Journal of Sport History* 35, no. 1 (2008): 119–40.
4. Thelin, *History of American Higher Education*, 215.
5. Elijah Wald notes the ubiquity of "college boy" dance bands and radio broadcasts by musicians associated with collegiate taste in the 1920s and 1930s in *How the Beatles Destroyed Rock 'n' Roll*, 65, 94. Allison McCracken analyzes the racialized, classed, and gendered reception of collegiate pop stars in the 1920s and 1930s in *Real Men Don't Sing: Crooning in American Culture* (Durham, NC: Duke University Press, 2015), and Andrew Berish discusses the dance band culture that marked 1930s college campuses in *Lonesome Roads and Streets of Dreams: Place, Mobility, and Race in Jazz of the 1930s and '40s* (Chicago: University of Chicago Press, 2012). While valuable, these books do not center the role of music publishing nor cover regional (specifically southern) dance band leaders in the 1930s collegiate music craze, as this chapter does.
6. Louis Reid, "Words without Music," *Mountain Echo* (Shickshinny, PA), August 26, 1938.
7. Appendix, copyright table of Thornton W. Allen's College Songs.
8. Thornton W. Allen Co. publicity materials enclosed with correspondence to University of Maine Alumni Association, January 4, 1937, University of Maine Alumni Association Records, 1872–1988, UA RG 0013.001, Box 5, Folder 3, University of Maine Special Collections.
9. "Grail Plans New Carolina Anthem," *Daily Tar Heel*, October 27, 1932.
10. "Composers of Music Honored at University," *Tampa Tribune*, November 17, 1935. Allen's 1935 copyright on this song refers to his arrangement of it; its tune was older. He credited himself and George Hamilton as the copyright holders for the lyrics (Appendix).
11. "Special: Gainesville," *Tampa Tribune*, May 24, 1935.

12. Library of Congress Copyright Records, New Series Vol. 26 for the year 1931 Nos. 1-12, 1932, 392, #7960, entered March 12, 1931.

13. Thornton W. Allen to Charles Crossland, February 27, 1931, University of Maine Alumni Association Records, 1872–1988, UA RG 0013.001, Box 5, Folder 3, University of Maine Special Collections.

14. Thornton W. Allen to Charles Crossland, February 11, 1931, University of Maine Alumni Association Records, 1872–1988, UA RG 0013.001, Box 5, Folder 3, University of Maine Special Collections.

15. Thornton W. Allen to Charles Crossland, February 11, 1931, University of Maine Alumni Association Records, 1872–1988, UA RG 0013.001, Box 5, Folder 3, University of Maine Special Collections.

16. Thornton W. Allen to Charles Crossland, February 27, 1931; August 12, 1931, University of Maine Alumni Association Records, 1872–1988, UA RG 0013.001, Box 5, Folder 3, University of Maine Special Collections.

17. Thornton W. Allen Co. publicity materials enclosed with correspondence of January 4, 1937, University of Maine Alumni Association Records, 1872–1988, UA RG 0013.001, Box 5, Folder 3, University of Maine Special Collections.

18. Thornton W. Allen Co. publicity materials enclosed with correspondence of January 4, 1937, University of Maine Alumni Association Records, 1872–1988, UA RG 0013.001, Box 5, Folder 3, University of Maine Special Collections.

19. Thornton W. Allen Co. publicity materials enclosed with correspondence of January 4, 1937, University of Maine Alumni Association Records, 1872–1988, UA RG 0013.001, Box 5, Folder 3, University of Maine Special Collections.

20. Thornton W. Allen Co. publicity materials enclosed with correspondence of January 4, 1937, University of Maine Alumni Association Records, 1872–1988, UA RG 0013.001, Box 5, Folder 3, University of Maine Special Collections.

21. "To Discuss Music," *Hartford (CT) Courant*, September 25, 1930.

22. Associated Press Release, "Campus Tunes to Thrill U.S.: Oct. 1–8 to Be College Song Week; Special Programs Are Planned," *Altoona (PA) Tribune*, September 30, 1932.

23. Associated Press Release, "Campuses Will Ring with College Songs Week of October 2," *Shreveport Journal*, September 29, 1933.

24. Associated Press Release, "Campuses Will Ring."

25. Thornton W. Allen Co. Royalty Statement to University of Maine Alumni Association, January 15, 1935; Thornton W. Allen to Charles Crossland, January 22, 1935. College football attendance shrank by 25% between 1929 and 1933. Watterson, *College Football*, 177.

26. AIC Copyright Agreement Form enclosed with correspondence, Thornton W. Allen to Charles Crossland, April 27, 1935, University of Maine Alumni Association Records, 1872–1988, UA RG 0013.001, Box 5, Folder 3, University of Maine Special Collections.

27. AIC Copyright Agreement Form enclosed with correspondence, Thornton W. Allen to Charles Crossland, April 27, 1935, University of Maine Alumni Association Records, 1872–1988, UA RG 0013.001, Box 5, Folder 3, University of Maine Special Collections.

28. Thornton W. Allen to Charles Crossland, April 27, 1935, University of Maine Alumni Association Records, 1872–1988, UA RG 0013.001, Box 5, Folder 3, University of Maine Special Collections.

29. Enclosed materials with correspondence, Thornton W. Allen to Charles Crossland, April 27, 1935, University of Maine Alumni Association Records, 1872–1988, UA RG 0013.001, Box 5, Folder 3, University of Maine Special Collections.

30. Thornton W. Allen to Charles Crossland, June 15, 1935, University of Maine Alumni Association Records, 1872–1988, UA RG 0013.001, Box 5, Folder 3, University of Maine Special Collections.

31. Thornton W. Allen to Charles Crossland, June 22, 1935, University of Maine Alumni Association Records, 1872–1988, UA RG 0013.001, Box 5, Folder 3, University of Maine Special Collections.

32. Unsigned permissions agreement between Thornton W. Allen Company and radio broadcasters, 194[_], Edmund Craney Papers, 1916–1979, MC 122, Box 15, Folder 2, Montana Historical Society, Research Center Archives.

33. Thornton W. Allen to Charles Crossland, January 22, 1935, University of Maine Alumni Association Records, 1872–1988, UA RG 0013.001, Box 5, Folder 3, University of Maine Special Collections.

34. Thornton W. Allen to Charles Crossland, July 25, 1936, University of Maine Alumni Association Records, 1872–1988, UA RG 0013.001, Box 5, Folder 3, University of Maine Special Collections.

35. Thornton W. Allen to Charles Crossland, September 23, 1937, University of Maine Alumni Association Records, 1872–1988, UA RG 0013.001, Box 5, Folder 3, University of Maine Special Collections.

36. Charles Crossland to Thornton W. Allen, September 28, 1937, University of Maine Alumni Association Records, 1872–1988, UA RG 0013.001, Box 5, Folder 3, University of Maine Special Collections.

37. Thornton W. Allen to Crossland, November 5, 1942, ,University of Maine Alumni Association Records, 1872–1988, UA RG 0013.001, Box 5, Folder 3, University of Maine Special Collections.

38. See earlier discussion of Allen's Eurocentric understanding of copyright and musical authorship.

39. Thornton W. Allen to Charles Crossland, August 12, 1931, University of Maine Special Collections: University of Maine Alumni Association Records, 1872–1988, UA RG 0013.001, Series 8: University of Maine Music Files, Box 5, Folder 3.

40. Thornton W. Allen to Adelbert W. Sprague, February 2 and 14; June 24; August 8 and 9, 1931, University of Maine Alumni Association Records, 1872–1988, UA RG 0013.001, Box 5, Folder 3, University of Maine Special Collections.

41. Thornton W. Allen, telegram to Charles Crossland, August 9, 1931; Thornton W. Allen, letters to Adelbert W. Sprague, June 24, 1931, University of Maine Alumni Association Records, 1872–1988, UA RG 0013.001, Box 5, Folder 3, University of Maine Special Collections.

42. Thornton W. Allen to Charles Crossland, June 24; August 8 and 9, 1931,

University of Maine Alumni Association Records, 1872–1988, UA RG 0013.001, Box 5, Folder 3, University of Maine Special Collections.

43. Thornton W. Allen to Adelbert W. Sprague, June 24, 1931, University of Maine Alumni Association Records, 1872–1988, UA RG 0013.001, Box 5, Folder 3, University of Maine Special Collections.

44. Thornton W. Allen to Adelbert W. Sprague, June 29, 1931, University of Maine Alumni Association Records, 1872–1988, UA RG 0013.001, Box 5, Folder 3, University of Maine Special Collections.

45. Thornton W. Allen, letters to Adelbert W. Sprague, June 24, 1931, University of Maine Alumni Association Records, 1872–1988, UA RG 0013.001, Box 5, Folder 3, University of Maine Special Collections.

46. "U.T. again Protecting 'The Eyes of Texas,'" *Austin American Statesman*, April 25, 1936. "Again" refers to legal action threatened months earlier by the University of Texas over copyright claims on an arrangement of "The Eyes of Texas" by a Boston publishing house ("Eyes of Texas on Song Tilt as M'Graw Maps Legal Act," *Austin American Statesman*, February 20, 1936); "Eyes of Texas Copyrighted Years Ago," *Fort Worth Star Telegram*, February 21, 1936; "Texas U. Will Protect Song: Students Obtain Copyright on Historic Tune of State School, *Times* (Shreveport, LA), April 23, 1936).

47. Thornton W. Allen to Charles Crossland, December 10, 1936 and January 4, 1937, University of Maine Alumni Association Records, 1872–1988, UA RG 0013.001, Box 5, Folder 3, University of Maine Special Collections.

48. Untitled clippings, *Battalion*, December 9, 1938, and *Battalion*, December 6, 1938; George Fuermann, "Backwash" column, *Battalion*, May 21, 1940, "Songs/Clippings of Texas War Hymn" vertical file, Cushing Memorial Library Archives and Special Collections, Texas A&M University.

49. "Publishing Firm Explains True Restrictions on Use of 'War Hymn,'" *Battalion*, January 6, 1939, "Songs/Clippings of Texas War Hymn" vertical file, Cushing Memorial Library Archives and Special Collections, Texas A&M University.

50. Untitled clipping, *Battalion*, December 6, 1938, "Songs/Clippings of Texas War Hymn" vertical file, Cushing Memorial Library Archives and Special Collections, Texas A&M University.

51. "Many Songs Are Submitted For Use By Aggies; Need for More Felt By Cadet Corps," *Eagle* (Bryan, TX), January 11, 1939, "Songs/Clippings of Texas War Hymn" vertical file, Cushing Memorial Library Archives and Special Collections, Texas A&M University.

52. "Publishing Firm Explains True Restrictions on Use of 'War Hymn,'" *Battalion*, January 6, 1939, "Songs/Clippings of Texas War Hymn" vertical file, Cushing Memorial Library Archives and Special Collections, Texas A&M University.

53. Untitled clipping, *Battalion*, January 6, 1939, "Songs/Clippings of Texas War Hymn vertical file," Cushing Memorial Library Archives and Special Collections, Texas A&M University.

54. Untitled clipping, *Battalion*, January 6, 1939, "Songs/Clippings of Texas War Hymn" vertical file, Cushing Memorial Library Archives and Special Collections, Texas A&M University.

55. George Fuermann, "Backwash" column, *Battalion*, May 21, 1940, "Songs/ Clippings of Texas War Hymn" vertical file, Cushing Memorial Library Archives and Special Collections, Texas A&M University.

56. Kenneth S. Clarke, "Everybody Up!" *Saturday Evening Post*, November 10, 1934, 23.

57. Clarke, "Everybody Up!," 23.

58. Clarke, "Everybody Up!," 23.

59. Thornton W. Allen to Charles Crossland, February 11, 1931 and September 23, 1937, University of Maine Alumni Association Records, 1872–1988, UA RG 0013.001, Box 5, Folder 3, University of Maine Special Collections.

60. McCracken, *Real Men Don't Sing*, 115; 117.

61. McCracken, *Real Men Don't Sing*, 127. There is no scholarly consensus about the historical meaning and historiographic utility of the hot-sweet jazz dance band binary. Elijah Wald writes that "the great fundamental truth of the 1930s [was that] whether remembered as jazz, swing, sweet, hot, novelty, corny, or 'Mickey Mouse,' all the bands played dance music." *How the Beatles Destroyed Rock 'n' Roll*, 98, 151. Andrew Berish states that the late 1920s through early 1940s were "dominated by dance bands, all of which to some degree or another incorporated elements of black vernacular music making," arguing in chapter 1 that the hot-sweet labels represented the extent to which bands drew on Black musical aesthetics. *Lonesome Roads*, 1. Stephanie Doktor interrogates the hot-sweet binary altogether in *Reinventing Whiteness: Race in the Early Jazz Marketplace* (unpublished manuscript).

62. McCracken, chapter 3, *Real Men Don't Sing*.

63. *Discography of American Historical Recordings*, s.v. "Vallée, Rudy," accessed March 30, 2022, https://adp.library.ucsb.edu/names/103912.

64. McCracken, *Real Men Don't Sing*, 103, 122–23; *Fred Waring's America*, Pennsylvania State University Libraries, Special Collections and Archives, accessed March 29, 2021, https://libraries.psu.edu/about/collections/fred-warings-america.

65. Peter T. Kiefer, *The Fred Waring Discography*, Discographies No. 65 (Westport, CT: Greenwood Press, 1996), 119–20.

66. "1920s—Rise to Fame" and "1930s and 40s—Radio Days," *Fred Waring's America*, Pennsylvania State University Libraries, Special Collections and Archives, accessed March 29, 2021, https://libraries.psu.edu/about/collections/fred-warings-america.

67. "Fred Waring's Music Library," *Fred Waring's America*, Pennsylvania State University Libraries, Special Collections and Archives, accessed March 29, 2021, https://libraries.psu.edu/about/collections/fred-warings-america. See for example, *College Memories* (Decca, 1954) and *Alma Mater Memories* (Capitol, 1963) (Kiefer, *Fred Waring Discography*, 34).

68. Turpie, "From Broadway to Hollywood," 133.
69. Victor Records advertisement, *Birmingham News*, April 3, 1930.
70. Andrew W. Smith (radio editor), "Following the Antenna," *Birmingham News*, October 20, 1930, 7; October 31, 1930.
71. "Rudy Vallee to Bring Orchestra to Fox for One Day, February 13," *Atlanta Constitution*, January 29, 1933.
72. Photo caption, "Rudy and Tampa Girl Rehearse," *Tampa Tribune*, February 12, 1931; "Rudy Vallee's Band to Broadcast from Dallas," *Tyler (TX) Morning Telegraph*, July 9, 1936.
73. "'Strange Interlude'; Vallee Here This Week," *Tampa Tribune*, February 5, 1933; Hugh Hough, "Hugh and Crye" column, *Miami Herald*, January 25, 1937.
74. "Rudy Vallee Talks about Miami," *Miami Herald*, January 25, 1931.
75. "Fred Waring's Glee Club to Play," *Tampa Times*, December 1, 1931.
76. "Gatwood Calls Glee Club Meet," *Vanderbilt Hustler*, October 2, 1936.
77. Robert Ikard, *Near You: Francis Craig, Dean of Southern Maestros* (Franklin, TN: Hillsboro Press, 1999), 15–17, 47.
78. Ikard, *Near You*, 38.
79. Ikard, *Near You*, 41.
80. The Francis Craig Collection, Box 1, Folders 1 and 2 contain fan mail and other documents demonstrating WSM's role in connecting Craig with listeners and consumers (MSS.0091, Vanderbilt University Archives and Special Collections).
81. Ikard, *Near You*, 56–59; *Colorado Greeters Guide and Denver Daily Doings* (vol. XI), Oct. 14–21, 1932, box 1, folder 14, Francis Craig Collection, MSS.0091, Vanderbilt University Archives and Special Collections.
82. Ben Austin, *The Forty Year Cycle* (South Pasadena, CA: Kilmarnock Press, 1980), cited in Ikard, *Near You*, 56–57.
83. Ikard, *Near You*, 72–73.
84. Ikard, *Near You*, 28, 48.
85. "'Long, Tall Gal From Dixie' Boosted Snooks Friedman," *Morning News* [Wilmington, DE], June 22, 1932.
86. McCracken, *Real Men Don't Sing*, 177. As Joshua Gailey argues, music associated with the school band movement, where some types of college song arrangements would fit, occupied a "middlebrow" tier in the US musical hierarchy, able to signify flexibly in different cultural and class contexts. Gailey, "Beginning Bands," 261. (Note: the terms "highbrow," "middlebrow," and "lowbrow," descriptors of hierarchical categories of cultural works and aesthetic tastes, derive from early twentieth-century phrenological discourse that linked intelligence and other optimal human traits to skull shapes thought to differ by race.)
87. McCracken, *Real Mean Don't Sing*, 215.
88. See for example a June 1937 issue of *Life* magazine devoted entirely to college life; in October 1937, *Life* ran an Albert Richard See advertisement that used a map of college football locations to advertise menswear. Similar features and advertisements were common in other 1930s national media outlets such as the *Saturday Evening Post*.

89. David Brackett, *Categorizing Sound: Genre and Twentieth-Century Popular Music* (Berkeley: University of California Press, 2016). Brackett contends that the emergence of the "foreign music" marketing category early in recorded sound history laid the foundation for four other categories built on ethnicity and identity to structure the US music industry in the 1920s: foreign, race, old-time, and mainstream popular music. Brackett's four-prong model became a three-prong model by the 1940s as foreign music dropped off the industry's radar (43).

90. Brackett, *Categorizing Sound: Genre and Twentieth-Century Popular Music.*

91. Miller, *Segregating Sound,* 8.

Chapter 8

1. Louis Reid, "Words Without Music," *Mountain Echo* (Shikshinny, PA), August 26, 1938, 3.

2. "Kenneth S. Clark, Composer, Editor," Obituary, *New York Times,* January 24, 1945; Kenneth S. Clarke, "Everybody Up!" *Saturday Evening Post,* November 10, 1934, 23, 72–73, 75.

3. Works Progress Administration and Public Works Administration funding improved athletic facilities at white southern flagship universities; see Jack Carey, "Ole Miss's New Deal: Building White Democracy at the University of Mississippi, 1933–1941" *Journal of Mississippi History* (Fall/Winter 2019): 185–220; and Carey, *Jim Crow U.* See Odum, *Southern Regions of the United States,* for an overview of southern higher education in the 1930s.

4. Thelin, *History of American Higher Education,* 210; Melvin Gruensfelder, "A History of the Origin and Development of the Southeastern Conference" (Master's thesis, University of Illinois, 1964), 64, 93; Charles H. Martin, "Integrating New Year's Day: The Racial Politics of College Bowl Games in the American South" in Miller, *Sporting World,* 179.

5. See book introduction for a list of founding SEC institutions.

6. John R. Tunis, "What Price College Football?" *American Mercury* 48 (October 1939): 129-142; John Sayle Watterson, chapter 10 in *College Football*; Eric Moyen, "Redefining Reform: Presidents, Football, and Athletic Policy in the SEC, 1929–1936" in Christian Anderson and Amber Fallucca, eds., *The History of American College Football* (London: Routledge, 2021), unpaginated e-book.

7. Thomas E. Douglass, "Biographical Sketch of William Edwin Douglass," February 2, 1993; University of Arkansas Orchestra program, April 29, 1911; W. D. McNair (Ozark Theatre) reference letter for William Douglass, May 1915, University of Arkansas Band Records, MC 2002-UA, Box 3, Folder 27, Special Collections, University of Arkansas Libraries.

8. "Field Song" manuscript, undated; Thomas E. Douglass, "Biographical Sketch of William Edwin Douglass," February 2, 1993, University of Arkansas Band Records, MC 2002-UA, box 3, folder 27, Special Collections, University of Arkansas Libraries. William Douglass's children believed this to be the original manuscript dating to his student days (Tom Douglass to Dale Millen, February

2, 1993, University of Arkansas Band Records, MC 2002-UA, box 3, folder 27, Special Collections, University of Arkansas Libraries).

9. Sporadic missing issues of the campus newspaper in the university's digitized collection warrant caution.

10. "College Spirit," *University Weekly*, May 2, 1918; "Page the Undertaker," *University Weekly*, February 3, 1921; "Snappy Program at Pep Meeting," *Arkansas Traveler*, November 3, 1921.

11. "Local Cast Will Present Comedy," *Arkansas Traveler*, November 15, 1923.

12. T. T. Tyler Thompson, *University of Arkansas Razorback Band: A History, 1874–2004* (Fayetteville: University of Arkansas Press, 2004), 44.

13. "Page the Undertaker," *University Weekly*, February 3, 1921.

14. "A Battle Song," *Arkansas Traveler*, November 16, 1922; "Untitled," *Arkansas Traveler*, November 22, 1923; "Homecoming Day is Greatest Ever Held," *Arkansas Traveler*, November 15, 1924.

15. "To Hold First 'Pep' Meeting 8:00 Tonight," *Arkansas Traveler*, October 11, 1923.

16. "And the Monkey . . .," *Arkansas Traveler*, January 22, 1925.

17. "Bandmen to Wear Colorful Uniforms," *Arkansas Alumnus*, September 1928, 10–11; "To Be Razorback Sports Announcer," *Arkansas Alumnus*, September 1928, 17.

18. "Listening in on KUOA," *Arkansas Alumnus*, October 1929, 6.

19. "KUOA Broadcasts Programs Every Day Except Sunday," *Arkansas Alumnus*, October 1929, 12; "Eight States Hear Games," *Arkansas Alumnus*, October 1929, 16; "Station KUOA to Broadcast Founder's Day Radio Program," *Arkansas Alumnus*, February 1930, 3: "KUOA Test Program Shows Station Can Cover Country If There's No Interference," *Arkansas Alumnus*, January 1929, 14.

20. "Rootin' Rubes Sell Razorback Pep Song," *Arkansas Traveler*, October 19, 1928.

21. "Prize for Pep Song Offered by Pi Kappa Journalism Society," *Arkansas Traveler*, November 15, 1928.

22. "Wanted—Words for a New Song!" *Arkansas Alumnus*, November 1928, 9–10; "There's Still Time to Give the University a New Song for Christmas," *Arkansas Alumnus*, December 1928, 6.

23. "Wanted—Words for a New Song!"; "There's Still Time."

24. List of alumni club chapters, front matter, *Arkansas Alumnus*, September 1929.

25. "Pi Kappa Extends Song Contest to March 1st," *Arkansas Alumnus*, December 13, 1928, 1.

26. "Victory (University of Arkansas Pep Song)," *Arkansas Alumnus*, June 1929, 16–17.

27. "New Pep Song in Use," *Arkansas Alumnus*, December 1929, 13.

28. "Try This On Your Piano," *Arkansas Alumnus*, June 1929, 15–17.

29. "Captain Bryan L. Milburn Wins Contest Conducted for New University Song," *Arkansas Alumnus*, January 1929, 3.

30. "Porker Pep Song Gains Popularity in Eastern Circle," *Arkansas Traveler*, September 15, 1932.

31. "New Arkansas Song Becomes National Hit," *Arkansas Traveler*, October 1, 1931.

32. "Graduates Write New Pep Song," *Arkansas Alumnus*, September 1931, 9.

33. "University to Feature Daily Radio Program," *Arkansas Traveler*, February 11, 1932. This account uses the title of Paisley's 1924 "Razorback Pep Song" but likely meant the 1931 "Razorback Rootin'." "Porker Pickups," *Arkansas Traveler*, February 18, 1932, also referred to the "new Razorback pep song" at a basketball game, likely meaning the 1931 "Razorback Rootin'."

34. The article attributed the "Field Song" arrangement to former student Richard Clayton rather than to music professor Henry Tovey, a discrepancy hard to reconcile with Tovey's name on the ca. 1913 manuscript, mentioned earlier. The article may have referred to a new 1932 "Field Song" arrangement no longer extant in the university's archives. "Douglass Field Song Favorite of Students," *Arkansas Alumnus*, May 1932, 4.

35. "Porker Pep Song Gains Popularity in Eastern Circle," *Arkansas Traveler*, September 15, 1932.

36. "Band Will Make Broadcast from Dallas," *Arkansas Traveler*, November 13, 1936.

37. Marjorie Moore, "Showmanship Is Appeal Used by Razorback Band," *Arkansas Traveler*, November 8, 1940.

38. "Twelfth Birthday of Homecoming Will Be Observed here Saturday when Razorbacks Face Rice Owls," *Arkansas Traveler*, November 8, 1934.

39. "Pep Song on Air," *Arkansas Traveler*, April 9, 1936.

40. "Pep Rally Parade, Dances to Feature 26th Celebration," *Arkansas Traveler*, October 31, 1947; "15 Tunes Are Ordered for New Chimes," *Arkansas Traveler*, February 11, 1949; "Advance Ticket Sale for Monroe [Dance] Starts Tomorrow," *Arkansas Traveler*, March 4, 1949.

41. "Pep Rally Will Be Held Friday Night; Hog Band Will Play," *Arkansas Traveler*, September 27, 1949.

42. "The Chicken or the Egg," *Arkansas Traveler*, October 8, 1943; "Ideas for the Student Senate," *Arkansas Traveler*, September 27, 1946; "Sparks from the Grindstone by Mac," *Arkansas Traveler*, September 24, 1948.

43. "UA Radio Show Broadcast from Union Ballroom," *Arkansas Traveler*, November 5, 1948.

44. "'Campus Circuit' Goes on Air Today for First Time," *Arkansas Traveler*, October 21, 1954; "Fight Song, Alma Mater Finally Break into Print for Homecoming," *Arkansas Traveler*, November 12, 1954.

45. Eldon Janzen to Joel Leach, October 23, 1972; Eldon Janzen to Col. Sam Kurtz, May 19, 1972; Tom Douglass to Dale Millen, February 2, 1993; "Arkansas Fight," arranged Dale Millen ca. 1993, University of Arkansas Band Records, MC 2002-UA, box 3, folder 27, Special Collections, University of Arkansas Libraries.

46. "We Want a New Pep Song," *Mis-A-Sip*, October 1936, 11; "Interest in Pep Song Increases," *Mis-A-Sip*, November 1936, 11.

47. "MSU Songs" vertical file, Mississippi State University Libraries, Archives and Special Collections.

48. "MSU Songs" vertical file, Mississippi State University Libraries, Archives and Special Collections.

49. "Frosh 'M' Books Insufficinet [*sic*] to Supply Demand," *Reflector*, September 19, 1934.

50. Purser Hewitt, "Hew-itt to the Line, Let the Chips Fall Where They May" *Clarion-Ledger*, October 10, 1936; "We Want a New Pep Song," *Mis-A-Sip*, October 1936, 11; "Interest in Pep Song Increases," *Mis-A-Sip*, November 1936, 10; "Pep Song Gathers Momentum," *Mis-A-Sip*, December 1936, 20; "Deadline on Song Contest Reset," *Mis-A-Sip*, January 1937 [n.p.]. *Mis-A-Sip* items in "MSU Songs" vertical file, Mississippi State University Libraries, Archives and Special Collections.
51. "Pep Song Gathers Momentum."
52. "Interest in Pep Song Increases"; "Pep Song Gathers Momentum."
53. "Interest in Pep Song Increases."
54. "Interest in Pep Song Increases"; "Pep Song Gathers Momentum."
55. "We Want a New Pep Song"; "Students to Vote on Leading Songs at Benefit Dance," *Reflector*, February 3, 1937. The Collegians played "dance novelties, tangos, waltzes, fox-trots, and special arrangements." "Collegians Now under Direction of Bell, Pianist," *Reflector*, September 19, 1934.
56. "Interest in Pep Song Increases."
57. "Interest in Pep Song Increases."
58. "Students Decide on Outstanding Song in Contest," *Reflector*, February 17, 1937.
59. Virginia Nash, "'Hail State, Born in the '30s, Still Thrilling MSU Fight Song," *Starkville (MS) Daily News*, November 26, 1969, "MSU Songs" vertical file, Mississippi State University Libraries, Archives and Special Collections.
60. "Students Decide."
61. "Students Decide."
62. "Students Decide."
63. "Local Orchestra Plans Delta Tour," *Reflector*, Dec. 9, 1936.
64. "Collegians Plan Vacation Tour," *Reflector*, March 10, 1937.
65. Grantland Rice profile, *Kansas City Times*, September 30, 1933, reprinted as "A Poet Despite the City," *Vanderbilt Alumnus*, December 1933, 9; Grantland Rice and Thornton W. Allen, "Vanderbilt Forever" (New York: Thornton W. Allen Co., 1933), Isabel Howell Papers, MSS.0216, Series: Sheet Music, flat box, Vanderbilt University Special Collections and University Archives. No correspondence between Rice and Allen is extant in the Grantland Rice Papers, MSS.0364, Vanderbilt University Special Collections and University Archives.
66. Grantland Rice, "Vanderbilt's New Marching Song," *Vanderbilt Alumnus*, October 1933, 5 (reprint of *Evening Tennessean* editorial), "Songs and Cheers" vertical file, Vanderbilt University Special Collections and University Archives.
67. Blinkey Horn, "One Flag or Two," *Tennessean*, September 6, 1933.
68. Vanderbilt Glee Club, Band Give Joint Concert," *Tennessean*, October 31, 1935; "Vanderbilt on the Air," *Vanderbilt Alumnus*, May 1937, 9; "The Whole Show Was Not on the Football Field, Candid Typewriter Man Reveals Colorful Crowd Had Big Role," *Tennessean*, November 26, 1937; "Drama of 'Curry's Good-Bye to McGugin,' before Battle, Assisted Commodores in Upsetting

Favored Rice," *Tennessean*, October 2, 1939; *Commodore* (Nashville, TN: Vanderbilt University, 1934), 92.

69. The Allen-Rice song was printed in a few 1930s Vanderbilt football programs. Vanderbilt Athletic Publications Collection: Football: Home Game Programs: 1922-1947, boxes unnumbered/no folders, Vanderbilt University Special Collections and University Archives.

70. A copy of the "Vanderbilt Forever" voice-piano sheet music with ukulele chords was inscribed to Morton Howell from the Secretary of the Vanderbilt Alumni Association at commencement 1935, suggesting some alumni interest in the song (cover inscription, "Vanderbilt Forever" [Thornton W. Allen Co., 1933], Isabel Howell Papers, MSS.0216, Series: Sheet Music, flat box, Vanderbilt University Special Collections and University Archives).

71. "Vanderbilt Alumni Gather in New York," *Vanderbilt Alumnus*, November 1935, 4.

72. "A Great Vanderbilt Reunion in Dallas" and "Vanderbilt Alumni Gather in Chicago," *Vanderbilt Alumnus*, November 1936, 3; 5.

73. "New Band Regalia, Stunts Stimulate College Spirit," *Vanderbilt Hustler*, October 28, 1936; "Bonfire, Parade to Top Pre-Game Cheering Rally," *Vanderbilt Hustler*, October 30, 1936.

74. "WSM to Broadcast Vanderbilt Games," *Vanderbilt Hustler*, October 2, 1936; "Varsity Squad Featured on Radio," *Vanderbilt Hustler*, September 24, 1937; "Gatwood Calls Glee Club Meet," *Vanderbilt Hustler*, October 2, 1936. See also from the *Vanderbilt Alumnus* "Vanderbilt's Weekly Program" (December 1933, 8) and advertisements and features in the March and April 1934 issues. The March 1937 issue documents Vanderbilt's appearance on the Pontiac Variety Show Night.

75. "Six Hundred 'Rebels' Arrive from Ole Miss," *Vanderbilt Hustler*, October 14, 1938.

76. "Band Outfitted with Striking New Uniforms," *Vanderbilt Hustler*, October 2, 1936; "Band to Present Stunts at Games," *Vanderbilt Hustler*, October 9, 1936 "New Band Regalia, Stunts Stimulate College Spirit," *Vanderbilt Hustler*, October 28, 1936.

77. "Freshmen to Fill Special Cheering Section at V.U. Games," *Vanderbilt Hustler*, October 9, 1936; "Yell!" (editorial), *Vanderbilt Hustler*, October 9, 1936.

78. "Junior Association in Action," *Vanderbilt Hustler*, September 24, 1937; "Spirit Already Revived by Junior Athletic Group," *Vanderbilt Hustler*, October 1, 1937; "Junior Association Reaches Peak in Arousing Spirit," *Vanderbilt Hustler*, November 24, 1937; "Pep Meetings," *Vanderbilt Hustler*, October 21, 1938; "Spirit Already Revived by Junior Athletic Group," *Vanderbilt Hustler*, October 1, 1937.

79. Austin, *The 40 Year Cycle*, 30, 65, 167, 268; Advertisement, Fletcher Henderson show at Nashville's Wagon Wheel nightclub, for which tickets were sold at the Vanderbilt bookstore, *Vanderbilt Hustler*, January 5, 1937; Advertisement, Duke Ellington show at Nashville's Silver Streak Ballroom, *Vanderbilt Hustler*, October 13, 1938.

80. Advertisement, 1937 Kentucky-Vanderbilt football dance at Nashville's Wagon Wheel nightclub, billed as a "battle of big bands," *Vanderbilt Hustler*,

September 24, 1937; "Red Nichols Plays for Script Dance," *Vanderbilt Hustler*,
November 3, 1938. After the 1940 Vanderbilt-LSU game, two bands played
at a dance positioned at opposite ends of the LSU gymnasium. One played
"sweet" and the other "hot" music. ("L.e S.U. [*sic*] Forget," *Vanderbilt Hustler*,
October 31, 1940.

81. Austin, *The 40 Year Cycle*; "Council Seeking Band for Prom," *Vanderbilt Hustler*,
January 22, 1937; "Red Nichols Plays for Script Dance," *Vanderbilt Hustler*,
November 3, 1938; "Jan Savitt Signed for Junior Prom Series," *Vanderbilt
Hustler*, November 22, 1940.

82. Austin, *The 40 Year Cycle*.

83. Austin, *The 40 Year Cycle*, 31, 188, 162, 169.

84. Austin, *The 40 Year Cycle*, 61, 89, 268, 270, 272, 294, 301.

85. Robert Ikard, *Near You*, 72.

86. Ikard, *Near You*, 72–73; "Dynamite" voice-piano score, undated, box 2, folder
23; "Dynamite," band arrangement with pen/pencil markings, undated, Box
3, Folder 2, Francis Craig Collection, MS.0091, Vanderbilt University Special
Collections and University Archives.

87. Francis Craig, "When Vandy Starts to Fight" ("Dynamite"), broadside
(Nashville, TN: Red Ace Gas, 1938), Mildred Simpson Scrapbook, AR-0085,
Betsey B. Creekmore Special Collections and University Archives, University
of Tennessee, Knoxville.

88. "When Vandy Starts to Fight" (Editorial), *Vanderbilt Hustler*, November 23,
1938; "Vandy's New Song," *Tennessean*, November 12, 1938.

89. "When Vandy Starts to Fight"; "New Marching Song, Key Figures in
Thanksgiving Classic," *Vanderbilt Hustler*, November 23, 1938.

90. "Vanderbilt Forever" still was used as late as 1941 ("Band to Attend Louisville
Game," *Vanderbilt Hustler*, November 14, 1941), the same year that the
band introduced a new fight song, "Vanderbilt Salute," at a game ("Band
to Introduce Vandy Fight Song," *Vanderbilt Hustler*, November 28, 1941).
"Dynamite" rarely appeared in late 1930s and early 1940s football programs
(Vanderbilt Athletic Publications Collection: Football: Home Game
Programs: 1922–1947, boxes unnumbered/no folders, Vanderbilt University
Special Collections and University Archives).

91. "Band! Wake Up!" *Vanderbilt Hustler*, October 17, 1941; "To Whom It May
Concern!," *Vanderbilt Hustler*, October 24, 1941; "The Bitter, the Sweet,"
Vanderbilt Hustler, December 5, 1941; "The War Is Over, Vandy," *Vanderbilt
Hustler*, November 16, 1945; "We Want the Best," *Vanderbilt Hustler*, October
26, 1945.

92. "Vandy Frosh to March with Band," *Vanderbilt Hustler*, October 10, 1941.

93. "Vanderbilt Band Open to Girls, Hill Announces," *Vanderbilt Hustler*,
November 4, 1943; "Vanderbilt Band, Skit Feature Turkey Game" [*sic*],
Vanderbilt Hustler, November 18, 1943; "Vanderbilt Band Returns to Campus,"
Vanderbilt Hustler, October 3, 1945.

94. Frances Craig, obituary, *Vanderbilt Alumnus*, folder 29, box 1, Francis Craig
Collection, MS.0091, Vanderbilt University Special Collections and University
Archives; *Vanderbilt Alumnus*, "The Dynamite Song," January–February

1947, 11. Edwin Morris's 1978 sale of Craig's catalogue to Paul McCartney's company caused consternation in the Vanderbilt community (untitled clipping, *Tennessean*, July 8, 1979, box 1, folder 28, Francis Craig Collection, MS.0091, Vanderbilt University Special Collections and University Archives).

95. "Radio Ban Forces Vandy Songs from Air Waves as Controversy Rages," *Vanderbilt Hustler*, January 10, 1941.

96. "Dynamite" was printed in nearly all Vanderbilt University home football programs between 1947 and 1955 (Vanderbilt University Athletic Records, Misc. Box; Vanderbilt University Athletic Publications Collection: Football: Home Game Programs: 1948-1958, Vanderbilt University Special Collections and University Archives).

97. "Band Needs More Members, *Vanderbilt Hustler*, October 21, 1949; "Band Organizes; Tulane Trip Set," *Vanderbilt Hustler*, September 29, 1950, 1; "Vandy Band Selects Military Officers," *Vanderbilt Hustler*, October 6, 1950.

98. "Vandy Band Shows Real Promise," *Vanderbilt Hustler*, October 3, 1952; "VU Band Schedules Concerts and Game Appearance, Elects Baker President," *Vanderbilt Hustler*, October 17, 1952.

99. "Pep Rally Launches Homecoming; New Band to Star Tonight," *Vanderbilt Hustler*, October 10, 1952.

100. "Cold Miss," *Vanderbilt Hustler*, October 15, 1948; "Pep Rally Launches Homecoming"; "VU Band Schedules Concerts and Game Appearance, Elects Baker President," *Vanderbilt Hustler*, October 17, 1952.

101. "New Fight Song Introduced at Game," *Vanderbilt Hustler*, October 30, 1953; "Around the Campus: Parnell and His Marching Music", *Vanderbilt Hustler*, November 6, 1953.

102. Early football songs included "Show Them Around, M.U." (tune: "Waltz Me Around, Willie") and texts sung to the tunes "Grand Old Flat" and "Rings on my Fingers" (Silas L. Dear and Clarence Leavell, eds., *The Mississippi Hand Book 1911–'12*, 18th ed., [University, MS: YMCA, 1911], 34–35); "Mississippi, U. of M." sung to "Maryland, My Maryland," associated with the Confederate army (S. Rosenthal, G. M. Jones, R. M. Guess, Iris Sweatt, eds., *The 'Ole Miss' Students' Handbook 1923–24* [University, MS: YMCA, 1923], 63); texts set to the minstrel number "Levee Song" and "Son of a Gondolier" (W. Alton Bryant, ed., *The "M" Book 1927–1928* [University, MS: YMCA and YWCA, 1927], 77), all items in "M-Books" Collection, MUM00590, box 1, 1911–1930, University of Mississippi Libraries, Department of Special Collections and University Archives. See also other texts and tunes written by students and alumni in box 1 (1911–1930) and box 2 (1930–1932), "M-Books" Collection, MUM00590, University of Mississippi Libraries, Department of Special Collections and University Archives. A student yearbook biography contained a reference to a 1930–31 songbook committee, *The Ole Miss* (Oxford, MS: 1931), 49. University of Mississippi football programs of the late 1920s and early 1930s do not contain any school songs (Football Programs Collection, MUM00556, box 1, folders 1-2, University of Mississippi Libraries, Department of Special Collections and University Archives).

103. "Ole Miss Closes Pep Song Contest March 15," *Clarion-Ledger* (Jackson, MS), February 11, 1931.

104. "Heard at the Alabama Dance," *Ole Miss* (Oxford, MS: 1932), 208.

105. *Ole Miss Alumni News*, October 1934, 1; 11.

106. *Ole Miss Alumni News*, December 1935, 5.

107. ". . . Needed—A March," *Mississippian*, November 14, 1936.

108. ". . . Good News, Director Whitfield," *Mississippian,* December 4, 1936.

109. "Band Concert Has Large Attendance," *Mississippian*, March 6, 1937; "Ole Miss Band Will Leave Monday on Annual State Tour," *Mississippian*, March 13, 1937; "New Song Will Cheer Fighting Rebs to Grid Victories in '37 Campaign," *Mississippian*, April 17, 1937.

110. "Victory March Will Be Played," *Clarion-Ledger* (Jackson, MS), February 28, 1937; "Free Band Concert Tuesday Night Features Proposed Victory March," *Mississippian*, February 27, 1937. E. F. Yerby did not donate papers to the University of Mississippi archives, and there appears to be no university band archival collection containing extant manuscripts or early arrangements of the song.

111. 1930s clippings, broadsides, and programs, Ole Miss Music Club Collection, MUM00600, folders 1-7, University of Mississippi Libraries, Department of Archives and Special Collections.

112. *The Ole Miss "M Book," 1934–35* (University, MS: YMCA and YWCA, 1934), 63, "M-Books" Collection, MUM00590, box 3, 1932-1947, University of Mississippi Libraries, Department of Special Collections and University Archives.

113. 1930s clippings, broadsides, and programs, Ole Miss Music Club Collection, MUM00600, folders 1-7, University of Mississippi Libraries, Department of Archives and Special Collections.

114. Harold Burson, "The Ole Miss Band," *The Rebel Kickoff* football program, University of Mississippi vs. Vanderbilt (University of Mississippi, November 4, 1939), 42-43, Athletic Publications: Football: Away Game Programs, 1939-1969, Vanderbilt University Special Collections and University Archives.

115. *The Ole Miss* (Oxford, MS: 1933), 77; *The Ole Miss* (Oxford, MS: 1934), 141; *The Ole Miss* (Oxford, MS: 1935), 122, 124, 182; *The Ole Miss* (Oxford, MS: 1936), 134–35, 128, 234.

116. "The Rebel Yells," *The Ole Miss* (Oxford, MS: 1937), 191.

117. "'Rebels' Is New Name for Athletic Team," *Ole Miss Alumni News*, October 1936, 6.

118. "Guider Wins Cup for Naming Team," *Ole Miss Alumni News*, October 1936, 10.

119. University of Mississippi Chancellor A. B. Butts privately expressed hesitation about the "Rebels" branding to Mississippi journalist Birney Imes, editor of the Columbus *Daily Commercial Dispatch* and vocal opponent of the branding. Butts' responses to Imes suggest he shared his concerns but felt the decision was forced on him by student, alumni, and sports media. See A. B. Butts to Birney Imes, August 4, 1936, folder 1; Birney Imes, "An Ole Miss Raw Spot," *Daily Commercial Dispatch*, n.d., folder 14; Birney Imes, "Hell Bent on It," *Daily Commercial Dispatch*, December 3, 1936, folder 14; Billy Gates to A. B. Butts,

June 30, 1936, folder 11; A. B. Butts to Billy Gates, July 10, 1936, folder 12; A. B. Butts to Birney Imes, December 17, 1936, folder 14; Birney Imes to A. B. Butts, December 22, 1936, folder 14; all items, Athletic Department Correspondence, MUM00517, University of Mississippi Libraries, Department of Archives and Special Collections.

120. Jack Carey, "Ole Miss's New Deal," 206, 207, 185.

121. "The Ole Miss Band," *The Ole Miss "M Book,"* 1937–38 (University, MS: YWCA and YMCA, 1937), 40–41; the new song appeared in the 1938 *M Book* in 1938 and thereafter through the early 1950s. See, for example, "Pep Song," *The Ole Miss "M Book,"* 1938–39 (University, MS: YWCA and YMCA, 1938), 141; "Pep Song," *Ole Miss M Book,* 1947–1948 (no publisher/editor info, 1947), 56; "Pep Song," *Ole Miss M Book,* 1948–49 (no publisher/editor info, 1948), 19, "M-Books" Collection, MUM00590, box 3, 1932–1947 and box 4, 1948–early 1950s, University of Mississippi Libraries, Department of Special Collections and University Archives.

122. For example, some 1940s football programs printed only the alma mater, such as the 1945 Ole Miss vs. University of Arkansas program (10), Football Programs Collection, MUM00556, box 1, folders 1-2, University of Mississippi Libraries.

123. *The Ole Miss* (Oxford, MS: 1950), 238; "Ole Miss Glee Club Ends Tour Here," *Clarion-Ledger*, April 7, 1949; "Ole Miss Glee Club Recordings Sell Fast," *Clarion-Ledger*, December 18, 1949.

124. *Ole Miss M Book,* 1949-1950 (no publication/editor info), 7, "M-Books" Collection, MUM00590, box 4, 1948–early 1950s, University of Mississippi Libraries, Department of Special Collections and University Archives.

125. Anne Buchanan, ed., "Exchange," *Clarion-Ledger*, December 22, 1940.

Chapter 9

1. "Louisiana: Jimmy the Stooge," *Time*, July 10, 1939.

2. There is little scholarly analysis of music's role in Huey Long's political career. Brief exceptions include a few pages in chapter 3 of Pete LaChapelle's *I'd Fight the World: A Political History of Hillbilly, Old-Time, and Country Music* (Chicago: University of Chicago Press, 2019) that link Long's use of varied genres to his varied political views, and Patrick B. Miller's mention of Long's relationship with the LSU band and football program, which Miller argues indexed Long's mythic persona and the "significance of . . . the rituals and spectacles of sporting competition" in the southern mind. Miller, *Sporting World*, 1–3. An example of typical retrospective journalism covering Long's musical activities at LSU is Jeremy Alford's "Sounds of the Kingfish," *gambit*, September 27, 2009, https://www.nola.com/gambit/commentary/article_ d29d4323-d895-5f66-b6ae-18fd08c7edba.html, which roots those activities in Long's personality rather than in a broader historical moment, as does the Louisiana Music Hall of Fame's description of Huey Long and Castro Carazo's musical collaborations. Del Moon and Mike Shepherd, "Huey P. Long & Castro Carazo," Louisiana Music Hall of Fame, accessed May 11, 2022,

https://louisianamusichalloffame.org/huey-p-long-castro-carazo. Biographies of Huey Long contain valuable anecdotes about music in Long's career, although they neither analyze their significance nor situate them in larger social and cultural contexts. Harry T. Williams, *Huey Long* (New York: Alfred Knopf, 1969) and Richard D. White Jr. *Kingfish: The Reign of Huey P. Long* (New York: Random House, 2006). Williams's biography should be regarded critically; see Michael S. Martin, "'We both Have Reason to Feel Good About the Book': Russell Long, T. Harry Williams, and Huey Long," *Historian*, 69, no. 4 (Winter 2007): 706–27.

3. Robert Penn Warren to Mr. ____ Stahley, November 7, 1962, MSs.5072, Louisiana State University Libraries, Special Collections. In the letter, Warren recounted LSU's focus on publicity in the Huey Long years when Warren was on the English faculty. Warren recalled of founding the *Southern Review* at LSU that even if its contents had upset Long, the journal likely would have been allowed to continue because it might have had "some advertising value" for the school.

4. On Long's policy proposals, political strategies and abuses, and impact on state politics, see Jerry P. Sanson, "'What He Did and What He Promised To Do . . .': Huey Long and the Horizons of Louisiana Politics," *Louisiana History: The Journal of the Louisiana Historical Society*, 47 no. 3 (Summer 2006): 261–76.

5. Huey P. Long, *Every Man a King: The Autobiography of Huey P. Long* (New Orleans: National Book Company, 1933); Williams, *Huey Long*; White, *Kingfish*; Historic Films Archive's F-A2905 contains footage of brass band music and singing at Huey Long's political events, usually with Long conducting and singing.

6. Don DeVol Oral History, Oct 7, 1982, Washington DC, 4700.0009, tape 9, 10: 8–9, Louisiana State University Libraries, Special Collections. DeVol worked as Long's private secretary in Washington, DC.

7. Long, *Every Man a King*; Williams, *Huey Long*; White, *Kingfish*.

8. Long, *Every Man a King*; Williams, *Huey Long*; White, *Kingfish*; Historic Films Archive's F-A2905.

9. Don DeVol Oral History, 22.

10. Footage of Huey Long with unknown pianist and vocalist singing "Every Man a King" in 1935, "Huey Long Collection | Every Man A King | Rare, Slowed Down," posted by @GeneralBurkhalter1, Dec. 27, 2017, https://www.youtube.com/watch?v=UePByx_jq44, and Huey Long with Ina Ray Hutton and her All-Girls Orchestra performing "Every Man a King," 1935, Historic Films Archive's F-A2905, 02:22:24. Both clips can be dated to 1935 due to the publication of "Every Man a King" in very early January 1935 and Long's September 1935 assassination.

11. Richard Munson, "Huey's Composer Still Dapper at 84," *Advocate* (Baton Rouge, LA), 1980, "Castro Carazo" vertical file, Louisiana State University Libraries, Special Collections.

12. Multiple revised drafts of press release about Huey Long's involvement with the band, Louisiana State University News Bureau, ca. 1930, Louisiana State

University School of Music Records, RG#A1600, box 13, folder 1, Louisiana State University Libraries, Special Collections.

13. Multiple revised drafts of press release about Huey Long's involvement with the band, Louisiana State University News Bureau, ca. 1930, Louisiana State University School of Music Records, RG#A1600, box 13, folder 1, Louisiana State University Libraries, Special Collections.

14. Huey P. Long, *My First Days in the White House* (Harrisburg, PA: Telegraph Press 1935), 8–9. Long's private secretary in Washington, DC, attested to Long's infatuation with brass band music in Don DeVol Oral History, 21.

15. White, *Kingfish*, 108.

16. A 1958 band hall fire at LSU likely destroyed many sources related to Huey Long and the band program, 1930–1935, although a few such sources survive in the Louisiana State University School of Music Records, RG#A1600, Louisiana State University Libraries, Special Collections, and are referenced in this chapter. According to longtime LSU university archivist Barry Cowan, the Huey P. Long Papers and other Long-related collections at the Louisiana State University Libraries contain few sources related to music in Long's career aside from copies of sheet music, which are referenced in this chapter.

17. Huey P. Long to Kurt Schwartz, September 27, 1933, Kurt S. Schwartz Papers, MSs.3740, Louisiana State University Libraries, Special Collections.

18. Continé and Phillips, *Golden Band*, 19; multiple revised drafts of press release about Huey Long's involvement with the band, Louisiana State University News Bureau, ca. 1930, Louisiana State University School of Music Records, RG#A1600, box 13, folder 1, Louisiana State University Libraries, Special Collections.

19. Multiple revised drafts of press release about Huey Long's involvement with the band, Louisiana State University News Bureau, ca. 1930; advertisement, Conn Instruments, *Musical Truth*, ca. 1930, 6–7, with photograph of LSU band captioned "Governor Long of Louisiana himself signed the order for a complete set of Conn instruments" from a New Orleans Conn dealer, Louisiana State University School of Music Records, RG#A1600, box 13, folder 1, Louisiana State University Libraries, Special Collections; Cadet Band to Travel With '31 L.S.U. Gridsters," press release, Louisiana State University News Bureau, 1931, Louisiana State University School of Music Records, RG#A1600, box 13, folder 1, Louisiana State University Libraries, Special Collections.

20. Continé and Phillips, *Golden Band*, 19; multiple revised drafts of press release about Huey Long's involvement with the band, Louisiana State University News Bureau, ca. 1930, Louisiana State University School of Music Records, RG#A1600, box 13, folder 1, Louisiana State University Libraries, Special Collections. I have not found scores or recordings of the march.

21. "To Instruct Huey's Band," *Tennessean*, December 19, 1934.

22. AP Report, "Row with Huey Long Culminates in Resignation of Jones as L.S.U. Coach," *New York Times*, December 19, 1934.

23. Munson, "Huey's Composer Still Dapper." Long's former secretary confirmed this pattern of behavior, noting that "when [Long] wanted

something he wanted it right then and there," demanding, for example, same-day turnaround on print materials (Don DeVol Oral History, 13–14).

24. "Senators Approve Official Marching Song for Louisiana," AP Release, *Town Talk* (Alexandria, LA), June 3, 1952.

25. "Carazo Leads On," *Reveille*, Nov. 3, 1939; "Carazo Returns from Band Conclave," *Reveille*, 1940[?]; "Carazo Will Judge in Band Festival," *Reveille*, 194[0?], "Famed ASCAP Invites Carazo," *Reveille*, Dec. 3 or 5, 1939; "Carazo's March Included in Folio," *Reveille*, Feb. 24, 1940; "Carazo Gets Band Honor," *Reveille*, March 30, 1940 ("Castro Carazo" vertical file, Louisiana State University Libraries, Special Collections). See also "WJBO to Present Marine Broadcast of Carazo March," *Morning Advocate* (Baton Rouge, LA), March 1, 1940.

26. "Bandmaster Began His Career at Age of Six," *Advocate* (Baton Rouge, LA), April 6, 1935. The Saenger company, initially based in Shreveport where they opened their first theater in 1925, eventually operated hundreds of theaters across the South. Saenger moved operations to New Orleans in 1927 and opened a theater there, where Carazo may have been its first music director. "Welcome to the Strand: Share your Memories!," Strand Theatre, accessed January 12, 2021, https://thestrandtheatre.com/about; "The Venue," Saenger Theatre, accessed January 12, 2021, https://www.saengernola.com/info/history.

27. Continé and Phillips, *Golden Band*, 22–23.

28. "Bandmaster Began His Career at Age of Six," *Advocate* (Baton Rouge, LA), April 6, 1935.

29. "L.S.U. Band Director," *Louisiana Leader*, April 1938; "Copies of Progress March for Bands," *Progress* (Hammond, LA), March 24, 1939; "Carazo March Will Be Played at National Guard Convention," *Progress* (Hammond, LA), November 5, 1939; "WJBO to Present Marine Broadcast of Carazo March," *Morning Advocate* (Baton Rouge, LA), March [?]1, 1940 ("Castro Carazo" vertical file, Louisiana State University Libraries, Special Collections).

30. Carazo conducted the Baton Rouge Symphony Orchestra in an arrangement of his "Overture to an Imaginary Play" and the Grieg Piano Concerto in A minor ("Former LSU Band Director Will Be Guest Conductor," *Reveille*, February 23, 1949). See also a list of Carazo's compositions in "WJBO to Present Marine Broadcast of Carazo March," *Morning Advocate* (Baton Rouge, LA), March [?]1, 1940; and Munson, "Huey's Composer Still Dapper." "Castro Carazo" vertical file, Louisiana State University Libraries, Special Collections.

31. Upon Carazo's removal, a Baton Rouge newspaper described his band directorship as a "dictatorship" (AP Release, "Castro Carazo Is Discharged as L.S.U. Band Head," *State Times* [Baton Rouge, LA], August 24, 1940, "Castro Carazo" vertical file, Louisiana State University Libraries, Special Collections). Carazo maintained ties with LSU, conducting high school bands on campus and returning for retrospective halftime shows.

32. Continé and Phillips, *Golden Band*, 19; Paul C. Young et al., oral history interview, 4700.0067, 1983, 24, 36, T. Harry Williams Center for Oral History Collection, Louisiana State University Libraries, Special Collections. According to this interview, Huey funded his own very specific ideas. When

he wanted a vocal quartet to perform at an early-1930s football banquet, possibly in Knoxville for a University of Tennessee-LSU game, Long bought train tickets for quartet members and their wives.

33. Photographs, Governor Huey Pierce Long handing out dollar bills to members of the Louisiana State University band, ca. 1933, State Library of Louisiana Historic Photograph Collection.

34. UP Feature, "LSU Band Faces Personnel Loss to Aid Military," *Pensacola News Journal*, November 21, 1953; Munson, "Huey's Composer Still Dapper."

35. Mary Hebert, oral history, "'I've Got a University': Huey Long and LSU's Golden Years," 1994, T. Harry Williams Center for Oral History, Louisiana State University.

36. On the band's use of jazz and ragtime in the 1910s and 1920s, see Continé and Phillips, *Golden Band*, and *Reveille* accounts such as "Medley of L.S.U. Songs Composed by Prof. Stropher," January 16, 1925; "KFGC Will Start Broadcasting on Thursday Nights," February 13, 1925; and "L.S.U. Station Broadcasts First Time This Week," February 20, 1925.

37. "From Forty Years Back," *Baton Rouge State Times*, October 5, 1972, "Castro Carazo" vertical file, Louisiana State University Libraries, Special Collections.

38. The 1936 LSU yearbook contained a two-page spread featuring the covers of two Long-Carazo songs ("Darling of LSU" and "Touchdown for LSU"), Carazo's headshot, and band photographs. The feature credited Carazo for expanding the band and diversifying its repertoire to encompass "military marches, pep songs, Alma Maters, symphonic overtures, classic and semi-classic fantasies, and popular selections." "Presenting Castro Carazo and the LSU Cadet Band," *Gumbo Yearbook* Class of 1936 (Louisiana State University and Agricultural & Mechanical College, 1936), n.p. See also Jack Troy, "'Sherman's Boys in Gray' March Here Saturday," *Atlanta Constitution*, November 15, 1935.

39. This may have reflected the governor's strained relationship with the student newspaper, discussed in the chapter's conclusion.

40. Eleanor Tatum, "Castro Carazo to Create Concert Band and Symphonic Dance Orchestras" and "Handsome Gift Presented to Wickboldt," *Reveille*, January 11, 1935.

41. "New Uniforms to be Adopted for LSU Band," *Reveille*, March 1, 1935.

42. Munson, "Huey's Composer Still Dapper."

43. "Song is Composed by Senator Long," *Miami Herald*, January 3, 1935. The report references published music for "Every Man a King."

44. No documentation of Long's and Carazo's songwriting seems extant in Louisiana State University Libraries Special Collections (Barry Cowan, University Archivist, Louisiana State University Libraries, email to author, May 10, 2018).

45. "Musical Memories," Louisiana Public Television, Baton Rouge, 1979; Munson, "Huey's Composer Still Dapper."

46. Munson, "Huey's Composer Still Dapper."

47. James E. Crown, "Long at Home: Spurring on the Solons," *New York Times*, July 21, 1935.

48. Don DeVol Oral History, 24.
49. "Farewell Is Said by Kingfish Long," *Morning Call* (Patterson, NJ), January 3, 1935.
50. Huey Long singing at outdoor political rally, [1935?], Historic Films Archive's F-A2905, 2:06:09.
51. Brad J. Burke, "Abraham Shushan: In the Shadow of Huey Long" (MA thesis, University of New Orleans, 2018), 3.
52. "Musical Memories" (Baton Rouge: Louisiana Public Television, 1979).
53. "Long and Carazo Publish 2 Songs of Old War Skule," *Reveille*, July 12, 1935.
54. "Company Buys L.S.U. Songs," *Reveille*, October 18, 1935.
55. "Castro Carazo Creates New Song; Students Invited to Write Verse; Winner of Contest to Have Name Copyrighted with Bandmaster's," *Reveille*, April 2, 1935; "Song Contest Regulations Are Announced" and "Melody Presented to Students by Carazo," *Reveille*, April 5, 1935.
56. "Song Contest Regulations"; "Melody Presented."
57. "Song Contest Regulations"; "Melody Presented."
58. "Song Contest Regulations"; "Melody Presented."
59. "Song Contest to be Extended Until Friday," *Reveille,* May 3, 1935.
60. "Cardenia Wins Lyric Contest," May 17, 1935.
61. "Cadet Band Wins Applause, Improvement Noted under New Leader," *Reveille*, April 9, 1935; "Univ. Band Will Give Concert at 1 O'clock Today," *Reveille*, May 3, 1935; LSU cadet band programs, March 18, 1935 and April 5, 1935, Kurt S. Schwartz Papers, MSs.3740, Louisiana State University Libraries, Special Collections.
62. Crown, "Long at Home."
63. Information about contents of LSU alumni magazine courtesy Barry Cowan, University Archivist, Louisiana State University Libraries (email to author, April 22, 2022).
64. The 1931–32 *L-Book* included "Tiger Swing," "LSU Swing," "Tulane Dirge," "Fight" (to the "Stein Song" tune), "Bengal Swing," and "Tigers" (*L-Book*, "Songs and Yells," 1931-32), 62–73, Louisiana State University Libraries, Special Collections. Other information about *L-Books* courtesy Barry Cowan, University Archivist, Louisiana State University Libraries (email to author, April 22, 2022).
65. *Louisiana State University Songs* (New York: Thornton W. Allen Company, 1937), Louisiana State University School of Music Records, RG#A1600, Box 11, Folder 7, Louisiana State University Libraries, Special Collections.
66. "LSU Program to Be Broadcast by Station WSM" and "LSU Program Is Broadcast from New York," *Reveille*, October 15, 1935; Decca Records #60081-50084, October 18, 1935.
67. Photographs of Huey Long at LSU football games show him on the field or sidelines, conferring with referees, posing with cheerleaders, or talking to coaches and university administrators. Huey P. Long Photograph Album, 1928–1935, Louisiana State University Libraries, Special Collections and Louisiana Digital Library, https://louisianadigitallibrary.org/islandora/object/

lsu-sc-hpl:collection. These appearances created affection for Long among LSU music and band students; they appreciated his formation of a "huge band," financial and logistical sponsorship of travel, parade appearances, and involvement with football music. One alumnus recalled that around 1933–34, Long appeared at an LSU choral rehearsal and ordered the group to learn a new alma mater to sing at the next football game (Young et al., oral history interview).

68. The 1934 Nashville trip is but one example of Long's well-publicized travels with the LSU band, often covered by the national press. For example, long before Carazo was hired, in October 1931, Long and the LSU contingent traveled to Houston for the Rice-LSU game, where Long led the band in a downtown parade.

69. Walter Greaves Cowan and Jack B. McGuire, *Louisiana Governors: Rulers, Rascals, and Reformers* (Jackson: University Press of Mississippi, 2008), 174-175.

70. "Nashville Stage All Set to Greet Senator Long and L.S.U. Tigers Today," *Tennessean*, October 27, 1934.

71. Cowan and McGuire, *Louisiana Governors*, 174.

72. "Huey Long May Swell Crowd for Vandy and L.S.U. to 18,000," *Tennessean*, October 27, 1934.

73. "Huey Long May Swell Crowd."

74. A police force was necessary; on other occasions when Long appeared with the LSU band, crowds had to be restrained by Louisiana police. "Huey Long and Band Awe Mississippians," *New York Times*, November 18, 1934. Long, a polarizing figure, likely wanted his own loyal force rather than relying on the twenty Tennessee officers provided in Nashville. "Nashville Stage All Set to Greet Senator Long and L.S.U. Tigers Today," *Tennessean*, October 27, 1934; "Huey Long May Swell Crowd."

75. "Nashville Stage All Set" with cartoon of Huey Long astride a train holding a lasso for a tiger, captioned "Football Puts on a Show," *Tennessean*, 1934.

76. "Huey Takes Coach, Mayor for a Walk," *Tennessean*, October 28, 1934.

77. Jack Monroe, "Kingfish Grins, Has Perfect Day, Pays Tribute to Coach McGugin as 20,000 Cheer in Stadium," *Tennessean*, October 28, 1934.

78. Photograph, Huey Long leading quartet at Vanderbilt-LSU football game, October 1934[?], Leon Trice Political Photographs, Tulane University Digital Library.

79. Huey Long singing in stands at football game, 193[?], Historic Films Archive's F-A2905, 02:15:23.

80. Monroe, "Kingfish Grins"; "Huey Long May Swell Crowd."

81. The next month, Long conducted a similar trip to Jackson, Mississippi, where LSU played the University of Mississippi. Long led a band parade to the Capitol, escorted by the Jackson mayor and by Governor Sennett Conner, whom a Long aide hauled off the front porch of the governor's mansion to join the procession. The parade concluded on the Capitol steps with a band concert led by Long, who also led the crowd in singing. "Huey Long and Band Awe Mississippians," *New York Times*, November 18, 1934.

82. Peterson, *Sound, Space, and the City*, 3.
83. Sandra Fink, "Spectacles of the Street: Performance, Power, and Public Space in Antebellum New Orleans" (PhD diss., University of Texas-Austin, 2004), 17.
84. Peterson, *Sound, Space, and the City*, 9.
85. White, *Kingfish*, 116; Young et al., 1.
86. On southern flagship universities as engines of regional white democracy in the 1930s, including augmented public relations initiatives and curricular, personnel, and physical plant expansions negotiated through fiscal relationships to state and federal governments, see Carey, *Jim Crow U*.
87. "History of LSU," Louisiana State University Libraries, Special Collections, accessed May 11, 2022, https://www.lib.lsu.edu/special/archives/historical-information.
88. *1931-32 L-Book* (Louisiana State University, 1932), 73, Louisiana State University Libraries, Special Collections.
89. Ina Ray Hutton and Her All-Girls Orchestra with Huey Long, "Every Man a King," 1935, Historic Films Archive's F-A2905, 02:22:24.
90. For a reconsideration of Long as racially progressive compared to contemporary southern governors, see Glen Jeansonne, "Huey Long and Racism," *Louisiana History: The Journal of the Louisiana Historical Association*, 33 no. 3 (Summer 1992): 265–82.
91. Chris Yacich and Frank Arena, "Follow Long" (New Orleans: National Book Company, 1935), Seymour Weiss Papers, MSs.4165, Sheet Music Box 1, Folder 17, Louisiana State University Libraries, Special Collections.
92. Patricia Sullivan, *Days of Hope: Race and Democracy in the New Deal Era* (Chapel Hill: University of North Carolina Press, 1996), 36–37.
93. Sullivan, *Days of Hope*, 36–37.
94. At 1930s football games, LSU performed "Tiger Rag," drawn from New Orleans's jazz culture, and starting in 1937 used a Black man as handler for the school's Bengal tiger mascot. After all, the LSU team name and mascot, "Louisiana Tigers," derived from the nickname of notable Confederate fighting regiments from Louisiana. The 1937 *Gumbo* yearbook vividly captures gendered and racialized dimensions of LSU's mid-1930s football pageantry, describing it as a "top-notch Broadway revue" that included women students dancing to "Tiger Rag" in support of the 207-piece male band. Meanwhile, Mike the Tiger was led roaring around the field by his "comic negro keeper," a toothless, smiling, suited Black man nicknamed "The Educated Vegetable Man" by students. Kimbrough Owen, ed., *Gumbo* (Baton Rouge: The Students of Louisiana State University, 1937), 268–75, 288. The soundscape of LSU football pageantry in the mid-to-late 1930s illuminates how cultural expressions, in tandem with law and policy, upheld southern white supremacy.
95. Williamson's framing is cited in Sullivan, *Days of Hope*, 155–56.
96. "L.S.U.: 26 Students Get Theirs in Huey Long vs. Press Row," *News Week* [sic], December 8, 1934.

Chapter 10

1. On World War II's impact on southern higher education, see Morton Sosna's introduction, James C. Cobb's "World War II and the Mind of the Modern South," and Clarence M. Mohr's "World War II and the Transformation of Southern Higher Education" in *Remaking Dixie: The Impact of World War II on the American South*, ed. Neil R. McMillen, (Jackson: University Press of Mississippi, 2007).
2. Mohr, "World War II."
3. These provisions aimed at retaining nominal amateurism in college sport by limiting universities' financial support for athletes. On SEC resistance to the sanity code, see Watterson, *College Football*, 213–18, and Mohr, "World War II," 41–42.
4. An October 1940 University of Pennsylvania game was the first television broadcast of college football, with TV deals for the sport in place by the late 1940s, monopolized by the NCAA for the next three decades. Zimbalist, *Unpaid Professionals*, 92, 94–96. The growing importance of college football TV broadcasts in the South are documented in the new column "On the Air" launched in September 1950 in the trade journal *Southern Coach and Athlete* 13, no. 1 (Sept. 1950), 58. On southern bowl games launched in the 1940s and 1950s, see Martin, "Integrating New Year's Day." On the postwar college football "arms race," see Walsh, *Where Football Is King*, 15–17, and Watterson, *College Football*, 209–18 and chapter 14.
5. Advertisements and articles in *Southern Coach and Athlete*, vol. 9 (September 1946 to June 1947) and vol. 10 (September 1947 to June 1948); on unequal postwar subsidization of public university football stadiums in the South, see White, *Blood, Sweat, and Tears*, 51, 92, 115–17.
6. *Southeastern Conference Press and Radio Dope Book* (Birmingham, AL: Southeastern Conference Office, 1948), Grantland Rice Papers, MSS.0364, box 20, folder 5, Vanderbilt University Special Collections and University Archives.
7. *Grantland Rice's Cities Service Football Guide*, launched in 1933 and published through the early 1950s, Grantland Rice Papers, MSS.0364, box 8, folder 25, Vanderbilt University Special Collections and University Archives.
8. Chapter 4 in Jeffrey Montez de Oca, *Discipline and Indulgence: College Football, Media, and the American Way of Life During the Cold War* (New Brunswick: Rutgers University Press, 2013).
9. Watterson, *College Football*, 201–2.
10. ". . . and they all went WILD," *Birmingham News*, December 2, 1956.
11. "Band to Feature TV Show Saturday for Georgia Game," *Auburn Plainsman*, November 14, 1951; football programs, Vanderbilt vs. Virginia Military Institute, September 21, 1968 and Vanderbilt vs. Army, September 27, 1969, Vanderbilt University Athletic Publications: Football: Home Game Programs, 1961-1969, Vanderbilt University Special Collections and University Archives; "Zarathustra" sheet music, 1969, Carolina Bands Collection, SCU-MUS-0001, Box 6, Folder 77, University of South Carolina Ernest F. Hollings Special Collections.

12. Football programs, Vanderbilt vs. Georgia Tech, September 23, 1967 and Vanderbilt vs. University of Tennessee-Chattanooga, September 12, 1970, Vanderbilt University Athletic Publications: Football: Home Game Programs, 1970–1972, Vanderbilt University Special Collections and University Archives; "Drill Charts, 1976," Carolina Bands Collection, SCU-MUS-0001, box 6, folder 88, University of South Carolina Ernest F. Hollings Special Collections.

13. Football programs, Vanderbilt vs. Army, September 27, 1969 and Vanderbilt vs. Mississippi State University, September 23, 1972, Vanderbilt University Athletic Publications: Football: Home Game Programs, 1961–1969 and 1970–1972, Vanderbilt University Special Collections and University Archives; "Media, 1968," Carolina Bands Collection, SCU-MUS-0001, box 5, folder 74, University of South Carolina Ernest F. Hollings Special Collections.

14. "Tigers Play at Home Saturday," *Alabama Journal*, October 6, 1944, mentioned the band playing the "Auburn Victory March"; "API Activities: Band Maps Plans for Tech Contest," *Opelika (AL) Daily News*, October 13, 1949, described the band playing "Auburn Victory March" in the halftime show; "API Activities," *Opelika Daily News*, November 30, 1951, documented the band playing "Auburn Victory March" and "Glory, Glory to Old Auburn"; Eldonna Brown, "Band Will Honor Miss Homecoming during API-State Halftime Show," *Auburn Plainsman*, November 7, 1952, stated that the halftime show included "Auburn Victory March," the alma mater, and "Tiger Rag"; "Tiger Rag" was mentioned in "500 Brave Rain, High Wind to Greet Touring API Band," *Dothan (AL) Eagle*, March 4, 1952; Les Ford, "Traditional Auburn Song Faces Death," *Auburn Plainsman*, October 2, 1953, described and printed the text for a "War Eagle Fight Song," claiming that although it once was used at games, parades, and pep rallies with the alma mater and the War Eagle cry, it had been neglected since Fall 1950; "Band to Perform at Tech, Benning," *Auburn Plainsman*, October 17, 1952, mentioned a halftime show with "Glory, Glory to Old Auburn" and "Dixie"; Herb White, "On the Rolling Plains of Dixie," *Auburn Plainsman*, October 30, 1953, called the alma mater the school's "most important song" and urged students to sing it at games ("if we can sing 'Glory, Glory to Old Auburn' we can surely sing it"); "Band to Execute X Plus Y Equals V Formation Saturday," *Auburn Plainsman*, October 15, 1954, mentioned "Auburn Victory March" played at halftime; "Band to Present New School Song," *Auburn Plainsman*, November 24, 1954, printed the text of a new song called "Spirit of API" with no tune, composer, or lyricist attribution and conveyed the band director's wish for students to learn it.

15. "New Victory Song [to] Be Presented at Next Pep Meeting," *Auburn Plainsman*, November 4, 1933.

16. "Songs Published," *Birmingham News*, October 16, 1936; "New Song at Auburn," *Montgomery Advertiser*, November 24, 1933. *Alabama Polytechnic Institute Songs* (New York: Thornton W. Allen, 1936) contained the alma mater, "Auburn Victory March," and "Fight 'Em Tiger" (sometimes spelled "Fight 'Um Tiger"). Other Auburn songs published in the first half of the twentieth century included Joe Marino's and William Sykes's "Fight 'Um

240 Notes to Page 133

Tiger" (Auburn A[lumni?] Club: 1931, Auburn University Libraries, Special Collections and Archives).

17. Untitled notice, *Opelika Daily News*, May 16, 1952, described a fall release for RCA Victor's Auburn album of school band and glee clubs performing the alma mater, "Auburn Victory March," "Tiger Rag," "Glory, Glory to Old Auburn," "Fight 'Em Tiger," and two new songs including "Hail to Auburn." One thousand albums would be pressed, with sales handled by the Alumni Association and college bookstore. "API Songs Ready in '45' Albums," *Auburn Plainsman*, September 25, 1952, stated that in addition to the 45s, RCA Victor would release 78s of Auburn songs. "New Record Album 'Songs of Auburn' Released for Sale," *Auburn Plainsman*, October 1, 1954, described an RCA Auburn band-choral album for sale at the campus bookstore, with many of the same songs listed in 1952 media coverage.

18. *Auburn Tiger Yells and Pep Songs* (Auburn University Student Association [?], ca. 1954) contains yells, the alma mater, and the song "Fight On, War Eagle," with no tune, text, or composer attribution. The book can be roughly dated with internal evidence of student names.

19. In the early and mid-1950s, the *Auburn Plainsman* advocated for band scholarships ("On the Auburn Band," December 3, 1954); urged students to cheer loudly and create new yells ("Tommy Burton Requests 'Give More War Eagles' for Florida Pep Rally," October 12, 1951; "Football Yell Contest Deadline Saturday," November 7, 1951; "Things Look Black as Student Spirit Sags to Record Low Mark," October 31, 1952); encouraged the creation of a school flag ("Florida Has Flag—Why Not Auburn?" November 7, 1952); praised band improvements (Eldonna Brown, "Auburn Band Pours Time, Effort into Grid Shows," November 21, 1952); and complained that students didn't know the alma mater well enough to sing it at games ("On Our Alma Mater," November 14, 1951). In assessing the university's financial, personnel, and maintenance needs during these years, many of which it deemed pressing, the student newspaper never called for a new song.

20. From 1950 to 1957, the years in which Sewell commissioned a new song, the *Auburn Alumnus* often mentioned his work on the Building Advisory Committee, in fundraising campaigns, and as an Alumni Association officer.

21. In addition to recommending adoption of coaching strategies and publicity approaches used at other southern schools (Roy Sewell to Auburn publicity director Bill Beckwith, August 2, 1958), Sewell corresponded with coaches about administrative and equipment minutiae. He suggested using head padding for a fragile player (Assistant Coach C. L. "Shot" Senn to Roy Sewell, March 15, 1952) and a dictating machine for office productivity, an idea the athletic staff adopted (Roy Sewell to Ralph Jordan, December 13, 1952; Ralph Jordan to Roy Sewell, August 31, 1954). Roy Sewell Correspondence, Athletic Department Records, RG 392, Auburn University Libraries, Special Collections and Archives.

22. In spring 1952, Jordan sent Sewell a list of 1952 football recruits and Sewell urged him to try the under-scouted cities of Montgomery, Huntsville, and Florence, Alabama (Roy Sewell to head coach Ralph "Shug" Jordan, March

8, 1952 and Ralph Jordan to Roy Sewell, April 18, 1952). Sewell visited recruits independently, then asked Auburn coaches to follow up (Roy Sewell to Ralph Jordan, April 21, 1952, November 25, 1952, and November 5, 1953). Sewell's maneuvers were informed by materials sent him by Auburn coaches: lists of scholarship recipients, assessments of prospects, and rosters of incoming freshmen (Ralph Jordan to Roy Sewell, January 21, 1953; Roy Sewell to Ralph Jordan, January 10, 1953; Roy Sewell to Ralph Jordan, July 22, 1953). Sewell kept tabs on players' academic performance (Roy Sewell to Ralph Jordan, January 4, 1957). In late spring 1957, Sewell wrangled with the Auburn registrar over the high school credentials of an out-of-state recruit. Sewell leaned on the recruit's high school principal to massage the athlete's GPA and asked the Auburn president and head coach to pressure the registrar to admit the student despite failing to meet Auburn's out-of-state class rankings criteria. Although Jordan told Sewell he was powerless in and ignorant of the situation, he forwarded his family's vacation itinerary to Sewell for ease of contact during the crisis (Ralph Jordan to Roy Sewell, May 30, 1957). Roy Sewell Correspondence, Athletic Department Records, RG 392, Auburn University Libraries, Special Collections and Archives.

23. Sewell sent inspirational quotations (Roy Sewell to Ralph Jordan, July 22, 1953; July 24, 1953; February 11, 1956) and religious books to Jordan, which the coach vowed he used daily (Roy Sewell to Ralph Jordan, August 29, 1952; Ralph Jordan to Roy Sewell, August 26, 1952). Mindful of the impact of Jordan's health on Auburn's football fortunes, Sewell wrote, "Ralph, I have a great interest in you and want to say to you at this time that whatever you are doing to gain weight you must discontinue . . . so you will be able to handle your coaching duties" (Roy Sewell to Ralph Jordan, May 19, 1954). Sewell followed this expression of concern with diagnostic self-help questions (Roy Sewell to Ralph Jordan, May 22, 1954). In 1957, Sewell suggested the Athletic Department retain a psychologist (Roy Sewell to Ralph Jordan, February 19, 1957) and funded a trip for Jordan to visit Dr. Norman Vincent Peale for private sessions in New York (Ralph Jordan to Roy Sewell, May 3, 1957). Sewell had encouraged Jordan to adopt Peale's perspectives for years, sending him a Peale book in 1952 (Roy Sewell to Ralph Jordan, August 25, 1952). Roy Sewell Correspondence, Athletic Department Records, RG 392, Auburn University Libraries, Special Collections and Archives. Sewell, interested in midcentury psychology and motivational thought, served on the Board of Governors of the American Foundation of Religion and Psychiatry. Roy Sewell, *One Sewell Family* (Atlanta, GA: Higgins-McArthur Company, 1960), 93.

24. Roy Sewell to Ralph Jordan, March 8, 1955, Roy Sewell Correspondence, Athletic Department Records, RG 392, Auburn University Libraries, Special Collections and Archives.

25. Sewell, *One Sewell Family*, 91–92.

26. "Atlanta Auburn Club Honors Loyal Son, Roy Sewell," *Atlanta Constitution*, May 15, 1963. Sewell reiterated these sentiments in his memoir, writing "As a youth at Auburn I was deeply impressed by the spirit of the place" and quoting George Petrie's "Auburn Creed" (Sewell, *One Sewell Family*, 86).

27. Ralph Jordan to Roy Sewell, May 9, 1952; Roy Sewell to Ralph Jordan, July 9, 1952, July 16, 1952, and October 14, 1953; Ralph Jordan to Roy Sewell, July 11, 1952. Sewell donated money to Auburn, sending $100 to its Educational Foundation and to the Tiger Club in spring 1954 (Roy Sewell to Ralph Jordan, April 5, 1954; Ralph Jordan to Roy Sewell, May 14, 1954). See also Roy Sewell to Bill Beckwith, October 14, 1958, which mentions a parking pass for the press box given to Sewell. Roy Sewell Correspondence, Athletic Department Records, RG 392, Auburn University Libraries, Special Collections and Archives.

28. Roy Sewell to Ralph Jordan, July 25, 1957, Roy Sewell Correspondence, Athletic Department Records, RG 392, Auburn University Libraries, Special Collections and Archives.

29. Ralph Jordan to Roy Sewell, July 1, 1955, Roy Sewell Correspondence, Athletic Department Records, RG 392, Auburn University Libraries, Special Collections and Archives. Extant correspondence between Auburn president Ralph Draughon and Roy Sewell from Fall 1954 contains no mention of Sewell's song plans, although the two men were in touch and socialized in Birmingham in December for a bowl game (Roy Sewell to Ralph Draughon, December 2, 1954; Ralph Draughon to Roy Sewell, December 3, 1954, Ralph Brown Draughon Papers, Series II, Box 1, Folders 21 and 22). The two did briefly discuss the song plans in Ralph Draughon to Roy Sewell, February 26, 1955, and Draughon made it clear that he was leaving the matter in Sewell's hands. Ralph Brown Draughon Papers, RG #107, Access. 1968, Series II, Box 1, Folder 22, Auburn University Libraries, Special Collections and Archives.

30. Roy Sewell to Ralph Draughon, February 24, 1955, Ralph Brown Draughon Papers, RG #107, Access. 1968, Series II, Box 1, Folder 22, Auburn University Libraries, Special Collections and Archives.

31. Dorothy Wanless, *The Auburn University Band: A Centennial History, 1897–1997* (Dallas, TX: Taylor Publishing Company, 1997), 76.

32. Obituary, "Robert Allen, 73, Whose Songs Were Sung by an Array of Stars," *New York Times*, October 5, 2000.

33. "I commissioned a song-writing team in New York to produce [a fight song]. One of those submitted was approved." In Sewell, *One Sewell Family*, 84.

34. Alan Patureau, "For Roy Sewell Sr., Auburn Is a Suitable Enthusiasm," *Atlanta Journal Constitution*, November 16, 1986.

35. Zipp Newman, "Dusting 'Em Off," *Birmingham News*, Sports, October 2, 1955, exemplifies midcentury Alabama press coverage of the supposed history of the Auburn "war eagle" yell, which Auburn's midcentury campus press also discussed frequently.

36. Al Stillman and Robert Allen, "War Eagle: A New Song for Auburn," voice-piano sheet music (Auburn Alumni Association, 1955), Auburn University Libraries, Special Collections and Archives.

37. The first page of the voice-piano score for "War Eagle" appeared on the front page of the *Birmingham News* Sunday sports section, September 4, 1955; see also Newman, "Dusting 'Em Off," and an untitled notice about new Auburn song, *Chattanooga Daily Times*, September 11, 1955.

38. "'War Eagle' Set to Music," *Alabama Journal*, September 5, 1955; "Fight Song Generates Enthusiasm Everywhere," *Alabama Journal*, November 9, 1956.

39. "'War Eagle' Set to Music."

40. Staff report, "Composer Proud of 'War Eagle' Fight Song," *Opelika-Auburn News*, October 11, 2000.

41. "'Big Orange Group' Incentive to Spirit," *Auburn Plainsman*, September 30, 1955; Auburn vs. University of Chattanooga football program, September 24, 1955, "Auburn's New Fight Song!" n.p., Auburn University Libraries, Special Collections and Archives.

42. "For Early Arrivals, Football Music," *Birmingham News*, October 5, 1955.

43. "Pep Rally, Dance Is Set Tonight by API Students," *Opelika (AL) Daily News*, September 30, 1955; "Band Scheduled for Seven Shows at Grid Contests," *Auburn Plainsman*, September 30, 1955; "Two Dances Set for Homecoming Next Week-End," *Auburn Plainsman*, October 28, 1955.

44. Bill Neville, "War Eagle Song—A New Tradition," *Auburn Plainsman*, October 28, 1955.

45. "Roy Sewell Is Selected by Alumni," *Anniston (AL) Star*, November 11, 1956.

46. Auburn News Bureau, "API Activities," *Opelika (AL) Daily News*, September 23, 1957.

47. "'War Eagle' Set to Music"; Bob Bozeman, "The Week's Wash," *Dadeville (AL) Record*, September 8, 1955; "Fight Song Generates Enthusiasm Everywhere."

48. "Darkness on the Plains," *Montgomery Advertiser*, September 10, 1955. Auburn student Bill Neville quoted part of the *Advertiser* critique in "War Eagle Song—A New Tradition."

49. "Fight Song Generates Enthusiasm Everywhere." The Auburn Alumni Association sponsored a .45 of "War Eagle" ca. late 1955. Wanless, *Auburn University Band*, 186.

50. "War Eagling Will Blanket the U.S.A.," *Birmingham News*, April 20, 1958. Previous recordings had been made ("Don't Run Over our Football Players," *Birmingham News*, January 24, 1956).

51. See numerous articles from the Alabama press cited in this section.

52. Andrea Walton, "What the Lens of Philanthropy Might Bring to the History of U.S. Higher Education," *History Teachers* 51 no. 1 (Nov. 2017): 9–36. Walton highlights the historiographic trend since the 1980s of historians of philanthropy in higher education focusing on large foundations. In contrast, this account of Roy Sewell's midcentury relationship with Auburn University explores the formative power of individual philanthropy in shaping university culture.

53. Sewell, *One Sewell Family*, 92.

54. Roy Sewell Scrapbook, "Homecoming '83," Alumni and Development Office Records, RG #385, Access. 96-64, Auburn University Libraries, Special Collections and Archives.

55. Reed Smith, "Carolina's Day," piano score, arr. P. S. Gilman (Columbia, SC: Reed Smith, 1914). Carolina Bands Collection, SCU-MUS-0001, Sheet Music: Box 1, Folder 7, Special Collections, University of South Carolina Libraries.

56. USC's 1964 band drill charts included "Carolina's Day," Carolina Bands Collection, SCU-MUS-0001, Box 3, Folder 45, Special Collections, University of South Carolina Libraries. Box and folder numbers for the Carolina Bands Collection are from the collection finding aid, although items digitized from the collection are often assigned different box and folder numbers in USC libraries' online entries.

57. F. E. Bigelow, "The NC-4 March," B♭ cornet and first clarinet parts (New York: Walter Jacobs, 1919); see James Pritchard's undated item annotations for the USC archives, Carolina Bands Collection, SCU-MUS-0001, Sheet Music: Box 1, Folder 8, Special Collections, University of South Carolina Libraries. USC's 1963 band drill charts included the "NC-4 March." Carolina Bands Collection, SCU-MUS-0001, Box 3, Folder 42, Special Collections, University of South Carolina Libraries.

58. Yates Snowden and Mrs. Leize F. B. Lockwood, "Carolina Hail!" (University of South Carolina Dean's Office, 1925); Carolina Bands Collection, SCU-MUS-0001, Sheet Music: Box 1, Folder 9, Special Collections, University of South Carolina Libraries.

59. Sanders R. Guignard (Class of 1932), "Carolina Football Song," late 1920s/early 1930s, text inserted under tune of Frances Shackelton, "Campus Song" (Ursinus College), *Intercollegiate Song Book* (New York: Thornton W. Allen, 1927), 205. Carolina Bands Collection, SCU-MUS-0001, Sheet Music: Box 1, Folder 10, Special Collections, University of South Carolina Libraries.

60. Text for four songs not mentioned here, and ten yells, were printed in the 1931–1932 *Carolina Students' Handbook* (University of South Carolina Young Men's Christian Association and Young Women's Christian Association, 1931–32), 88–94. Carolina Students' Handbook Collection, 1920–1940, University Archives, University of South Carolina.

61. M. Carrére Salley to James Pritchard, May 16, 1969, dates song contest to ca. 1933 but confesses uncertainty about exact year; James Pritchard to M. Carrére Salley, May 20, 1969; undated Permissions Card for "Carolina Fight Song" dating the song to 1936, Carolina Bands Collection, SCU-MUS-0001Box 6, Folder 49, Special Collections, University of South Carolina Libraries.

62. M. Carrére Salley "Carolina Fight Song" manuscript (melody and piano accompaniment), ca. 1936, and SATB arrangement by James Pritchard, 196[?]. Pritchard supplied the USC archives with information about arrangements and alterations made to the song throughout the 1950s and 1960s. Carolina Bands Collection, SCU-MUS-0001, Sheet Music: Box 1, Folder 11, Special Collections, University of South Carolina Libraries. Extant marching band drill charts from Pritchard's tenure document the use of "Carolina Fight Song" in 1961 and 1962 (Carolina Bands Collection, SCU-MUS-0001, Programs and Scripts, 1959: Box 1, Folder 20; Box 2, Folder 26; Box 3, Folder 33, Special Collections, University of South Carolina Libraries).

63. Fred Waring, "The Gamecocks of SCU," sheet music, 1940, Carolina Bands Collection, SCU-MUS-0001, Sheet Music: Box 1, Folder 13, Special Collections, University of South Carolina Libraries.

64. In the 1966 and 1967 football seasons, Pritchard used a at least three new
    songs. First was "Fight!!! USC!" written in 1966 by a sergeant stationed in
    Columbia, SC (Carolina Bands Collection, SCU-MUS-0001, Box 5, Folder
    62, Special Collections, University of South Carolina Libraries). In 1967,
    Pritchard went to great lengths to locate music for, and arrange for band,
    the German march "Frei Weg!" by C. Latann (Carolina Bands Collection,
    SCU-MUS-0001, Box 5, Folder 60; folders 69 and 70 document his efforts
    to obtain the score). In 1967, Pritchard introduced a band arrangement
    of "Fighting Gamecock Song" by E. Z. "Buzz" Purcell, first published for
    piano by Whippoorwill Music of Lexington, SC, in 1967. Carolina Bands
    Collection, SCU-MUS-0001, Box 5, Folder 61, Special Collections, University
    of South Carolina Libraries.

65. Pritchard's arrangement of "Step to the Rear" lists copyright by Carwin
    Music, Inc. with permission authorized, copyright 1967. Carolina Bands
    Collection, SCU-MUS-0001Box 5, Folder 71, Special Collections, University
    of South Carolina Libraries; James Pritchard, notes on "Step to the Rear,"
    Carolina Bands Collection, SCU-MUS-0001, Box 5, Folder 71, Special
    Collections, University of South Carolina Libraries.

66. Pritchard, notes on "Step to the Rear."

67. Pritchard, notes on "Step to the Rear."

68. James Pritchard to Edwin Morris, Band Arrangement Request Form, "Step
    to the Rear," October 30, 1968; James Pritchard to Sol Reiner (Edwin Morris
    Co.), October 30, 1968, with song lyrics enclosed, Carolina Bands Collection,
    SCU-MUS-0001, Box 6, Folder 49: "Correspondence and Notes, 1969," Special
    Collections, University of South Carolina Libraries.

69. Pritchard, notes on "Step to the Rear"; James Pritchard to Edwin Morris,
    Band Arrangement Request Form, "Step to the Rear," October 30, 1968;
    James Pritchard to Sol Reiner (Edwin Morris Co.), October 30, 1968, Carolina
    Bands Collection, SCU-MUS-0001, Box 6, Folder 49: "Correspondence and
    Notes, 1969," Special Collections, University of South Carolina Libraries.

70. James Pritchard to Harry Fox (Agent and Trustee, Edwin Morris Co.),
    October 20 and 21, 1969, cited an early January 1969 correspondence regarding
    royalties and indicated a Fall 1968 conception date for USC's plan to record
    "Step to the Rear." James Pritchard to Sol Reiner [Edwin Morris Co.], October
    30, 1968, Carolina Bands Collection, SCU-MUS-0001, Box 6, Folder 49, Special
    Collections, University of South Carolina Libraries.

71. M. Carrére Salley to James Pritchard, May 16, 1969, and James Pritchard to
    Sol Reiner [Edwin Morris Co.], October 30, 1968, Carolina Bands Collection,
    SCU-MUS-0001, Box 6, Folder 49, Special Collections, University of South
    Carolina Libraries.

72. James Pritchard to M. Carrére Salley, May 20, 1969, stated that the USC
    band recorded Salley's "Carolina Fight Song" that spring and would add the
    university choir to the recording that fall, hoping to release a *Songs of Carolina*
    album in the mid-1969 football season; see also undated Permissions Card
    for "Carolina Fight Song" dating the song to 1936, Carolina Bands Collection,

SCU-MUS-0001, Box 6, Folder 49, Special Collections, University of South Carolina Libraries.

73. M. Carrére Salley to Paul Dietzel, December 10, 1968, and James Pritchard to Sol Reiner [Edwin Morris Co.], October 30, 1968, Carolina Bands Collection, SCU-MUS-0001, Box 6, Folder 49, Special Collections, University of South Carolina Libraries.

74. James Pritchard to M. Carrére Salley, May 20, 1969, and James Pritchard to Sol Reiner [Edwin Morris Co.], October 30, 1968, Carolina Bands Collection, SCU-MUS-0001, Box 6, Folder 49, Special Collections, University of South Carolina Libraries.

75. Pritchard, notes on "Step to the Rear"; Paul Dietzel's poem "Sissy" quoted in Ted Ownby, "Manhood, Memory, and White Men's Sports in the American South," in Miller, *Sporting World*, 326–27.

76. Paul Dietzel, "Straight Talk from the Roundhouse," *Gamecock*, September 11, 1967.

77. Band Directions and Drill Charts, Halftime Music, 1966 Homecoming, Carolina Bands Collection, SCU-MUS-0001, Box 4, Folder 53, Special Collections, University of South Carolina Libraries.

78. Band Budget Memo, 1969-70, James Pritchard to Paul Dietzel, April 12, 1969, Carolina Bands Collection, SCU-MUS-0001, Box 6, Folder 49: "Correspondence and Notes, 1969," Special Collections, University of South Carolina Libraries.

79. James Pritchard to Paul Dietzel, June 6, 1969, and Paul Dietzel to James Pritchard, June 6, 1969, Carolina Bands Collection, SCU-MUS-0001, Box 6, Folder 49: "Correspondence and Notes, 1969," Special Collections, University of South Carolina Libraries.

80. USC band director James Copenhaver wrote "Go Carolina" and premiered it at the 1980 Gator Bowl, stating that USC was looking for another fight song. Musical score, Carolina Bands Collection, SCU-MUS-0001, Box 9, Folder 118: "Sheet Music, 1980," Special Collections, University of South Carolina Libraries.

81. "Football Songs," football program, University of Tennessee vs. Central University of Kentucky, Oct 2, 1909, n.p.; "Tennessee Songs and Yells," football program, University of Tennessee vs. Sewanee, Oct 18, 1913, n.p.; "Cheers and Songs," football program, University of Tennessee vs. Carson-Newman, Oct 18, 1924, n.p. (Football Programs Digital Collection, University of Tennessee Libraries).

82. "Cheers and Songs," football program, University of Tennessee vs. Carson-Newman, Oct 18, 1924, n.p.; football program, University of Tennessee vs. Sewanee, Nov 6, 1926, n.p.; "Songs and Yells," football program, University of Tennessee vs. University of Mississippi, Oct 12, 1929, n.p. (Football Programs Digital Collection, University of Tennessee Libraries).

83. "U.T. Students to Publish 'Tennessee Song Book,'" *Tennessean*, January 11, 1929; Erle Stapleton, ed., *Songs of the Volunteers: Songs of the University of Tennessee* (Knoxville, TN: The All-Students' Club, University of Tennessee), 1929.

84. David C. Turpie documents how the 1939 University of Alabama-University of Tennessee game thrust the Tennessee football program into the national

spotlight with a dual CBS-NBC radio broadcast and the convergence of sports media on Knoxville. Bing Crosby also discussed the game and sang UT's "Spirit of the Hill" on his NBC radio show *Kraft Music Hall* on October 26, 1939. That year, the UT Athletic Department created a publicity department, hired a publicity director, and expanded the stadium's press box. In Turpie, "From Broadway to Hollywood." Turpie argues that these events "demonstrate[d] the greater integration of the South into the nation and into American popular culture that occurred in the late 1930s" (135).

85. Appendix, Thornton W. Allen's college song copyrights.

86. Cassandra Sproles, "Tennessee Songs," *Torchbearer*, March 20, 2017.

87. "Neyland's Boys March against Sooners to Tune of New Song 'Fight, Vols, Fight,'" *Tennessean*, December 20, 1938; an identical article, suggestive of a UT press release, ran in the *Atlanta Constitution* on December 20, 1938. Betsy B. Creekmore, "Fight Vols Fight!" Volopedia, University of Tennessee Libraries, last updated Oct. 7, 2018, https://volopedia.lib.utk.edu/entries/fight-vols-fight.

88. The undated broadside "Songs of UT" contains typed lyrics for "Fight Vols Fight," "Spirit of the Hill," Tennessee Victory March, "Aloha OE, "To Tennessee," and "Here's to Old Tennessee," extant in the memorabilia of a woman who attended UT in the late 1930s. Mildred Simpson Scrapbook, AR-0085, Betsy B. Creekmore Special Collections and University Archives, University of Tennessee Libraries.

89. 1970s UT pregame shows nearly always included "Fight, Vols, Fight," "Down the Field," and the "Tennessee Waltz," closing with "Spirit of the Hill" and the alma mater. Series Three, Box 64, 1960s and 1970s Game Scripts, UT Marching Band Collection, AR-0785, Betsey C. Creekmore Special Collections and University Archives, University of Tennessee Libraries.

90. The Vanderbilt band played a retrospective country medley of "Wildwood Flower," "Wabash Cannonball," "Foggy Mountain Breakdown," "I Saw the Light," and "Jambalaya." Football program, Vanderbilt vs. University of Alabama, October 9, 1971, 96, Vanderbilt University Athletic Publications, Football: Home Game Programs, 1970–1972.

91. Boudreaux and Felice Bryant Songwriting Ledger #9, December 1967, 122–23, Country Music Hall of Fame; Patricia A. Hall, interview with Boudreaux and Felicia Bryant (Nashville TN: Country Music Foundation Oral History Project OH18, November 19, 1975), 48–49; "'Rocky Top' Writer Sings Praises of Song's Legacy," *Tennessean*, December 5, 1998.

92. Bryant Ledger #9, 122–123; Hall, interview with Bryants, 48–49; "'Rocky Top' Writer Sings Praises."

93. Hall, interview with Bryants, 4; Lee Wilson, *All I Have to Do Is Dream: The Boudleaux and Felice Bryant Story* (Nashville, TN: Two Creeks Press/House of Bryant Publications, 2017), 6–7, 10–12.

94. Hall, interview with Bryants, 49; Wilson, *All I Have to Do Is Dream*, 109–10.

95. Bobbie Malone and Bill C. Malone, *Nashville's Songwriting Sweethearts: The Boudreaux and Felice Bryant Story* (Norman: University of Oklahoma Press, 2020), 118.

96. Box 64, Folder 71, UT Game Scripts: October 21 1972 vs. Alabama, UT Marching Band Collection, AR-0785, Betsey C. Creekmore Special Collections and University Archives, University of Tennessee Libraries.

97. Box 64, Folder 71, UT Game Scripts: October 21 1972 vs. Alabama, UT Marching Band Collection, AR-0785, Betsey C. Creekmore Special Collections and University Archives, University of Tennessee Libraries.

98. Roy Acuff and the Carter Family recorded and performed the nineteenth-century song "Wabash Cannonball" in the 1930s, while the old song "Columbus Stockade Blues," performed and recorded by many artists long before this period, received renewed attention in 1970 due to Willie Nelson's album of the same title.

99. Photograph, "Rocky Top" with Marching Band, Neyland Stadium (Knoxville TN, September 23, 1978), Bryant Collection, Accession 2017.74, Box 001, Country Music Hall of Fame, Nashville, Tennessee.

100. Even after the UT band introduced "Rocky Top" in 1972, pregame shows in the 1970s continued to use "Fight, Vols, Fight," "Down the Field," and the "Tennessee Waltz," usually closing with "Spirit of the Hill" and the school's alma mater. Series Three, Box 64, 1960s and 1970s Game Scripts, University of Tennessee Marching Band Collection, AR-0785, Betsey C. Creekmore Special Collections and University Archives, University of Tennessee Libraries.

101. UT Game Scripts: LSU (Bluebonnet Bowl), 1972 Dec. 30, Box 64, Folder 76, UT Marching Band Collection, AR-0785, Betsey C. Creekmore Special Collections and University Archives, University of Tennessee Libraries.

102. Henrietta W. Chandley (Mrs. E. L. Jr.) to Pride of the South Band, October 29, 1977, Box 2, Folder 9, UT Marching Band Collection, AR-0785, Betsey C. Creekmore Special Collections and University Archives, University of Tennessee Libraries.

103. George M. Livers to Dr. Julian, October 17, 1979, Box 2, Folder 9, UT Marching Band Collection, AR-0785, Betsey C. Creekmore Special Collections and University Archives, University of Tennessee Libraries.

104. *Volunteer* (Knoxville: University of Tennessee, 1979), 419.

105. For example, in October 1972, the month the band debuted "Rocky Top," the Beacon printed a radio editorial by James Brown urging African Americans to eschew violence and pursue education. "James Brown Speaks Out," *UT Daily Beacon*, October 18, 1972. See also chapter 5 in T. R. C. Hutton, *Bearing the Torch: The University of Tennessee, 1794–2010* (Knoxville: University of Tennessee Press, 2022).

106. "Is Dixie Worth the Violence?" letter to editor, November 10, 1972, and "Anger at Symbols Is Ridiculous," letter to editor, November 29, 1972, *UT Daily Beacon*.

107. See issue of the UT *Library Development Review* (University of Tennessee Libraries Marketing and Communications Team, 2017–2018) dedicated to documenting the school's embrace of "Rocky Top" as an institutional symbol, including exhibits of song memorabilia, archival collections of band history, and alumni events celebrating the song.

108. Fall *UT Daily Beacon* coverage of 1972 Homecoming festivities.

109. "This Is Knoxville Now," *UT Daily Beacon,* October 31, 1972.

110. Marching band photographs, 1972, Box 2, Folder 14, UT Marching Band Collection, AR-0785, Betsey C. Creekmore Special Collections and University Archives, University of Tennessee Libraries.

111. Mildred Acuff to Dr. Julian, July 27, 1979, and Mildred Acuff to Dr. Julian, November 5, 1979, Box 2, Folder 9, UT Marching Band Collection, AR-0785, Betsey C. Creekmore Special Collections and University Archives, University of Tennessee Libraries.

112. UT Game Scripts: Kentucky 1972 November 25, Box 64, Folder 74 and UT Game Scripts, Duke 1973 September 15, Box 64, Folder 79, UT Marching Band Collection, AR-0785, Betsey C. Creekmore Special Collections and University Archives, University of Tennessee Libraries.

113. Marching band photographs, 1972, Box 2, Folder 13; UT Game Scripts, Duke 1973 September 15, Box 64, Folder 79; Drill Charts: Pregame and Halftime: Kentucky/Vandy 1973 and Special Pregame, Bengals Chart #3, 1973, Box 62, Folder 13; Drill Charts, Colorado/Ole Miss 1975, Box 62, Folder 27; Drill Charts: Ole Miss, Kentucky, Vandy 1977, Box 62, Folder 41; September 7, 1974, UCLA, Box 64, Folder 91; UT Game Scripts: Auburn 1975 September 27: pregame, Box 64, Folder 103; UT Game Scripts: Duke 1976 September 11, Box 64, Folder 113. UT Marching Band Collection, AR-0785, Betsey C. Creekmore Special Collections and University Archives, University of Tennessee Libraries. Non-uniform citation data replicates item titles as they appear in this collection.

114. Anthony Harkins, *Hillbilly: A Cultural History of an American Icon* (Oxford: Oxford University Press, 2004), 4.

115. Harkins, *Hillbilly,* 71–72.

116. Harkins, *Hillbilly,* 71–72. Joti Rockwell emphasizes continual genre contestation and negotiation in bluegrass discourse, practice, and fandom, "especially given [its] hybrid status . . . as a folk music, a progressive concert music, and a commercially mediated form" in "What Is Bluegrass Anyway? Category Formation, Debate and the Framing of Genre," *Popular Music* 31 no. 3 (Oct 2012), 364. UT's use of "Rocky Top" demonstrates the rich cultural, symbolic, and economic possibilities enabled by bluegrass's "hybrid status."

117. Hutton, *Bearing the Torch,* 136.

118. Malone, *Nashville's Songwriting Sweethearts,* 121.

119. M. Helen Rosko, "Drinking and (Re)making Place: Commercial Moonshine as Place-Making in East Tennessee," *Southeastern Geographer* 57 no. 4 (Winter 2017), 353–54.

120. Emelie K. Peine and Kai A. Schafft, "Moonshine, Mountaineers, and Modernity: Distilling Cultural History in the Southern Appalachian Mountains," *Journal of Appalachian Studies* 18, no. 1 (Spring/Fall 2012), 93.

Chapter 11

1. Demas, *Integrating the Gridiron*, 72–87.
2. Kurt Edward Kemper, *College Football and American Culture in the Cold War Era* (Urbana: University of Illinois Press, 2009), 136–37.
3. White, *Blood, Sweat, and Tears*, 166, 191. On SEC academic desegregation, see Peter Wallenstein, ed., *Higher Education and the Civil Rights Movement: White Supremacy, Black Southerners, and College Campuses* (Gainesville: University of Florida Press, 2009) and Melissa Kean, *Desegregating Private Higher Education in the South: Duke, Emory, Rice, Tulane, and Vanderbilt* (Baton Rouge: Louisiana State University Press, 2013). On SEC athletic desegregation see Martin, "Desegregating New Year's Day"; chapters 3 and 4 of Kemper, *College Football and American Culture*; Charles H. Martin, "Hold That (Color) Line!: Black Exclusion and SEC Football, in Wallenstein, *Higher Education and the Civil Rights Movement*; chapter 4 in Demas, *Integrating the Gridiron*; Charles H. Martin, *Benching Jim Crow: The Rise and Fall of the Color Line in Southern College Sports, 1890–1980* (Urbana: University of Illinois Press, 2010); Andrew Maraniss, *Strong Inside: Perry Wallace and the Collision of Race and Sports in the South* (Nashville, TN: Vanderbilt University Press, 2016); and chapter 5 in T. R. C. Hutton, *Bearing the Torch: The University of Tennessee, 1794–2010* (Knoxville: University of Tennessee Press, 2022).
4. Demas, *Integrating the Gridiron*, 3.
5. Hutton, *Bearing the Torch*, 108.
6. Derrick White, "Race, Football, and 'Dixie' at the University of Florida," *Florida Historical Quarterly* 88 no. 4 (Spring 2010): 469–96; chapter 8 in Christian McWhirter, *Battle Hymns;* Craig A. Warren, *The Rebel Yell: A Cultural History* (Tuscaloosa: University of Alabama Press, 2014); Jack Carey, chapter 6 in "The Design of the Southern Future: The Struggle to Build White Democracy at the University of Mississippi, 1890–1948" (PhD diss., University of Mississippi, 2014); Carey, *Jim Crow U.*
7. Bill DeJournett, *The Pride of the South, 1928–2014: The Ole Miss Rebel Band, A History* (Oxford: University of Mississippi, 2015).
8. "Feel of Old South" (photograph caption), *Delta Democrat Times*, November 13, 1958.
9. Hutton, *Bearing the Torch*, 111.
10. "API Features Minstrel Show at Tiger-'Dog Contest," *Auburn Plainsman*, November 14, 1952.
11. "Band to Feature Stephen Foster's Music at Game," *Arkansas Traveler*, October 23, 1953.
12. Emily Bingham, *My Old Kentucky Home: The Astonishing Life and Reckoning of an Iconic American Song* (New York: Alfred A. Knopf, 2022), 169–71.
13. Football programs, Vanderbilt vs. University of Kentucky, November 10, 1956, 41, and September 8, 1958, n.p., contained sheet music for "My Old Kentucky Home" with the original term "darkies." Athletic Publications: Football: Away Game Programs, 1939-1969, Vanderbilt University Special Collections and University Archives.

14. University of Florida Centennial Homecoming Half-Time Show, 1952, Production #20, Earl Jarnigan Film Archives, University of Florida Archives Moving Image Collection.

15. "Band Directions and Drill Chart, USC vs. Georgia, Oct. 6, 1962," Carolina Bands Collection, SCU-MUS-0001, Ernest F. Hollings Special Collections, University of South Carolina Libraries.

16. For context on national and state Civil War Centennial commemorations, see Robert J. Cook's *Troubled Commemoration: The American Civil War Centennial, 1961–1965* (Baton Rouge: Louisiana State University Press, 2007). Cook documents how centennial events in southern states often expressed Lost Cause and other sectional sentiment, whereas federal government and some northern state centennial events attempted to project a stance of reconciliation. Related to the USC halftime show described here, see Chapter 3, which documents political and social controversies around South Carolina's 1961 centennial celebrations.

17. 1961 University of South Carolina halftime show, University of South Carolina Moving Image Research Collections, SCAR 90. For context on the rebel yell, see Warren, *The Rebel Yell*; for context on most Confederate songs mentioned here, see earlier chapters of this book.

18. Mohr, "World War II," 52.

19. Chapter 4 in John Thelin, *Going to College in the Sixties* (Baltimore, MD: John Hopkins University Press, 2021).

20. Wallenstein, *Higher Education and the Civil Rights Movement*, 21.

21. William Tate, "The University Cannot Win with Either Way in Controversy over Playing 'Dixie,'" *Athens Observer*, September 23, 1976, and *Athens Observer Sportsview*, September 11, 1976.

22. "Band Will Continue Playing 'Dixie,'" *Northwest Arkansas Times*, November 4, 1968; "Arkansas Had Wrangle over 'Dixie,'" *Austin American-Statesman*, November 29, 1970.

23. Christian K. Anderson and Amber C. Fallucca, eds., *The History of American College Football: Institutional Policy, Culture, and Reform* (London: Routledge, 2021), 13.

24. University of Georgia Black Student Union to President Fred Davison, February 26, 1969, Hargrett Rare Book and Manuscript Library, University of Georgia.

25. A. Levert Hood, Chief of Staff, University of Georgia Black Student Union, to President Fred Davison, February 21, 1971, Hargrett Rare Book and Manuscript Library, University of Georgia.

26. Chronology of "Dixie" Controversy, n.d., Box 78, Folder 10, William Tate Papers, UA97-085, Hargrett Rare Book and Manuscript Library, University of Georgia.

27. Chronology of "Dixie" Controversy; Buddy Waller, "UAP Member Says 'Dixie' Not Racist," *Red and Black*, November [?], 1974, Box 50, Folder 6, William Tate Papers, UA97-085, Hargrett Rare Book and Manuscript Library, University of Georgia.

28. President Fred Davison, Memo to University of Georgia Faculty and Staff, October 31, 1975, Alumni Society Collection, UA97-108, Box 18, Folder 2, Hargrett Rare Book and Manuscript Library, University of Georgia.

29. Chronology of "Dixie" Controversy and letters in Alumni Society Collection, UA97-108, Box 18, Folder 2, Hargrett Rare Book and Manuscript Library, University of Georgia.

30. Clippings in Alumni Society Collection, UA97-108, Box 18, Folder 2, Hargrett Rare Book and Manuscript Library, University of Georgia.

31. Steve Dancz to William Tate, October 3, 1976, Box 78, Folder 10, William Tate Papers, UA97-085, Hargrett Rare Book and Manuscript Library, University of Georgia.

32. Tate, "The University Cannot Win."

33. Fall 1976 letters to William Tate in Box 50, Folder 6, William Tate Papers, UA97-085, Hargrett Rare Book and Manuscript Library, University of Georgia.

34. Herbert B. Kimzey to William Tate, July 21, 1976, Box 78, Folder 10, William Tate Papers, UA97-085 and _____ Wells, political cartoon depicting UGA marching band member in "Turn-Coat Band" uniform stomping on Confederate battle flag, October 12, 1975, *Athens Banner-Herald*, Alumni Society Collection, UA97-108, Box 18, Folder 2, Hargrett Rare Book and Manuscript Library, University of Georgia.

35. Chronology of "Dixie" Controversy, n.d., Box 78, Folder 10, William Tate Papers, UA97-085, Hargrett Rare Book and Manuscript Library, University of Georgia.

36. Phil Jones to Tyus Butler, Director of Alumni Relations, University of Georgia Alumni society, April 30, 1976, Box 78, Folder 10, William Tate Papers, UA97-085, Hargrett Rare Book and Manuscript Library, University of Georgia.

37. Dean John C. Stephens Jr., to William Tate, September 27, 1976, Box 78, Folder 10, William Tate Papers, UA97-085, Hargrett Rare Book and Manuscript Library, University of Georgia.

38. Tate, "The University Cannot Win."

39. Tate, "The University Cannot Win," described how Georgia Tech coach Bobby Dodd asked the Tech band to drop "Dixie" because it hurt recruitment of Black players.

40. Angie Maxwell, *The Indicted South*, 18. For a historicization of "tackiness" and its regional, class-based, and racial inflections, especially in opposition to mainstream and middle-class aesthetics, see Charles Reagan Wilson, Foreword, and Katherine Burnett and Monica Carol Miller, "Introduction: What Would Dolly Do?" in *The Tacky South*, ed. Katherine Burnett and Monica Carol Miller (Baton Rouge: Louisiana State University Press, 2022).

41. Andrew Doyle, "An Atheist in Alabama Is Someone Who Doesn't Believe in Bear Bryant: A Symbol for an Embattled South," in Miller, *Sporting World*, 248.

42. Brad Green, curator, Paul W. "Bear" Bryant Museum (Tuscaloosa, AL), email to author, September 9, 2021.

43. McCluskey, "'Rough! Tough!," 29–57; McCluskey, "This is Ghetto Row": Musical Segregation in American College Football," *Journal of the Society for American Music* 14, no. 3 (August 2020): 337–63,

44. Zachary J. Lechner, Introduction, *The South of the Mind: American Imaginings of White Southernness, 1960–1980* (Athens: University of Georgia Press, 2018), unpaginated e-book.

45. Travis Stimeling, "'Stay Out of the Way of the Southern Thing': The Drive-By Truckers' Southern Gothic Soundscape," *Popular Music and Society* 36 no. 1 (2013), 22.

46. Nadine Hubbs, "'Redneck Woman' and the Gendered Poetics of Class Rebellion," *Southern Cultures* 17, no. 4 (Winter 2011), 47, surveys the "redneck pride" phenomenon in popular music of the 1970s. Chapter 4 in Lechner, *The South of the Mind*, documents Skynyrd's use of Confederate flags and recordings of "Dixie," journalists' reaction to their hypermasculine, hardcore white southern persona, and group members' ambiguous political stances in song and real life. For a review of varied perspectives on southern rock's cultural politics, see Bartow J. Elmore, "Growing Roots in Rocky Soil: An Environmental History of Southern Rock," *Southern Cultures* 16 no. 3 (Fall 2010): 102–28; interpretations of "Sweet Home Alabama" are discussed on 121. For more on the band's 1970s image and reception, see Mark Ribowsky, *Whiskey Bottles and Brand-New Cars: The Fast Life and Sudden Death of Lynyrd Skynyrd* (Chicago: Chicago Review Press, 2015). Charles Hughes argues that interracial southern music studios such as Muscle Shoals, where Lynyrd Skynyrd often recorded, obscured the extent of racial inequality in the post–civil rights South; see chapter 6 of *Country Soul: Making Music and Making Race in the American South* (Chapel Hill: University of North Carolina Press, 2015).

47. Richard Dyer, *Stars*, 3rd ed. (London: BFI Publishing), 1979.

48. Charles Hughes, *Country Soul*, 162.

49. Erin C. Tarver, *The I in Team*, 3.

50. Nell Irvin Painter, *Southern History across the Color Line*, 2nd ed. (Chapel Hill: University of North Carolina Press: 2021), 4.

51. Watts, *White Masculinity*, 15.

52. Christopher Cooper and H. Gibbs Knotts, "South Polls: Rethinking the Boundaries of the South," *Southern Cultures*, 16 no. 4 (Winter 2010), 74.

53. For an overview of southern exceptionalism as a historiographic concept and a popular, mythic belief, see the introduction in Andrew J. Huebner and John M. Giggie, eds., *Dixie's Great War: World War I and the American South* (Tuscaloosa: University of Alabama Press, 2021), 1–2.

54. In "This Is Ghetto Row," McCluskey argues that music selections in Power Five college football are racialized, with in-game music coding white to appeal to predominantly white fan bases and recruiting/pre-game music coding Black to appeal to predominantly Black athletes. McCluskey argues that this musical "segregation" echoes racialized power hierarchies of college football management and administration.

55. McCluskey, "This Is Ghetto Row," 338.

56. Matthew D. Lassiter and Joseph Crespino, introduction to *The Myth of Southern Exceptionalism* ed. Lassiter and Crespino (Oxford: Oxford University Press, 2010), 27. Although this collection primarily explores the limits of the framework of southern exceptionalism as a tool of historical analysis for the South's political, economic, religious, and social development, its interrogation of this framework has productive implications for the study of southern cultural products and expressions.
57. Miller, *Segregating Sound*, 8.
58. Natalie Ring, *The Problem South*, 14.

Epilogue

1. Andrew Smith, "SEC Expansion: Why Missouri Makes Neither Sense nor Cents for League," *Bleacher Reports*, October 6, 2011, https://bleacherreport.com/articles/882367-sec-expansion-why-missouri-makes-neither-sense-nor-cents-for-league.
2. Charles Reagan Wilson, "Whose South? Lessons Learned from Studying the South at the University of Mississippi," *Southern Cultures* 22, no. 4 (Winter 2016), 104.
3. Thomas T. Railey, "When the Varsity Band Plays Dixie" (tune from *Missouri Harmony*), Thomas T. Railey, ed., *Around the Columns: 1929 Missouri Songbook*, 16. "Dixie" appeared in printed university football materials such as a 1952 University of Missouri vs. University of Maryland football program ("Missouri Songs") and the undated song booklet *On the Quad* that contained "Dixie" and the Civil War tune "Marching Through Georgia," "Songs and Cheers" vertical files, University Archives and Special Collections, University of Missouri Libraries.
4. "A New M.U. Song," *Missouri Alumnus*, May 1914, mentions a pep songbook compiled by the Young Women's Christian Association at the University of Missouri, "Songs and Cheers" vertical file, University Archives and Special Collections, University of Missouri Libraries.
5. Typed memo containing information about "Old Missouri" [early twentieth century], "Songs and Cheers" vertical file, University Archives and Special Collections, University of Missouri Libraries.
6. "Fifty Dollars for a Song," *The Independent*, May 27, 1905; sheet music, "Old Missouri" [1921?]; "Tiger Pep" in University of Missouri Song Booklet (1920-1921); *Alumnus* announcement of song contest (1926); "M.U. Song Book Started in 1873," University of Missouri student paper [?], September 19, 1929, describes the "modern edition" of the school songbook as beginning in 1924, sponsored by the Alumni Association, "Songs and Cheers" vertical file, University Archives and Special Collections, University of Missouri Libraries.
7. "New Song Accepted by Pres. Middlebush," *Columbia Missourian*, November 29, 1946, describes the unusual ratification of "Fight Tiger" (written by two students) by the university president at a pep rally. The song was selected by a student judging board which selected it from roughly fifty entries. The

text printed in the article was neither sectional nor regional. By the 1950s, it was regularly used, along with "Every True Son" and a handful of others. "Songs and Cheers" vertical file, University Archives and Special collections, University of Missouri Libraries.

BIBLIOGRAPHY

Allen, Thornton W., ed. *Intercollegiate Songbook*. New York: Thornton W. Allen Company, 1927.

Allen v. Walt Disney Productions, Ltd. et al., 41 F. Supp. 134. Southern District, New York. June 27, 1941.

Anderson, J. A., city attorney. *Code of the City of Atlanta, Adopted by the Mayor and General Council, September 4, 1899, and Approved the Same Day*. Atlanta, GA: Byrd Printing Co., 1899.

Andre, Naomi, and Denise Von Glahn. "Colloquy: Shadow Culture Narratives: Race, Gender, and American Music Historiography," *Journal of the American Musicological Society* 73, no. 3 (Fall 2020): 711–84.

Austin, Ben. *The Forty Year Cycle*. South Pasadena, CA: Kilmarnock Press, 1980.

Baily, Dee. "College Songs." *Grove Music Online/Oxford Music Online*, 2012.

Bain-Selbo, Eric. *Game Day and God: Football, Faith, and Politics in the American South*. Macon, GA: Mercer University Press, 2018.

Bayor, Ronald H. *Race and the Shaping of Twentieth Century Atlanta*. Chapel Hill: University of North Carolina Press, 2000.

Bell, Andrew McIlwaine. *The Origins of Southern College Football: How an Ivy League Game Became a Southern Tradition*. Baton Rouge: Louisiana State University Press, 2020.

Berish, Andrew. *Lonesome Roads and Streets of Dreams: Place, Mobility, and Race in Jazz of the 1930s and '40s*. Chicago: University of Chicago Press, 2012.

Bernstein, Mark. *Football: The Ivy League Origins of an American Obsession*. Philadelphia: University of Pennsylvania Press, 2001.

Biggs, Elizabeth W. "Everyone Play: Sound, Public Space, and the (Re)Making of Place." PhD diss., Princeton University, 2009.

Bingham, Emily. *My Old Kentucky Home: The Astonishing Life and Reckoning of an Iconic American Song*. New York: Alfred A. Knopf, 2022.

Born, Georgina, ed. *Music, Sound and Space: Transformations of Public and Private Experience*. New York: Cambridge University Press, 2013.

Bradford, J. C. *Charter of the City of Nashville and Other Acts of Assembly Relating Thereto, Published by the Authority of the Mayor and City Council*. Nashville, TN: 1885.

Bradley, Regina. *Chronicling Stankonia: The Rise of the Hip-Hop South*. Chapel Hill: University of North Carolina Press, 2021.

Brackett, David. *Categorizing Sound: Genre and Twentieth-Century Popular Music*. Berkeley: University of California Press, 2016.

Bronner, Simon J. *Campus Traditions: Folklore from the Old-Time College to the Modern Mega University*. Jackson: University Press of Mississippi, 2012.

Bull, Michael, and Les Back, eds. *The Auditory Culture Reader*. 2nd ed. London: Bloomsbury Academic, 2016.

Burke, Brad J. "Abraham Shushan: In the Shadow of Huey Long." MA thesis, University of New Orleans, 2018.

Burnett, Katherine, and Monica Carol Miller, eds. *The Tacky South*. Baton Rouge: Louisiana State University Press, 2022.

Carby, Hazel V. Foreword to *Silencing the Past: The Power and Production of History* by Michel-Rolph Trouillot. 20th anniversary ed. Boston, MA: Beacon Press, 2015.

Carey, Jack. "The Design of the Southern Future: The Struggle to Build White Democracy at the University of Mississippi, 1890–1948," PhD diss., University of Mississippi, 2014.

———. "Ole Miss's New Deal: Building White Democracy at the University of Mississippi, 1933-1941." *Journal of Mississippi History* 81, no. 3 and 4 (Fall/Winter 2019): 185–220.

———. *Jim Crow U: White Authority and the Idea of the Southern University*. Unpublished manuscript, 2020.

Clark, Robert H. "A Narrative History of African American Marching Band: Toward a Historicultural Understanding." *Journal of Historical Research in Music Education* 41, no. 1 (October 2019): 5–32

Cobb, James. *Away Down South: A History of Southern Identity*. Oxford: Oxford University Press, 2005.

Cobb, James C. "World War II and the Mind of the Modern South." In McMillen, *Remaking Dixie*, 3–20.

Cohan, Noah. *We Average Unbeautiful Watchers: Fan Narratives and the Reading of American Sports*. Lincoln: University of Nebraska Press, 2019.

Connolly, James. "Bringing the City Back In: Space and Place in the Urban History of the Gilded Age and Progressive Era." *The Journal of the Gilded Age and Progressive Era* 1, no. 3 (July 2002): 258–78.

Continé, Tom, and Faye Phillips. *The Golden Band from Tigerland: A History of LSU's Marching Band*. Baton Rouge: Louisiana State University Press, 2016.

Conyers, C. T., ed. *Georgia Songs and Airs*. Athens: Georgia Glee and Mandolin Clubs, 1922.

Cook, Robert J. *Troubled Commemoration: The American Civil War Centennial, 1961–1965*. Baton Rouge: Louisiana State University Press, 2007.

Cooper, Christopher and H. Gibbs Knotts. "South Polls: Rethinking the Boundaries of the South." *Southern Cultures* 16, no. 4 (Winter 2010): 72–88.

Cornelius, Steven. *Music of the Civil War Era*. Westport, CT: Greenwood Press, 2004.

Cowan, Walter Greaves and Jack B. McGuire. *Louisiana Governors: Rulers, Rascals, and Reformers*. Jackson: University Press of Mississippi, 2008.

Cox, Karen. *Dixie's Daughters: The United Daughters of the Confederacy and the Preservation of Confederate Culture*. 2nd ed. Gainesville: University Press of Florida, 2019.

———. *Dreaming of Dixie: How the South Was Created in American Popular Culture*. Chapel Hill: University of North Carolina Press, 2011.

Crawford, Richard. *America's Musical Life: A History*. New York: W.W. Norton, 2001.

Crespino, Joseph and Matthew D. Lassiter, eds., *The Myth of Southern Exceptionalism*. Oxford: Oxford University Press, 2010.

Crowther, Edmund R., ed. *The Enduring Lost Cause: Afterlives of a Redeemer Nation*. Knoxville: University of Tennessee Press, 2020.

DeJournett, Bill. *The Pride of the South, 1928–2014: The Ole Miss Rebel Band, A History*. Jackson: University Press of Mississippi, 2015.

Demas, Lane. *Integrating the Gridiron: Black Civil Rights and American College Football*. New Brunswick, NJ: Rutgers University Press, 2011.

Discography of American Historical Recordings. University of California, Santa Barbara and Packard Humanities Institute, copyright 2008–2023, https://adp.library.ucsb.edu.

Doktor, Stephanie. *Reinventing Whiteness: Race in the Early Jazz Marketplace*. Unpublished manuscript.

Domby, Adam. *The False Cause: Fraud, Fabrication, and White Supremacy in Confederate Memory*. Charlottesville: University of Virginia Press, 2020.

Dorr, Lisa Lindquist. "Fifty Percent Moonshine and Fifty Percent Moonshine: Social Life and College Youth Culture in Alabama, 1913–1933." In *Manners and Southern History*, edited by Ted Ownby, 45–76. Jackson: University Press of Mississippi, 2007.

Doyle, Andrew. "Foolish and Useless Sport: The Southern Evangelical Crusade Against Intercollegiate Football." *Journal of Sport History* 24, no. 3 (Fall 1997): 317–40.

———. "Causes Won, Not Lost: Football and Southern Culture, 1892–1983." PhD diss., Emory University, 1998.

———. "An Atheist in Alabama is Someone Who Doesn't Believe in Bear Bryant: A Symbol for an Embattled South." In Miller, *Sporting World*, 247–75.

Doyle, Don H. *New Men, New Cities, New South: Atlanta, Nashville, Charleston, Mobile, 1860–1910*. Chapel Hill: University of North Carolina Press, 1990.

Duttlinger, Carolin. "Walter Benjamin: Fragments, Salvage, and Detours." *Times Literary Supplement* online, August 2019.

Dyer, Richard J. *Stars*. 3rd ed. London: BFI Publishing, 1979.

Dyreson, Mark. *Making the American Team: Sport, Culture, and the Olympic Experience*. Urbana: University of Illinois Press, 1998.

Elmore, Bartow J. "Growing Roots in Rocky Soil: An Environmental History of Southern Rock." *Southern Cultures* 16, no. 3 (Fall 2010): 102–128.

Fass, Paula. *The Damned and the Beautiful: American Youth in the 1920s*. Oxford: Oxford University Press, 1977.

Finebaum, Paul. *My Conference Can Beat Your Conference: Why the SEC Still Rules College Football*. New York: Harper, 2014.

Fink, Sandra. "Spectacles of the Street: Performance, Power, and Public Space in Antebellum New Orleans." PhD diss., University of Texas-Austin, 2004.

Frith, Simon and Lee Marshall, eds. *Music and Copyright*, 2nd ed. New York: Routledge and Edinburgh University Press, 2004.

Gailey, Joshua. "Beginning Bands: Progressive Reform and the Birth of the American School Band Industry, 1907–1940." PhD diss., Yale University, 2019.

Gems, Gerald R. *For Pride, Profit, and Patriarchy: Football and the Incorporation of American Cultural Values*. Lanham, MD: Rowman and Littlefield, 2000.

Gioia, Ted. *Jazz Standards: A Guide to the Repertoire*. Oxford: Oxford University Press, 2012.

Gitelman, Lisa. "Recording Sound, Recording Race, Recording Property." In *Hearing History: A Reader*, edited by Mark M. Smith, 279–94. Athens: University of Georgia Press, 2004.

Glier, Ray. *How the SEC Became Goliath: The Making of College Football's Most Dominant Conference*. New York: Howard Books, 2012.

Goehr, Lydia. *The Imaginary Museum of Musical Works: An Essay in the Philosophy of Music*. Rev. ed. Oxford: Oxford University Press, 2007.

Goldfield, David. *Region, Race, and Cities: Interpreting the Urban South*. Baton Rouge: Louisiana State University Press, 1997.

Goldschmitt, Kaleb. Review of *Music, Sound and Space: Transformations of Public and Private Experience*, by Georgina Born. *Ethnomusicology Forum* 24, no. 3 (2015): 485–87.

Graham, Sandra. *Spirituals and the Birth of the Black Entertainment Industry*. Urbana: University of Illinois Press, 2018.

Grasso, John. *Historical Dictionary of Football*. Lanham, MD: Scarecrow Press, 2013.

Gruensfelder, Melvin. "A History of the Origin and Development of the Southeastern Conference." MS thesis, University of Illinois, 1964.

Harkins, Anthony. *Hillbilly: A Cultural History of an American Icon*. Oxford: Oxford University Press, 2004.

Hatchett, Thomas. "Race Shapes the New South City." *Journal of Urban History* 26, no. 2 (January 2000): 259–66.

Hillyer, Reiko. *Designing Dixie: Tourism, Memory, and Urban Space in the New South*. Charlottesville: University of Virginia Press, 2014.

Hobson, J. Hardin. "Football Culture at New South Universities: Lost Cause and Old South Memory, Modernity, and Martial Manhood." In *The History of American College Football: Institutional Policy, Culture, and Reform*, edited by Christian Anderson and Amber Fallucca, e-book. London: Routledge, 2021.

Hubbs, Nadine. "'Redneck Woman' and the Gendered Poetics of Class Rebellion," *Southern Cultures* 17, no. 4 (Winter 2011): 44–70, 122.

Huebner, Andrew J. and John M. Giggie, eds. *Dixie's Great War: World War I and the American South*. Tuscaloosa: University of Alabama Press, 2021.

Hughes, Charles L. *Country Soul: Making Music and Making Race in the American South*. Chapel Hill: University of North Carolina Press, 2015.

Hutton, T.R.C. *Bearing the Torch: The University of Tennessee, 1794–2010*. Knoxville: University of Tennessee Press, 2022.

Ikard, Robert. *Near You: Francis Craig, Dean of Southern Maestros*. Franklin, TN: Hillsboro Press, 1999.

Ingrassia, Brian. *The Rise of Gridiron University: Higher Education's Uneasy Alliance with Big Time Football*. Lawrence: University of Kansas Press, 2012.

Jabir, Johari. *Conjuring Freedom: Music and Masculinity in the Civil War's "Gospel Army."* Columbus: Ohio State University Press, 2017.

Jeansonne, Glen. "Huey Long and Racism." *Louisiana History: The Journal of the Louisiana Historical Association* 33, no. 3 (Summer 1992): 265–82.

Johnson, Mark A. Johnson. *Rough Tactics: Black Performance in Political Spectacles, 1877–1932*. Jackson: University Press of Mississippi, 2021.

Kean, Melissa. *Desegregating Private Higher Education in the South: Duke, Emory, Rice, Tulane, and Vanderbilt*. Baton Rouge: Louisiana State University Press, 2013.

Kemper, Kurt Edward. *College Football and American Culture in the Cold War Era*. Urbana: University of Illinois Press, 2009.

Kiefer, Peter T. *The Fred Waring Discography*, Discographies No. 65. Westport, CT: Greenwood Press, 1996.

Knepper, Steven. "Unveiling Black Labor: Sterling Brown, Charles Johnson, and the Depression Era Critique of the Plantation Myth." In *Reassessing the 1930s South*, edited by Karen Cox and Sarah Gardner, 13–29. Baton Rouge: Louisiana State University Press, 2018.

Kyriakoudes, Louis. *The Social Origins of the Urban South: Race, Gender, and Migration in Nashville and Middle Tennessee, 1890–1930*. Chapel Hill: University of North Carolina Press, 2003.

LaChapelle, Pete. *I'd Fight the World: A Political History of Hillbilly, Old-Time, and Country Music*. Chicago: University of Chicago Press, 2019.

Lanford, Michael. "'When the Band Plays 'Dixie' Over Our Team, It Can Whip Eleven Red Granges: The Origin of Civil War Melodies in College Fight Songs." Paper presented at the Thirty-Sixth Annual Conference of the Society for American Music, Ottawa, Ontario, March, 2010.

Lechner, Zachary J. *The South of the Mind: American Imaginings of White Southernness, 1960–1980*. Athens: University of Georgia Press, 2018.

Levine, David O. *The American College and the Culture of Aspiration, 1915–1940*. Ithaca, NY: Cornell University Press, 1986.

Long, Huey P. *Every Man a King: The Autobiography of Huey P. Long*. New Orleans: National Book Company, 1933.

———. *My First Days in the White House*. Harrisburg, PA: Telegraph Press 1935.

MacCambridge, Michael, ed. *ESPN Encyclopedia: Southeastern Conference Football*. New York: Ballantine, 2009.

Mahar, William. *Behind the Burnt Cork Mask: Early Blackface Minstrelsy and Antebellum American Popular Culture*. Urbana: University of Illinois Press, 1999.

Mahoney, Antron D. "Reclaiming the Beat: The Sweet Subversive Sounds of HBCU Marching Bands." *Southern Cultures* 27, no. 4 (Winter 2021): 78–97.

Malone, Bobbie and Bill C. Malone. *Nashville's Songwriting Sweethearts: The Boudreaux and Felice Bryant Story*. Norman: University of Oklahoma Press, 2020.

Maraniss, Andrew. *Strong Inside: Perry Wallace and the Collision of Race and Sports in the South*. Nashville, TN: Vanderbilt University Press, 2016.

Martin, Charles H. "Integrating New Year's Day: The Racial Politics of College Bowl Games in the American South." In Miller, *Sporting World*, 358–77.

———. "'Hold That (Color) Line!': Black Exclusion and SEC Football." In *Higher Education and the Civil Rights Movement: White Supremacy, Black Southerners, and College Campuses,* edited by Peter Wallenstein, 166–198. Gainesville: University of Florida Press, 2009.

———. *Benching Jim Crow: The Rise and Fall of the Color Line in Southern College Sports, 1890–1980*. Urbana: University of Illinois Press, 2010.

Martin, Michael S. "'We both Have Reason to Feel Good About the Book': Russell Long, T. Harry Williams, and Huey Long." *The Historian* 69, no. 4 (Winter 2007): 706–27.

Mathieu, Jane. "'The Injustice of the Thing': Negotiating the Song Market in the U.S. Copyright Debates of 1906–1910." *Popular Music* 44, no. 3 (2021): 292–305.

Maxwell, Angie. *The Indicted South: Public Criticism, Southern Inferiority, and the Politics of Whiteness*. Chapel Hill: University of North Carolina Press, 2014.

May, Christ. "Jurisprudence v Musicology: Riffs from the Land Down Under." *Music and Letters* 97, no. 4 (Nov 2016): 622–46.

McCandless, Amy Thompson. "Maintaining the Spirit and Tone of Robust Manliness: The Battle Against Coeducation at Southern Colleges and Universities, 1890–1940." *NWSA Journal* 2, no. 2 (Spring 1990): 199–216.

McCluskey, John Michael. "Music as Narrative in American College Football." PhD diss., University of Kentucky, 2016.

———. "'Rough! Tough! Real Stuff!': Music, Militarism, and Masculinity in American College Football." *American Music* 37, no. 1 (2019): 29–57.

———. "'This is Ghetto Row': Musical Segregation in American College Football." *Journal of the Society for American Music* 14, no. 3 (2020): 337–63.

McCracken, Allison. *Real Men Don't Sing: Crooning in American Culture*. Durham, NC: Duke University Press, 2015.

McKindra, Frederick. "The Rich, Black, Southern Heritage of Hip-Hop Majorettes." BuzzfeedNews, May 7, 2019, https://www.buzzfeednews.com/article/frederickmckindra/marching-bands-hip-hop-majorettes-jsettes-prancing-elites.

McLeod, Ken. *We Are the Champions: The Politics of Sports and Popular Music*. New York: Routledge, 2011.

McMillen, Neil R., ed. *Remaking Dixie: The Impact of World War II on the American South*. Jackson: University Press of Mississippi, 2007.

McNamara, Daniel ed. *The ASCAP Biographical Dictionary of Composers, Authors, and Publishers*. 2nd ed. New York: Thomas Y. Crowell Company, 1952.

McWhirter, Christian. *Battle Hymns: The Power and Popularity of Music in the Civil War*. Chapel Hill: University of North Carolina Press, 2012.

Miller, Karl Hagstrom. *Segregating Sound: Inventing Folk and Pop Music in the Age of Jim Crow*. Durham, NC: Duke University Press, 2010.

———. "Revisiting Minstrelsy: *Love and Theft* at Twenty," *American Music* 33, no. 2 (Summer 2015): 274–80.

Miller, Patrick, ed. *The Sporting World of the Modern South.* Urbana: University of Illinois Press, 2002.

———. "The Manly, the Moral, and the Proficient: College Sport in the New South. In Miller, *Sporting World,* 17–51.

Mohr, Clarence M. "World War II and the Transformation of Southern Higher Education." In McMillen, *Remaking Dixie,* 33–55.

Monson, Ingrid. *Saying Something: Jazz Improvisation and Expression.* Chicago: University of Chicago Press, 1996.

Montez de Oca, Jeffrey. *Discipline and Indulgence: College Football, Media, and the American Way of Life During the Cold War.* New Brunswick, NJ: Rutgers University Press, 2013.

Morelock, Kolan Thomas. *Taking the Town: College and Community Culture in the Bluegrass, 1880–1917.* Lexington: University of Kentucky Press, 2008.

Morrison, Matthew D. "Race, Blacksound, and the (Re)Making of Musicological Discourse," *Journal of the American Musicological Society* 72, no. 3 (Fall 2019): 781–823.

———. "Blacksound." In *Oxford Handbook of Western Music & Philosophy,* edited by Tomás McAuley, Nanette Nielsen, Jerrold Levinson, and Ariana Phillips-Hutton, online. Oxford: Oxford University Press, 2021.

Moyen, Eric. "Redefining Reform: Presidents, Football, and Athletic Policy in the SEC, 1929 1936." In *The History of American College Football,* edited by Christian Anderson and Amber Fallucca, e-book. London: Routledge Press, 2021.

"Musical Memories." Baton Rouge: Louisiana Public Television, 1979.

O'Brien, Robert F. *School Songs of America's Colleges and Universities: A Directory.* New York: Greenwood Press, 1991.

O'Callaghan, Casey. *Sounds: A Philosophical Theory.* Oxford: Oxford University Press, 2008.

O'Connor, Flannery. *Mystery and Manners: Occasional Prose.* New York: MacMillan, 1969.

Odum, Howard. *Southern Regions of the United States.* Chapel Hill: University of North Carolina Press, 1936.

Oriard, Michael. *King Football: Sport and Spectacle in the Golden Age of Radio and Newsreels, Movies and Magazines, the Weekly and the Daily Press.* Chapel Hill: University of North Carolina Press, 2001.

———. *Bowled Over: Big-Time College Football from the Sixties to the BCS Era.* Chapel Hill: University of North Carolina Press, 2009.

Ownby, Ted. *Subduing Satan: Religion, Recreation, and Manhood in the Rural South, 1865–1920.* Chapel Hill: University of North Carolina Press, 2014.

Painter, Nell Irvin. *Southern History Across the Color Line.* 2nd ed. with new preface. Chapel Hill: University of North Carolina Press, 2021.

Peine, Emelie K. and Kai A. Schafft. "Moonshine, Mountaineers, and Modernity: Distilling Cultural History in the Southern Appalachian Mountains." *Journal of Appalachian Studies* 18, no. 1 (Spring/Fall 2012): 93–112.

Percy, Walker. Introduction to William Alexander Percy, *Lanterns on the Levee: Recollections of a Planter's Son* [1941]. Baton Rouge: Louisiana State University Press, 1973.

Peterson, Marina. *Sound, Space, and the City: Civic Performance in Downtown Los Angeles.* Philadelphia: University of Pennsylvania Press, 2012.

Powell, Donald B. and Mary Jo. *The Fightin' Texas Aggies Band.* College Station: Texas A&M University Press, 1994.

Price, Edwin A., City Attorney, and K. T. McConnico, Asst. City Attorney. *Digest of the Ordinances of the City of Nashville.* Nashville, TN: Boylin Printing Co., 1901.

Ribowsky, Mark. *Whiskey Bottles and Brand-New Cars: The Fast Life and Sudden Death of Lynyrd Skynyrd.* Chicago: Chicago Review Press, 2015.

Richards, Robin J. *The University of Georgia Redcoat Marching Band: 1905–2005.* Charleston, SC: Arcadia Press, 2004.

Ring, Natalie. *The Problem South: Region, Empire, and the New Liberal State, 1880–1930.* Athens: University of Georgia Press, 2012.

Roberts, Brian. *Blackface Nation: Race, Reform, and Identity in American Popular Music, 1812–1925.* Chicago: University of Chicago Press, 2017.

Robinson, Zandria. *This Ain't Chicago: Race, Class, and Regional Identity in the Post-Soul South.* Chapel Hill: University of North Carolina Press, 2014.

Rockwell, Joti. "What Is Bluegrass Anyway? Category Formation, Debate and the Framing of Genre." *Popular Music* 31, no. 3 (Oct 2012): 363–81.

Rose, Steven. *Musical Authorship from Schütz to Bach.* Cambridge: Cambridge University Press, 2021.

Rosko, M. Helen. "Drinking and (Re)making Place: Commercial Moonshine as Place-Making in East Tennessee." *Southeastern Geographer* 57, no. 4 (Winter 2017): 351–70.

Russell, Fred, and Maxwell E. Benson, eds., *Fifty Years of Vanderbilt Football.* Nashville, TN: Russell and Benson, 1938.

Saerchinger, Cesar ed. *International Who's Who in Music and Musical Gazetteer.* New York: Current Literature Publishing Co., 1918.

Samson, Jim. *The Cambridge Guide to Nineteenth-Century Music.* Cambridge: Cambridge University Press, 2002.

Sanson, Jerry P. "'What He Did and What He Promised To Do . . .': Huey Long and the Horizons of Louisiana Politics, *Louisiana History: The Journal of the Louisiana Historical Society* 47, no.3 (Summer 2006): 261–76.

Scafidi, Susan. *Who Owns Culture? Appropriation and Authenticity in American Law.* New Brunswick, NJ: Rutgers University Press, 2005.

Schafer, R. Murray. *The Soundscape: Our Sonic Environment and the Tuning of the World.* Rochester, VT: Destiny Books, 1994.

Scherzer, Kenneth A. "Southern Cities—How Exceptional?" *Journal of Urban History* 26, no. 5 (July 2000): 692–706.

Schmidt, Raymond. *Shaping American Football: The Transformation of an American Sport, 1919–1930.* Syracuse, NY: Syracuse University Press, 2007.

Sewell, Roy. *One Sewell Family.* Atlanta, GA: Higgins-McArthur Company, 1960.

Shephard, Thomas G., ed. *College Songs and Glees: Including the Most Admired Songs, New and Old, Used in the Colleges of America*. Cincinnati, OH: The John Church Co., 1896.

Smilor, Raymond W. "American Noise." In *Hearing History: A Reader*, edited by Mark M. Smith, 319–330. Athens: University of Georgia Press, 2004.

Smith, Christopher. *The Creolization of American Culture: William Sidney Mount and the Roots of Blackface Minstrelsy*. Urbana: University of Illinois Press, 2013.

Smith, Mark M. *Listening to Nineteenth Century America*. Chapel Hill: University of North Carolina Press, 2001.

———, ed. *Hearing History: A Reader*. Athens: University of Georgia Press, 2004.

Solberg, Winton U. *Creating the Big Ten: Courage, Corruption, and Commercialization*. Urbana: University of Illinois Press, 2018.

Solis, Gabriel. "'A Unique Chunk of Jazz Reality': Authorship, Musical Work Concepts, and Thelonious Monk's Live Recordings from the Five Spot, 1958." *Ethnomusicology* 48, no. 3 (Fall 2004): 315–47.

Songs of Yale. New Haven, CT: T. H. Pease, 1853.

Sosna, Morton. Introduction to McMillen, *Remaking Dixie*, xiii–xix.

Stevens, C. Wistar, ed. *College Songbook: A Collection of American College Songs with Piano forte Accompaniment*. Boston, MA: Russell and Tolman, 1860.

Stimeling, Travis. "'Stay Out of the Way of the Southern Thing': The Drive-By Truckers' Southern Gothic Soundscape." *Popular Music and Society* 36, no. 1 (2013): 19–29.

Stoevall, Jennifer Lynn. *The Sonic Color Line*. New York: New York University Press, 2016.

St. John, Warren. *Rammer Jammer Yellow Hammer: A Journey into the Heart of Fan Mania*. New York: Broadway Books, 2004.

Strickland, Jeffrey. "Race and Ethnicity in Mobile, Alabama." *Journal of Urban History* 33, no.1 (November 2006): 130–39.

Studwell, William and Bruce Schueneman, eds., *College Fight Songs: An Annotated Anthology*. New York: Routledge, 2011.

———. *College Fight Songs II: A Supplementary Anthology*. New York: Routledge, 2013.

Sullivan, Patricia. *Days of Hope: Race and Democracy in the New Deal Era*. Chapel Hill: University of North Carolina Press, 1996.

Syrett, Nicholas. *The Company He Keeps: A History of White College Fraternities*. Chapel Hill: University of North Carolina Press, 2009.

Tarver, Erin C. *The I in Team: Sports Fandom and the Reproduction of Identity*. Chicago: University of Chicago Press, 2017.

Thelin, John. *A History of American Higher Education*. 3rd ed. Baltimore, MD: Johns Hopkins University Press, 2019.

———. *Going to College in the Sixties*. Baltimore, MD: John Hopkins University Press, 2021.

Thompson, Katrina Dyonne. *Ring Shout, Wheel About: The Racial Politics of Music and Dance in North American Slavery*. Urbana: University of Illinois Press, 2014.

Thompson, T. Tyler. *University of Arkansas Razorback Band: A History, 1874–2004*. Fayetteville: University of Arkansas Press, 2004.

Tipton, Carrie Allen. "Minstrel Songs Like 'The Eyes of Texas' Were Once Common on College Football Saturdays in the South." *The Andscape* [formerly *The Undefeated*], November 24, 2021. https://andscape.com/features/minstrel-songs-like-the-eyes-of-texas-were-once-common-on-college-football-saturdays-in-the-south.

———. "Battle Sounds." *Deep South Magazine*, September 2, 2015. Digital edition.

Tranquada, Jim. *The 'Ukulele: A History*. Honolulu: University of Hawaii Press, 2012.

Travis, Clay. *Dixieland Delight: A Football Season on the Road in the Southeastern Conference*. New York: Harper Entertainment, 2007.

Turpie, David. "From Broadway to Hollywood: The Image of the 1939 University of Tennessee Football Team and the Americanization of the South." *Journal of Sport History* 35, no. 1 (2008): 119–40.

Vats, Anjali. *The Color of Creatorship: Intellectual Property, Race, and the Making of Americans*. Palo Alto, CA: Stanford University Press, 2020.

Veblen, Thorstein. *The Theory of the Leisure Class* [1899]. New York: Routledge/Taylor & Francis, 2017.

Wald, Elijah. *How the Beatles Destroyed Rock 'n' Roll: An Alternative History of American Popular Music*. Oxford: Oxford University Press, 2011.

Waite, Henry Randall, ed. *College Songs: A Collection of New and Popular Songs of the American Colleges*. New York: Oliver Ditson & Co., 1887.

Wallenstein, Peter, ed. *Higher Education and the Civil Rights Movement: White Supremacy, Black Southerners, and College Campuses*. Gainesville: University of Florida Press, 2009.

Walsh, Christopher J. *Where Football Is King: A History of the SEC*. Lanham, MD: Taylor Trade Publishing, 2006.

Walton, Andrea. "What the Lens of Philanthropy Might Bring to the History of U.S. Higher Education." *The History Teachers* 51, no. 1 (Nov 2017): 9–36.

Wanless, Dorothy. *The Auburn University Band: A Centennial History, 1897–1997*. Dallas, TX: Taylor Publishing Company, 1997.

Warren, Craig A. *The Rebel Yell: A Cultural History*. Tuscaloosa: University of Alabama Press, 2014.

Watkins, Billy. *University of Mississippi Football Vault: The History of the Rebels*. Atlanta, GA: Whitman Publishing, 2009.

Watterson, John Sayle. *College Football: History, Spectacle, Controversy*. Baltimore, MD: Johns Hopkins Press, 2000.

Watts, Trent, ed. *White Masculinity in the Recent South*. Baton Rouge: Louisiana State University Press, 2008.

White, Derrick. "Race, Football, and 'Dixie' at the University of Florida," *Florida Historical Quarterly* 88, no. 4 (Spring 2010): 469–96.

———. *Blood, Sweat, and Tears: Jake Gaither, Florida A&M, and the History of Black College Football*. Chapel Hill: University of North Carolina Press, 2019.

White, Richard D., Jr. *Kingfish: The Reign of Huey P. Long*. New York: Random House, 2006.

Williams, Harry T. *Huey Long*. New York: Alfred Knopf, 1969.

Williamson, Samuel R. *Sewanee Sesquicentennial History: The Making of the University of the South*. Sewanee, TN: University of the South, 2008.

Wilson, Charles Reagan. *Baptized in Blood: The Religion of the Lost Cause, 1865–1920.* 2nd ed. Athens: University of Georgia Press, 2009.

———. "Bryant, Paul W. 'Bear.'" In *New Encyclopedia of Southern Culture,* vol. 16, *Sports and Recreation,* 264–65. Chapel Hill: University of North Carolina Press, 2011.

———. "Whose South? Lessons Learned from Studying the South at the University of Mississippi," *Southern Cultures* 22, no. 4 (Winter 2016): 96–110.

Wilson, Lee. *All I Have to Do Is Dream: The Boudleaux and Felice Bryant Story.* Nashville, TN: Two Creeks Press/House of Bryant Publications, 2017.

Winstead, J. Lloyd. *When Colleges Sang: The Story of Singing in American College Life.* Tuscaloosa: University of Alabama Press, 2013.

Woodruff, Fuzzy. *History of Southern Football 1890–1928.* Atlanta, GA: Walter W. Brown, 1928.

Zimbalist, Andrew. *Unpaid Professionals: Commercialism and Conflict in Big-Time College Sports.* Princeton, NJ: Princeton University Press, 2001.

Manuscript Collections and Oral Histories

Alumni Society Collection, UA97–108. Hargrett Rare Book and Manuscript Library, University of Georgia.

Emma L. Ashford Papers, MSS.0027. Vanderbilt University Special Collections and University Archives.

Athletic Department Correspondence, MUM00517. University of Mississippi Libraries, Department of Archives and Special Collections.

Kathleen Baldwin Collection, MUM00518. University of Mississippi Libraries, Department of Archives and Special Collections.

Black Student Union Correspondence. Hargrett Rare Book and Manuscript Library, University of Georgia.

Boudreaux and Felice Bryant Songwriting Ledger #9, December 1967. Country Music Hall of Fame, Nashville, Tennessee.

Bryant Collection, Accession 2017.74. Country Music Hall of Fame, Nashville, Tennessee.

Carolina Bands Collection, SCU-MUS-0001. University of South Carolina Ernest F. Hollings Special Collections.

Francis Craig Collection, MSS.0091. Vanderbilt University Special Collections and University Archives.

Johnny DeDroit, interview. December 4, 1969. *Oral History Files,* edited by Betty B. Rankin, Richard B. Allen, and Keith V. Abramson. New Orleans: William Ransom Hogan Jazz Archive, Tulane University.

Don DeVol oral history. Oct 7, 1982, Washington DC, 4700.0009. Louisiana State University Libraries, Special Collections.

Ralph Brown Draughon Papers, RG #107, Access. 1968. Auburn University Libraries, Special Collections and Archives.

Football Programs Collection, MUM00556. University of Mississippi Libraries, Department of Archives and Special Collections.

Georgia Tech Songs Collection, U318. Georgia Tech University Archives

Patricia A. Hall, interview with Boudreaux and Felicia Bryant, November 19, 1975. Nashville, TN: Country Music Foundation Oral History Project OH18.

Mary Hebert, oral history, 1994. "'I've Got a University': Huey Long and LSU's Golden Years." T. Harry Williams Center for Oral History, Louisiana State University.

Historic Films Archive, LLC, Stock Footage F-A2905.

Isabel Howell Papers, MSS.0216. Vanderbilt University Special Collections and University Archives.

Huey P. Long Photograph Album, 1928–1935. Louisiana State University Libraries, Special Collections and Louisiana Digital Library.

Earl Jarnigan Film Archives. University of Florida Archives Moving Image Collection.

Louisiana State University School of Music Records, RG#A1600. Louisiana State University Libraries, Special Collections.

"M-Books" Collection, MUM00590. University of Mississippi Libraries, Department of Archives and Special Collections.

Miscellaneous vertical files, football programs, broadsides, songbooks, recordings, sheet music.

Ole Miss Music Club Collection, MUM00600. University of Mississippi Libraries, Department of Archives and Special Collections.

Presidents Record Group, Series 6: Dinwiddie, Albert Bledsoe. University Archives, Tulane University Special Collections.

Thomas Walter Reed. *History of the University of Georgia* (unpublished manuscript, 194[?]). Hargrett Rare Book and Manuscript Library, University of Georgia.

Grantland Rice Papers, MSS.0364. Vanderbilt University Special Collections and University Archives.

Richard B. Russell, Jr. Papers, RBRL/001/RBR. Richard B. Russell Library for Political Research and Studies, Special Collections Libraries, University of Georgia

Kurt S. Schwartz Papers, MSs.3740. Louisiana State University Libraries, Special Collections.

Roy Sewell Correspondence, Athletic Department Records, RG 392. Auburn University Libraries, Special Collections and Archives.

Roy Sewell Scrapbook, "Homecoming '83," Alumni and Development Office Records, RG #385, Access. 96–64. Auburn University Libraries, Special Collections and Archives.

State Library of Louisiana Historic Photograph Collection.

Mildred Simpson Scrapbook, AR-0085. Betsey B. Creekmore Special Collections and University Archives, University of Tennessee, Knoxville.

Alec Brock Stevenson Papers, MSS.0418. Vanderbilt University Special Collections and University Archives.

Tennessee State Library and Archives Map Collection.

William Tate Papers, UA97–085. Hargrett Rare Book and Manuscript Library, University of Georgia.

Leon Trice Political Photographs. Tulane University Digital Library.

University of Arkansas Band Records, MC 2002-UA. Special Collections, University of Arkansas Libraries.

UF Songs and Yells. University of Florida George A. Smathers Libraries, University Archives.

University of Maine Alumni Association Records, 1872–1988. University of Maine Special Collections.

University of the South Athletics Records, UA 2. William R. Laurie University Archives and Special Collections, Sewanee University.

University of South Carolina Moving Image Research Collections. University of South Carolina Libraries.

University of Tennessee Football Programs. Digital Collections, University of Tennessee Libraries.

UT Marching Band Collection, AR-0785. Betsey C. Creekmore Special Collections and University Archives, University of Tennessee Libraries

Vanderbilt Athletic Publications Collection. Vanderbilt University Special Collections and University Archives.

Fred Waring's America. Pennsylvania State University Libraries, Special Collections and Archives Digital Exhibits.

Robert Penn Warren to Mr. _____ Stahley, November 7, 1962, MSs.5072. Louisiana State University Libraries, Special Collections.

Seymour Weiss Papers, MSs.4165. Louisiana State University Libraries, Special Collections.

Paul C. Young, et al., oral history interview, 4700.0067. 1983. T. Harry Williams Center for Oral History Collection, Louisiana State University.

University Student and Alumni Publications

University of Alabama
  Corolla
  Crimson White
  Rammer Jammer

University of Arkansas
  Arkansas Alumnus
  Arkansas Traveler
  Razorback
  University Weekly

Auburn University
  Auburn Alumnus
  Auburn Plainsman
  Glomerata

University of Florida
  The Alligator
  "F" Books
  The Florida Alligator
  The Orange and Blue Daily Bulletin
  The Seminole

University of Georgia
  Pandora
  Red and Black

Georgia Institute of Technology
  Blue Print
  Georgia Tech Alumni Magazine
  The Technique

University of Kentucky
The Idea
Kentuckian
Kentucky Kernel

Louisiana State University
Gumbo
L-Books
Reveille

Mississippi State University
Mis-A-Sip
Reflector
Reveille

University of Mississippi
M-Books
The Mississippian
The Ole Miss
The Ole Miss Alumni News

University of North Carolina
The Daily Tar Heel

University of South Carolina
Carolina Students' Handbooks
Gamecock
Garnet and Black

University of Tennessee
UT Daily Beacon
Volunteer

Tulane University
Tulane Hullaballoo

Texas A&M University
The Battalion
The Longhorn

Vanderbilt University
Commodore
Hustler
Vanderbilt Alumnus

Washington and Lee University
Alumnus
Calyx
The Ring-Tum Phi

Newspapers, Magazines, and Trade Journals

Abilene (TX) Reporter-News
Advocate (Baton Rouge, LA)
Alabama Journal
Altoona (PA) Tribune
American Mercury
Athens (GA) Banner-Herald
Athens (GA) Observer
Atlanta (GA) Constitution
Atlanta (GA) Journal
Austin-American (TX) Statesman
Bangor (ME) Daily News
Billboard
Birmingham (AL) News
Bleacher Report
Brownsville (TX) Herald
The Chat (Brooklyn, NY)
Clarion-Ledger (Jackson, MS)
Concord (NC) Daily Tribune

Courier-Journal (Louisville, KY)
Denton (TX) Record-Chronicle
Dayton (OH) Daily News
Dayton (OH) Herald
Decatur (IL) Herald
Delta Democrat Times (Greenville, MS)
The Eagle (Bryan, TX)
Fort Worth Star-Telegram
Gainesville (FL) Sun
gambit
Great Falls (MT) Tribune
Hartford (CT) Courant
Kansas City Times
Miltonian (Milton, PA)
Miami News
Miami Herald
Minneapolis Journal
Montclair (NJ) Times

Montgomery (AL) Advertiser
Morning Advocate (Baton Rouge, LA)
Morning Call (Paterson, NJ)
Morning News (Wilmington, DE)
Mountain Echo (Shickshinny, PA)
Musical Courier
Nashville American
Newarker (NJ)
Newport News (VA)
News and Observer (Raleigh, NC)
Newsweek
New York Times
Northwest Arkansas Times
Orlando Sentinel
Opelika-Auburn (AL) News
Owensboro (KY) Messenger
Pensacola News-Journal
Phi Delta Theta Scroll
Pittsburgh Post-Gazette
Presto: The American Music Trade Weekly

San Antonio Express-News
San Antonio News
Saturday Evening Post
Shiner (TX) Gazette
Southern Coach and Athlete
Starkville (MS) Daily News
Saint Louis Post-Dispatch
Tampa Times
Tampa Tribune
Tennessean (Nashville)
Time
Times (Shreveport, LA)
Times-Democrat (New Orleans)
Times-Dispatch (Richmond, VA)
Topeka Daily Herald
Town Talk (Alexandria, LA)
Valentine (NE) Democrat
Washington Post
Wilmington (NC) Morning Star
Wireless Age

US Government Documents

Census Records
Library of Congress Copyright Office, *Catalogue of Copyright Entries*
Records of Congressional Hearings
World War I Draft Registration Cards

ACKNOWLEDGMENTS

It is neither a negligible nor a solo feat to research and write an academic book during a global pandemic and was possible only with the generous and selfless help of those named here. Many thanks are due former dean Mark Wait and current dean Lorenzo Candelaria of Vanderbilt University's Blair School of Music for their support through a Visiting Scholar appointment, research funding, and hiring me to develop and teach a course rooted in the book project. Vanderbilt colleagues Andrew Maraniss and musicology-ethnomusicology faculty members were tremendously supportive, as were my students. Special thanks to Stephanie Doktor for an insightful grant recommendation letter that startled me into seeing the project's potential; to Douglas Shadle for invaluable advice and mentorship at every stage of the process; to Jack Carey for boundless patience in suggesting southern studies literature and reading and commenting on early chapter drafts; and to Gianna Mosser and Zachary Gresham in taking a chance on an entire (but hopefully not tiresome) book about college fight songs. I am also grateful for the interest in and support of the project from my American Bach Society colleagues. Many other colleagues inquired often and encouragingly about my project, giving much-needed mental fuel for the next stage of the journey. Two anonymous readers improved the manuscript and my grasp of the project's contours with their thoughtful critiques, for which I am thankful.

I am deeply grateful to archivists at the universities covered in the book, many of whom exceeded the call of duty to scan materials or arrange visits for me or my research assistants during COVID restrictions; among these are Barry Cowan (Louisiana State University Libraries), John

Varner (Auburn University Libraries), Leigh McWhite (University of Mississippi Libraries), Jessica Perkins-Smith (Mississippi State University Libraries), Steven Armour (University of Georgia Libraries), Matthew Reynolds (Sewanee-University of the South), Ann Case (Tulane University Libraries), Desiree Butterfield-Nagy (University of Maine Libraries), and staff at the University of Tennessee-Knoxville Special Collections and Archives and Vanderbilt University Special Collections and Archives. Research assistants Austin Nicholson and Stuart Simms ably and nimbly located and documented archival materials not otherwise easily obtained, at times suggesting collections or sources I had not previously considered. A project of this scope would have been impossible without the rich and deep source base of student and alumni publications digitized by many SEC schools in recent years, and I want to recognize the anonymous work of librarians who have made these sources available to scholars and to an interested public.

To my extended and immediate family and friends: your support and encouragement the past few years has been invaluable. My eternal thanks go especially to Debbie Allen, to the Rev. Dr. Aubrey Blaine Allen, who gets a big "Roll Tide" from me, and to the many people who made it psychologically and practically possible for a parent of small children to research and write a book during a global pandemic. Thank you, Rebecca Martin, for always understanding. In some mystical sense, you are always my coauthor. My special thanks and love to Joe, Anne, and Markus, who tolerated both me and my book for several years with notable patience. I love to write, but I love you more.

Printed in the USA
CPSIA information can be obtained
at www.ICGtesting.com
LVHW071536190923
758675LV00004B/303